**Dr Vincent Powell-Smith**, LLM, DLitt, FCIArb, sometime Lecturer in Law at the University of Aston Management Centre, now acts as a consultant specialising in building contracts and as a practising arbitrator. A well-known conference speaker, he has been Legal Correspondent of *Contract Journal* for the past twelve years and is a regular contributor to *The Architects' Journal* and *International Construction*. A former member of the Council of the Chartered Institute of Arbitrators, for several years he was a member of the Minister's Joint Advisory Committee on Health and Safety in the Construction Industry. He has written a number of highly successful titles on construction law topics. He is joint editor of *Construction Law Reports* and co-author of *The Encyclopedia of Building Control*, both to be published by the Architectural Press.

**Dr David Chappell**, RIBA, MA, PhD, currently lectures in construction, building law and contractual procedures. He has previously worked as an architect in public and private sector practice and has experience as contracts administrator for a building contractor. He has written *Contractual Correspondence for Architects* (1983), *Contractor's Claims: an architect's guide* (1984) and *Report Writing for Architects* (1984), all of which have been published by the Architectural Press.

# Building Contract Dictionary

VINCENT POWELL-SMITH and DAVID CHAPPELL

The Architectural Press: London

First published in 1985 by the Architectural Press Ltd, 9 Queen Anne's Gate, London SW1H 9BY
Reprinted 1986

**British Library Cataloguing in Publication Data**

Powell-Smith, Vincent
    Building contract dictionary.
    1. Building——Contracts and specifications——
    Great Britain——Dictionaries
    I. Title   II. Chappell, David
    692'.8'0941      TH425

    ISBN 0-85139-758-1

Typeset by Halpen Typesetting & Database Management, London
Printed by Mackays of Chatham Ltd.

**By Norman Royce FRIBA PPCIArb**
Formerly Chairman of The Joint Contracts Tribunal

It is seldom that one feels the justification for another dictionary, but this is more than a dictionary. It is a book which gives succinct explanations of the terms used in building contracts which both satisfies as a quick reference and also sharpens the appetite of all involved in the construction industry for more information on the various topics embraced. In its primary objective of giving an exposition of terms in present use it has avoided the barren and unsatisfactory pitfall of being a mere description of a word or phrase by the welcome addition of referring to relevant legal decisions. With the growth in the number of standard forms of contract in the industry during recent years, it is difficult enough for those involved in contract administration to be aware of the meaning of all the terminology used. A great deal of mystery and misunderstanding surrounds the different forms, and many involved in building are often ignorant of the meaning and ramification of the contractual terms highlighted in this book.

The book has been compiled primarily for the layman – although it will I know commend itself to lawyers involved in the industry – as an easy reference. It would, however, be a pity and a loss if others – particularly clients, expert witnesses and students – were deprived of the instruction and sheer value of the book in the mistaken belief that it is intended for contract administrators alone. Those who advise clients have a special problem when comparing the respective merits of contracts for differing projects.

The terms used in the building industry have evolved by usage and have been adopted by the courts. They vary in interpretation and those involved in the building process should have a detailed knowledge of the whole range of expressions used in law and in court procedure if disputes are to be minimized.

I particularly welcome this book for its clear, readable and highly practical treatment. Moreover, the entries are in sufficient depth to be useful but not tedious. As a reference work it is an invaluable guide of manageable proportions, and deals with most aspects of contracts.

I am honoured and delighted to have been asked to write a brief foreword to a book which will be positively helpful to all connected with building.

Our object in writing this book is to provide a handy reference for architects, quantity surveyors and other professionals, as well as for contractors and their staff. Students in the appropriate disciplines will also find it helpful. It is, as its title suggests, a *Dictionary* and nothing more. Our treatment is not exhaustive and we do not claim that the definitions are authoritative. The book is a *vade mecum* and not a legal textbook – there are a good many of those and we have included a selected list of further reading.

We have taken a very broad view of the words and phrases to be included so that, although they are not all purely contractual, they are all likely to be encountered in connection with building contracts. With a few exceptions, we decided against including definitions of Latin terms because good legal dictionaries are readily available and we wish to keep this book to a manageable size. The final selection of words, phrases and concepts for inclusion is our own, but the publishers helpfully circulated fifteen leading professional practices and we have valued their suggestions.

It need hardly be said that we are indebted to the authors of the leading standard textbooks, but there are a number of people to whom we owe especial thanks. First, to Norman Royce, FRIBA, PPCIArb, distinguished arbitrator and architect, for reading the text and for writing a Foreword. Next, to Maritz Vandenberg, Director in charge of Book Publishing at The Architectural Press Ltd, who has supported us enthusiastically throughout and who, indeed, was instrumental in bringing us together.

L.C.H. Bunton, FRICS, FCIArb; John Sims, FRICS, FCIArb; and Geoffrey Trickey, FRICS, ACIArb, read and commented upon the entries from a quantity surveyor's point of view and made a number of useful comments. Professor Michael Furmston, TD, MA, BCL, LLM, FCIArb, also scrutinized the text from the point of view of the contract lawyer. We are grateful to all of them for their help.

Diagrams from the *Manual of the BPF System* are reproduced by permission of The British Property Federation, the copyright holders.

Certificates for use with the ACA Form of Building Agreement are reproduced by permission of the Association of Consultant Architects Ltd, the copyright holders.

Any book of this kind will omit words which should be included and vice versa. We will be glad to receive, care of the publishers, any suggestions for inclusions or deletions for incorporation in a future edition.

Vincent Powell-Smith
David Chappell

The following abbreviations appear throughout the text:

ACA 2       The Association of Consultant Architects Form of Building Agreement 1982, 2nd edn., 1984.

GC/Works/1   The General Conditions of Government Contracts for Building & Civil Engineering Works, 2nd edn., 1977.

IFC 84       The JCT Intermediate Form of Building Contract 1984

JCT 80       The JCT Standard Form of Building Contract 1984 edn.

MW 80      The JCT Form of Agreement for Minor Building Works 1980.

**ACA Form of Building Agreement**

The ACA Form of Building Agreement was first published in October 1982. The second edition was published in September 1984.

By providing alternatives in a number of key clauses, the standard terms allow a variety of contractual arrangements. The employer, in conjunction with the architect, will decide which of the alternatives is to apply.

The contractor's basic obligation (clause 1.1) is to 'execute and complete the works in strict accordance with the contract documents' (contract drawings (q.v.), the time schedule (q.v.), either a schedule of rates or bills of quantities/schedule of activities (q.vv.), and, optionally, a specification (q.v.)). The contractor must 'comply with and adhere strictly to the architect's instructions' issued under the agreement and is entitled to payment for compliance unless the matter is already covered by the contract sum or results from his default.

Clause 2, covering contract documentation, gives two alternatives. Alternative 1 is traditional and requires the architect to issue further information. Alternative 2 applies where the contractor undertakes to supply further information. It must be submitted to the architect for comment.

The time schedule sets out important stages of the job and provides a list for the insertion of key dates. Where he has undertaken to provide additional drawings, etc., the contractor warrants under clause 3.1 that:

—The works will comply with any performance specification or requirements contained in the contract documents (q.v.).

—Any part of the works to be designed by him will be fit for its intended purpose.

If he is responsible for the design in whole or in part, clause 6.6 requires him to take out professional indemnity insurance in respect of his negligence or that of his sub-contractors, suppliers, etc.

Clause 11.1 states that, once possession of the site (or appropriate part) is given by the employer, the contractor shall then immediately begin the works and proceed 'regularly and diligently' (q.v.) and in accordance with the time schedule so that the works are completed 'fit and ready for taking-over by the employer' by the due or extended date. General damages are provided for as an alternative to liquidated damages for delay. In both cases the architect's clause 11.2 certificate of delay must be issued before deduction.

Extensions of time are dealt with under clause 11.5 which provides alternative criteria. Alternative 1 limits the grounds to 'any act, instruction, default or omission of the employer or of the architect on his behalf' whether authorized by the agreement or not. Alternative 2 is more traditional and lists such things as *force majeure* (q.v.) and insurance contingencies. Clause 11.7 provides for a mandatory review of extensions of time granted by the architect. It also gives the architect power to order acceleration or postponement. The architect's decisions are reviewable on arbitration (if the arbitration option applies) or by the adjudicator if appointed. The time schedule must be revised (clause 11.8) if the contract period is extended or an acceleration or a postponement instruction is issued.

The contractor is responsible for his sub-contractors and suppliers (clause 9.9), but the architect's consent must be obtained to sub-letting (clause 9.2). Provision is made in clauses 9.4 and 9.5 for sub-contractors to be named either in the contract documents or by way of an architect's instruction regarding provisional sums.

Clause 5 is important. It provides for the contractor to ensure proper management of the works, appoint a site manager and employ only appropriately skilled and qualified people on the works. This duty is backed up by the sanction that the architect (clause 8.1(b)) may require the dismissal from the works of any incompetent person.

Architect's instructions are dealt with by clause 8. Certain instructions can be issued at any time up to completion of all the contractor's obligations. Procedures for valuation are covered in clause 17 which requires the contractor to submit written estimates of the value of the adjustment, the length of any extension of the time and the amount of any loss or expense. Work not forming part of the contract may be carried out by the employer's own contractors subject to certain provisos.

The claims clause (clause 7) is very broad, dealing with any act, omission, default or negligence of the employer or the architect which disrupts the regular progress of the whole or part of the works. Loss or expense resulting from architect's instructions is excepted, being dealt with under clause 17.

The scheme of certificates and payments requires the contractor to submit interim applications, with supporting documents, on the last working day of each month up to and including the month in which taking-over occurs and thereafter, as and when further amounts become due either to the contractor or to the employer (clause 16.1). The architect is to issue his certificate within 10 working days of the contractor's application. Payment of 95% of the amount stated as due must be made by the employer within a further 10 working days. Failure to pay is a ground for termination under clause 20.2 (a). Final payment is governed by clause 19. The contractor must submit his final account with vouchers within 60 working days after the end of the maintenance period (q.v.) and the architect must issue his final certificate (q.v.) within 60 working days after the contractor has completed all his contractual obligations. No certificate relieves the contractor of any liability under the contract.

A unique feature is the optional provision for disputes to be settled by a named adjudicator (see: *Adjudication*) with the possibility of arbitration on his decision. It is one of three options. The others are arbitration (q.v.) and litigation (q.v.). If litigation is adopted, the contract confers on the courts 'full power to open up, review and revise' the architect's opinions. In the absence of that provision, they have no such power, as shown by *North Western Regional Health Authority v. Derek Crouch Ltd* (1984).

Tables 1, 2 and 3 give summaries of the clauses and the architect's and contractor's powers and duties under the contract.

A special edition of this contract (BPF edition of the ACA Form of Building Agreement) is also available, and is adapted for use with the British Property Federation system of contracting (see: *BPF System*). It contains some minor differences, such as fewer alternative clauses, the use of the term 'client's representative' (q.v.) rather than 'architect', and the mandatory use of adjudication followed by arbitration for the settlement of disputes.

| A fortiori argument | *A fortiori* means so much more; or, with stronger reason. It is commonly heard in judicial utterances when a particular case is being considered. Reference is made to a rule which applies to another case and it is thought that the case under consideration shows a stronger reason for application of the same rule and, therefore, the rule should apply to the case under consideration as well.

Such an argument is open to a variety of logical criticisms, notably that there may well be reasons why one rule should apply to the first case and a different rule to the case under consideration.

# Table 1 Summary of Clauses

**Clause 1 Contractor's general obligations**
In BPF/ACA an alternative clause 1.4 allows for either bills of quantities or schedule of activities

**Clause 2 Drawings, details, documents and information**
In ACA only, there are alternative clauses. BPF/ACA corresponds to ACA alternative two. In both versions, there is a new clause 2.6 dealing with ground conditions and artificial obstructions

**Clause 3 Obligations in respect of drawings, details, documents and information**
Clause 3.4 makes plain that architect's comments or advice do not relieve the contractor of responsibility for drawings, etc. Clause 3.5, new and common to both versions, deals with samples

**Clause 4 Visits to the works by the architect**
In BPF/ACA this is entitled 'The client's representative' and contains an additional sub-clause dealing with CR's assistants. The CR may delegate all or any of his duties to any number of persons or firms

**Clause 5 Supervision of works by the contractor**
Sub-clause 5.3 details the duties of the site manager

**Clause 6 Vesting of property, contractor's indemnity and insurance**
Clause 6.1 optionally allows for vesting of property where contract documents contain provision for the payment of unfixed goods and materials. Clause 6.6 (professional indemnity insurance) is mandatory in BPF/ACA, optional in ACA. Insurance clauses extensively revised

**Clause 7 Employer's liability**
In BPF/ACA, clause 7.6, adjudication is mandatory – optional in ACA. If contractor fails to submit estimates, he has no right to interest or financing charges on sums claimed

**Clause 8 Architect's (client's representative's) instructions**

**Clause 9 Assignment and sub-letting**
In BPF/ACA no sub-clauses 9.4 and 9.5 (provisional sums, etc.) or involvement with named sub-contractor negotiations. BPF/ACA has a special clause (9.6) dealing with substitute sub-contractors

**Clause 10 Employer's licensees**

**Clause 11 Commencement and delays in the execution of the works**
In BPF/ACA only liquidated damages are allowed. Grounds for extension of time correspond to ACA alternative two

**Clause 12 Taking-over and defective work**

**Clause 13 Taking over of part of the works**

**Clause 14 Antiquities**

**Clause 15 The Contract Sum**
In ACA 2 only there is an optional provision for the appointment and duties of the QS

**Clause 16 Payment**
In BPF/ACA alternatives for payment based on schedule of activities or bills of quantities. ACA 2, clause 16.4 makes the placing of the retention in a separate bank account optional for local authorities. ACA(BPF has no clause 16.6 dealing with provisional sums)

**Clause 17 Valuation of architect's (client's representative's) instructions**
ACA 2 has optional provision for reference to an adjudicator if contractor's estimates are not agreed. Mandatory in BPF/ACA

**Clause 18 Fluctuations**
Optional in both cases. ACA Index used and only 80 per cent payable

**Clause 19 Payment of final contract sum**

**Clause 20 Termination**
Reference to an adjudicator optional in ACA 2

# Table 1  Summary of Clauses (continued)

**Clause 21 Termination due to causes outside control of both parties**

**Clause 22 Consequences of termination**

**Clause 23 Notices and interpretation**

**Clause 24 Finance (No. 2) Act 1975**

**Clause 25 Disputes**

ACA 2 has alternatives – adjudication, arbitration and litigation. BPF/ACA has only adjudication

In both cases the contract conditions are preceded by Articles of Agreement and conclude with the vital time schedule. The differences between ACA 2 and BPF/ACA are minimal

# Table 2 Architect's powers and duties under ACA 2

| Clause | Architect's power or duty | Comment/Precondition |
|---|---|---|
| 1.4 | **Duty** Correct any mistake in quantities or omission or misdescription of *items* in the bills and certify a fair adjustment to the contract sum | Where bills of quantities form part of the agreement |
| 1.5 | **Power** Issue instructions regarding ambiguities or discrepancies in the contract documents | |
| 1.6 | **Duty** Issue instructions about infringement of statutory requirements | |
| 2.1 | **Duty** Supply contractor with two copies of the contract documents immediately after the execution of the agreement | Applies to both alternatives |
| 2.2 | **Duty** Supply contractor with two copies or a negative of such drawings or details as are, in his opinion, reasonably necessary to explain or amplify the contract drawings or to enable the contractor to execute and complete the works | Alternative one: contractor must make specific application at the right time unless a date for supply is listed in the time schedule Alternative two: duty limited to supplying drawings, etc., expressly stated to be the architect's responsibility |
| 2.3 | **Duty** Return one copy of contractor's drawings, etc., with comments or 'no comment' within 10 working days or other period specified in time schedule | Contractor's submission of drawings, etc. |
| 2.6 | **Duty** Issue instructions as to how adverse ground conditions or artificial obstruction at the site are to be dealt with | Contractor's written notification with details |
| 3.5 | **Power** Instruct contractor to provide samples of quality of goods and/or materials or standards of workmanship to be used in works | |
| 4.2 | **Power** Visit site and workshops, etc., from time to time or as specified in contract documents | |
| 5.2 | **Power** Consent in writing to appointment of site manager or to substitute | Notification by contractor |
| 5.3 | **Power** Request contractor's site manager, employees, and sub-contractors or suppliers to attend meetings | |
| 6.4 | **Duty** Ascertain and certify a fair and reasonable adjustment to the contract sum in respect of restoration, etc., by the contractor of damaged works | Alternative two: where employer has undertaken to insure |
| 7.4 | **Power** Require contractor to submit vouchers, receipts, etc., necessary for computing the contractor's estimate of the adjustment of the contract sum as a result of disturbance to regular progress **Duty** Give notice to contractor of acceptance of estimate or of wish to negotiate *and* Adjust contract sum when agreement is reached | |

# Table 2 Architect's powers and duties under ACA 2 (continued)

| Clause | Architect's power or duty | Comment/Precondition |
|---|---|---|
| 8.1 | **Power** Issue written instructions at any time up to taking-over in respect of any matter connected with the works, *and* Issue instructions at any time up to completion of all defective outstanding work in respect of: removal from site of defective work, etc.; dismissal from the works of incompetent people; opening up of work for inspection and testing; altering obligations to restrictions as regards working hours, space or site access or use | |
| 8.3 | **Power** Issue oral instructions **Duty** Confirm any oral instructions in writing | Oral instructions can only be issued in an emergency |
| 9.2 | **Power** Consent in writing to sub-letting any portion of the works | If so requested by the contractor |
| 9.4 | **Power** Issue instructions requiring contractor to sub-let work to person named | Contract documents must provide that work priced as provisional is to be carried out by person(s) named |
| 9.5 | **Power** Issue instructions requiring sub-letting | As above, but sub-contractor or supplier need not be named |
| 9.6 | **Power** Attend negotiation meetings between contractor and named sub-contractor, *and* Inspect and check accounts and payment records in respect of named sub-contractors and suppliers **Duty** Consent to alternative sub-contractor where proposed named sub-contractor is unable to contract | The sub-contractor or supplier must be named in contract documents or under clause 9.5

The contractor must select another person and reason for failure must be beyond the control of the contractor |
| 9.7 | **Duty** Consent to substitute sub-contractor if named sub-contractor's employment is properly determined by main contractor | Determination or discharge must be in accordance with sub-contract terms |
| 10.2 | **Power** Issue instructions in relation to employer's contractors | Contractor is not bound to comply if he makes reasonable objection within five working days |
| 11.2 | **Power** Issue certificate that works or section of them not fit and ready for taking over | Date specified in time schedule or any extended period must have elapsed |
| 11.3 | **Power** Deduct damages from amount otherwise payable to contractor on any certificate | Only applies where alternative one (liquidated damages) is operative. Certificate under clause 11.2 is a prerequisite to deduction |
| 11.6 | **Duty** Grant in writing such extension of time as he estimates to be fair and reasonable | It must be reasonably apparent that the works will not be completed by the due date, *and* Contractor must have submitted written notice *unless* delay is caused by act, instruction, omission or default of employer or architect on his behalf, *and* Reasons for delay must be within the terms of whichever alternative applies |
| 11.7 | **Duty** Review extensions of time granted within a reasonable time after taking over and notify contractor of final decision | Architect *must* do this and confirm dates even if no extension is granted |

# Table 2 Architect's powers and duties under ACA 2 (continued)

| Clause | Architect's power or duty | Comment/Precondition |
|---|---|---|
| 11.8 | **Power** Instruct contractor to accelerate or postpone dates shown on time schedule for taking over any section of part of the works **Duty** Ascertain and certify a fair and reasonable adjustment of contract sum in respect of contractor's compliance | Must not be done unreasonably; cannot be used to reduce original total contract period Architect may require contractor to give estimate of adjustment required before instructing acceleration |
| 12.1 | **Power** Issue taking over certificate, *or* Notify contractor of items of work required to be done to render works fit and ready for taking over, *or* Approve contractor's list of outstanding items of work, *or* Add items to the contractor's list | Contractor must have given notification that works are fit and ready for taking over In last three cases the taking over certificate must be issued as soon as contractor has completed outstanding items Taking over certificate may be issued even if items are outstanding provided contractor gives written undertaking to complete outstanding items with due diligence |
| 12.2 | **Power** Instruct during maintenance period or 10 working days thereafter the making good of defects, etc. | |
| 12.3 | **Duty** Ascertain and certify a fair and reasonable adjustment of contract sum where remedial works are not contractor's fault | Defective work is at contractor's cost unless due to employer's use or occupation or his or the architect's negligence, omission or default |
| 13.3 | **Duty** Certify a fair and reasonable reduction of liquidated damages where employer takes over part of the works | Contractor's consent to partial taking-over is required. This duty only applies where clause 11.3, alternative one applies |
| 14.2 | **Duty** Issue instructions if antiquities, etc., are discovered | Written notification from contractor |
| 15.2 | **Power** Assign duties to QS where appointed | |
| 16.2 | **Duty** Certify interim payments at monthly intervals until month when taking over occurs and thereafter as further amounts fall due | Contractor's interim application, supported by vouchers, etc. |
| 17.2 | **Duty** Take reasonable steps to agree contractor's estimates of value of compliance with instructions, *and* Grant appropriate extension of time and appropriate adjustments to contract sum | Wherever in the opinion of either architect or contractor certain instructions will require adjustment to the contract sum and/or affect the time schedule, the contractor is to provide the architect with estimates of the adjustments required. The qualifying instructions are: 1.5 Ambiguities or discrepancies 1.6 Statutory requirements 2.6 Ground conditions, etc. 3.5 Samples 8.1 (c) Opening up, soil testing, etc.; (d) Alteration of obligations as to working spaces, hours, etc; (e) Variations as such; (f) Other matters connected with the works 14 Finding antiquities |
| 17.3 | **Power** Instruct contractor to comply with instruction where estimates not agreed, *or* Instruct him not to comply, *or* Refer him to adjudicator for decisions | Clause 17.5 will apply and contractor is reimbursed Contractor has no claim Only if adjudication option applies |

# Table 2 Architect's powers and duties under ACA 2 (continued)

| Clause | Architect's power or duty | Comment/Precondition |
|---|---|---|
| 17.5 | **Power** By notice to the contractor dispense with need for contractor to submit estimates **Duty** Ascertain and certify a fair and reasonable adjustment to contract sum and grant a fair and reasonable extension for the contractor's compliance | |
| 18.3 | **Duty** Calculate substitute indices for fluctuations | Only where clause 18 applies and ACA index is not published or publication is delayed |
| 19.2 | **Duty** Issue final certificate stating final contract sum | This must be done within 60 working days after completion by the contractor of all his obligations. The contractor must submit his vouched and documented final account within 60 working days after the maintenance period expires |
| 19.5 | **Power** Delete, modify or correct any sum which he has previously certified. This he may do in *any* certificate | |
| 22.1 | **Duty** Certify the amount of any loss, damage and/or expense suffered or incurred by the employer where the contract has been terminated by the employer for contractor's fault | Exercisable only when the full and final cost of completion by others has been ascertained |
| 22.2 | **Duty** Ascertain and certify the total amount due to contractor on termination by him for employer's fault | Also where termination through no one's fault, but in that case no loss or expense is payable |
| 25.1 | **Power** Settle matters in dispute **Duty** Give written notice to both parties of his decision about any dispute referred to him | Only where alternative two (settlement of disputes by arbitration) applies |

# Table 3 Contractor's powers and duties under ACA 2

| *Clause* | *Contractor's power or duty* | *Comment/Precondition* |
|---|---|---|
| 1.1 | **Duty** Execute and complete the works in strict accordance with the contract documents | |
| 1.1 | **Duty** Comply with and strictly adhere to the architect's instructions issued under the contract | |
| 1.2 | **Duty** In performing his contractual obligations to exercise all the skill, care and diligence to be expected of a proper qualified and competent contractor, who is experienced in carrying out work of a similar scope, nature and size to the works. | |
| 1.5 | **Duty** Notify the architect of any ambiguity or discrepancy contained in the contract documents | Compliance with the architect's subsequent instruction qualifies for payment unless the ambiguity, etc., could reasonably have been foreseen at the date of contract by a contractor exercising the prescribed standard of skill, care and diligence |
| 1.6 and 1.7 | **Duty** Comply with statutory requirements for the works. Notify architect of any infringement, *and* Make duty all statutory applications, give notices and pay fees unless otherwise instructed by architect, *and* Indemnify employer against all damage, loss and/or expense incurred as a result of contractor's breach | Compliance with the architect's subsequent instruction qualifies for payment |
| 2.1 | **Duty** Apply specifically to the architect for necessary drawings and details at a reasonable time | Alternative one only: unless a date is shown on the time schedule for supply of the information |
| 2.2 | **Duty** Submit to the architect two copies or a negative of all drawings, etc., which are reasonably necessary to explain and amplify the contract drawings or specification, *or* To enable the contractor to execute and complete the works, *or* Are stated in the contract documents as being provided by the contractor | Alternative two only: where the contractor is to prepare further drawings, details or documents necessary to build the works. This must be done at a reasonable time |
| 2.4 | **Duty** Take account of any comments by the architect on the drawings, etc., submitted and resubmit to the architect under clause 2.2 | |
| 2.5 | **Duty** Ensure that all work shown on the drawings, etc., submitted by him, complies with statutory requirements | |
| 2.6 | **Duty** Notify the architect if adverse ground conditions or artificial obstructions are encountered on site, *and* Comply with any architect's instructions | Compliance with the architect's instructions qualifies for payment unless competent contractors could reasonably have foreseen the situation |

# Table 3  Contractor's powers and duties under ACA 2 (continued)

| Clause | Contractor's power or duty | Comment/Precondition |
|--------|---------------------------|----------------------|
| 3.1 | **Duty** Responsible for the accuracy of all drawings, etc., prepared by him, *and* Must ensure that the works comply with any performance specification or requirement in the contract documents, *and* That the parts designed by the contractor must be reasonably fit for their intended purpose | This express obligation is 'without prejudice to any express or implied warranties or conditions' and is therefore an additional obligation |
| 3.3 | **Duty** Must preserve confidentiality of information and not disclose to unauthorised third parties | |
| 3.5 | **Power** Request the architect to accept samples in lieu of drawings, etc. **Duty** Comply at his own cost with any procedures set out in architect's consent to submission of samples | The architect's consent must not be unreasonably withheld or delayed |
| 4.1 | **Duty** Give the architect and his representatives full access to the works and his own workshops and those of his sub-contractors, etc. | |
| 4.2 | **Duty** Assist the architect and his representatives during site visits | |
| 5.1 | **Duty** Provide all necessary inspection, supervision, planning and management to ensure proper performance of his contractual obligations | |
| 5.2 | **Duty** Appoint a competent full-time site agent or manager | The architect must approve the appointment and any subsequent change |
| 5.3 | **Duty** Ensure that the site agent or his other employees or sub-contractors, etc., attend meetings convened by the architect in connection with the works | Only if the architect so requests |
| 5.4 | **Duty** Employ only appropriately skilled personnel on the works | |
| 6.1 | **Duty** Ensure that any goods or materials valued and included in an interim certificate are not removed except for delivery to site | Only applies if contract documents contain provision for payment of goods and materials before incorporation in the works |
| 6.3 | **Duty** Indemnify the employer and insure against personal injury or death or damage to property as described in the agreement, *and* Ensure that his sub-contractors insure as described in the agreement | Does not apply to property to be insured under clause 6.4 |
| 6.4 | **Duty** Insure in joint names of employer and contractor against all risks stated | There are alternative versions |
| 6.5 | **Duty** Insure in joint names against subsidence and collapse, etc., where so required by the contract documents | Exceptions are where damage is caused by contractor's negligence, *or* Errors or omissions in design, *or* Where damage could reasonably have been foreseen having regard to the nature of the work to be executed or the manner of its execution |

# Table 3 Contractor's powers and duties under ACA 2 (continued)

| Clause | Contractor's power or duty | Comment |
|---|---|---|
| 6.6 | **Duty** Take out professional indemnity insurance as required by contract documents | Only where contractor is responsible for preparing details, drawings, etc., and so assumes design liability: see clause 2, alternative two |
| 6.8 | **Duty** Pay insurance premiums promptly and produce insurance policies and premium receipts if requested by the employer | |
| 7.2 | **Duty** Notify the architect | If it becomes apparent that there is likely to be disturbance to regular progress If an event giving rise to a money claim is likely to occur or has occurred |
| 7.2 | **Duty** Submit estimate of required adjustment to contract sum with supporting documentation | On presentation of the next interim application for payment following the giving of notice |
| 7.6 | **Power** Refer estimate, etc., to adjudicator if appointed | If agreement cannot be reached within 20 working days of the architect's notice of his wish to negotiate an adjustment |
| 8.1 | **Duty** Immediately comply with all the architect's instructions | Instructions must be issued in writing, except in an emergency |
| 9.1 | **Power** Assign the contract | If the employer consents in writing |
| 9.2 | **Power** Sub-let any portion of the works | If the architect consents in writing |
| 9.3 | **Duty** Sub-let work to or obtain goods or materials from named sub-contractors | Where the contract documents so provide |
| 9.4 | **Duty** Comply with the architect's instructions as to named sub-contractors | There must be a provisional sum and a person or a list of named persons in the contract documents |
| 9.5 | **Duty** Comply with the architect's instructions requiring sub-letting | There must be a provisional sum, *and* The contractor has a right to make reasonable objection within five working days of the date of the instruction |
| 9.6 | **Duty** Negotiate and agree a price with any named sub-contractor or supplier Notify the architect of negotiations, meetings, etc., and permit him to attend them Supply the architect with copy correspondence and documents | |
| 9.6 | **Duty** Select someone to carry out the specified work and obtain architect's consent to substitute, *and* Keep proper and detailed accounts and records of all payments to named sub-contractors and suppliers and make available for inspection by the architect | Only if negotiations do not result in a sub-contract, *and* If this is for reasons beyond contractor's control |
| 9.7 | **Duty** Select another sub-contractor or supplier if the named sub-contractor fails and obtain the architect's consent to the substitution | |
| 9.8 | **Duty** Responsible for any design carried out by all sub-contractors and suppliers | The contractor should obtain appropriate indemnities and/or insurance cover |

# Table 3 Contractor's powers and duties under ACA 2 (continued)

| Clause | Contractor's power or duty | Comment |
|---|---|---|
| 9.9 | **Duty** Responsible for all sub-contractors, etc. | |
| 10.1 | **Duty** Permit work to be done on site by employer's licensees as provided in the contract documents | The work done must not form part of the contract work |
| 10.2 | **Duty** Permit work, etc., to be done by others engaged by the employer | The work must not form part of the contract, *and* The contractor has a right of reasonable objection |
| 10.3 | **Duty** Permit work to be executed on site by statutory undertakers | The work must not form part of the contract, *and* It must be done pursuant to statutory obligation, for example mains installation |
| 11.1 | **Duty** Immediately start the works when possession of the site is given and proceed regularly and diligently with it in accordance with the time schedule so that the works (or sections) are fit and ready for taking over on the due date | Subject to any extensions of time granted by the architect or adjudicator (if appropriate) |
| 11.3 | **Duty** Pay or allow to the employer liquidated damages at the rate specified in the time schedule | If the works are not fit and ready for taking over, *and* The architect has issued a clause 11.2 certificate to that effect (alternative one only) |
| 11.5 | **Duty** Notify the architect immediately, specifying the event(s) in question, *and* Submit to the architect as soon as possible after the notice full and detailed particulars of the extension of time to which he considers himself entitled, *and* Submit any further particulars necessary to keep the architect up to date | If it becomes reasonably apparent that taking over by the prescribed date(s) will be prevented by one or more of the listed events |
| | Prove to the satisfaction of the architect that taking over is prevented by the specified event(s) | The architect may request additional details Note that there are alternative versions of clause 11; alternative one is more limited Alternative two only |
| 11.9 | **Duty** Submit revised time schedule to the architect | Where date for taking over is adjusted |
| 12.1 | **Power** Submit to the architect a list of any outstanding works required to render the works fit and ready for taking over | If appropriate |
| 12.1 | **Power** Give a written undertaking to complete outstanding items with all due diligence **Duty** Notify the architect when in his opinion the works (or a section) are fit and ready for taking over | |
| 12.2 | **Duty** With all due diligence complete any defective outstanding work during the maintenance period, *and* Immediately carry out any remedial work ordered by the architect | This may be instructed during the maintenance period or within 14 days of its expiry |

# Table 3 Contractor's powers and duties under ACA 2 (continued)

| Clause | Contractor's power or duty | Comment/Precondition |
|---|---|---|
| 12.3 | **Duty** Remedy all defective work at his own expense | Unless, in the architect's opinion, it is due to the employer's use or occupation or the negligence, etc., of the employer or the architect |
| 12.4 | **Duty** Bear the costs of remedying defective work by others | If contractor is in default, *and* Notice of default has been served on him |
| 13.1 | **Duty** Consent to employer's request to take over part of the works | Consent must not be unreasonably withheld Damages will be proportionately reduced |
| 14.2 | **Duty** Immediately notify architect if antiquities, etc., are found on site, and not disturb or damage them | Compliance with any architect's instruction issued as a result will qualify for payment |
| 16.1 | **Duty** Submit interim applications for payment to the architect with supporting documentation | On the last working day of each month (or other agreed intervals) up to and including the calendar month in which taking over occurs. Thereafter, as due |
| 17.1 | **Duty** Supply the architect with estimates of value, extension of time, and loss and expense of compliance with architect's instruction | If requested by architect or in the contractor's opinion the contract sum, etc., will require adjustment |
| 17.2 | **Duty** Take reasonable steps to agree those estimates with the architect | |
| 19.1 | **Duty** Submit vouchered final account to architect | Within 60 working days after the expiry of the maintenance period |
| 19.4 | **Duty** Deliver to the employer all drawings, etc., prepared by or on behalf of contractor for the works | Must be done before the issue of the final certificate |
| 20.1 | **Power** Refer validity of default notice to adjudicator **Duty** Comply with employer's default notice | If adjudication option applies |
| 20.2 | **Power** Serve a default notice on the employer | If the employer: Fails to pay any amount properly due and payable on any certificate, *and* Obstructs the issue of any certificate, *or* Is otherwise in breach of contract *and* the breach has prevented the contractor carrying out any of his obligations for a continuous period of 20 working days |
| 20.2 | **Power** Serve a termination notice on the employer terminating his employment under the contract forthwith | If the employer fails to remedy the default specified in the default notice within 10 working days. If the adjudication option applies and the employer has referred the dispute to the adjudicator, the termination notice cannot be served until the adjudicator has given his decision |
| 20.3 | **Power** Serve a termination notice on the employer | Only applicable to insolvency, no previous default notice is required |
| 21 | **Power** Serve a termination notice on the employer | If the contractor is prevented or delayed from executing the works for a period of 66 consecutive working days by *force majeure, or* Occurrence of an insurance risk listed in clause 6.4, *or* War and allied causes |

## Table 3  Contractor's powers and duties under ACA 2 (continued)

| Clause | Contractor's power or duty | Comment/Precondition |
|--------|----------------------------|----------------------|
| 22.4 | **Duty** Immediately deliver to the employer possession of the site and properly protect and secure the works | When a termination notice is served by either party, even if the contractor disputes its validity |
| 22.6 | **Duty** Deliver to the employer all drawings, etc., prepared by or on behalf of contractor for the works | Upon any termination of the contractor's employment |
| 22.7 | **Duty** To do all things necessary to effect assignment of sub-contracts, etc. | Upon any termination of the contractor's employment |
| 24.3 | **Duty** Forthwith supply the employer with Inland Revenue form 715 | If the contractor receives a payment from the employer without statutory tax deduction, *and* If the contractor is not the holder of Inland Revenue form 714c |
| 24.4 | **Duty** State in any interim certificate application or in final account the amount included in respect of the true and accurate direct cost to the contractor, etc., of the materials and goods used in executing the works | Only where contractor does not provide form 714c or form 715 |
| 24.5 | **Duty** Indemnify employer against any damage, etc., suffered by non-compliance with clause 24 obligations | |
| 25.1 | **Power** Refer any dispute, etc., to the architect in writing for decision | If arbitration option applies service of notice does not relieve either party of liability for due and punctual performance |
| 25.2 | **Power** Refer any dispute, etc., to the named adjudicator **Duty** Provide any evidence required by adjudicator | If adjudication provision applies alternative one |
| 25.3 | **Power** Refer dispute, etc., to arbitration | If dissatisfied with architect's decision |
| 25.5 | **Power** Give notice of arbitration | If dissatisfied with adjudicator's decision |

| | |
|---|---|
| **Abandonment of work** | A phrase used in the arbitration (q.v.) provisions of JCT 80 (article 5), GC/Works/1 (clause 61) and ACA 2 (clause 25, alternative 2). Completion or abandonment of the work marks the point at which any reference to arbitration may be opened. Abandonment of the works must entail complete stoppage of all the works and the clear intention not to continue at some future date. It implies removal of all the contractor's men and sub-contractors from the site and may be construed as intention to repudiate the contract. See also: *Repudiation*. |
| **Abatement** | Used alone, the term refers to the interruption of legal proceedings following an application, usually by the defendant, stating reasons why the proceedings should not continue. The most common instance in the construction industry is probably the application of the limitation period (see: *Limitation of actions*), but it could be an objection to the form or place of the plaintiff's (q.v.) claim. Abatement in relation to nuisance (q.v.) refers to the right of the person who suffers injury or damage by reason of the nuisance to act personally to remove the cause. Care must be taken not to interfere with another party's rights and, in any case, abatement of nuisance is not looked upon with favour by the courts, unless there is an emergency, because other remedies are available by application to the courts. Local authorities may serve abatement notices in respect of statutory nuisances. |
| **Abeyance** | Technically, where a right is not presently vested in anyone, and in this sense of no importance in building contracts. Generally, when something is said to be 'in abeyance' what is meant is that it is in a state of being suspended or temporarily put aside. |
| **Abrogate** | To repeal or annul, and hence *abrogation* which refers to the annulling or repealing of a law by legislation. |

| | |
|---|---|
| **Absolute** | Full, complete and unconditional. Absolute liability is liability irrespective of the degree of care taken. No proof of negligence or default is required. It is sufficient only that a particular incident has occurred. This type of liability may be imposed by statute (q.v.). See also: *Liability; Strict liability.* |
| **Absolute assignment** | The assignment (q.v.) or transfer of an entire debt (q.v.), as opposed to merely part of it, and without any conditions attached. |
| **Abstract of particulars** | The phrase used in GC/Works/1 to refer to the supplement which contains important terms and details which, in other forms of contract, are usually set out in an Appendix (q.v.). It lists modifications to the printed conditions, gives the date for completion, the amount of liquidated damages and the length of the maintenance period (q.v.). It also names the employer ('the Authority') and the 'Superintending Officer' (q.v.). Two addenda set out dates after acceptance for the provision of certain information which is relevant in the case of a disruption claim and the length of time for any sub-contract nominations. |
| **Abut** | In physical contact with. There must be actual contact between part of the premises and the road or other feature which will produce some measurable frontage. |
| **Acceleration of work** | Under the general law, the architect has no power to instruct the contractor to accelerate work. The contractor's obligation is to complete the work within the time specified, or – where no particular contract period is specified – within a reasonable time (q.v.). The contractor cannot be compelled to complete earlier than the agreed date unless there is an express contract term authorizing the architect to require acceleration.<br>ACA 2, clause 11.8 empowers the architect to issue an instruction to bring forward dates shown on the |

Time Schedule (q.v.) for the taking-over (q.v.) of any part of the Works, but this power may not be exercised unreasonably and an appropriate adjustment must be made to the contract sum.

In other cases, if the employer wishes the work to be completed earlier (or more usually to be completed on time despite unavoidable delays) a special agreement must be negotiated, and will generally involve extra payment.

Architects sometimes believe that JCT 80, clause 25.3.4.2, and GC/Works/1, clause 28(2)(iv) give them the power to instruct acceleration measures because both clauses state that the contractor must 'do all that may reasonably be required' to the satisfaction of the architect to proceed with the works. A clause like this is often erroneously referred to by architect and contractor alike as the 'acceleration clause'. That, however, is not its true function. It is there to ensure that the contractor proceeds with the work diligently (q.v.), taking notice of the architect's wishes but not to an extent involving the use of additional resources.

If the architect does issue an instruction to accelerate and the contractor obeys, the legal position could be:
—The contractor is not entitled to payment.
—The contractor is entitled to reasonable payment on the basis of an implied contract or *quantum meruit* (q.v.).

Because the architect has no implied authority to issue acceleration instructions or make a new contract, he could find himself paying for the measure himself directly or indirectly. If the employer has authorized the instruction, the contractor is more likely to be able to make a successful claim. See also: *Postponement*.

| | |
|---|---|
| **Acceptance** | The act of agreeing to an offer (q.v.) which constitutes a binding contract. Acceptance may be made in writing, orally or by conduct. Acceptance by conduct would occur if the offeree acted in such a way as to observe the terms of the offer and clearly show that |

he intended to be bound by it. Acceptance must be unqualified or there is no contract. A qualified acceptance may amount to a counter-offer (q.v.). Thus, if contractor A offered to build a house for employer B for the sum of £20,000 and B 'accepted' subject to a reduction in price for the omission of the garage, B is said to have made a counter-offer. The original offer is terminated and B cannot later decide to accept it.

If the form of acceptance is stipulated by the offeror, no other form will suffice. Thus, oral acceptance of an offer stipulating written acceptance will not form a binding contract. If acceptance is made by post, it becomes operative from the moment it is posted, no matter that the offeror has already posted a letter withdrawing his offer.

If a tender is received by the employer and a letter of acceptance sent, all the terms of the contract are immediately in force even though the formal signing of the contract documents has not taken place unless the parties have agreed that there shall be no contract until the formal documents are signed. This is a point often overlooked by architects who, for example, refuse to issue interim certificates until the contract documents are signed. See also: *Letter of intent; Subject to contract; Incorporation of Documents.*

**Accepted risks**

The term used in GC/Works/1, clauses 1(2), 25(1) and 28 to describe the risks which may affect the works but which are outside the contractor's control. Clause 1(2) defines 'accepted risks' as fire or explosion; storm, lightning, tempest, flood or earthquake; aircraft or other aerial devices or objects dropped from them, including pressure waves caused by aircraft or such devices whether travelling at sonic or supersonic speeds; ionising radiations or contamination from radioactivity from any nuclear fuel or from nuclear waste from the combustion of nuclear fuel, radioactive, toxic, explosive or other hazardous properties of any explosive nuclear assembly or nuclear component thereof; riot, civil commotion, civil war, rebellion, revolution, insurrection, military or usurped power or King's enemy risks (q.vv.).

Under clause 25(1) the contractor is under a duty to take all reasonable precautions to prevent loss or damage from any of the accepted risks and to minimize the amount of loss or damage so caused. Provided he does so the Authority pays for loss or damage so caused and the contractor is entitled to an extension of time under clause 28.

---

**Access to works**

The contractor has an implied right of access to the works in so far as the access is controlled by the employer, otherwise it would be impossible for him to carry them out.

Under clause 25.4.12 of JCT 80, failure by the employer to give ingress or egress to or from the site is a ground for extension of time. It may also give rise to a money claim under clause 26.2.6. There are several provisos attached:

—The access must be across adjoining or connected land, buildings, way or passage.

—Such land, etc., must be in the possession *and* control of the employer

—The means of access must have been stated on the drawings or in the bills of quantities (q.v.).

—The contractor must have given such notice, if any, that he is required to give.

It is not a breach of contract where access is impeded by third parties over whom the employer has no control, e.g., pickets: *LRE Engineering Services Ltd v. Otto Simon Carves Ltd* (1981). Similarly, no extension could be awarded or money claim allowed if the employer failed to obtain permission for the contractor to cross a third party's property, though that might well amount to a breach of contract by the employer if he has expressly undertaken to obtain such access. There is also a strange provision in the clause for extension of time and money if the employer has failed to give such access as the *architect* and the contractor have agreed between them. This seems to be a surprising extension of the architect's power to bind the employer.

ACA 2 makes no specific provision for extension of time or money on the ground that the employer has failed to provide access, but failure to provide agreed access would give rise to such claims on the ground of the employer's default: clause 11.5, both alternatives; clause 7.

The position under GC/Works/1 is similar: clause 28 (2)(c). Clause 56 (Admission to the Site) is not relevant. It merely refers to the power of the Authority to refuse admission to such persons as the Authority shall think fit.

| | |
|---|---|
| **Accident** | An unlooked-for mishap or an untoward event neither designed nor expected (*Fenton v. Thorley* (1903)). Its actual meaning in a contract or elsewhere is a question of interpretation ( *J. & J. Makin Ltd v.London & North Eastern Railway Co.* (1943)). In general, accident is no defence to action in tort (q.v.) and in some cases the happening of an accident may itself give rise to a *prima facie* case of liability. This is known as *res ipsa loquitur* ('the thing speaks for itself') which was explained in *Scott v. London & St Catherine's Docks Co.*(1865): |

'Where the thing is shown to be under the management of the defendant or his servants, and the accident is such as in the ordinary course of things does not happen if those who have the management use proper care, it affords reasonable evidence in the absence of explanation by the defendants, that the accident arose from want of care.'

For example, objects do not usually fall from scaffolding unless there is negligence, so if a visitor to site is injured by a bucket falling on his head from scaffolding, the maxim will apply. See also: *Inevitable accident.*

| | |
|---|---|
| **Accommodation works** | Works such as bridges, fences, gates, etc., which are carried out and maintained by statutory undertakers (q.v.), e.g., the Department of Transport, British Rail, |

etc., for the accommodation or convenience of the owners or occupiers of adjoining land. For example, there is a statutory obligation on British Rail (as successor to the former railway companies) to fence off land used for the railway from adjoining land.

| | |
|---|---|
| **Accord and satisfaction** | 'The purchase of a release from an obligation whether arising under contract or tort by means of any valuable consideration, not being the actual performance of the obligation itself. The accord is the agreement by which the obligation is discharged. The satisfaction is the consideration which makes the agreement operative': *British Russian Gazette & Trade Outlook Ltd v. Associated Newspapers Ltd* (1933). Accord and satisfaction bars any right of action. If a contractor agrees to accept part payment and to release the employer from payment of the balance, this will be valid if the agreement is supported by fresh consideration (q.v.) or if the agreement is under seal (q.v.). There must be true accord, under which the creditor *voluntarily* agrees to accept a lesser sum in satisfaction: *D. & C. Builders Ltd v. Rees* (1966). The essential point is that the creditor must voluntarily accept something different from that to which he is entitled (*Pinnel's Case* (1602)). Although writing is not legally necessary it is prudent to arrange that the agreement should be recorded formally in a letter or other document, e.g., if a legal action is being compromised a suitable formula would be 'I accept the sum of £x in full and final settlement of all or any claims ... and I will forthwith instruct my solicitors to serve notice of discontinuance.' |
| **Accrued rights or remedies of either party** | This is a phrase used in JCT 80, clause 28.2 ( JCT 63, clause 26 (2)) with reference to the rights and duties of the parties following the contractor's determination of his employment under the contract. It does not refer merely to cases where the right or remedy is a claim for breach of contract but also to other rights and remedies, e.g., the architect's right to issue an instruction requiring rectification of |

defective work (*Lintest Builders Ltd v. Roberts* (1980)). Since under the contract the employer acquires a right to have the defective work remedied at the time it was carried out, this is an 'accrued right' for the purposes of the clause. See also: *Rights and remedies*.

## Act of bankruptcy

The outward sign that an individual is insolvent (see: *Insolvency*). Before a person can be made bankrupt (see: *Bankruptcy*) he must commit what is technically called 'an act of bankruptcy' which is statutory recognition of his insolvent state. Several acts of bankruptcy are specified in s.1 of the Bankruptcy Act 1914, as amended. They include presenting a bankruptcy petition to the court, failing to comply with a bankruptcy notice served on him by a judgment creditor, or allowing his goods to be seized to enforce a judgment.

Within three months of the act of bankruptcy, a creditor may petition the court for a receiving order (q.v.). Bankruptcy is deemed to have begun on the day the act was committed.

## Act of God

An archaic legal phrase meaning a sudden and inevitable occurrence caused by natural forces. The test is whether or not human foresight and prudence can reasonably recognize its possibility so as to guard against it (*Greenock Corporation v. Caledonian Railway Co.* (1917)). Lightning, earthquake (at least in the United Kingdom) and very extraordinary weather conditions come within the concept. An Act of God does not in itself excuse contractual performance, but it may do so on the true interpretation of the terms of the contract. Some insurance policies and contracts for the carriage of goods provide that there is no liability for losses caused by Act of God. There appear to be no reported cases involving Act of God in the context of the construction industry, although some contractors may refer to it as an excuse for non-performance or a ground for terminating the contract. What they usually mean is the similar but wider concept of *force majeure* (q.v.). See also: *Frustration; Vis major*.

| **Act of Parliament** | A Statute (q.v.). It is the formal expression of the will of Parliament and sets out the law in written form, e.g., the Building Act 1984. |
|---|---|

A Statute (q.v.). It is the formal expression of the will of Parliament and sets out the law in written form, e.g., the Building Act 1984.

Proposed legislation is introduced in the form of a Bill which must pass through all the requisite stages in both Houses of Parliament and then receive the Royal Assent. The majority of modern Acts of Parliament are public general statutes which are of general application.

An Act of Parliament is divided into several parts:

—The *short title* by which the Act is known.

—The *long title* which sets out the purpose of the Act in general terms.

—The *enacting formula* which runs 'Be it enacted by the Queen's most Excellent Majesty, by and with the advice and the consent of the Lords Spiritual and Temporal, and Commons, in this present Parliament assembled, and by the authority of the same, as follows':

—The *numbered sections* which contain the substance of the Act. Each is divided into sub-sections, paragraphs and sub-paragraphs as appropriate.

—The *marginal notes* to each section.

—Various *Schedules* which contain matters of detail, repeals, etc.

The modern practice is for Acts to state broad general principles leaving matters of detail to be covered by regulations made by a Minister by Statutory Instrument (q.v.)

Figure 1 shows the first page of an Act of Parliament.

**Action**

A civil legal proceeding by one party against another. The purpose may be to gain a remedy, enforce a right, etc. Actions may be *in personam* (against an individual – the defendant) or *in rem* (against an item of property). Criminal proceedings are termed 'prosecutions'. See also: *Defendant; Plaintiff; Pleadings*.

**Ad hoc**

For this purpose. The Latin term used to refer to an appointment for a particular purpose and usually in contrast to an appointment *ex officio* (by virtue of office).

**Figure 1**
First page of an Act of Parliament

ELIZABETH II

# Arbitration Act 1979 —— short title

### 1979 CHAPTER 42

An Act to amend the law relating to arbitrations and for — long title
purposes connected therewith.     [4th April 1979] — date of royal assent

B E IT ENACTED by the Queen's most Excellent Majesty, by and
with the advice and consent of the Lords Spiritual and
Temporal, and Commons, in this present Parliament — enacting formula
assembled, and by the authority of the same, as follows:—

section —— **1.**—(1) In the Arbitration Act 1950 (in this Act referred to as Judicial
"the principal Act") section 21 (statement of case for a decision review of
of the High Court) shall cease to have effect and, without pre-arbitration
judice to the right of appeal conferred by subsection (2) below, awards.
the High Court shall not have jurisdiction to set aside or remit an 1950 c. 27.
award on an arbitration agreement on the ground of errors of fact
or law on the face of the award. — side note

(2) Subject to subsection (3) below, an appeal shall lie to the
High Court on any question of law arising out of an award
made on an arbitration agreement ; and on the determination of
such an appeal the High Court may by order—

(*a*) confirm, vary or set aside the award ; or ——————— paragraph

(*b*) remit the award to the reconsideration of the arbitrator
or umpire together with the court's opinion on the
question of law which was the subject of the appeal ;

and where the award is remitted under paragraph (*b*) above
the arbitrator or umpire shall, unless the order otherwise directs,
make his award within three months after the date of the order.

sub-
section

| | |
|---|---|
| **Ad idem** | Literally, at the same point, but also 'agreed' or 'of the same mind'. Negotiating parties are said to be *ad idem* when they have reached agreement on all the terms of contract. |
| **Addendum bills** | A term used to describe bills of quantities (q.v.) produced to modify the bills originally prepared. Common reasons for preparing addendum bills are:<br>—To make a reduction on the lowest tender figure if it exceeds the employer's budget. In this case they are usually termed 'reduction bills' (q.v.).<br>—When standard house types are designed and standard bills of quantities prepared, addendum bills are often necessary for use on individual contracts to quantify minor variations from the standard to accommodate such items as steps and staggers in terraces or otherwise identical dwellings. A point is reached when it becomes more convenient to take off a completely fresh set of quantities and the process of amendment starts again.<br>Addendum bills of the first type are not popular with any of the parties to the construction process. They can be confusing and lead to errors unless both are fully cross-referenced. For example, the original bills may include an item for pointing in a particular type of mastic. The addendum bills may show that the mastic has been omitted and a different, superior mastic added back. The addendum bills are, of course, referenced to the originals but the originals are often not referenced to the addendum. It is possible, therefore, that the contractor may overlook the change unless he checks through both documents. Some alterations will be clear from the drawings, which should reflect the situation shown in the original bills plus addendum bills. Unfortunately an item such as mastic will often simply be termed 'mastic' on the drawing, without any indication of the type. The contractor would be required to correct his mistake at his own cost, but he would be understandably angry about it. When faced with addendum bills, contractors should take care to go through their |

working copy of the original bills, noting in the margin where the addendum bills take effect.

If possible, addendum bills should be avoided unless they are very short. Their advantages – cheapness and speed – could be negatived if they lead the contractor to make a major blunder.

**Addition**

See: *Extra work.*

**Adjacent**

Lying near to but not necessarily adjoining: *Wellington v. Lower Hutt Corporation* (1904). It is a phrase sometimes found in building contracts in relation to access (q.v.) to the site and is contrasted with 'adjoining' which suggests a degree of contiguity. JCT 80, clause 25.4.12, for example, recognizes as a ground for extension of time the employer's failure to give access to the site over land which is in his possession and control and which is 'adjoining or connected with the site'. That sub-clause does not extend to an agreement to give access over *adjacent* land, though failure by the employer to do so where he had agreed access with the contractor might well amount to a breach of contract at common law and give rise to a common law claim by the contractor.

**Adjoining property**

Few building sites stand in isolation and so the rights of owners of adjoining property must always be considered. There is no general right of access over adjoining property, even for the purpose of carrying out essential repairs. Care must therefore be taken to ensure that the works are set out so that no trespass (q.v.) to neighbouring property occurs. See also: *Party walls; Support, right of.*

**Adjudication**

In English law, it refers to the decision of a court, especially in regard to bankruptcy. In Scots law, it is concerned with the attachment of land, usually in relation to a debt. In the special context of building contracts it means to decide an issue judicially. ACA 2 makes provision for the appointment of an adjudicator (clause 25, alternative 1.) His duties are clearly described in the clause. Broadly, he is to settle disputes which may arise between the employer and the contractor prior to the taking-over of the works. Clause 25.3 expressly provides that the adjudicator shall be deemed (q.v.) to be acting as an expert (q.v.), not as an arbitrator. He must give his decision in writing within 5 working days of being asked to do so by either party. Either party may require that the decision be referred to arbitration (q.v.) within 20 working days (10 working days in the case of termination) of receiving the adjudicator's decision, otherwise it becomes final and binding. The following disputes are referable to the adjudicator:

— Adjustment or alteration of the contract sum.

— Entitlement to and length of extensions of time.

— Whether the works are being executed in accordance with the contract documents (q.v.).

— Either party's entitlement to terminate the contract.

— The reasonableness of any of the contractor's objections to a change of architect, architect's instruction requiring sub-letting, or in relation to work to be carried out by the employer's own contractors.

The adjudicator can call for evidence and has the widest possible powers.

The BPF *Manual* refers to the appointment of an adjudicator in two instances:

— During the pre-tender stage.

— During the construction process.

His decisions are open to arbitration after taking-over of the project. In the BPF edition of the ACA Contract adjudication subject to subsequent arbitration is *the* method of dispute settlement.

Standard form sub-contracts, e.g., the JCT Nominated Sub-contract NSC/4 (1980), clause 24, often provide for main contractor's claims not agreed by the sub-contractor to be referred to an adjudicator who is named in the sub-contract. The object is to enable the sub-contractor to dispute the main contractor's right to set-off (q.v.) and the procedure is relatively speedy, but the adjudicator's powers are severely limited. See also: *BPF System*.

| **Admissibility of evidence** | The purpose of evidence (q.v.) is to establish facts in court or before a tribunal. In England and Wales the law of evidence is mainly exclusionary, i.e., it deals largely with what evidence may or may not be introduced. Admissibility deals with the items of evidence which may be brought before the court. The main basic rule is that the evidence must be *relevant* to the matter under enquiry.<br>—Hearsay (q.v.) evidence is generally excluded.<br>—Extrinsic evidence (q.v.) is generally inadmissible. |
| --- | --- |
| **Advances** | A term used in GC/Works/1, clause 40, to refer to the payments which the contractor is entitled to receive during the progress of the execution of the works at not less than monthly intervals. The provision is similar to those clauses in other contracts providing for payment through *Interim certificates* (q.v.). |
| **Adverse possession** | Occupation of land inconsistent with the rights of the true owner; commonly called 'squatter's rights'. Title to land may be acquired by adverse possession under the Limitation Act 1980. If a landowner allows a third party to remain in possession of his land for twelve years (thirty years in the case of Crown Land) without payment of rent or other acknowledgment of title the squatter may acquire a possessory title and the original owner's title is excluded.<br>Acquiring a possessory title is not easy. Mere occupation of the land is insufficient. 'Acts must be done which are inconsistent with the (owner's) enjoyment of the soil for the purpose for which he intended to use it': *Leigh v. Jack* (1879). There is much relevant case law. Periodical cultivation of a piece of unmarked land was held to be insufficient to establish a possessory title in *Wallis's Cayton Bay Holiday Camp Ltd v. Shell-Mex & B P Ltd* (1975) where Lord Denning MR summarized the position aptly:<br>'Possession by itself is not enough to give a title. It must be adverse possession. The true owner must have discontinued possession or have been dispossessed and another must have taken it adversely |

to him. There must be something in the nature of an ouster of the true owner by the wrongful possessor ... Where the true owner of land intends to use it for a particular purpose in the future, and so leaves it unoccupied, he does not lose his title simply because some other person enters on to it and uses it for some temporary purpose, like stacking materials, or for some seasonal purpose, like growing vegetables.'

In contrast, in *Rudgwick Clay Works Ltd v. Baker* (1984), the incorporation of a piece of land into the curtilage of a house showed an intention to possess the land permanently and was capable of amounting to adverse possession. The incorporation was inconsistent with the use of the land for future mining operations. The question as to whether adverse possession has been established is one of fact.

Boundaries (q.v.) are frequently varied by adverse possession, e.g., when a fence is re-erected by a householder, and it is in this connection that problems are caused in building contract situations.
See also: *Adjoining property; Boundaries; Possession; Site; Title.*

| **Adverse weather conditions** | The changing nature of the weather has always been the enemy of building work which generally takes place exposed to the elements. At common law, bad weather as such does not excuse the contractor if he is delayed as a result *(Maryon v. Carter* (1830)). *Extraordinary* weather 'such as could not reasonably be anticipated' may amount to an Act of God (q.v.) or *force majeure* (q.v.). |

The realities of the situation are recognized by most forms of contract which allow for bad weather to varying degrees and provide for an extension of time (q.v.) to be awarded under certain circumstances. JCT 80, clause 25.4.2. lists 'exceptionally adverse weather conditions' as a relevant event (q.v.) entitling the contractor to claim an extension of time. JCT 63, clause 23 (b) refers to 'exceptionally inclement weather'. The change in wording makes clear that the new wording is intended to cover an exceptionally hot summer, which might well not be regarded as 'inclement weather', although excessive heat and drought can be just as damaging to progress as snow or frost.

Adverse weather conditions would embrace any weather conditions which were contrary to the ideal in any particular circumstance, and the contractor must be taken to have contemplated the possibility of such weather as part of his contractual risk (*Jackson v. Eastbourne Local Board* (1885)). The qualifying word 'exceptionally' is, therefore, of the utmost importance.

In order to show that weather conditions were *exceptionally* adverse, the contractor may have to provide meteorological records for a lengthy period – 10 or 20 years – to show that the weather was 'exceptional' for the area. It is the kind of weather which may be expected at the particular site which is important at the particular time when the delay occurs.

Thus, in most areas of England and Wales snow is not exceptional in January, but it is in July. In some areas, however, and at some altitudes, snow would not necessarily be exceptional in early summer. Even if the weather conditions are exceptional, they may not necessarily be 'adverse' because the weather must interfere with the works at the particular stage when the exceptionally adverse weather occurs. This depends on the stage of the construction work at the particular time. If some internal works can continue, for example, the contractor would generally have no valid claim.

The contractor is expected to allow in his tender and his programme (q.v.) for anticipated weather conditions in the area, having regard to historical data, the time of year and the location of the site. This allowance is or should be reflected in the tender price. Often the situation is not clear-cut and, for example, some work may continue on internal fittings at the same time as external work is delayed due to exceptionally adverse weather conditions. In such cases, the architect must enquire carefully into the contractor's master programme (q.v.) before reaching a decision.

GC/Works/1, clause 28 (2)(b) allows 'weather conditions which make continuance of the work impracticable' as a circumstance entitling the contractor to claim an extension of time. At first sight the provision appears wider than its JCT 80 equivalent in the sense that it covers any situation where the weather conditions seriously interfere with the carrying out of the work. The conditions need not be 'exceptional', i.e., unusual, nor need they be 'adverse' in the sense of 'contrary' or 'hostile'; but the keyword is 'impracticable', i.e., incapable of being carried out, which means in effect that the weather must interfere with the work at the stage it has reached and make it infeasible to proceed. However, it seems that it is irrelevant whether or not the contractor could have foreseen the possibility of delay from such a cause.

GC/Works/1, clause 23 empowers the superintending officer (q.v.) to order suspension of the work or any part of the work to avoid the risk of damage from frost or inclement weather. In such circumstances the contractor may be entitled to make a financial claim.

ACA 2 makes no specific references to the weather. However, clause 11.5 (alternative 2) allows *force majeure* (q.v.) as a basis for a claim for extension of the time and wholly exceptional and unanticipated weather conditions, e.g., extraordinary rainfall, extraordinary snow, etc., could qualify under this head. This is not, however, as wide as under JCT 80 or GC/Works/1. See also: *Extension of time.*

| | |
|---|---|
| **Affidavit** | A sworn written statement of evidence sometimes used in civil actions. Affidavit evidence is given: |

A sworn written statement of evidence sometimes used in civil actions. Affidavit evidence is given:
— By agreement.
— If the judge or arbitrator so decides.
— Always in relation to applications for summary judgment (q.v.) in the High Court.

The content of the affidavit may be strictly factual or simply the opinion of the person swearing to it. The architect who is required to give affidavit evidence will give his solicitor a statement of the points he wishes to make. The solicitor will prepare the actual documents, then the architect (referred to as 'the deponent') swears (or affirms) that it is true and signs it before an authorized person. Authorized persons include a justice of the peace, a solicitor (other than the one who has drawn up the affidavit) or a court official. Documents attached to, and referred to in, an affidavit are called exhibits. See also: *Evidence; Oaths and affirmations.*

## Affirmation of contract

Where there is a breach of contract of a kind which entitles the innocent party to terminate (q.v.), the innocent party may affirm the contract and treat it as still being in force. The breach itself does not bring the contract to an end automatically; it must be accepted by the other party, who has an option. If he refuses to accept the breach, the contract continues in force. In such circumstances the innocent party will still have a right to damages (q.v.), and in an appropriate case, e.g., a contract for the sale of land, he may obtain an order of specific performance against the other party *(Hasham v. Zenab* (1960)).
A not dissimilar situation arises where there is an actionable misrepresentation (q.v.) and the innocent party may likewise elect to affirm the contract. He then loses his right to rescind the contract.
Lapse of time may be evidence that the contract has been affirmed, but in general it may be said that clear words or actions are required, although standing by idly and remaining silent may also be sufficient. See also: *Rescission.*

## Agency

An agent is a person exercising contractual powers on behalf of someone else, the important point being that the principal is bound by the acts of his agent. The architect is the employer's agent under the ordinary building contract, even though he has a duty to act fairly between the parties (*Sutcliffe v. Thackrah* (1974)).

The agency relationship can be created by express appointment or by implication. It may also arise where someone, without prior authority, contracts on someone else's behalf and the latter ratifies or adopts the contract. Agency may also sometimes be implied from a particular relationship between the parties where one has apparently held out the other as his agent. This situation commonly arises where employees holding administrative functions contract on behalf of their employers.

The key concept is that of the agent's authority. An agent has *actual authority* according to the terms of his appointment, but he has *apparent authority* according to the type of functions he performs. It is therefore important to determine what acts fall within an agent's usual or apparent authority. For example, the manager of a building merchant's depot may act for the owner in all matters connected with the business. Those dealing with him are not bound by any limitations placed upon his authority by his employer unless they have notice of those limitations. An agent's primary duty is to see that he acts in his principal's interests and he must not abuse his position. He is in a fiduciary (q.v.) relationship to his principal. Thus, if an agent makes an unauthorized profit for himself in the course of his agency he can be compelled to hand over any profit wrongfully made. He also forfeits any agreed remuneration. Similarly an agent is under a strict duty to account for all property coming into his hands on the principal's behalf. In carrying out his duties the agent must use ordinary skill and diligence and, except in certain circumstances, he cannot delegate the performance of his duties to another – *delegatus non potest delegare* (q.v.). Delegation may be expressly or impliedly authorized by the principal.

In general, an agent is not personally liable on a contract made on behalf of his principal, except where he fails to disclose the principal's existence or it is intended that he should be personally liable. However, if in fact the agent had no authority to contract, the aggrieved party may bring an action against him for breach of implied warranty of authority (q.v.). Usually, the agent drops out of the transaction once he has brought about a contract between his principal and the third party.

The agency relationship can be brought to an end by mutual consent or by performance. The principal may revoke the agent's authority and, in some cases, the relationship comes to an end automatically, e.g., on the death of the agent.

In the context of building contracts, the employer is only liable to the contractor for acts of his architect which are within the scope of his authority (*Stockport Metropolitan Borough Council v. O'Reilly* (1978)) and this principle is of importance since all the standard form contracts define closely the architect's powers. However, in *Rees & Kirby Ltd v. Swansea City Council* (1983) it was pointed out that in many cases – particularly where the architect is an employee of the building owner – there will be instances where the exercise of his professional duties is sufficiently linked to the employer's attitude and conduct that he becomes the employer's agent so as to make the employer liable for his default. In *Croudace Ltd v. London Borough of Lambeth* (1985), the local authority's Chief Architect named in a JCT contract was held to be the employer's agent and his failure to ascertain or instruct the quantity surveyor to ascertain a contractor's money claim was held to be a breach of contract for which the council was liable in damages.

| Agreement | Although an agreement between two parties, in the sense of a meeting of minds, has no legal significance in itself, agreement is necessary for there to be a valid contract. Possibly for this reason, the word is often used to mean a contract. JCT 80 refers to 'articles of agreement' (q.v.) at the beginning of the contract, but from then on refers to 'contract' or 'conditions' (q.v.). ACA 2, however, uses 'agreement' rather than |

'contract' throughout the contract, e.g.: 'This Agreement is made the ...' at the very beginning of the document.

## Agreement for Minor Building Works

The JCT Agreement for Minor Building Works was first published in June 1968, the current version being dated January 1980, reprinted with minor amendments in October 1981. Practice Note M 2, issued in August 1981, says that it is designed for use where minor building works are to be carried out for an agreed lump sum and where an architect or supervising officer has been appointed on behalf of the employer. It is for use where a lump sum offer has been obtained based on drawings and/or specifications and/or schedules but without detailed measurements. It is suggested that the form is generally suitable for projects up to a value of £50,000 at 1981 prices. Contract value is not, however, the deciding factor which is probably the complexity of the job rather than its value.

The form should *not* be used where any of the following are required:
—Nominated sub-contractors or suppliers (q.v.).
—Bills of quantities (q.v.).
—Fluctuations (q.v.) in the value of labour or materials. Certainly, substantial amendments would need to be made to the form as printed if any of these items were desired, although Practice Note M 2 does envisage the use of Bills in certain circumstances.

The Form consists of only 8 clauses, as follows:
1.    *Intentions of the parties.*
1.1.  Contractor's obligation.
1.2.  Architect's/Supervising Officer's duties.
2.    *Commencement and completion.*
2.1.  Commencement and completion.
2.2.  Extension of contract period.
2.3.  Damages for non-completion.
2.4.  Completion date.
2.5.  Defects liability.
3.    *Control of the Works.*
3.1.  Assignment.

There are also the usual Articles of Agreement (q.v.) and Recitals (q.v.), the first of which defines the contract documents (q.v.).

The express provisions are very much in common form. The contractor's basic obligation (clause 1.1 ) is to carry out and complete the works in accordance with the contract documents. He is to do this with all due diligence (q.v.) 'and in a good and workmanlike manner'. There are no provisions for money claims (q.v.) for disruption or prolongation, and under the form such claims will have to be dealt with at common law. The extensions of time (q.v.) clause (2.2) only applies while the Works are in progress and the architect has no power to grant an extension of time after the Works have been completed.

An interesting feature of the form is clauses dealing with the final certificate (especially clause 4.4). Unlike JCT 80 (q.v.) the certificate is not stated to be conclusive evidence of performance to any extent. The final certificate referred to in clause 4.4 is merely the final certificate of payment and is issued on the basis of documentation submitted by the contractor. Similarly, in the defects liability certificate issued under clause 2.5 there is no requirement for the architect to state that the works have been completed to his satisfaction and after the end of the defects liability period questions as to liability must be dealt with at common law.

JCT Minor Works is a very short term of contract and no attempt has been made to cover all the situations envisaged by JCT 80. In particular, it should be noted:

—Although there is provision for a quantity surveyor to be appointed, there is no indication of his duties. In most cases, there will be no quantity surveyor associated with the contract. If it is thought necessary to appoint one, he would no doubt act in an advisory capacity to the architect in valuing work done and variations.

— There is no provision for bills of quantities (q.v.). Valuation of variations is to be carried out by using priced specification (q.v.), priced schedules or a schedule of rates (q.v.) provided by the contractor. Alternatively, the price may be agreed before the variation is carried out.

—There is no provision for the use of nominated sub-contractors or suppliers.

—The contract is on a fixed price basis with no provision for fluctuations in the price of labour or materials. Provision is made (Clause 4.5 and Supplementary Memorandum) for contribution, levy and tax fluctuations, if appropriate.

—There is no provision for dealing with contractors' claims for loss and/or expense.

—There is no provision for the use of a clerk of works. This is a strange omission because it is more than likely that a clerk of works would be employed, part time, on the larger of the 'minor' works. However, the point is easily rectified by a suitable insertion.

—The extension of time clause (2.2) is very broad and the contractor may claim an extension provided only that it is apparent that the works will not be completed by the completion date, he notifies the architect (not necessarily in writing although it is clearly advisable), and the reasons for the delay are beyond his control. Such things as bad weather, strikes, late instructions, etc., are all covered by this clause. On a job where there may be considerable expense caused to the employer as a result of late completion this clause would be inadequate to safeguard his interests. The contract must be used with care by employer and contractor. Unforeseen problems invariably arise during construction and this form presupposes a considerable measure of goodwill on both sides.

The respective powers and duties of the architect, employer and contractor are summarized in Tables 4, 5 and 6.

| Agreement to negotiate | English law does not recognize 'a contract to negotiate a contract'. In the context of the construction industry this is illustrated by *Courtney & Fairbairn Ltd v. Tolaini Brothers (Hotels) Ltd* (1974) where an agreement 'to negotiate fair and reasonable contract sums' was held not to amount to a binding contract. There was no agreement on the price or any method by which the price was to be calculated. Since the law does not recognize a contract to make a contract, it cannot |

## Table 4 Architect: powers and duties under MW 80

| Clause | Power or duty |
| --- | --- |
| **1.1** | Approve materials and workmanship if to be to his approval |
| **1.2** | Issue any further information necessary<br>Issue all certificates<br>Confirm instructions in writing |
| **2.2** | Make written extensions of time |
| **2.4** | Certify practical completion date |
| **2.5** | Certify making good of defects date after defects liability period |
| **3.2** | Consent in writing to the sub-contracting of the works or part thereof |
| **3.4** | Issue instructions to exclude from the works any person employed thereon |
| **3.5** | Issue written instructions<br>Confirm oral instructions in writing in 2 days<br>Issue written notification requiring compliance with instructions within 7 days |
| **3.6** | Order a variation in the works, order or period of time<br>Value variations<br>Agree the price of a variation with the contractor before execution |
| **3.7** | Issue instructions regarding the expenditure of provisional sums |
| **4.1** | Correct inconsistencies in or between the contract documents |
| **4.2** | Certify progress payments at intervals of not less than 4 weeks |
| **4.3** | Certify 97½ per cent of the total amount to be paid to the contractor within 14 days after practical completion |
| **4.4** | Issue a final certificate |
| **6.3B** | Issue instructions for reinstatement and making good of loss or damage |

# Table 5  Employer: powers and duties under MW 80

| Clause | Power or duty |
| --- | --- |
| 3.1 | Give consent to the contractor to assign the contract |
| 3.2 | Employ and pay other persons to carry out the works and deduct the cost from monies due to the contractor |
| 4.2 | Pay certified amounts within 14 days |
| 4.3 | Pay the certified amount within 14 days |
| 5.2 | Pay VAT properly chargeable |
| 5.5 | Cancel the contract if the contractor indulges in corrupt practices<br>Recover the amount of any loss from the contractor |
| 6.3A | Pay received insurance monies to the contractor |
| 6.3B | Maintain adequate insurance against clause 6.3B risks |
| 6.4 | Require the contractor to produce evidence of insurance<br>Produce evidence of insurance if the contractor requires it |
| 7.1 | Forthwith determine the employment of the contractor under certain conditions<br>Withhold further payment until after completion of the works |
| 7.2 | Pay to the contractor a fair and reasonable sum after taking into account certain circumstances |

# Table 6  Contractor: powers and duties under MW 80

| Clause | Power or duty |
|---|---|
| **1.1** | With due diligence and in a good and workmanlike manner carry out and complete the works in accordance with the contract documents or to the approval of the architect where specified |
| **2.1** | Commence the works on the stated date<br>Complete the works by the stated date |
| **2.2** | Notify the architect of delays beyond the contractor's control which would cause the completion date to be exceeded |
| **2.3** | Pay liquidated damages if the completion date or any later fixed completion date is exceeded |
| **2.5** | Make good defects which appear during the defects liability period |
| **3.1** | Give consent to the employer to assign the contract |
| **3.2** | Sub-contract the works with the architect's consent |
| **3.3** | Keep a competent person in charge upon the works at all reasonable times |
| **3.5** | Forthwith carry out the architect's written instructions |
| **3.6** | Agree the price of a variation with the architect before execution |
| **4.2** | Request and receive payment at not less than 4-weekly intervals |
| **4.3** | Receive 97½ per cent of the total amount to be paid within 14 days of practical completion |
| **4.4** | Supply within 3 months from the date of practical completion all documentation reasonably required to calculate the final amount to be certified |
| **5.1** | Comply with and give all notices required by statute etc.<br>Pay all fees and charges<br>Give written notice to the architect specifying any divergence between statutory requirements and contract documents or instructions |
| **5.2** | Receive VAT properly chargeable |
| **5.4** | Comply with the Fair Wages Resolution in respect of any persons employed by the contractor |
| **5.5** | Pay the employer's loss after the contract has been cancelled due to corruption |
| **6.1** | Indemnify the employer against expense, liability, loss or claim in respect of personal injury or death<br>Maintain and cause sub-contractors to maintain insurance |
| **6.2** | Indemnify the employer against and insure and cause sub-contractors to insure against expense, liability, loss or claim in respect of damage to property |
| **6.3A** | Maintain adequate insurance against clause 6.3A risks<br>Restore or replace damaged work or materials and complete the works<br>Receive payment of insurance monies |
| **6.4** | Produce evidence of insurance if the employer requires it<br>Require the employer to produce evidence of insurance |
| **7.1** | Immediately give up possession of the site of the works upon determination of employment |
| **7.2** | Forthwith determine the contractor's employment under certain conditions<br>Receive a fair and reasonable sum taking into account certain circumstances |

recognize a contract to negotiate a contract.

In fact, this proposition may not be as far-reaching as it appears because in some cases the courts may find means of filling gaps left in a contract: *Foley v. Classique Coaches Ltd* (1934). The importance of the principle in building contracts is, however, that the parties should be agreed on all the essential terms of the contract. The problem is largely important in relation to letters of intent (q.v.) and, in practical terms, it is essential to ensure that vital terms should not be left 'to be agreed' or 'subject to agreement' – phrases which are often seen in practice. See also: *Conditional contract; Subject to contract.*

---

**Alien enemy**

A person whose State is at war with the United Kingdom, or a person, including a British subject, who is voluntarily resident or carrying on business in enemy or enemy-occupied territory.

Such persons are not permitted to bring actions in tort (q.v.) although they may defend an action against them. They may be allowed to leave the country or they may be interned. They cannot enter into a contract with a British subject and if a contract was made before the outbreak of war (q.v.), an alien enemy's rights are suspended except that he may defend an action in contract brought against him. Alien enemies may contract and enforce contracts if they are present in the U.K. by Royal licence.

---

**Alteration or amendment of contract**

The forms of contract in common use in the construction industry have been carefully drafted to take account of most of the situations which regularly arise during the course of building works. The forms are regularly updated in line with decisions of the courts. The employer may wish to incorporate some special provisions in a particular contract to suit his own requirements. It is perfectly feasible to alter or amend a standard form provided:

— The contractor is aware of the alterations or amendments at the time of tender.

— The amendments are carried out carefully so that no inconsistencies result.

It is always advisable to obtain the assistance of a lawyer specializing in building contracts if anything but minor amendments are needed.

Most forms provide for certain deletions to be carried out (for example, the insurance provisions in clause 22 of JCT 80) and the printed instructions must be followed minutely. There are pitfalls, however, if more radical alterations are required. The principal danger concerns the JCT forms which are negotiated with all sides of industry and, therefore, are not caught by the provisions of the Unfair Contract Terms Act 1977. Extensive tampering with the terms of the JCT contracts may well cause them to be considered as the employer's 'written standard terms of business' under s.3 of the Act and/or to be construed *contra proferentem*(q.v.). Two other common problems are worth mention.

The employer sometimes wishes to stipulate that the building must be completed in sections on particular dates. In order to do this effectively, great care must be taken to make the appropriate alterations throughout the contract, otherwise the employer may find himself, for example, unable to deduct liquidated damages (q.v.) for late completion of some or all of the sections (see: *Trollope & Colls Ltd v. North West Metropolitan Regional Hospital Board* (1973) and *Bramall & Ogden Ltd v. Sheffield City Council* (1985)). The JCT form has a Sectional Completion Supplement to overcome these problems.

If the employer wishes to amend clause 25 of the JCT form, he will lose his entitlement to 'freeze' fluctuations after completion date (q.v.) unless he also strikes out the appropriate clause in the fluctuation provisions (clauses 38.4.8.1, 39.5.8.1 or 40.7.2.1).

Any amendments must be made on the printed form itself and signed or initialled by both parties. It is not sufficient merely to refer to amendments in the bills of quantities (q.v.) or specification (q.v.) because most forms contain a clause giving priority to the provisions of the printed form over any of the other contract documents (q.v.). See also: *Priority of documents*.

**Ambiguity**  Something which is of unclear or of uncertain meaning; a word, phrase or description which may have more than one meaning.

ACA 2, clause 1.5, refers to ambiguities in the contract documents. This clause is somewhat broader than the similar clause 2.3 in JCT 80 which refers to discrepancies (q.v.). If a clause in, say, the specification (q.v.) can read so as to have two very different meanings, it is possible to argue, under the JCT form, that one of the meanings would give rise to no discrepancy and, therefore, that is the meaning to be used. Under the ACA form, however, it would appear to be sufficient to bring the clause into operation that an ambiguity exists. It might conceivably be to the contractor's advantage to plead ambiguity, although he would have to show that it could not have been found or foreseen at the date of the agreement.

**Ancient monument**  An historical or archaeological building or site scheduled by the Secretary of State for the Environment under s. 1 of the Ancient Monuments and Archaeological Areas Act 1979, as amended. In the case of monuments in England this duty is in fact carried out by the Ancient Monuments Branch of the Department of the Environment after consultation with the Historic Buildings and Monuments Commission. Under s. 2 of the 1979 Act it is an offence to carry out construction work to the scheduled monument without consent. The 1979 Act also introduced the concept of 'areas of archaeological importance' or archaeological areas (q.v.). See: *JCT 80, clause 34.3, ACA 2, clause 14 and GC/Works/1, clause 20 (2)*, as to what is to happen if 'fossils, antiquities (q.v.) and other objects of interest or value' are found on site.

**Anticipatory breach of contract**  When one party to a contract states that he will not carry out his obligations before the time for carrying out the obligations has arrived. The other party may accept the breach immediately and sue for breach of contract (q.v.) or he may wait until the time for carrying out the obligations has passed and then sue. The latter could be a dangerous course to pursue because events could turn in favour of the defaulting party during the intervening period. See also: *Repudiation*.

**Antiquities**     Ancient relics of various kinds. In building works, they could be parts of ancient structures or artifacts, coins or works of art.

Most standard forms of contract have provision for ownership on discovery and for safeguarding such items until they can be examined and removed from site. ( JCT 80, clause 34; ACA 2, clause 14; GC/Works/1, clause 20(2)). In practice, many small items such as coins are easily 'lost' unless the likelihood of discovery is appreciated and constant supervision of excavation is maintained. The discovery of larger antiquities, such as ancient pavements, etc., is often greeted with dismay by employer and contractor alike because of the probable delay to the works.

For a fuller consideration of discoveries upon the site see also: *Ancient monuments; Archaeological areas; Fossils; Treasure trove.*

**Appeal**     An application to a court or tribunal higher than the one which has decided an issue for reconsideration or review of a decision.

At common law there is no right of appeal from a superior court (see: *Courts*), but rights of appeal have been created by various Acts of Parliament. In most cases appeals, whether from the High Court or the County Court, go to the Court of Appeal. Appeal lies on both questions of law and questions of fact.

In civil matters appeal lies from the Court of Appeal to the House of Lords. Before an appeal may be heard the appellant (q.v.) must obtain the leave of the Court of Appeal or of the House of Lords itself. In practice only important points of law come up on appeal to the House of Lords.

An appeal is not a re-hearing: it is a reconsideration

of the case, although in certain circumstances fresh evidence may be admitted. The Court of Appeal has wide powers to order a new trial in appropriate cases. See also: *Courts*.

**Appearance**

In litigation in the High Court, this is the defendant's formal act indicating his intention to defend the case. This he does, personally or through his solicitor, by returning to the Court office a Form of Acknowledgment of Service.

The term is also used of the parties to an action being present in court when the proceedings are heard, either personally or by Counsel or a solicitor.

**Appendix**

An addition to a book or document, usually subsidiary to the main work.

The Appendix is an integral part of the JCT 80 form, and in clause 2.1. it is expressly stated to be part of the contract documents. It is to be filled in, in accordance with the information given in the documents accompanying the invitation to tender, before the contract documents are signed or sealed (q.v.). IFC 84 contains a similar Appendix.

ACA 2 has a similar appendage entitled the 'Time Schedule'. It is expressly stated to be one of the contract documents in part C of the recitals (q.v.). If entries in the Appendix are filled in so as to be inconsistent with the provisions of the contract terms themselves then, at least under JCT terms, those entries will be construed *contra proferentem* (q.v.) and the printed contract terms will prevail (*Bramall & Ogden Ltd v. Sheffield City Council* (1985)).

**Appropriation of payments**

Setting apart money for a specific purpose out of a larger sum. It usually arises when there are different debts between the same debtor and creditor or when payments are made on account of work done by a contractor to particular items of work, e.g., variations. This cannot be done if there is only one contract and the variations have been ordered under it. The question can only arise if extra work was ordered outside the terms of the contract and if the employer has paid money generally on account.

For example, a contractor is due to be paid £5,000 on contract A, £150 on contract B and £50 on contract C with the same employer. The employer may send a single cheque for £5,150. The employer should state how he has made up the payment, e.g., £5,000 for contract A, £100 for contract B and £50 for contract C, leaving £50 owing for contract B. If the person making the payment fails to appropriate it, it is open to the person receiving the payment to do so. In some cases this may be advantageous, for example where one of the debts has become statute-barred (q.v.).

| **Approval and satisfaction** | Most contracts, either in the printed conditions or in annexed documents such as bills of quantities (q.v.) or specification (q.v.), make provision for approval to be obtained to materials, workmanship or operations. The extent of the approvals required varies from contract to contract. It is sometimes expressed as being 'to the satisfaction of...' The provision is extremely important, with implications which are not always obvious. |

In building contracts there are three possible sources of approval:

— The employer.
— The architect.
— A statutory authority, e.g., through building control.

Unless expressly excluded, the expression of satisfaction by employer or architect is binding on the parties to the contract. Approval by a statutory authority is not final and binding because it represents only an additional safeguard for the employer. The architect, for example, may require a higher standard than the building control officer.

Where the architect's approval is specified in addition to the requirement that the work is to be in accordance with the contract, his approval will override the latter requirement. Thus, if the architect approves of some materials which are not strictly in conformity with the contract, the employer cannot require the contractor to substitute different materials at a later stage, although in some cases courts have held the two requirements to be cumulative. Even though the contract may not expressly state it, the courts will expect the architect's satisfaction to be reasonable (q.v.). For example, if the specification required one priming coat, one undercoat and one coat of gloss paint to be applied to internal doors, to the architect's satisfaction, it would not be considered reasonable if two coats of gloss paint were required to obtain a finish which met with his approval. However, the architect is entitled to withhold his approval until the best possible finish is achieved, given the limited specification.

Neither the architect nor the employer is entitled to withhold approval without a genuine reason. For example, the architect's refusal to accept the contractor's making good at the end of the defects liability period (q.v.) simply to avoid the release of retention money is not a genuine reason.

The architect must be acting within his authority when he requires work or materials to be to his satisfaction. As far as the contractor is concerned, that authority can only be discovered by examining the contract documents. If there is no requirement for the architect's approval then, strictly, his approval need not be sought. However, the contractor will still have express and implied obligations under the contract to carry out the work correctly. Moreover, the architect should not certify for payment work which is defective. In practice, many aspects of the contract imply the architect's approval.

JCT 80, clause 30.9.1.1 makes the Final Certificate conclusive evidence (except in regard to certain matters concerning arbitration or other proceedings or fraud) that 'where the quality of materials or the standard of workmanship are to be to the reasonable satisfaction of the Architect/Supervising Officer, the same are to such satisfaction'. Neither ACA 2 nor GC/Works/1 has a similar provision. The provision is of enormous importance for the architect. Many specifications are littered with provisos that work or materials must be to the architect's satisfaction or 'to the architect's approval'. Often a 'catch-all' clause will be attempted such as:

'Unless otherwise stated, all materials and workmanship must be to the architect's satisfaction.' In the context of the JCT 80 form, these clauses have the opposite effect to what the architect probably intended. Instead of being limited in effect, the Final Certificate becomes conclusive evidence that all materials and workmanship are to the architect's satisfaction.

There is no obligation upon the architect to express his approval of the work as it progresses, indeed he would be most unwise to do so. His approval cannot be implied through silence. Approval may be implied through the issue of certificates (q.v.), but usually there is a clause restricting such implication (e.g., JCT 80, clause 30.10). In practice, the architect can hardly escape from giving certain approvals as the work proceeds, otherwise he may rightly be regarded as extremely uncooperative, and probably in breach of his duties under the contract.

Depending upon the particular terms of the contract, the architect's approval or satisfaction will be subject to review on arbitration (q.v.).

**Approved documents**  Documents issued under s. 6 of the Building Act 1984 giving 'practical guidance with respect to the requirements of any provision of building regulations' (q.v.). Their legal effect is stated in the Act. If proceedings are brought against a contractor by a local authority (q.v.) for contravention of the building regulations and he has complied with the requirements of an 'approved document', his compliance will tend to remove liability. Conversely, he is not automatically liable if he fails to comply, but the onus is then on the contractor to show that he has met the relevant functional requirements of the regulations in some other way. See also: *Building control*.

**Arbitration**

The settlement of disputes by referring the matters at issue to the decision of an independent person, called an arbitrator (q.v.). It is an essential feature of arbitration that the parties agree to be bound by the decision of the third party, which is called an award (q.v.). In Scotland, the arbitrator is styled 'the arbiter' and his award is called a 'decree arbitral' and different statutory provisions apply.

Arbitration requires agreement. Under s. 32 of the Arbitration Act 1950, the arbitration agreement must be in writing if it is to fall within the Act, though the agreement (see: *Arbitration agreement*) can be entered into before or after the dispute has arisen.

All the standard forms of building contract contain an arbitration clause: JCT 80, article 5; ACA 2, clause 25 (alternatives 1 and 2); GC/Works/1, clause 61 are typical. Such provisions make it a term of the contract that disputes between them shall be settled by arbitration and neither party can refer the dispute to litigation unless the other party agrees. This is, of course, subject to the power of the High Court to refuse a stay of proceedings (q.v.) in limited circumstances.

The arbitrator may be appointed by agreement or else by an agreed third party, e.g., the President of the RIBA or other professional body.

Arbitration is an excellent method of settling construction industry disputes, although in the majority of cases it is no cheaper than litigation (q.v.) and may be marginally more expensive, since the parties are responsible for the arbitrator's fees and expenses.

The usual standard form contracts confer very wide powers on the arbitrator to 'open up, review and revise any decision, opinion, instruction, certificate', etc., of the architect. No corresponding power is available to the court (*Northern Regional Health Authority v. Derek Crouch Construction Ltd* (1984)) unless the contract confers that express power on the court. Essentially, arbitration is a voluntary process and so the powers of the arbitrator are limited, especially as regards joining third parties, compelling the attendance of witnesses, etc., although s. 5 of the Arbitration Act 1979 does enable the arbitrator himself to apply to the High Court to be given certain powers.

Arbitration procedure is flexible and may be adapted by agreement to suit the needs of the parties, but in practice in most arbitrations normal court procedures are followed. The normal stages in a hearing are:

— Preliminary meeting at which the parties agree with the arbitrator to determine procedure, time-table, etc.

— Service of pleadings (q.v.). These define the matters in dispute.

— Discovery of documents (q.v.) followed by each party inspecting the other's documents.

— Exchange of reports of expert witnesses in appropriate cases.

— The Hearing when each party or his advocate presents his case, calling witnesses. Although the normal rules of evidence (q.v.) are generally followed, there is some flexibility.

— The arbitrator makes his Award (q.v.)which is final and binding on the parties.

The courts retain wide powers to control arbitrations, and under the Arbitration Act 1979 there is in effect a system of appeals against an arbitrator's Award for errors of law. The court can order the arbitrator to give reasons for his decision but, as a result of case law development, it is difficult to obtain leave to appeal against an Award except on substantial matters of law which it is in the public interest that they should be resolved. In practice, the courts are reluctant to interfere unless it can be shown, e.g., that the arbitrator has made a serious error.

| | |
|---|---|
| **Arbitration agreement/clause** | Section 32 of the Arbitration Act 1950 defines an 'arbitration agreement' as 'a written agreement to submit present or future differences to arbitration, whether an arbitrator is named therein or not'. The arbitration agreement must be in writing if the |

arbitration is to be governed by the Arbitration Acts 1950 and 1979.

The majority of standard form building contracts contain a clause or provision committing the parties to submit future disputes to arbitration, and these are sometimes called 'agreements to refer'. JCT 80, article 5; IFC 84, article 5; MW 80, article 4; ACA 2, clause 25 (alternatives 1 and 2) and GC/Works/1, clause 61 are typical arbitration agreements. The essential point is that there must be a contractual obligation to arbitrate.

If a contract contains no arbitration clause, there is nothing to prevent the parties coming to an *ad hoc* agreement after the dispute has arisen, but this is rare in practice.

**Arbitrator**
An impartial referee selected or agreed upon by the parties to a dispute to hear and determine the matter in dispute between them. In one sense, an arbitrator resembles a judge, but unlike a judge he derives his jurisdiction from the consent of the parties. The procedure which he follows is a matter to be determined from the express or implied terms of the arbitration agreement (q.v.) and extensive powers are conferred on arbitrators by Act of Parliament. The arbitrator must be impartial – he owes duties equally to both parties – and he must act in a judicial manner. 'He stands squarely between the two parties, having no special affiliation to either': Mustill & Boyd, *Commercial Arbitration* (1982), p.189.

In building contracts, it is usual for there to be an arbitration clause providing for the parties to agree on an arbitrator but, failing agreement, the standard form contracts provide for an arbitrator to be appointed by the President or Vice-President of some appropriate professional body, e.g., the Royal Institute of British Architects or the Chartered Institute of Arbitrators.

The arbitrator may be chosen for his professional expertise or technical knowledge, but certain important basic rules must be observed:

—The arbitrator must not have an interest in the dispute or a subsisting relationship with either party which might affect his impartiality.

— He must have a general technical knowledge of the technicalities of the matter in dispute.

— He must be able to act judicially.

The Chartered Institute of Arbitrators, 75 Cannon Street, London EC4N 5BH, is the professional organization concerned with arbitration. It runs training courses for prospective arbitrators and training now includes a period of pupillage. The selection of an arbitrator who is listed on one of the Institute's panels of arbitrators is some guarantee of his professional competence as an arbitrator and, in fact, the majority of appointing bodies nominate as arbitrators only those who are members of one of the Institute's panels.

An arbitrator is essentially the servant of the parties and his fees are paid by them. There is no recommended scale of fees.

| | |
|---|---|
| **Arbitrator's award** | See: *Award*. |

| | |
|---|---|
| **Archaeological areas** | 'Areas of archaeological importance' may be designated by the Secretary of State for the Environment and certain local authorities under s.33 of the Ancient Monuments and Archaeological Areas Act 1979. Once an area has been designated, it is an offence to carry out any operations in it which disturb the ground without serving 'an operations notice' on the borough (district) council. This brings various controls into play. Few such areas have been designated except in historic cities, e.g., York and Chester. |

| | |
|---|---|
| **Architect's Appointment** | Introduced in July 1982 by the Royal Institute of British Architects (RIBA) (q.v.) to assist in the agreement of fees, services and responsibilities between the architect and his client. It is the successor to the RIBA *Conditions of Engagement* (q.v.) and follows the report of the Monopolies and Mergers |

Commission on architects' and surveyors' services, which recommended the abolition of the mandatory fee scale. There is also a Small Works Edition (effective from September 1982) for jobs where the total construction cost will not exceed £50,000 (1981 prices).

The architect is recommended, but not bound, to use the Architect's Appointment. It is a convenient way of settling the terms of appointment. The recommended fee scale is a useful guide, but the architect is not precluded from agreeing a fee which is more or less than the scale nor from altering the stages at which it is payable. The document is arranged in four parts:

One — Preliminary and Basic Services provided by the architect. The sequence may be varied or two or more services combined to suit circumstances.

Two — Other Services normally charged on a time or lump sum basis.

Three — Conditions of Appointment, normally applying. If different or additional conditions are to apply, they should be set out in the separate Schedule of Services and Fees or in a letter of appointment.

Four — Recommended methods of calculating fees for services and expenses. Fees may be based on a percentage of total construction cost, time expended or a lump sum. Graphs are included to show recommended scales for new and existing buildings according to a table showing groupings into five classifications.

A *Memorandum of Agreement* (q.v.) is produced to tie up the appointment on a firm legal basis. Although no longer mandatory, architects would be wise to use the document as a basis for every appointment because it covers virtually every possible situation which might arise and forms a valuable source of information for the client.

**Architects Registration Council (ARCUK)**

Set up by the Architects (Registration) Act 1931 to control the architectural profession in England, Wales, Scotland and Northern Ireland. The Act was followed by the Architects Registration Acts of 1939 and 1969. Persons wishing to use the title 'Architect' for business purposes must be registered with ARCUK.

ARCUK has three principal duties:

— To maintain and annually publish a register of architects.

— To maintain proper standards of professional conduct.

— To award scholarships to students without means.

Registration may be achieved by one of the following methods:

— Passing a recognized examination.

— By a resolution of a constituent body of the Council recommended for acceptance in accordance with regulations.

Architects may be removed from the register for the following reasons:

— Conviction of a criminal offence or being found guilty of disgraceful conduct.

— Failure to pay the annual retention fee in due time.

— Failure to notify a change of address after being requested to do so.

It is an offence, punishable by a heavy initial fine and a continuing fine if the offence continues, for an unregistered person to practise or carry on a business which contains the word 'architect' in its title. It is important to note, therefore, that although membership of the RIBA enables a person to style himself or herself 'chartered architect', it would be an offence to do so if that person were not also registered with ARCUK. The Council has a Professional Purposes Committee to investigate minor complaints and advise architects, and a Discipline Committee to deal with serious offences.

ARCUK publishes a Code of Professional Conduct (q.v.) which is similar to but not identical with the RIBA Code. The constituent bodies on the Council are:

— Royal Institute of British Architects. (41)

— Incorporated Association of Architects and Surveyors. (1)
— Faculty of Architects and Surveyors. (1)
— Architectural Association. (2)
— STAMP section of UCATT. (1)
— Council of Provisional Associations. (1)
— Unattached Architects. (12)
— Royal Society of Ulster Architects. (1)
— Secretary of State for Education and Science. (1)
— Department of Environment. (2)
— Secretary of State for Scotland. (1)
— Secretary of State for Northern Ireland. (1)
— Royal Institution of Chartered Surveyors. (1)
— Institution of Structural Engineers. (1)
— Institution of Municipal Engineers. (1)
— Society of Engineers. (1)
— Chartered Institute of Building. (1)
— Building Employers Confederation. (1)
— National Federation of Construction Unions.
(Figures in brackets refer to the number of seats apportioned to each body).

---

**Arrangement, deed or scheme of**

Someone who is unable to pay his debts may agree with his creditors to discharge his liabilities by composition or part payment. This can be done privately or by application to the High Court or County Court. If the deed of arrangement is executed privately, the provisions of the Deeds of Arrangements Act 1914 must be complied with. A deed of arrangement is a contract and its effect depends on its own terms. In some circumstances a deed of arrangement may amount to an act of bankruptcy (q.v.).

A Scheme of Arrangement is an insolvent debtor's proposal for dealing with his debts by applying his assets or income in proportionate payment of them. The scheme must be approved by the creditors or the majority of them. The court has power in bankruptcy (q.v.) proceedings to approve a scheme in lieu of adjudging the debtor bankrupt. The term is often confined to schemes proposed by limited companies in like circumstances. A statutory procedure is laid down and a company Scheme of Arrangement requires the approval of the court. It may compromise claims, alter the rights of shareholders or resolve other difficulties.

JCT 80, clause 27.2 lists the contractor 'making a composition or arrangement with his creditors' as a ground for determination of the contract by the employer and, indeed, provides that the contract 'shall be forthwith automatically determined'. ACA 2, clause 20.3 lists as a ground for termination by either party if the other 'shall make or offer to make an arrangement or composition with its creditors', but notice is required. GC/Works/1, clause 45(a)(i) and (ii) also list compositions and arrangements as a ground for determination.

| | |
|---|---|
| **Articles of agreement** | 'Articles' generally means clauses. The 'articles of agreement' are the formal opening parts and recitals (q.v.) of the JCT and ACA forms of contract. |
| **Artificial person** | An entity, other than a human being, which is recognized in law as a legal person capable of acquiring rights and duties. A corporate body, such as a local authority, a limited company, or the bishop of a diocese. In general, a corporate body can only exist if it has been formed under the authority of the State and today the only methods of incorporation are a charter from the Crown and an Act of Parliament. See also: *Corporation; Limited company ; Local authority.* |
| **Artists and tradesmen** | A phrase found in JCT 63, clauses 23(h) and 24(1)(d). The full phrase reads: 'artists, tradesmen or others'. It has been held that the words 'or others' were not to be construed *ejusdem generis* (q.v.) and could refer to statutory authorities engaged by the employer under contract and *not* carrying out their statutory duties. (*Henry Boot Construction Ltd v. Central Lancashire Town Development Corporation* (1980)). Thus, in practice, the phrase refers to anyone engaged by the employer under a separate contract. |

The phrase has been completely removed from the JCT 80 form and clauses 25.4.8 and 26.2.4 substitute a much clearer wording which is wider in scope than the JCT 63 provisions.

| | |
|---|---|
| **Ascertain** | To find out for certain. Compare the use of this word with *estimate* (q.v.). |

It is used in the JCT 80, IFC 84, ACA 2, and GC/Works/1 forms in relation to financial claims. The contracts intend that the calculation of money due to the contractor is to be an extremely accurate process rather than a rough assessment or the expression of an opinion or a fortuitous guess.

The JCT 80 and ACA 2 forms, clauses 26.1, 34.3.1 and 15.3, 17.5 respectively, make clear that it is the architect's duty to ascertain the amount of a claim. He can, if he wishes, delegate the ascertainment to the quantity surveyor. He is well advised to do so because the quantity surveyor is specially qualified to carry out this work. However, in *R. B. Burden Ltd v. Swansea Corporation* (1957), under an earlier version of what is now JCT 80, it was indicated that the architect need not accept the quantity surveyor's quantification. Note that the architect has no power to delegate the initial decision to the quantity surveyor; that is: whether or not there is a valid claim.

GC/Works/1 provides, clauses 9 and 53(1), for the quantity surveyor to ascertain the expense. The architect (if such is the S.O.) has no power to carry out the ascertainment himself even if he so wishes. The limited nature of the quantity surveyor's powers under JCT contracts were confirmed in the judgment of Webster J. in *County & District Properties Ltd v. John Laing Construction Ltd* (1982):

'His authority and function under the contract are confined to measuring and quantifying. The contract gives him authority, at least in certain instances, to decide quantum. It does not in any instance give him authority to determine liability, or liability to make any payment or allowance.'

| | |
|---|---|
| **Assent** | Agreement or compliance. It is also used to describe the formal act of a deceased person's executor to give effect to a gift made to a legatee. |

| | |
|---|---|
| **Assignment and sub-letting** | Assignment is the legal transfer of a right or duty from one party to another. In the absence of an express term to the contrary, any party to a contract is entitled to assign the benefit of his rights to another party. This may be done by means of a special contract for the purpose, in which case consideration (q.v.) must be present. For example, a contractor might assign his rights to receive payment in exchange for financial assistance from an outside source. It is not permitted to assign *duties* under a contract, and this is a matter of general law. Personal claims for damages may not be assigned but a claim arising out of a business transaction may (*Trendtex Trading Corporation v. Crédit Suisse* (1980)). An assignee has the right to sue to recover the debt assigned to him. If a party is permitted to assign a duty, he still remains primarily liable for the performance of that duty.<br>Many building contracts include clauses restricting the right to assign. If a party purports to assign in such circumstances without consent, the assignment is of no legal effect (*Helstan Securities Ltd v. Hertfordshire County Council* (1978)). JCT 80, clause 19.1 forbids either party to assign 'the contract' without the other's written consent. ACA 2, clause 19.1 also forbids assignment with the proviso that the contractor may assign any moneys due or to become due to him under the contract and the employer may assign any of his rights after Taking-Over of the works. This is a perfectly sensible provision. The employer, for example, may wish to assign the building to someone else after it is completed. However, he remains liable to the contractor for any further payments as they become due.<br>Following traditional practice in the building industry, most contracts allow the contractor to sub-let part of the work with the consent of the employer. Unlike the provision governing assignment, it is |

common for the contract to warn that consent to sub-letting must not be unreasonably withheld (see: JCT 80, clause 19.2, and ACA 2, clause 9.2). See also: *Sub-contract; Sub-contractor*.

**Attachment of Debts**  Another name for garnishee proceedings. The procedure is employed in High Court actions where a judgment for the payment of money has been obtained against a debtor to whom money is owing by another person. The judgment creditor can then obtain an order that sums owing by the third party should be attached to satisfy the judgment debt. This has the effect of preventing the third party from paying his creditor until the court has considered the matter. See also: *Garnishee order*.

**Attendance**  Sub-contract NSC/4, clause 27.1.1 states: 'General attendance shall be provided by the Contractor free of charge to the Sub-Contractor and shall be deemed to include only use of the Contractor's temporary roads, pavings and paths, standing scaffolding, standing power operated hoisting plant, the provision of temporary lighting and water supplies, clearing away rubbish, provision of space for the sub-contractor's own offices and for the storage of his plant and materials and the use of messrooms, sanitary accommodation and welfare materials.' If the nominated sub-contractor requires any items of special attendance, he is to set them out in tender NSC/1. A further definition of the terms 'general attendance' and 'special attendance' can be found in the *Standard Method of Measurement* (q.v.).

**Attestation**  The practice of having contracts or other documents signed or sealed in the presence of a witness who also signs and adds his address and description as evidence that the document was properly signed or sealed. One witness is generally sufficient. A dictionary definition of 'attest' is 'to witness any act or event'. Different forms of attestation clause are used in the case of contracts under seal and those which are merely executed by hand. Figures 2 and 3 are specimen attestation clauses.

**Figure 2**

Specimen attestation clause: contract under seal

**The Common Seal** *of the above-named*
*Contractor was hereunto affixed in the presence*
*of*

..................................................................................

..................................................................................

**Figure 3**

Specimen attestation clause: simple contract

**Signed** by the above-named Contractor
in the presence of

..................................................................................

..................................................................................

**Figure 4**

Specimen award

IN THE MATTER OF THE ARBITRATION ACTS 1950-1979
- and -
IN THE MATTER OF AN ARBITRATION

BETWEEN:

|  |  |
|---|---|
| JOHN DOE & CO LTD | Claimants |
| - and - | |
| RICHARD ROE | Respondent |

WHEREAS by an agreement in writing made the 17th day
of October 1983 between the Claimants of the one part
and the Respondent of the other part it was agreed
inter alia that any disputes or differences between
the parties arising out of the said agreement should be
referred to the arbitration and final decision of a person
to be appointed at the request of either party by the
President for the time being of the Chartered Institute
of Arbitrators.

AND WHEREAS such disputes or differences having arisen
between the parties to the said agreement, at the
request of the Claimants, the President of the said
Chartered Institute appointed me, Albert Edward Campion,
to be the sole Arbitrator on the 13th day of March 1984.

NOW I, the said Albert Edward Campion, having accepted
the said appointment and having heard and considered
the allegations, witnesses and evidence of both parties
and the addresses made to me by the Counsel on their behalf
DO HEREBY MAKE AND PUBLISH my final Award.

I AWARD AND DIRECT THAT:-

1. The Respondent shall pay to the Claimants within 28
days from the date on which this Award is taken up by
either party the sum of £14,852 in full and final
settlement of all claims and counterclaims herein.

2. The Respondent shall pay the Claimants' costs and
the costs of this arbitration upon a party and party
basis such costs, failing agreement, to be taxed.

3. The Respondent shall also pay and bear the costs
of this Award which I tax and settle at £4,600
(including £600 Value Added Tax) or if such costs
have already been paid by the Claimants forthwith to
repay such costs to the Claimants.

Fit for Counsel.

MADE AND PUBLISHED by me this 30th day of October 1984.

Signed

*A. E. Campion*

Arbitrator

In the presence of:-
*Herbert Gussett,*
*Much Binding, Blankshire*

| | |
|---|---|
| **Avoidance** | Setting aside or making void (q.v.), especially a contract, e.g., when one party withdraws from a voidable (q.v.) contract. Where a bond (q.v.) contains a condition providing that it is void on the happening of a certain event it is said to be 'conditioned for avoidance'. |
| **Award** | The decision of an arbitrator (q.v.). The arbitrator's Award must be:<br>— Final.<br>— Certain in its meaning.<br>— Consistent in all its parts.<br>It must:<br>— Deal with all matters referred to arbitration.<br>— Comply with any special directions in the submission.<br>Provision is made in s. 14 of the Arbitration Act 1950 for *interim awards* to be made at any time, e.g., in respect of matters of principle or for part of the sum claimed.<br>The Award is usually in writing and is published as soon as it is signed by the Arbitrator. The Award does not usually contain reasons, unless the parties have specially requested this, but s. 1(5) of the Arbitration Act 1979 empowers the High Court to order an arbitrator to state the reasons for his Award if there is any appeal on a question of law under the Act. Section 26 of the 1950 Act provides for an Award to be enforced in the same way as a judgment or order of the Court. Figure 4 is a specimen Award. |

| | |
|---|---|
| **BPF System** | In December 1983 the British Property Federation – which is representative of the interests of property owners – published a manual describing a new system for the organization of contract management. The BPF System divides the design and building process into five stages – concept, preparation of brief, development of design, tender documentation and construction. The *Manual* specifies these stages and notes the duties of the parties. |

The system re-defines traditional roles, introducing a Client's Representative (q.v.) who manages the project on behalf of the client, a Design Leader (q.v.) who has overall responsibility for pre-tender design and for sanctioning any contractor's design. A significant feature of the new system is that, in general, payment is based on a Schedule of Activities (q.v.) rather than on traditional Bills of Quantities.

The BPF system aims to remedy the main problems which arise under the traditional system of contracting:

— Incomplete initial design, leading to extensive variations and disruption of the building programme.
— Higher costs than expected.
— Delays in completion.

The system emphasizes the need for production of a detailed brief at the outset and for the client to determine his full requirements at an early stage. It also sets out to establish clear lines of communication and demarcation of responsibilities (see Figure 5) as well as the notion of fixed fees for consultants and

**Figure 5**
BPF design contract showing contractual
relationships (solid line) and functional
ones (broken line)

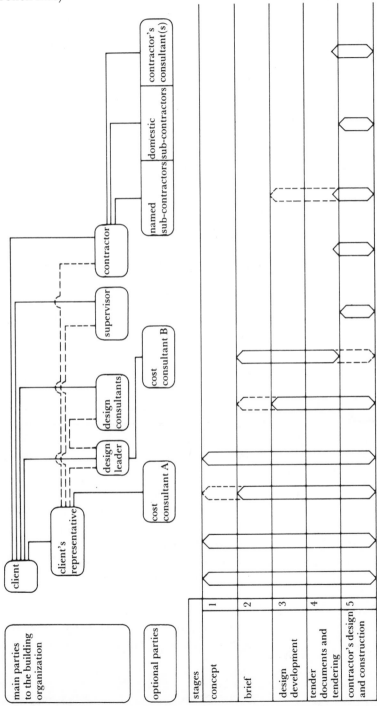

essentially a fixed-price contract. The system is intended to be flexible and is not a rigid formula suitable in its entirety for every project. Properly operated, it may save time and cost and achieve high quality in building.

Subsequent to the publication of the *Manual*, a BPF edition of the ACA Form of Building Agreement (q.v.) has been published, together with a Model Consultancy Agreement and various forms for use with the system.

Major changes to the traditional procedure introduced are shown in Table 7. Copies of the BPF *Manual* are obtainable from: The British Property Federation, 35 Catherine Place, London, SW1E 6DY.

| | |
|---|---|
| **Bailee** | A person to whom the possession (q.v.) of goods is entrusted by the owner for a particular purpose, with no intention of transferring the ownership (q.v.). A common example in the construction industry is that of the hirer of plant. The bailee (hirer) receives both possession of the plant and the right to use it, in return for a price to be paid to the bailor (owner). In fact, most plant is hired under the *Model Conditions for the Hiring of Plant* (1979 edition) or a variation of them and these conditions affect the common law position. A bailee has qualified ownership in the goods. See also: *Hire*. |
| **Bailment** | The legal relationship which exists where goods are lent to or deposited with another person on the condition that they will be re-delivered to him or to his order in due course. Bailment may be gratuitous, e.g., a simple loan, or as a pledge or pawn. It may also be for reward, e.g., hire. A common example of bailment is where goods are left with someone for repair and in such a case the bailee of uncollected goods is given a power of sale under the Torts (Interference with Goods) Act 1977. |
| **Bankruptcy** | The procedure by which the State takes over the assets of an individual who is unable to meet his debts (see also: *Insolvency*). The purpose is two-fold: |

# Table 7 Major changes proposed in the BPF Manual

**Adjudication**
Disputes arising during the contract to be settled within 5 working days by an independent adjudicator. His decisions are subject to post-contract arbitration. The aim is to provide speedy settlement of disputes and prevent any clash of interests

**Architect**
Provides pre-contract conceptual and architectural design and advises on architectural and design aspects of variations during construction. Has no authority to issue instructions to the contractor

**Bills of quantities**
Not used in the recommended system although the contract makes provision for them as an option. Tenders are invited against drawings and specifications produced by the design team

**Consultants**
Specialists — including architects and engineers — contracted by the client to produce design and cost services as well as those provided by the design leader

**Client's representative**
The person or firm managing the project on the client's behalf. He may delegate his duties under the contract to any number of assistants

**Design leader**
Has overall responsibility for pre-tender design, etc., and sanctions any contractor's design through the client's representative. The team leader

**Design liabilities**
Option for contractor to undertake a proportion of design

**Fixed-fee contracts**
Professionals to work for a fixed-fee. All contracts on a fixed-price basis unless they last for more than two years when 80 per cent only of fluctuations payable based on ACA Index

**Schedule of activities**
Prepared by the contractor it replaces priced Bills. It is a priced schedule of the contractor's activities and forms the basis of his tender. Used to manage the project, monitor progress and for payment. Payment made on the basis of each completed activity, with provision for pro rata payment of preliminaries

**Sub-contractors**
'Named sub-contractors' and suppliers if client wishes. Otherwise choice left to main contractor with whom full responsibility remains

**Variations**
Special procedure laid down, based on contractor's estimates of cost

— To ensure equal distribution of assets among creditors, subject to an order of preference (see: *Liquidation*).

— To protect the debtor from the pressing demands of his creditors and to enable him to start again. The process is started by a debtor making a declaration of his inability to pay his debts or by the debtor or his creditor presenting a bankruptcy petition to the court. If the court, after enquiry, is satisfied, it will make a receiving order which makes the official receiver (q.v.) receiver of the debtor's assets until the creditors have appointed a trustee in bankruptcy. If the receiving order is not rescinded (because, for example, the debtor becomes able to meet his debts) or a composition or scheme of arrangement (q.v.) between the debtor and his creditors is not approved by the court, the court will adjudicate the debtor a bankrupt. The adjudication order may subsequently be cancelled or the bankrupt may apply to the court for an order of discharge from his bankruptcy. Bankrupts are precluded from holding certain offices and carrying out certain functions.

The property of the bankrupt individual vests in his trustee in bankruptcy (q.v.).

| | |
|---|---|
| **Banwell Report** | A report produced by a government committee under the chairmanship of Sir Harold Banwell. The proper title of the report is: *The Placing and Management of Contracts for Building and Civil Engineering Work* (HMSO, 1964). Far-reaching recommendations were made for tendering and contract procedures. Following the report, open tendering (where tenders are invited from any contractor who cares to apply) was discouraged and the membership of the National Joint Consultative Committee for Building was broadened to embrace a wider spectrum of the industry. The Codes of Practice for Single and Two Stage Selective Tendering (q.v.) resulted. |
| **Basic method; Alternative method** | Refers to the systems of nominating sub-contractors under JCT 80, clause 35. The systems of nomination are intricate. Very briefly, the difference is that, under |

the 'basic method', the employer uses NSC/1 and NSC/2 to obtain tenders and the employer/nominated sub-contractor agreement before nomination and the signing of sub-contract NSC/4. In the 'alternative method' some other method of picking the sub-contractor is used, NSC/2a is used for the employer/nominated sub-contractor agreement and sub-contract NSC/4a is signed. See also: *Nominated sub-contractor*.

| | |
|---|---|
| **Basic prices** | See: *Schedule of rates.* |
| **Best endeavours** | A phrase used in the JCT 80, IFC 84 and GC/Works/1 contracts, in clauses 25.3.4.1 and 28(2)(iv) respectively. It must be read in the context of the contract in order to determine its meaning. In these contracts it is the duty of the contractor to use his best endeavours to prevent delay. The carrying out of the duty is a precondition to the awarding by the architect (or authority in the case of GC/Works/1) of an extension of time. |

Best endeavours, in this context, means that the contractor must constantly do everything reasonably practicable to prevent delay, short of incurring additional expenditure. In the majority of cases, best endeavours means simply that the contractor must continue to work regularly and diligently (q.v.) and nothing more. Put another way, provided the contractor has not contributed to the delay by his own fault, he can be said to have used his best endeavours. The point is often disputed. If, for example, the contractor could reduce delay by switching a gang of bricklayers from one portion of the work to another and does not do so, it could reasonably be said that he is not using his best endeavours. Similarly, if the contractor foresees delay, he must reprogramme if it is practicable to do so.

| | |
|---|---|
| **Bias** | A tendency or inclination to decide an issue influenced by external considerations and without regard to its merits. It is essential that the architect avoids actual |

or apparent bias in exercising his functions under the building contract, especially as regards certifying or giving or withholding approval or consent. The architect as certifier must act fairly, reasonably and independently as between employer and contractor. Failure to act fairly or acting as a result of improper pressures or influence will result in the decision being of no effect. For example, in *Hickman & Co. v. Roberts* (1913) the architect was instructed by the employer not to issue a certificate until the contractor's account for extras was received, and the architect advised the contractor accordingly. The House of Lords held that the need for the architect's certificate was dispensed with and the contractor was entitled to sue without a certificate.

In arbitration proceedings, the arbitrator must show no bias and, if he does so, may be removed by the court for misconduct: Arbitration Act 1950, s. 23 (1). This covers situations where unfairness might be suspected or foreseen, as where a person with close links with one of the parties accepts an appointment as arbitrator: *Veritas Shipping Corporation v. Anglo-American Cement Ltd* (1966). Bias against one party will also disqualify a person from appointment as an arbitrator, but an interest alone is not sufficient to disqualify. The question always is whether there is a predisposition to decide for or against one party without proper regard to the merits of the dispute. If that question is answered affirmatively, then the courts can intervene.

Apparent animosity to one party or his witnesses amounts to bias: *Catalina v. Norma* (1938). See also: *Arbitration; Arbitrator.*

| | |
|---|---|
| **Bid** | A contractor's price for carrying out work, submitted in competition with others. Another name for the contractor's tender (q.v.). The buyer at an auction sale makes a bid, i.e., offer, which the auctioneer is free to accept or reject. |
| **Bill of sale** | A document under which a person transfers his property in personal chattels (q.v.) to someone else without transferring possession (q.v.) of them. In |

general terms it is a document creating a security and a bill of sale is a document of title (q.v.). The general position of the parties is similar to that of parties to a legal mortgage of land.

It is the substance of the transaction rather than its form which is decisive, e.g., where an owner of goods sells them to someone else and agrees to take back the goods on hire-purchase and the real object of the transaction is to provide security, no title in the goods will pass to the 'purchaser': *North Central Wagon Finance Co. Ltd v. Brailsford* (1962)).

The rules governing bills of sale are complex. The Bills of Sale Acts 1878 and 1892 apply to most bills of sale. They must be registered in the Central Office of the Supreme Court in London within seven days of their execution. If not registered the security is void (q.v.). The Acts apply only where the bill of sale is made by an individual, but s. 45 of the Companies Act 1948 requires company charges to be registered.

| | |
|---|---|
| **Bill of variations** | Sometimes known as the 'Final Account' or 'computation of the adjusted Contract Sum'. It is prepared by the quantity surveyor and completed within the period named in the contract and before the issue of the Final Certificate (q.v.). |

The contractor must present the quantity surveyor with all the documents necessary for him to produce a detailed list of all the variations from the original bills of quantities (q.v.). These documents may take the form of invoices, sub-contractors' accounts, measurements, etc. The quantity surveyor normally prices all the items which have already been agreed or which he can price using the method set out in the particular contract. Any remaining items are often settled by negotiation, although in most contract forms, e.g., JCT 80, the quantity surveyor makes the decision. It is good practice to send the finished bill to the contractor prior to the final certificate, but there is generally no requirement to do so.

JCT 80 refers to the procedure in clause 30.6. ACA 2 refers to 'computing the Final Contract Sum' in clause 19.1. GC/Works/1 refers to the Final Account in clause 41(2). See also: *Final account.*

**Bills of quantities**

A very detailed list of all the work and materials required to produce a building. Its main purpose is to allow rates to be fixed for every item of work and materials and thus to arrive at a total price; the resultant rates become the basis for valuing variations. The bill is commonly divided into two sections:
— The Preliminaries.
— The measured work.

The Preliminaries contain factual information of a general nature to help the contractor to arrive at a price for the work. Among items to be included are the following:
— Name and address of the employer.
— Name and address of the architect.
— Name and address of the quantity surveyor.
— Description of the site including access and working space.
— Visiting the site.
— Trial holes.
— Inspection of drawings.
— Possession.
— General description of the works.
— Form and type of contract.
— Plant, tools and vehicles.
— Safety, health and welfare.
— Notices and fees.
— Setting out.
— General foreman, person-in-charge.
— Maintenance of roads.
— Safeguarding the works.
— Police regulations.
— Obligations and restrictions imposed by the employer.
— Water for the works.
— Lighting and power for the works.
— Injury to persons and property and damage to the works.
— Insurance of employer's liabilities.
— Clearing away.
— Temporary roads, etc.
— Temporary sheds, offices, messrooms, sanitary accommodation, etc.

— Temporary offices for use of architect, quantity surveyor, clerk of works.

— Temporary telephone facilities.

— Temporary screens, fencing, hoardings, etc.

— General scaffolding.

— Works by the local authority or statutory undertaking.

— Nominated sub-contract works.

— Nominated suppliers.

— Protecting the works.

— Drying the works.

— Removal of rubbish.

A full description of the items to be included in the Preliminaries can be found in the *Standard Method of Measurement*, 6th edition, pp. 17-19.

The quantities, together with the relevant description of the item, make up the major portion of the bills and they are usually arranged under trades, approximately in the order in which they will be carried out. Each trade has a preamble which provides a general description of the work for the contractor followed by a detailed series of descriptions of every part of the particular trade. Alongside each description, the quantity is expressed in lineal, square or cubic measurement (e.g.: lin m or m, sq m or $m^2$, cu m or $m^3$ or enumerated (e.g.: No.5). Weights are given in kg. Space is provided for the contractor to insert a rate opposite each item and to arrive at a total for each item by multiplying the quantity by the rate. The prices can be totalled by the contractor at the foot of each page and the totals carried to a collection at the end of each trade. The collections are gathered together on a sheet at the end of the document and totalled to arrive at a price for the whole work.

The method of measurement adopted for the bills should be clearly stated therein. Usually this is the *Standard Method of Measurement of Building Works* (SMM), compiled by the Royal Institution of Chartered Surveyors and the Building Employers

Confederation (formerly the National Federation of Building Trades Employers). A shortened version, for use with small structures such as housing, is also produced. It is usually referred to as the Small Code. Use of the SMM is mandatory on JCT contracts and thus, if on such contracts, it is desired to depart from the SMM for any reason, the departure must be clearly stated at the beginning of the bills.

The preparation of bills of quantities is normally undertaken by a quantity surveyor from the architect's production information: drawings, schedules and specifications (q.v.). The process is complex and usually involves the following stages:

— Taking off, i.e., taking the measurements from the architect's drawings.

— Abstracting, i.e., the gathering together of quantities for like items.

— Billing, i.e., writing up the final bills of quantities. A detailed specification (q.v.), which should be prepared by the architect, is commonly bound into the bills between the Preliminaries and the quantities and is usually referred to as the Trade Preambles.

Bills of quantities are included as one of the contract documents in JCT 80 (With Quantities editions), ACA 2 and GC/Works/1 contracts. They are often referred to as the 'contract bills'.

It is sometimes useful to prepare what is known as *Bills of Approximate Quantities* in order to determine rates for various items of work and materials when the precise quantity cannot be established before tenders are required to be submitted. By this method a rough idea of the total price can be obtained before work begins and the individual rates are applied to the actual quantities once these are fixed, which enables fast, accurate and indisputable remeasurement to proceed as the job progresses. Such a bill is often used for works of alteration or renovation or in the rarer instances where work must begin before the architect's production information can be completed. See also: *Bill of variations; Discrepancies; Schedule of activities; Schedule of rates.*

# Figure 6

Specimen performance bond

BY THIS BOND We Cosdon Contractors Ltd
whose registered office is at Cosdon House, Cosdon
Blankshire                         (hereinafter called 'the Contractor')
and Jorrocks Securities Ltd ————————————
whose office in the United Kingdom is at Surtees House
Handley Cross, Wessex      (hereinafter called 'the Surety') are
held and firmly bound unto Sponge Enterprises Ltd
————————————————— (hereinafter called 'the Employer')
in the sum of One hundred and twenty thousand
pounds (£120,000) ————————————————————
for the payment of which sum the Contractor and Surety bind
themselves their successors and assigns jointly and severally by these
presents.

Sealed with our respective seals and dated this First day of
February 1985

WHEREAS the Contractor by an Agreement
made between the Employer of the one part and the Contractor of the
other part has entered into a Contract (hereinafter called 'the said
Contract') for the construction completion and maintenance of certain
Works as therein mentioned in conformity with the provisions of the
said Contract.

NOW THE CONDITION of the above-written Bond is such
that if the Contractor shall duly perform and observe all the terms
provisions conditions and stipulations of the said Contract on the
Contractor's part to be performed and observed according to the true
purport intent and meaning thereof or if on default by the Contractor
the Surety shall satisfy and discharge the damages sustained by the
Employer thereby up to the amount of the above-written Bond then
this obligation shall be null and void but otherwise shall be and
remain in full force and effect but no alteration in terms of the said
Contract made by agreement between the Employer and the Contractor or in the extent or nature of the Works to be constructed
completed and maintained thereunder and no allowance of time by
the Employer or the Architect under the said Contract nor any
forbearance or forgiveness in or in respect of any matter or thing
concerning the said Contract on the part of the Employer or the said
Architect shall in any way release the Surety from any liability under
the above-written Bond.

The Common Seal of
Cosdon                                    L.S.
Contractors Ltd
was hereunto affixed
in the presence of:

*Tobias James*

The Common Seal of
Jorrocks Securities Ltd          L.S.
was hereunto affixed
in the presence of:

*John Jorrocks*

| | |
|---|---|
| **Body of deed** | The operative parts of a deed (q.v.) which set out the terms of the agreement between the parties. |
| **Bonds** | A bond is a contract under seal (q.v.) to pay a sum of money, usually on the happening of some specified event. There are several different types of bond, but in general their purpose is to guarantee payment of a fixed sum by way of compensation for non-performance of a contractual obligation. In this context, a *performance bond* is an undertaking given by an insurance company, bank or other surety to indemnify the beneficiary (usually the employer) against the contractor's failure to perform the contract. There are few English cases relating to performance bonds, although they are common in the building industry and are commonly required by local and other public authorities. A performance bond is a strong weapon in the employer's hands to ensure prompt completion and is, in effect, a thinly-disguised solvency guarantee (Figure 6). |
| **Bonus clause** | A clause included in a contract with the object of encouraging the contractor to complete the works before the contractual completion date by offering additional money for early completion. The SIAD Works Agreement (q.v.) is the only current standard form which includes a bonus for early completion. This is at a set amount per day and is payable to the contractor for each day by which completion of the works, as certified by the Supervising Officer, precedes the date for completion or extended completion. Unlike liquidated damages (q.v.), the amount of |

money specified is not legally required to bear any relationship to the amount gained by the employer through early completion. The employer may stipulate any sum he thinks fit.

Problems may arise if the amount of the bonus is not as great as any figure for liquidated damages in the contract. Moreover, default by the employer which prevents the contractor from earning the bonus may result in the contractor recovering its amount as damages for breach of contract (*Bywaters v. Curnick* (1906)) but, unless the clause expressly provides to this effect, circumstances beyond the builder's control which delay completion will not entitle him to the bonus (*Leslie v. Metropolitan Asylums Board* (1901)).

It is also open to question whether a bonus clause is a significant incentive to the contractor. It is perhaps better to specify a shorter contract period at the tendering stage so that the contractor may price accordingly. Many contractors argue that a bonus clause must always be present in any contract which includes a liquidated damages clause – presumably on a 'carrot and stick' principle. This argument is without any legal foundation.

The BPF System (q.v.) recommends the sharing of any savings achieved by the contractor between him and the employer. This is not the same as a bonus clause but it operates on the same principle, i.e., that the contractor will be rewarded if he gains some advantage for the employer. There is no clause to give effect to this recommendation in the BPF edition of ACA 2 and so a separate agreement would be required.

---

**Boundaries**

The demarcation lines between the ownerships of land. Boundaries should be defined in the title deeds although frequently they are obscure. Common reference is to walls, fences, hedges and watercourses. Ownership usually, but not invariably, extends to the centre line of highways (q.v.) and watercourses. If the boundary is not clear from the title, it may be possible to settle the matter on site in the presence of both owners. There are certain presumptions which may be useful (see Figure 7). If the parties cannot agree, the matter can be settled, expensively, in court.

Encroachment over or under a boundary will give rise to an action for trespass (q.v.), but may also give rise to variation of the boundary by adverse possession (q.v.).

| | |
|---|---|
| **Breach of contract** | An unjustified failure to carry out obligations under the contract or a repudiation of contractual obligations. The breach may be total, i.e. refusing to perform the contract at all, in which case it is known as 'repudiation' (q.v.) or it may be partial. The breach may be of varying degrees of seriousness depending upon whether it is breach of a condition or a warranty (q.vv.). The common law remedies are to sue for damages or for a decree of specific performance (q.v.), or the right to treat the contract as discharged. The remedies applied by the court will depend upon the seriousness of the breach. Breach does not itself discharge the contract; the breach must be accepted by the other party.<br><br>A number of events which are breaches of contract are expressly provided for under the terms of all the standard forms of contract together with remedies. For example JCT 80, at clause 26, provides for the contractor to obtain financial recompense for certain specified breaches of the employer. It must be noted, however, that it is always open to the injured party to seek damages at common law rather than through the contractual provisions if he so desires. See also: *Anticipatory breach of contract*. |
| **Bribery and corruption** | Promising, offering or giving money, secret commission, gifts, etc., to someone to influence his conduct. Secret dealings of this type as between, e.g., architect and contractor, would entitle the employer to terminate the architect's employment and to recover any commission paid (*Reading v. Attorney-General* (1951)). The employer could also treat the building contract as at an end. |

## Figure 7
Boundaries: presumption of ownership

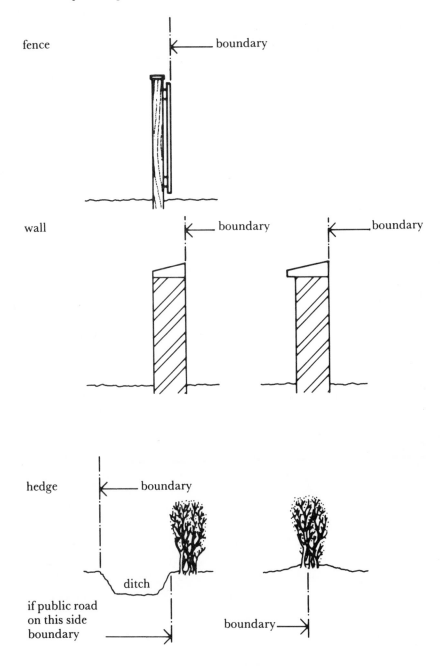

fence — boundary

wall — boundary — boundary

hedge — boundary

ditch

if public road
on this side
boundary

boundary

acts of ownership may partially settle
uncertainty, e.g. rebuilding a wall
or cutting a hedge (on both sides)

Some building contracts deal expressly with this matter, e.g., GC/Works/1, clause 55; JCT 80, clause 27.3 , and entitle the employer to determine the contracts which he could already do at common law. Corrupt practices are a criminal offence under the Prevention of Corruption Acts 1889 to 1916.

**Builder**

The individual, partnership or firm carrying out building works. Most contracts now refer to the 'contractor' (q.v.).

**Building control**

The system of controls over the construction and design of buildings, other than planning controls. In England and Wales the basic framework is contained in the Building Act 1984, which consolidates all earlier primary statutory material, and in the building regulations (q.v) which set out legal and constructional rules in greater detail. In Scotland, the system of control is based on the Building (Scotland) Acts 1959-1970, as amended, and in regulations made under them, i.e., the Building Standards (Scotland) Regulations 1981. See also: *Approved documents; Building regulations.*

**Building line**

An imaginary line drawn parallel to the highway at a specified distance from the back of the footpath (if any). The dimensions are specified by the local planning authority as part of their overall responsibility for development control. The significance of the line is that no building or part of any building (with certain minor exceptions) may be erected between the building line and the highway. The authority has considerable discretion in fixing the line, depending upon all the circumstances. The main purpose of a building line is to ensure privacy and sightlines. Thus the building line on a housing estate may be generally five metres, while in a town centre the building line may well be the back of the footpath. Individual consultation with the local planning officer is necessary to establish the line required in any particular situation.

**Building owner**

Usually, but not invariably, the person or firm known in most forms of building contract as 'the employer'. It is the person or firm which owns the site or will own the structure on completion (q.v.).

Section 5 of the London Building Act 1930 defines 'building owner' as 'such one of the owners of adjoining land as is desirous of building or such one of the owners of buildings, storeys or rooms separated from one another by a party wall or party structure as does or is desirous of doing a work affecting that party wall or party structure, and includes assigns', thus, giving the term a technical significance for the purposes of the London party wall (q.v.) legislation.

**Building regulations**

The Building Regulations 1985 form the basis of the system of building control (q.v.) in England and Wales. They are set out in the form of functional requirements and are supported by a wide range of 'approved documents' which give practical guidance in respect of their provisions.

The Regulations came into effect on 11 November 1985 and apply to Inner London with effect from 6 January 1986. They contain important definitions and procedural requirements.

It should be noted that, in the context of building contracts, the contractor must comply with the building regulations: *Street v. Sibbabridge Ltd* (1980). Most of the standard form contracts make this clear, e.g., JCT 80, clause 6.1, imposes on the contractor an express duty to comply with all statutory obligations; such a term would be implied in any event.

**Burden of a contract**

The obligation which rests upon one party to a contract, e.g., under a building contract the contractor's obligation to execute and complete the works. A contracting party cannot assign a contract so as to relieve himself of its burdens without the consent of the other party (*Tolhurst v. Associated Portland Cement Manufacturers Ltd* (1902)). See also: *Assignment; Novation.*

**Byelaws**

A form of delegated legislation (q.v.) made by local authorities and certain other public bodies and confirmed by some central government department. They are a kind of local law enforceable in the courts which have power to review them and determine whether or not they have been properly made. Building control (q.v.) was formerly exercised through local building byelaws (now replaced by building regulations (q.v.)) and this is still the case in the Inner London area where there are fundamental differences between the system of building control there and that in the rest of England and Wales, although it is intended to extend building regulation control to Inner London in due course.

**Capacity to contract**   The general law is that any person can enter into a binding contract. To this general rule there are a number of exceptions or qualifications. They may be summarized under the following heads:
— Corporations.
— Minors.
— Insane persons.
— Drunkards.
— Aliens.
— Agents.

*Corporations:* All corporations are restricted in their actions by the rules by which they were formed. For example, a company registered under the Companies Acts is restricted by its Memorandum of Association, a local authority is restricted by various statutes (q.v.). They may make binding contracts if such contracts are within the powers conferred upon them. If they attempt to make contracts outside their powers, such contracts are *ultra vires* (q.v.) and void.

*Minors:* Persons under the age of eighteen. As a general rule a minor may only enter into a binding contract:
— For necessaries.
— For his benefit.

'Necessaries' include such things as food and clothing, but the concept is by no means clear-cut because items falling into the category of 'necessaries' will depend upon circumstances. Contracts for the minor's benefit include contracts of apprenticeship and education. As with 'necessaries', the court will take all the circumstances into account in deciding whether a contract is for the minor's benefit.

All other contracts entered into by a minor are invalid. Thus contracts for the supply of goods or for payment of money cannot be enforced. Contracts which are of a long-term nature, such as the acquiring of an interest in land or a firm will become binding upon the minor unless he repudiates them before or soon after reaching the age of eighteen.

*Insane Persons:* Contracts are generally voidable, i.e., they may be repudiated, provided the person was insane when he made the contract and the other party was aware of it. If the insane person recovers his sanity, he may be bound by a contract made during the period of his insanity unless he repudiates the contract within a reasonable time.

*Drunkards:* Contracts with drunken persons fall under the same rules as contracts with insane persons.

*Aliens:* Generally, in peacetime, an alien has the same capacity to contract as a British national (but see: *Alien enemy*).

*Agents:* Capacity to form a binding contract on behalf of a principal depends upon the terms of the agency (q.v.).

---

**Care, standard of**

In actions for negligence (q.v.) it is necessary to establish that the defendant has failed to meet the standard of care to be expected of him. This is the standard of the 'reasonable man', who is a hypothetical creature of ordinary prudence and intelligence.

'Negligence is the omission to do something which a reasonable man, guided upon those considerations which ordinarily regulate the conduct of human affairs, would do, or doing something which a prudent and reasonable man would not do': Alderson B. in *Blythe v. Birmingham Waterworks Co.* (1856).

However, if someone holds himself out as being capable of attaining a certain standard of skill, e.g., an architect, a contractor, or an engineer, he must show the skill which is generally possessed by people in his trade or profession. So, when discharging the duties which he has contracted to do, the contractor or professional man is to be judged by the generally accepted standards prevalent at the time he carried out his work.

'Where you get a situation which involves the use of some special skill or competence, then the test as to whether there has been negligence or not is not the test of the man on the top of the Clapham omnibus, because he has not got this special skill. The test is the standard of the ordinary skilled man exercising and professing to have that special skill; it is well established law that it is sufficient if he exercises the ordinary skill of an ordinary competent man exercising that particular art': McNair J. in *Bolam v. Friern Hospital Management Committee* (1957).

This test has been approved time and time again. The terms of the contract may impose a higher standard, but generally the contractor must exercise in relation to his work the standard of care which is to be expected of a reasonably competent building contractor (*Worlock v. SAWS* (1982)).

The basic test establishes the degree of knowledge or awareness which the professional man ought to have. The fact that he has a higher degree of knowledge or awareness and acts in a way which, in light of that actual knowledge, he ought reasonably to have foreseen would cause damage, does not of itself make him liable in negligence (Webster J. in *Wimpey Construction U.K. Ltd v. Poole* (1984)). See also: *Reasonable forseeability.*

| | |
|---|---|
| **Case stated** | A procedure under the Arbitration Act 1950 by which the arbitrator could make his award in the form of alternatives hinging upon the interpretation of a point of law. The point was put to the High Court for resolution as a 'case stated'. <br><br> The procedure was abolished by the Arbitration Act 1979. See also: *Arbitration; Point of law.* |
| **Cash discount** | A discount for prompt payment by the main contractor. It is allowed by sub-contractors and suppliers, usually for payment within thirty days. It |

is not usually refundable to the employer and he does not guarantee its payment. The purpose is to assist the contractor in his forward financing of the work. Some contractors look upon it as additional profit. Usual cash discounts are 2½% from sub-contractors and 5% from suppliers. These percentages are stipulated in the JCT series of forms for nominated sub-contractors (NSC/4, clause 21.3.1.1, for payment within seventeen days) and nominated suppliers (JCT 80, clause 36.4.4, for payment within thirty days of the end of the month in which delivery is made). It is important to remember that the contractor has no right to the discount unless he makes payment within the stipulated period. If a provisional sum, on which the contractor expected to make money from cash discounts, is omitted, the contractor has no claim to the lost discount.

| **Causa causans** | The immediate cause. It is the last link in the chain of causation (q.v.) and must be recognized as different from the *causa sine qua non*, which is some earlier link but for which the *causa causans* would not have operated. In relation to monetary claims for direct loss and/or expense under building contracts, it means that the loss and/or expense must have been caused by the breach or act relied on and not merely be the occasion for it (*Weld-Blundell v. Stevens* (1920)). Many contractors have a very confused view of causation which leads them to submit claims which have no hope of success. For example, where there is a claim for direct loss and/or expense arising under JCT 80, clause 26.2.7 in respect of a variation, the loss and expense must flow from the variation order as a *causa causans*. If a variation order requires the contractor to obtain materials from a specified supplier who, in breach of his contract of sale with the contractor, delivers late or delivers defective materials, the *causa causans* is the supplier's breach of contract and not the variation order which is no more than a *causa sine qua non*. The simple precedence diagram at Figure 8 should clarify the point. To take a quite different |

**Figure 8**
Chain of causation

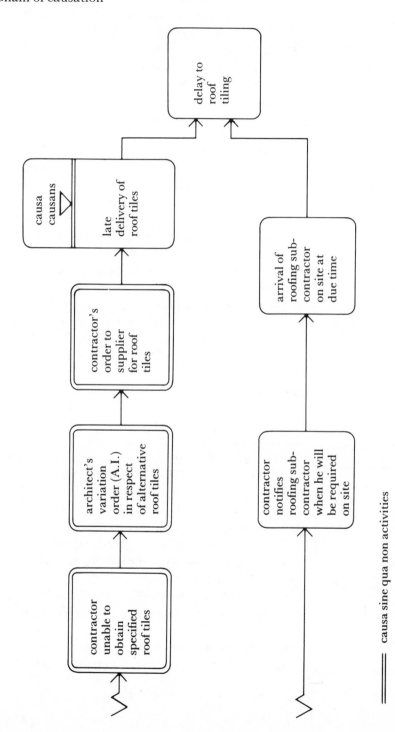

delay to roof tiling

causa causans

late delivery of roof tiles

contractor's order to supplier for roof tiles

architect's variation order (A.I.) in respect of alternative roof tiles

contractor unable to obtain specified roof tiles

arrival of roofing sub-contractor on site at due time

contractor notifies roofing sub-contractor when he will be required on site

══ = causa sine qua non activities

example, a Post Office driver, involved in an accident, would blame his delivery instructions (a *causa sine qua non*) only at the risk of appearing ridiculous if the fault lay with his careless driving (the *causa causans*). See also: *Causation; Foreseeability; Remoteness of damage.*

**Causation**

The relationship between cause and effect. The concept is very important in the context of liability for negligence (q.v.). In many cases, the doing of a wrongful act starts off a series of events which lead to damage being suffered, and this is called by lawyers a 'chain of causation'. If liability is to be established, the original wrongful act must be connected, without interruption, to the loss or damage suffered or incurred by the injured party. Thus, if the effective cause of the damage was not the original event but some intervening event, the defendant will not be liable. (The legal term is *novus actus interveniens* – a new act coming in between.)

In the context of building contracts, for example, in making a claim for loss and/or expense or for breach of contract, the contractor must establish that the loss or expense was actually *caused* by the event or breach on which he relies.

An example will help to clarify the position. Assume that the contractor makes a claim for loss and/or expense under JCT 80, clause 26.2.1 (late instructions). The circumstances are:

1. The architect has issued an instruction during the course of the work to vary all door furniture.
2. The contractor promptly places his order and the supplier confirms a satisfactory delivery date.
3. The supplier fails to deliver on time.
4. The contractor suffers loss and expense.

The late instruction is not the *cause* of the contractor's loss. There has been an intervening event (late delivery) which caused the loss. The contractor may well argue that he would not have suffered the loss had the architect's late instruction not set the chain in motion, but the intervening event prevents recovery of damages from the employer. (The contractor's redress is against the supplier). The intervening event might well be the contractor's own inefficiency. If, however, the architect's late instruction resulted in the contractor being unable to obtain a satisfactory delivery date and the supplier correctly delivered to such later date as was agreed, the late instruction would be the *cause* of the damage suffered by the contractor and a successful claim could result. See also: *Causa causans; Foreseeability; Remoteness of damage.*

**Caveat emptor**

Let the buyer beware. The basic common law rule in law of sale of goods that the buyer purchases at his own risk and relies on his own judgment as to suitability or quality. Modern legislation has attenuated this principle particularly in the case of purchases by ordinary consumers, e.g., in most situations the Sale of Goods Act 1979 implies a condition that goods are of merchantable quality (q.v.) and will be reasonably fit for their intended purpose. See also: *The Unfair Contract Terms Act 1977.*

**Certificates**

All the standard forms of contract provide for the architect to issue certificates at various times (see Tables 8, 9, 10, 11, and 12). It is crucial that all certificates are issued promptly by the architect, otherwise the contractor may have a claim in damages since failure by the architect to issue a certificate required by the contract is a breach of contract for which the employer is liable. Standard certification forms are available for use with some contracts and it is wise to use them. Where no form is available, a certificate must be specially prepared. A certificate may take the form of a letter, but to avoid any doubt, the letter should be headed 'Certificate of...' and begin 'This is to certify...'
If the certificate is to be issued by an architect, it must be signed by a registered architect. Because a certificate is a contractual document, once issued it may not be altered or amended (except probably for obvious errors) unless this is empowered by the contract, e.g., ACA 2, clause 19.5.

## Table 8  Certificates to be issued by the architect under JCT 80

| *Clause* | *Certificate* |
| --- | --- |
| **17.1** | Practical completion |
| **17.4** | Making good defects |
| **18.1.1** | Partial possession |
| **18.1.3** | Making good of partial possession |
| **22A.4.2** | Payment of insurance money |
| **24.1** | Contractor's failure to complete on the due date |
| **27.4.4** | Expenses incurred by employer on determination of contract by employer |
| **30.1.1.1** | Interim certificates |
| **30.7** | Interim certificates including finally adjusted sub-contract sums |
| **30.8** | Final certificate |
| **35.15.1**<br>**35.16** | Delay by nominated sub-contractor |

## Table 9  Certificates to be issued by the architect under IFC 84

| *Clause* | *Certificate* |
| --- | --- |
| **2.5** | Certificate of non-completion |
| **2.8** | Practical completion |
| **2.9** | Making good of defects |
| **4.2** | Interim certificates |
| **4.3** | Interim payment on practical completion |
| **4.5** | Final certificate |

## Table 10  Certificates to be issued by the architect under ACA 2

| Clause | Certificate |
| --- | --- |
| 1.7 | Payment of fees by contractor according to clause 1.7 |
| 6.4 (Alt. 2) | Adjustment to contract sum in respect of restoration, repair and/or removal |
| 11.2 | Works not fit and ready for taking-over |
| 12.1 | Taking-over certificate |
| 12.3 | Adjustment to contract sum in respect of clause 12.2 |
| 13.3 | Reduction of the liquidated and ascertained damages sum |
| 16.2 | Interim certificates |
| 17.5 | Adjustment to contract sum in respect of instructions and damage, loss and/or expense |
| 19.2 | Final certificate |
| 22.1 | Damage, loss and/or expense incurred by employer after termination |
| 22.2 | Amount due to contractor after termination |

## Table 11  Certificates to be issued by the architect under MW 80

| Clause | Certificate |
| --- | --- |
| 2.4 | Practical completion |
| 2.5 | Making good of defects |
| 4.2 | Progress payments |
| 4.3 | Penultimate certificate |
| 4.4 | Final certificate |

## Table 12  Certificates to be issued by the S.O. under GC/Works/1

| Clause | Certificate |
| --- | --- |
| 24 | Vouchers for daywork |
| 28A(1) | Satisfactory completion of part of the works |
| 40(3) | Certification of advances on account |
| 40(6)(b) | Amount not paid to nominated sub-contractor or supplier |
| 42(1) | Certificate of payment under clauses 40 and 41<br>Satisfactory completion of the works<br>Works in a satisfactory state at the end of the maintenance period |
| 46(1)(e) | Cost of completion after determination |

The effect of a certificate depends upon the actual wording of the contract (see: *East Ham Borough Council v. Bernard Sunley & Sons Ltd* (1965)). In most standard form contracts an architect's certificate is a condition precedent (q.v.) to payment to the contractor, but if the architect refuses to issue the certificate, the contractor can sue without it (*Page v. Llandaff RDC* (1901); *Croudace Construction Ltd v. London Borough of Lambeth* (1985)).

Interference or obstruction with the issue of a certificate is, under most standard contracts, a ground on which the contractor may terminate his employment under the contract, e.g., JCT 80, clause 28.1.2. Figure 9 is an example of a certificate. See also: *Final certificate; Interim certificate.*

| | |
|---|---|
| **Change of parties** | See: *Assignment and sub-letting; Novation.* |
| **Charging order** | A judgment creditor can apply to the court for an order imposing a charge on a debtor's property as a means of enforcing his judgment. The court's discretion to charge a debtor's property in this way is derived from s.1 of the Charging Orders Act 1979. The creditor is not entitled to the order as of right but the order will usually be made unless the debtor can persuade the court that in all the circumstances it should not be made. The charge may be enforced by an order for sale. |
| **Chattels** | Any property other than freehold land. *Chattels real* are leasehold interests in land in contrast to *chattels personal* which are all other things capable of being owned, e.g., goods and materials. See also: *Personal property.* |
| **Cheque, payment by** | Payment by cheque is only conditional payment. A creditor is not bound to accept a cheque in payment of his debt, but if he does so the debt will be discharged, provided the cheque is not dishonoured by the bank. Theoretically, under most of the standard form contracts, payment of amounts due on certificate |

## Figure 9
Taking-over certificate

**TAKING-OVER CERTIFICATE**

Architect's name:   A.W.Pugin

Address:   Gothic Buildings, St Chad's, Birmingham

To –

Employer's name:   The Duke of Omnium

Address:   Trollope House, Belstead

And to –

Contractor's name:   Buildrite Contractors Ltd

Address:   The Crescent, Belstead

Date   28 June 1985

Job reference   AWP/DO/1234

I/We certify in accordance with Clause 12.1 (a) of the Agreement dated  1 August 1984

for the Works   New Factory, Anytown, West Midlands

that the Section of the Works described hereunder was/that the Works were/
fit and ready for taking-over by the Employer on
(delete whichever does not apply)

Date  27 June 1985

Signed   A.W.Pugin   Architect

[X]  Employer   [X]  Q.S.   [ ]

[X]  Contractor   [ ]   [ ]

[X]  Architect   [ ]   [ ]

ought to be made in legal tender (q.v.) because none of the standard forms makes provision for payment by cheque. There is nothing to prevent a special contract provision being drawn up to that effect.

In practice, payment by cheque (if the cheque is honoured) is sufficient, and it might well be argued that there is an established custom (q.v.) in the industry to that effect, and certainly if certificated payments have been accepted by cheque, and the cheques have been duly honoured, it is not thought that the courts would look kindly on a claim that a later payment by cheque amounted to a breach of contract (q.v.).

| | |
|---|---|
| **Choses in action; in possession** | Personal rights of property which are enforceable by legal action. They are intangible rights, such as a debt or the right to recover damages, in contrast with choses in possession (things in possession) which are items of personal property capable of physical possession. In general, they can be assigned (q.v.) and are transferred on death or bankruptcy (q.v.). See also: *Personal property*. |
| **Civil commotion** | A phrase used to describe a situation which is more serious than a riot (q.v.) but not as serious as civil war (q.v.): *Levy v. Assicurazioni Generali* (1940). The essential element is one of turbulence or tumult, though it is not necessary to show that the acts were done at the instigation of an outside organization. Civil commotion may amount to *force majeure*. The activities of anti-nuclear protesters at military bases may well amount to civil commotion. JCT 80, clause 25.4.4 provides that civil commotion which delays the works is a ground for extension of time. Civil commotion which causes suspension of the works for a specified period is a ground on which the contractor may determine his employment (clause 28.1.3.3) and it is also referred to in clause 1.3 as being one of the insurable risks under clause 22. See also: *Commotion; Disorder; Riot*. |

| | |
|---|---|
| **Civil Liability (Contribution) Act 1978** | Section 1(1) of this Act enables 'any person liable in respect of any damage suffered by another person (to) recover contribution from any other person liable in respect of the same damage (whether jointly with him or otherwise)'. For example, the building owner sues the architect for negligence (q.v.). The architect may bring in the contractor and sub-contractors for contribution. This does not, however, apply against someone entitled to be indemnified by the tortfeasor, e.g., the employer under the JCT contracts.<br>A contribution can also be recovered by someone who has made a payment in *bona fide* settlement of a claim 'without regard to whether or not he himself is or ever was liable in respect of the damage'.<br>In all cases, the amount of contribution is a matter for the court's discretion. The amount is to be 'just and equitable' having regard to the person's liability for the damage in question. See also: *Indemnity clauses.* |
| **Civil war** | A continuous and large-scale state of hostilities, greater in scope than an insurrection (q.v.), between two or more sets of armed forces within a single State, often between the Government and an insurgent group. Civil war is a ground for awarding an extension of time (q.v.) under ACA 2, clause 11.5, alternative 2. In other forms of contract the situation is covered by *force majeure* (q.v.). See also: *Civil commotion; Commotion; Disorder; Riot.* |
| **Claims** | The dictionary defines 'claim' as 'an assertion of a right' and, under standard building contracts, the word conveys the concept of additional payment which the contractor seeks to assert outside the contractual machinery for valuing the work itself. The word is also used in respect of the contractor's applications for an award of extensions of time (q.v.). The main types of claim which may be made by a contractor are:<br>*Contractual claims* which are those made under specific provisions of the contract, e.g., one for 'direct loss and/or expense' under JCT 80, clause 26, or for 'direct |

expense' under GC/Works/1, clause 53. This type of claim is also described as being *ex contractu*, i.e., arising from the contract. Under JCT terms – and most other forms of contract – it is only claims of this type which the architect has authority under the contract to settle.

*Common law claims,* which are those which arise apart from the express provisions of the contract. They include claims in tort (q.v.), claims for a *quantum meruit* (q.v.), claims for breach of express or implied terms of the contract, and those for breach of a collateral contract or warranty (q.v.). All the current standard forms allow additional or alternative claims for breach of contract, based on the same facts. Usually they are based on implied terms relating to non-interference with the contractor's progress (see: *Hindrance and prevention*). They are sometimes called ex contractual or extra contractual claims.

*Ex gratia claims* are those without legal foundation and are usually made on moral or hardship grounds. Very rarely, there may be an advantage to meeting such a claim as a matter of grace, e.g., if the contractor is on the brink of insolvency (q.v.) and, as a result, the employer would face greater expense.

In order to obtain payment under the provisions of the contract, any procedural requirements as to notices, etc., must be observed. Typically, such a clause sets out (a) the grounds on which sums can be claimed (b) requirements as to notice (c) provision for payment, e.g., JCT 80, clause 26. All the current forms in use require notice in writing and impose restrictions on what is recoverable. Under JCT terms, the sums claimed must represent 'direct' loss and/or expense and must not be recoverable elsewhere under the contract. GC/Works/1 (clauses 53 (1) and 9 (2)(a) uses the word 'expense' which must be 'beyond that otherwise provided for in or reasonably contemplated by the contract'. This is an objective test.

There is no necessary link between money claims and extensions of time: most standard forms allow claims for both disruption and prolongation.

Contractors are often labelled 'claims conscious' on the basis that they are alive to their rights and make claims envisaged by the contract. The label takes no note of the validity or otherwise of such claims, and it is an unfair view of matters since the employer desires and has a right to expect an efficient contractor and an efficient contractor will be efficient in all things – including his own claims. There are, of course, some contractors who make totally unjustified, but time-consuming, claims as a matter of routine on the basis that some will hit the target. They are their own worst enemies and should not be labelled 'claims conscious', for they are nothing of the kind. They are simply inefficient.

Clauses which may give rise to claims are summarized in Tables 13, 14 and 15. The tables cannot be complete because, given the correct circumstances, any clause could give rise to a claim.

**Clause**

The numbered divisions or terms in a legal document or in a Bill presented to Parliament are called clauses. All standard forms of contract have numbered terms for ease of reference. A new clause normally indicates a change in subject matter. Thus in ACA 2, clause 4 deals with 'Visits to the works by the architect' and the following clause, 5, deals with 'Supervision of the works by the contractor'. The JCT 80 standard forms refer to all clauses as 'conditions'. This is misleading because contract terms can be sub-divided broadly into 'conditions' (q.v.), and 'warranties' (q.v.) and the distinction is legally significant.

**Clerical errors**

*Clerical* errors in a contract will usually be disregarded. See: *Errors*.

**Clerk of works**

An inspector employed on the works to ensure compliance with the contract provisions with regard to standards of materials and workmanship.

The clerk of works is specifically mentioned in JCT 80, IFC 84 and GC/Works/1 forms of contract in clauses 12, 3.10 and 16 respectively. JCT 80 states that he is to be

# Table 13  JCT 80 clauses which may give rise to claims

| Clause | Event |
|---|---|
| 2.2.2.2 | Departure from SMM or error in description or quantity |
| 2.3 | Discrepancy between any two or more of: drawings, bills, instructions (not being a variation) |
| 3 | Failure to take ascertainment into account in next interim certificate* |
| 4.1.1 | Additions, omissions, alterations of materials, workmanship or order of work |
| 4.1.2 | Employer employs others to carry out work without going through procedure* |
| 4.3 | Instructions by employer (or architect orally)* |
| 5.2 | Failure to provide correct documents* |
| 5.3 | Documents purporting to impose obligations beyond contract documents* |
| 5.4 | Failure to provide information as necessary* |
| 5.8 | Failure to send duplicate copies of certificates to contractor* |
| 6.1 | Divergence between statutory requirements and contract documents in 2.3 |
| 6.2 | Statutory fees and charges |
| 7 | Failure to provide levels or accurate dimensioned drawings for setting out* |
| 8.1 | Materials, goods or workmanship not procurable |
| 8.3 | Opening up of work or testing of materials or goods found to be in accordance with the contract |
| 8.4 | Wrongly phrased instructions* |
| 8.5 | Unreasonable or vexatious instructions* |
| 9.2 | Royalties and patent rights |
| 12 | Clerk of works exceeding duties* |
| 13.1.3 | Nomination of a sub-contractor* |
| 13.2 | Variations |
| 13.3 | Expenditure of provisional sums |
| 13.4 | Failure to value* |
| 13.5.1 – 5 | Failure to value in accordance with the rules* |
| 13.5.6 | Valuations not otherwise included |
| 13.6 | Contractor not given the opportunity to be present at time of measurement* |
| 13.7 | Failure to give effect to a valuation* |
| 15 | Recovery of VAT or loss of input tax |
| 16.1 | Unreasonable withholding of consent to removal of materials and goods* |
| 17.1 | Failure to issue certificate of practical completion* |
| 17.2 | Failure to deliver a schedule of defects* |
| 17.3 | Issue of instructions to make good defects after delivery or after 14 days from the expiration of the defects liability period* |

## Table 13  JCT 80 clauses which may give rise to claims (continued)

| Clause | Event |
|---|---|
| 17.4 | Failure to issue certificate of making good defects* |
| 17.5 | Instruction to make good damage by frost appearing after practical completion not caused by injury before practical completion |
| 18.1 | Possession without contractor's consent* |
| 18.1.1 | Failure to issue certificate of partial possession* |
| 18.1.2 | Failure to give effect to all the results of the certificate* |
| 18.1.3 | Failure to issue certificate of making good defects* |
| 18.1.5 | Failure to reduce liquidated damaged correctly* |
| 19.1 | Assign by employer without consent* |
| 19.2 | Unreasonably withholding consent to sub-letting* |
| 21.2 | Special insurances under a provisional sum |
| 22A.4.2 | Accepted insurance claims |
| 22B.2.2 | Restoration of damaged work |
| 22C.2.3.3 | Restoration of damaged work |
| 23.1 | Failure to give possession of site on due date* |
| 24.2.2 | Repayment of liquidated damages deducted Interest* |
| 25 | Financial claims* |
| 26 | Loss and/or expense |
| 27.1 | Invalid determination of the contractor's employment* |
| 28.2 | Payment after contractor's determination |
| 29 | Works by employer |
| 30 | Certificates Failure to observe rules* Interest on retention* |
| 31 | Failure to observe the requirements of this clause* |
| 32 | Invalid determination of the contractor's employment* |
| 32.3 | Payment for protective work |
| 33.1 | Making good war damage |
| 34.3 | Loss and/or expense in regard to antiquities |
| 35 | Nominated sub-contractors* |
| 36 | Nominated suppliers* |
| 38 – 40 | Fluctuations |

* Common law claims

# Table 14 ACA 2 clauses which may give rise to claims

Note: Due to the broad provisions of clause 7, all the events listed may be the subject of contractual claims. However, there is nothing to prevent the contractor pursuing any claim through the courts if he considers it offers him a better chance of success or more money. All the following claims would be dealt with by the architect.

| Clause | Event |
| --- | --- |
| 1.4 | Mistake in contract bills |
| 1.5 | Discrepancy or ambiguity in drawings or documents comprising the contract documents |
| 1.6 | Compliance with statutory requirements |
| 2.1 (Alts. 1 and 2) | Failure to supply drawings or details |
| 2.3 | Failure to deal with documents in due time |
| 3.2 | Failure to comply with clause 2 |
| 6.4 (Alts 1 and 2) | Accepted insurance claims |
| 7.1 | Damage, loss and/or expense |
| 8.1 | Instruction by employer |
| 8.2 | Architect's instructions |
| 9.1 | Assignment by employer without consent |
| 9.2 | Unreasonably withholding consent to sub-letting |
| 10.4 | Disruption of progress |
| 11.1 | Failure to give possession of the site on the due date |
| 11.2 | Failure to issue certificate |
| 11.5 (Alt. 1) | Failure to complete due to causes beyond the control of the contractor and liquidated damages deducted |
| 11.8 | Acceleration or postponement |
| 12.1 | Failure to issue certificates in due time |
| 12.3 | Defective work due to employer or architect |
| 12.4 | Wrongful deduction |
| 13.1 | Taking-over without consent |
| 13.3 | Failure to issue certificate within due time |
| 16.2 | Failure to issue certificate or failure to issue it in proper form |
| 16.4 | Failure to hold retention in separate account |
| 16.6 | Failure to properly adjust the contract sum |
| 16.7 | Recovery of VAT |
| 17.1 | Variations<br>Damage, loss and/or expense |

# Table 14 ACA 2 clauses which may give rise to claims (continued)

| Clause | Event |
|---|---|
| **17.3** | Failure to act after time limit |
| **18.1** | Fluctuations |
| **19.2** | Failure to issue Final Certificate in proper form or at proper time |
| **20.1, 20.3 and 21** | Invalid termination |
| **22.2** | Payment after contractor's termination |
| **23.1** | Failure to properly serve notices |

# Table 15  GC/Works/1 clauses which may give rise to claims

| Clause | Event |
|---|---|
| 5(2) | Error in bills of quantities |
| 6 | Failure to give possession of the site* |
| 7(1)(a) | Variation or modification of design, quality or quantity or addition, omission or substitution of any work |
| 7(1)(b) | Discrepancy in or between specification, bill of quantities, drawings |
| 7(1)(c) | Removal from site of goods for incorporation and substitution of other goods |
| 7(1)(e) | Order of execution of any part of the work |
| 7(1)(f) | Hours of working and extent of overtime or nightwork |
| 7(1)(i) | Opening up for inspection of work found to be in accordance with the contract |
| 7(1)(k) | Emergency work |
| 7(1)(m) | Any instruction other than those in 7(1)(a) – 7(1)(i) inclusive |
| 9 | Variations |
| 9(1) | Failure to value in accordance with the rules* |
| 9(2)(a)(i) | Expense not otherwise included, in complying with instructions |
| 12 | Failure to supply dimensioned drawings, levels or other information for setting out* |
| 13(3) | Tests on goods found to be in accordance with contract |
| 15 | Royalties and patent rights |
| 21 | Failure to examine and/or approve excavations for foundations* |
| 23 | Making good defects due to frost or inclement weather not the fault of the contractor |
| 26(2)(b)(i) | Damage to works or other things caused by the authority |
| 26(2)(b)(ii) | Damage to works or other things caused by any of the accepted risks |
| 28 | Financial claims* |
| 28A(1) | Possession without the contractor's consent* |
| 28A(3) | Failure to certify* |
| 28A(5) | Failure to release reserve* |
| 38 | Prime cost sums |
| 38(2) | Fixing goods |
| 38(3) | Failure to adjust contract sum* |
| 39 | Provisional sums |
| 40(1)(2) | Failure to pay 97 per cent of value of work executed or goods brought onto site for incorporation* |
| 40(3) | Failure to value or certify in accordance with the rules* |
| 41(1) | Failure to pay the Final Sum less one half the reserve on completion* |

## Table 15 GC/Works/1 clauses which may give rise to claims (continued)

| Clause | Event |
| --- | --- |
| **41(3)** | Failure to pay sum remaining due after certification of satisfaction and sum has been agreed* |
| **41(4)** | Failure to pay in accordance with this clause* |
| **42(1)** | Failure to certify* |
| **44(3)** | Failure to operate provisions after determination* |
| **44(3) and 46(2)** | Payment after determination |
| **50** | Works by authority* |
| **53** | Prolongation and disruption |

\* Common law claims

appointed by the employer and be under the direction of the architect. He may give 'directions' provided that they are in respect of matters for which the architect is expressly empowered by the contract to issue instructions, but they are of no effect unless the architect confirms them within 2 working days. The duty of the clerk of works is to act solely as an inspector. GC/Works/1 outlines duties in broadly similar terms without being specific on the matter of directions. ACA 2 and the JCT Agreement for Minor Building Works (q.v.) do not refer to a clerk of works but there is no reason why a clerk of works should not be employed if a suitable clause is inserted in the Specification (q.v.) or Bills of Quantities (q.v.).

The Architect's Appointment (q.v.) refers to the employment of a clerk of works, in clause 3.11, where frequent or constant inspection is required. In practice, his duties will be somewhat broader than laid down in the contract as far as the architect is concerned. They will often include inspecting, reporting in detail, advising and generally being the eyes and ears of the architect on site. He must have a wealth of practical experience supplemented by sound technical knowledge.

The clerk of works is liable if he is negligent in the performance of his duties and this will reduce the architect's responsibility for inspection (q.v.) in appropriate cases. In *Kensington & Chelsea & Westminster Health Authority v. Wettern Composites Ltd* (1985) the vicarious liability (q.v.) of the employer for the negligence of the clerk of works was considered.

Although the clerk of works is under the architect's direction and control, it was found on the facts that the clerk of works had been negligent, though to a lesser extent than the defendant architects. The judge described the relationship between clerk of works and architect as that 'of the Chief Petty Officer as compared with that of the Captain of the ship'. The clerk of works was held 20% responsible and the employers were held to be contributorily negligent to the same extent, since they were vicariously liable for their employee's negligence. Damages were reduced accordingly. The negligent architects were responsible for the balance of 80% of the damages. It is very important that the duties of the clerk of works are clearly defined at the first site meeting to avoid difficult situations and misunderstandings arising during the contract.

The Institute of Clerks of Works of Great Britain Incorporated (ICW ) was formed in 1882. It admits members, after examination, as Licentiate, Associate and Fellow. Useful publications are the *Clerk of Works' Manual* produced by the RIBA and ICW and the *Handbook* produced by the GLC.

---

**Client**

This word is used in the BPF System (q.v.) to describe the building owner or employer. He is specifically described as being 'the person or firm responsible for commissioning and paying for the design and construction of the building'. In the BPF edition of the ACA Contract and in other standard form contracts he is referred to as the Employer. (q.v.).

The *Architect's Appointment* (q.v.), published by the RIBA, sets out the recommended fees and conditions to govern the relationship between architect and client.

---

**Client's representative**

The term used, under the BPF System (q.v.) and its supporting form of contract, to describe the person or firm responsible for managing the project on behalf of and in the interests of the client (q.v.).

He may be an architect or other professional, or a project manager but, contractually, he performs the functions under the contract usually allotted to the architect. Under the BPF System, as far as his employer is concerned, he has a more extensive role, but under BPF edition of the ACA contract (q.v.) his authority and powers are the same as those of the architect, although the client's representative is given a specific right to delegate his functions which the architect does not have.

**Code of procedure for single-stage selective tendering 1977**

A document produced for the benefit of all who commission building work and which aims to introduce generally accepted standards into the traditional tendering procedure.

The code is prepared by the National Joint Consultative Committee for Building in collaboration with:
— The Department of the Environment.
— The Joint Standing Committee of Architects, Surveyors and Building Contractors in Scotland.
— The Joint Consultative Committee for Building, Northern Ireland.

The code assumes that standard forms of building contract are to be used. If other forms of contract are used, some modification of detail may be necessary.

There are clear benefits to all parties in the knowledge that a standard procedure will be followed in inviting and accepting tenders (q.v.). The Code recommends that the number of tenderers for a contract should be based on the following scale:

| Size of Contract | Maximum Number of Tenderers |
| --- | --- |
| Up to £50,000 | 5 |
| £50,000 – £250,000 | 6 |
| £250,000 – £1 million | 8 |
| Over £1 million | 6 |

The number of tenderers is restricted because the cost of preparing abortive tenders will be reflected in prices generally throughout the building industry. In preparing a short list of tenderers, the following must be borne in mind:
— The firm's financial standing.
— Recent experience of building over similar contract periods.
— General experience and reputation of similar building types.
— Adequacy of management.
— Adequacy of capacity.

Each firm on the short list should be sent a preliminary enquiry to determine if it is willing to tender. The enquiry should contain:
— Job title.
— Name of employer.
— Name of architect.
— Name of quantity surveyor.
— Name of consultant and note of duties.
— Location of site including plan.
— General description of work.
— Approximate cost range.
— Principal nominated sub-contractors.
— Form of contract noting important additions or deletions.
— Procedure for correction of priced bills.
— Contract under seal or under hand.
— Anticipated date for possession.
— Contract period.
— Anticipated date for despatch of tender documents.
— Length of tender period.
— Length of time tender must remain open for acceptance.
— Amount of liquidated damages (q.v.).
— Bond (q.v.).
— Special conditions.

Once a contractor has confirmed his intention to tender, he should do so. If circumstances arise which make it necessary for him to withdraw, he should notify the architect before the tender documents are issued or, at the latest, within 2 days thereafter. If a contractor has expressed willingness to tender but is not chosen for the final short list, he must be informed immediately.

Note:
— Tender documents should be despatched on the stated date.
— Tenders must be submitted on the same basis.
— Alternative offers based on alternative contract periods may be admitted if requested on date of despatch of documents.
— Standard forms of contract should not be amended.

— A time of day should be stated for receipt of tenders and tenders received late should be returned unopened.

— The tender period should depend on the size and complexity of the job, but be not less than 4 weeks. If any tenderer requires clarification of a point, he must notify the architect who should inform all tenderers of his decision. If a tenderer submits a qualified tender, he should be given the opportunity to withdraw the qualification without altering his tender figure, otherwise his tender should normally be rejected.

Under English law, a tender may be withdrawn at any time before acceptance (q.v.). Under Scottish law, it cannot be withdrawn unless the words 'unless previously withdrawn' are inserted in the tender after the stated period of time the tender is to remain open for acceptance.

After tenders are opened, all but the three lowest tenderers should be informed immediately. The lowest tenderer should be asked to submit his priced bills within 4 days. The other two are informed that they may be approached again. After the contract has been let, each tenderer should be supplied with a list of tender prices.

The quantity surveyor must keep the priced bills strictly confidential. If there is an error in pricing, the Code sets out alternative ways of dealing with the situation:

— The tenderer should be notified and given the opportunity to confirm or withdraw his offer (i.e., the total sum). If he withdraws, the next lowest tenderer is considered. If he confirms his offer, an endorsement should be added to the priced bills that all rates, except preliminary items, contingencies, prime cost and provisional sums, are to be deemed reduced or increased, as appropriate, by the same proportion as the corrected total exceeds or falls short of the original price.

— The tenderer should be given the opportunity of confirming his offer or correcting the errors. If he corrects and he is no longer lowest tenderer, the next tender should be examined. If he does not correct, an endorsement is required.

Corrections must be initialled or confirmed in writing and the letter of acceptance must include reference. The lowest tender should be accepted, after correction or confirmation, in accordance with the alternative chosen. Problems sometimes occur because the employer will see that a tender will still be the lowest even after correction. If the first alternative has been agreed upon and notified to all tenderers at the time of invitation to tender, the choice facing the tenderer should clearly be to confirm or withdraw. The employer may require a great deal of persuading to stand by the initial agreement in such circumstances. The answer to the problem is to discuss the use of the alternatives thoroughly with the employer before the tendering process. He must be made aware that the agreement to use the Code and one of the alternatives is binding on all parties. It is possible that an employer who stipulated alternative one and subsequently allowed price correction could be sued by, at least, the next lowest tenderer for the abortive cost of tendering.

The employer does not usually bind himself to accept any tender nor does he take responsibility for the costs of tendering. It may be that there are reasons why he will decide to accept a tender which is not the lowest. Although he is entitled to do so, it will not please the other tenderers. The Code is devised to remove such practices.

If the tender under consideration exceeds the estimated cost, negotiations should take place with the tenderer to reduce the price. The quantity surveyor then normally produces what is called 'Reduction Bills' or 'Adjustment Bills'. They are priced up and signed by both parties as part of the Contract Bills. See also: *Errors*.

**Code of procedure for two-stage selective tendering 1983**

Single stage selective tendering is considered to be appropriate for most building contracts. Where it is thought desirable to involve the contractor in the design stage, two stage tendering is usual. This document is produced for the benefit of all who commission building work and aims to introduce generally accepted standards into the procedure. The Code is prepared by the National Joint Consultative Committee for Building in collaboration with:

— The Joint Standing Committee of Architects, Surveyors and Building Contractors in Scotland;

— The Joint Consultative Committee for Building, Northern Ireland;

and in consultation with the Department of the Environment.

The Code is not concerned with any responsibility for design which may involve the main contractor. It assumes the use of standard forms of building contract after the second stage. If other forms of contract are to be used, some modification of detail may be necessary.

Two stage tendering involves a first-stage competitive tendering procedure to select the contractor on the basis of pricing of documents related to the preliminary design. Thus a level of pricing is provided for use in subsequent negotiations. During the second stage, a tender is produced, using the first-stage pricing on bills of quantities (q.v.) which properly document the finished design. The process is most suited to large or complex schemes where the involvement of the contractor at an early stage is desirable. It is important to remember that, although the system is often used when designs are fairly crude and time is short, the often long process of negotiation may not give any overall saving in time over single-stage tendering at a later point in the design process. During the first stage it is important to:

— Provide a competitive basis for selection.

— Establish the layout and design.

— Provide clear pricing documents which are flexible enough to be the basis for the pricing of the first-stage tender. Provision must be made for fluctuations between the first- and second-stage tenders.

— Clearly state the respective obligations and rights,

the programme for the second stage and the conditions of contract.

The exact nature of the first-stage documents will depend upon the circumstances. It is not intended that any contract for the execution of the work will be entered into at the end of the first stage.

The number of tenderers for the first stage should be restricted to six. In preparing a short list of tenderers, the following must be borne in mind:

— The firm's financial standing.

— Recent experience of building over similar contract periods.

— General experience and reputation of similar building types.

— Adequacy of management.

— Adequacy of capacity.

Each firm on the short list should be sent a preliminary enquiry to determine if it is willing to tender.

The enquiry should contain:

— Job title.

— Name of employer.

— Name of architect.

— Name of quantity surveyor.

— Name of consultant and note of duties.

— Location of site including plan.

— General description of work.

— Approximate cost range.

— Two-stage tendering procedure envisaged including the contractor's participation in the second stage.

— Principal nominated sub-contractors.

— Form of contract noting important additions or deletions.

— Second-stage contract under seal or under hand.

— Anticipated date for possession.

— Contract period.

— Anticipated date for despatch of tender documents.

— Length of tender period.

— Length of time tender must remain open.

— Amount of liquidated damages (q.v.).

— Bond (q.v.).
— Special conditions.
— Reimbursement of costs to employer/contractor if second-stage procedures fail.
— Adjustment for price fluctuation between first and second stages.

Once a contractor has confirmed his intention to tender, he should do so. If circumstances arise which make it necessary for him to withdraw, he should notify the architect before the tender documents are issued. If a contractor has expressed willingness to tender but is not chosen for the final short list, he must be informed immediately.

Note:
— Tender documents should be despatched on the stated date.
— Tenders must be submitted on the same basis.
— Standard forms of contract should not be amended.
— A time of day should be stated for receipt of tenders and tenders received late should be returned unopened.
— The tender period should depend on the size and complexity of the job, but should be not less than five weeks.

If any tenderer requires clarification of a point, he must notify the architect who should inform all tenderers of his decision. If a tenderer submits a qualified tender, he should be given the opportunity to withdraw the qualification without altering his tender figure, otherwise his tender should normally be rejected.

Under English law, a tender may be withdrawn at any time before acceptance (q.v.). Under Scottish law, it cannot be withdrawn unless the words 'unless previously withdrawn' are inserted in the tender after the stated period of time the tender is to remain open for acceptance.

After the tenders are examined, all the tenderers except the three adjudged most favourable should be informed immediately.

The quantity surveyor must keep the priced

documentation (which should be submitted at the same time as the tender) strictly confidential. If there is an error in pricing, the tenderer should be given the opportunity to confirm the offer or correct genuine errors. If he corrects and he is no longer the most favourable tenderer, the next tender should be examined. If he does not correct, an endorsement is required. Corrections must be initialled or confirmed in writing and if recommended for the basis of the second stage, reference must be made.

If one tender is not clearly the most favourable, two or more tenders may be given to the employer, together with recommendations, for his decision. Acceptance of the first-stage tender is recommended to be confirmed in writing and the intentions of the parties clearly defined with regard to:

— Grounds for withdrawal from the second stage.

— Entitlement to costs and methods of ascertaining them if the parties fail to conclude second-stage negotiations to their mutual satisfaction.

— Reimbursement for any work done on site if second-stage procedures are abortive.

Acceptance of the first-stage tender is a particularly delicate operation. The employer, in particular, does not wish to find himself in the position of having accepted a contract sum at that stage. The terms of the letter of acceptance must be carefully worded to avoid such an eventuality. Depending upon the circumstances, it may be that a contract has been entered into. The question may be: What are the terms of the contract? There are two pitfalls:

— No real contract may exist. This is likely in many cases.

— A contract exists binding the employer to pay and the contractor to build. This would be far the worse of the two situations which could arise if insufficient care is given to the drafting of the invitation to tender, the tender and the acceptance.

The second stage is the completion of the design, production drawings and bills of quantities and the pricing of the bills from the first-stage tender prices.

The total of the priced bills will be recommended to the employer for acceptance as the contract sum. The Code states that no contract will have been entered into until the employer has accepted the sum.

If agreement cannot be reached, second-stage procedures may be restarted with the next most favourable tenderer or new first-stage tenders invited. After a contractor is appointed, all unsuccessful tenderers should be notified and, if feasible, a list of first-stage tender offers should be provided. If cost has not been the sole reason for acceptance, the fact should be stated.

A model preliminary enquiry for invitation to first-stage tender is appendixed to the Code, together with a model formal invitation to tender and form of tender. Notes are included for use in Scotland.

The Code apparently works well in practice and this is probably because both parties, after the completion of the first stage, have an interest in bringing the procedure to a successful conclusion. The two stages can be summarized as reaching an agreement to try and form a contract. The contractor and the employer's professional advisers should be aware of the possible legal and financial traps involved and make due provision in the documentation. See also: *Contract*.

## Collateral contract/ Collateral warranty

An independent contract which is collateral to another contract can be created in several ways. 'The purpose of the device usually is to enforce a promise given prior to the main contract and but for which the main contract would not have been made': Cheshire & Fifoot, *Law of Contract*, 10th edn, p.58.

Promises made by the employer to the contractor during pre-contractual negotiations may give rise to such a contract or warranty, e.g., *Bacal (Midlands) Ltd v. Northampton Development Corporation* (1976) where statements about ground conditions were held to give rise to such a warranty. The classic case is *Shanklin Pier Ltd v. Detel Products Ltd* (1951) where the employer

116

contracted with a third party to paint the pier. The defendants induced the employer to specify their paint and gave assurances as to its quality. The paint was properly applied by the third party but did not live up to the defendants' promises. It was held that there was a collateral contract between the parties under which the employer could recover the amount it had to spend to put matters right.

In the construction industry, the use of formal collateral contracts between employer and a proposed sub-contractor is common. In the normal way, there is no privity of contract (q.v.) between employer and *any* sub-contractor, nominated or otherwise. But when a main contract is entered into in JCT 80 standard form, it is usual for a proposed nominated sub-contractor to be required to enter into the JCT Standard Form of Employer/Nominated Sub-contractor Agreement (NSC/2 or NSC/2a) which is collateral contract. This gives each party (employer and nominated sub-contractor) certain direct contractual rights against each other. Such collateral contracts are highly desirable in order to protect the employer both as regards nominated sub-contractors and nominated suppliers in three main areas:

— Where the nominated sub-contractor has carried out design work.

— Where the main contractor has a valid claim for extension of time under the main contract.

— Where the main contractor has a valid money claim under the main contract.

In these circumstances, delay by the nominated sub-contractor, or design failure, may be costly to the employer who, under JCT terms, has no claim against the main contractor. These and other defects are remedied by the collateral contract which gives the employer direct rights against the defaulting sub-contractor, and in return the nominated sub-contractor is given various rights against the employer, e.g., rights to direct payment.

A similar, but not identical, formal collateral contract is created by the RIBA/CASEC Form of Employer/Specialist Agreement ESA/1 for use under IFC 84.

The contractual situation is illustrated in Figure 10.

**Figure 10**

Diagram showing the contractual situation
where there is a collateral contract/warranty

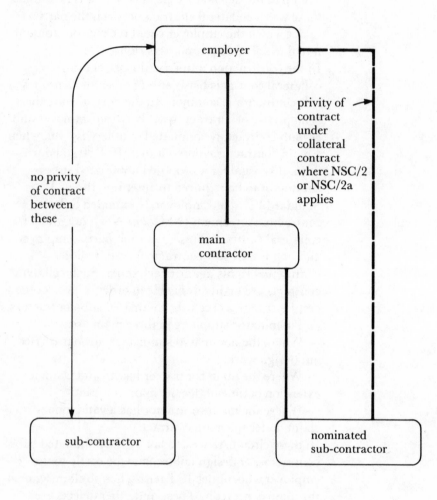

contractual relationship ━━━━━

| **Commercial Court** | Part of the Queen's Bench Division of the High Court staffed by judges with special knowledge of commercial law and commercial matters. It deals largely with legal matters arising out of the financial and commercial activities of the City of London. The procedure is more flexible than the ordinary procedure and by consent the strict rules of evidence are often relaxed.<br>Many important questions arising from arbitration (q.v.) are determined in the Commercial Court, especially since the Arbitration Act 1979. |
|---|---|
| **Commission** | — A body set up by the Crown or other authority, generally to enquire into and report upon something.<br>— An order, especially to an agent, to do something. Thus an architect is said to have received a commission when a client requests him to act on his behalf, for example, to prepare designs for a building.<br>— A form of remuneration which is related to the value or type of business generated. It is a common way of paying sales representatives. The theory is that if a man is paid in proportion to what he sells, he will sell more. An agent must not take any secret commission, i.e., one of which his principal is unaware. See also: *Agency*. |
| **Common law** | The rules and principles expressed in judicial decisions over the centuries. It is unwritten law and covers all law other than law made by statute (q.v.). Its essential feature is the doctrine of judicial precedent (q.v.) which is one of the most important sources of English law. Even where there is a comprehensive written contract, such as JCT 80, there may be implied terms (q.v.) which derive from common law. Thus, at common law, unless the parties have agreed to the contrary, a building contractor, where no architect is employed, impliedly undertakes that:<br>— He will do his work in a good and workmanlike manner.<br>— He will supply good and proper materials.<br>— The completed structure will be reasonably fit for |

its intended purpose: *Hancock v. B. W. Brazier (Anerley) Ltd* (1966). See also: *Equity.*

| | |
|---|---|
| **Commotion** | A term used in ACA 2, clause 11.5, alternative 2, as a ground for awarding extension of time (q.v.). Various stages of violence are listed ranging from war (q.v.) to disorder (q.v.). In this context, it seems that the term refers to a violent disturbance between a riot (q.v.) and a disorder, although the dictionary allows both 'violent disturbance; upheaval' and 'political insurrection' as definitions. In other contracts, commotion in this sense probably comes under the head of *force majeure* (q.v.). See also: *Civil commotion; Civil war; Insurrection.* |
| **Company** | See: *Corporation.* |
| **Competent** | Properly qualified. The word is used in a strictly legal context about a court, to denote the extent of its jurisdiction, or of a witness, to show that he is able to give evidence. It is also used in contracts to stress that a particular person must be suitably qualified to do a particular job. So JCT 80, clause 10 refers to a 'competent person-in-charge'. The intention is clearly that such a person must be able to do his work with skill and care and also that he is the contractor's representative on the site. Clause 1.2. of ACA 2 requires the contractor to exercise 'all the skill, care and diligence to be expected of a properly qualified and competent contractor experienced in carrying out work of a similar scope, nature and size' to the project in hand. It is a question of fact whether or not a person is 'competent', i.e., has the necessary qualities and skills. |
| **Completion** | In general, the point in time at which the contract works are finished. Different forms of contract qualify completion in various ways. For a fuller discussion see also: *Completion date; Practical completion; Taking-over.* |

**Completion date**     All standard forms of contract make provision for
stating a specific date by which or a period within
which the work is to be completed. Usually, failure
by the contractor to so complete will result in his
having to pay or allow the employer liquidated
damages (q.v.) at a specified rate, subject to the
contract provisions for extensions of time (q.v.).
In the absence of such a contractual provision and
where no completion date is expressly agreed, the
contractor would be under an obligation to complete
within a 'reasonable time'. In that case, the employer
would be unable to recover liquidated damages
although he might, with difficulty, recover liquidated
damages although he might, with difficulty, recover
unliquidated or general damages on proof of loss.
JCT 80, clause 17 refers to practical completion
(q.v.) as discharging the contractor's obligations
with regard to the completion date. The completion
date is referred to in clause 23.1 and the actual date
is to be inserted in the Appendix (q.v.).
ACA 2 does not refer to a completion date but to a
date on which the works are fit and ready for taking-
over (clause 12), which clearly amounts to the same
thing. The date for taking-over is to be inserted in
the Time Schedule (q.v.).
GC/Works/1 refers to completion in clause 28, and
clause 1(2) refers to the date for completion being the
date set out in or ascertained in accordance with the
Abstract of Particulars (q.v.). See also: *Essence of the
contract.*

**Compromise**     See: *Settlement.*

**Conclusive evidence**     The final certificate under JCT 63 (until the 1976
revision) was final in two senses:
— The last occasion on which the architect could
certify payment.
— The final certification that the works had been
carried out in accordance with the contract.
The operative clause was 30 (7) which stipulated
that the final certificate was to be conclusive evidence
(unless proceedings had been commenced before

issue or an arbitration request was made within 14 days of issue) in any proceedings that the works had been properly carried out and completed in accordance with the terms of the contract. This meant that the employer had no redress against the contractor if, for example, a month after the issue of the final certificate the employer discovered that all the ceilings were 150mm lower than specified. Even if the employer sued through the courts, the final certificate was conclusive ('in any proceedings'). The employer could, of course, sue the architect, which was why architects waited as long as possible before issuing the final certificate. Sometimes the final certificate was never issued, a small sum being left outstanding in the hope that the contractor would not consider it worth his while to take legal action and the architect would never have to certify. Certain things were excluded from the conclusiveness of the final certificate – fraud, dishonesty or fraudulent concealment, any defect, including omissions, in the works which reasonable inspection (q.v.) at any reasonable time before the issue of the final certificate would not have revealed. The last are sometimes known as 'latent defects' (q.v.).

The position under JCT 80 (clause 30.9) and IFC 84 (clause 4.7) is different. The final certificate is conclusive evidence:

— That where the quality of materials or the standard of workmanship are to be to the reasonable satisfaction of the architect, they are to such satisfaction.

— That any necessary effect has been given to all the terms of the contract which require adjustment of the contract sum, except for accidental errors in arithmetic.

The proviso regarding fraud (q.v.) and proceedings remains. The difference is important because it means that if nothing is left in the contract to the satisfaction of the architect, the conclusiveness affects only the financial aspects of the certificate. In any action brought by the employer after the issue of the final certificate, the contractor is no longer able to point to the certificate as proof that the works are in accordance with the contract. Architects will, no doubt, limit the situations in which they require work or materials to be to their satisfaction.

ACA 2 (clause 19.5) expressly states that the final certificate does not relieve the contractor of any liability under the contract. GC/Works/1 (clause 42(2)) states that no interim certificate (q.v.) is to be conclusive. Although it makes no mention of the conclusiveness of the final certificate, it is thought that the position must be the same. MW 80 does not make the final certificate conclusive. See also: *Approval and satisfaction; Final certificate.*

| **Condition** | A term in a contract which is of fundamental importance to the contract as a whole. If such a term is broken by one party, the other party may repudiate the contract. He may elect to treat the contract as at an end and sue for damages (q.v.). It is, therefore, crucial to appreciate which terms are conditions and which are simply warranties (q.v.). It is for the court to decide the question. |
|---|---|
| | The JCT and GC/Works/1 forms refer to the body of the printed contract form as 'conditions'. They are not all conditions in the legal and contractual sense; some of them are warranties or minor terms. The ACA 2 form refers to its terms as 'clauses', which is less liable to give rise to misunderstanding. |
| | Clause 2.1 of the JCT 80 is a good example of a condition, since it sets out the contractor's fundamental obligations. See also: *Condition precedent; Condition subsequent.* |
| **Condition precedent** | A condition which makes the rights or duties of the parties depend upon the happening of an event. The right or duty does not arise until the condition is fulfilled. For example, under JCT 80, clause 26.1, the making of a written application by the contractor at the proper time is a condition precedent to payment under the contractual machinery for reimbursement |

of direct loss and/or expense. Similarly, before the employer can claim liquidated damages under many forms of building contract, the architect's certificate of delay is a condition precedent, e.g., JCT 63, clause clause 22; JCT 80, clause 24; IFC 84, clause 2.7; ACA 2, clause 11.3.

There are many other examples in the standard forms It should be noted, however, that it is sometimes open to question whether or not a term is a condition precedent unless it is expressly stated to be such. An example of this is to be found in JCT 80, clause 25. Although, at first sight, the requirement of written notice by the contractor appears to be a condition precedent to the awarding of an extension of time, most commentators believe that is not the case. If the architect fails to carry out his duties under clause 25, the employer may lose his right to recover liquidated damages (q.v.). See also: *Condition; Condition subsequent.*

| | |
|---|---|
| **Condition subsequent** | A provision which terminates the rights of the parties upon the happening of an event, e.g., a contract clause providing for the termination of the contract on the outbreak of war (q.v.). See also: *Condition; Condition precedent.* |
| **Conditional contract** | Where an offer (q.v.) is made subject to a condition and is accepted by the other party, differing legal consequences may result:<br>— Where the parties have not settled all the terms or the agreement is conditional on a further agreement, there is no contract. This interpretation is always adopted where the parties express their agreement as being 'subject to contract' (q.v.). Another possibility is that the agreement will be void for uncertainty, e.g., as in *Lee-Parker v. Izzet* (1972) where agreement was reached 'subject to the purchaser obtaining a satisfactory mortgage'.<br>— Where there is complete agreement but it is suspended until the happening of a stated event (see: *Condition precedent*) such as the obtaining of an |

export licence. In some cases this may impose an obligation on one party to bring about the stipulated event or at least not to prevent it happening: *Mackay v. Dick* (1881).

— Dependent on the wording used, the condition does not prevent the contract coming into existence, but merely suspends some aspect of contractual performance until the condition is satisfied.

| | |
|---|---|
| **Conditions of contract** | The clauses or terms in the main body of the contract, e.g., in JCT 80 that portion of the contract between the recitals (q.v.) and the appendix (q.v.). They are sometimes referred to as 'operative clauses'. The word 'condition' used in this sense must be differentiated from the same word used to denote a term of fundamental importance to the contract as a whole. See also: *Condition; Condition precedent; Condition subsequent.* |
| **Conditions of Engagement (RIBA)** | A document issued by the Royal Institute of British Architects for the benefit of clients and architects. It determined the minimum fees for which RIBA members could undertake work and the professional services which clients could expect to receive in return. The Conditions of Engagement were mandatory upon members of the RIBA. They were replaced in July 1982 by the *Architect's Appointment* (q.v.). |
| **Confidence, breach of** | See: *Confidentiality.* |
| **Confidential communications** | See: *Privilege.* |
| **Confidentiality** | The law recognizes that certain relationships give rise to a duty to maintain confidentiality and will award damages (q.v.) or an injunction as appropriate. 'The obligation to respect confidence is not limited to cases where the parties are in contractual relationship... If the defendant is proved to have used confidential information, directly or indirectly |

obtained from the plaintiff without consent… he will be guilty of an infringement of the plaintiff's rights': Lord Greene MR in *Saltman Engineering Co. Ltd v. Campbell Engineering Co. Ltd* (1948).

This is a developing area of the law and protection is not confined to business relationships. Some standard form contracts deal expressly with the matter, e.g., ACA 2, clause 3.3 which is in very plain terms, but even where the contract is silent it is clear that the relationships in contracting give rise to a duty to maintain confidentiality.

The principle is that someone who has received information in confidence should not take unfair advantage of it, but it is now established that the courts can take the public interest into account: See: *Lion Laboratories Ltd v. Evans* (1984).

| | |
|---|---|
| **Consequential loss** | Many supply contracts contain terms purporting to exclude the supplier's liability for 'consequential loss or damage' caused by such matters as late delivery, defects in materials supplied and so on. The use of the word 'consequential' causes much debate but, in the context of building and related contracts, its meaning is quite clear. |

In *Croudace Construction Ltd v. Cawoods Concrete Products Ltd* (1978) the Court of Appeal decided that 'consequential loss or damage' means the loss or damage which does not result directly and naturally from the breach of contract complained of. Damages are not consequential if they result directly and naturally from the breach or event on which reliance is put. Loss which directly and naturally results in the ordinary course of events from a breach of contract is recoverable as 'direct loss and/or expense' under JCT 80, clause 26, and similar provisions in other contracts.

'Consequential loss' clauses merely protect suppliers, etc., 'from claims for special damages which would be recoverable only on proof of special circumstances and for damages contributed to by some supervening cause': Atkinson J. in *Saint Line Ltd v. Richardsons, Westgarth & Co. Ltd* (1940).

In *Millar's Machinery Co. Ltd v. David Way & Son* (1934) a contract provided that suppliers did 'not accept responsibility for consequential damages'. It was held that this clause did not exclude liability for the buyer's expenses in obtaining other machinery to replace the defective machine. See also: *Causation; Damages; Direct loss and/or expense; Foreseeability.*

| | |
|---|---|
| **Consideration** | Something which is given, done or foreborne by one party in return for some action or inaction on the part of the other party. It must have some legal value. It is a vital part of a simple contract (but not of a contract under seal, i.e., a specialty contract (q.v.)). There are some general rules which apply to consideration. It must be: |

— Genuine; it must not be a vague promise or one in which there is no real benefit to the other party.

— Legal; it must not be unlawful.

— Possible; it must be capable of fulfilment at the time the contract is made. This must be distinguished from the consideration becoming impossible during the course of the contract (see: *Frustration* ).

— Present or future; it cannot be something already done or given at the time the contract is made.

— Moving from the promisee; the parties entering into the contract must provide the consideration. The consideration need not be adequate. If two parties have entered into a genuine contract where that given by one of the parties does not appear to be equivalent to that given by the other, the courts will rarely intervene. There are exceptions to some of these general rules and in some instances the existence of consideration may be difficult to prove. In the case of building contracts the consideration will be the carrying out of the works by the contractor and the payment by the employer.

*Executed consideration* exists where the consideration on one side consists of the doing of an act, the doing of which brings the contract into existence. A good example is a typical estate agent's contract to sell a house. The client says 'I will pay you 2½% if you sell my house.' There is no contract until the house is sold, and so the estate agent is not liable if he does not try to sell the house and the client can withdraw the agency before the house is sold.

*Executory consideration* exists where the consideration consists of an exchange of promises. See also: *Contract*.

## Consultant

Literally, a specialist who gives expert advice or assistance. None of the standard forms of building contract mention consultants specifically. It is important to remember, therefore, that a consultant will have no express authority to issue instructions under any of the standard forms unless a suitable clause is written in to the contract. It is not advisable to do this because it is essential that the control of the work rest in the hands of one man: the architect, supervising officer or, in the case of the BPF edition of ACA 2, the client's representative (q.v.). It must be recognized, however, that the dubious practice of consultants visiting site and giving instructions directly to a sub-contractor does exist.

Under the BPF System (q.v.), consultants are defined as persons or firms contracted by the client (q.v.) to produce design and cost services additional to those provided by the design leader (q.v.). They may be experts in any relevant field and are paid a fixed fee to cover all costs and expenses. Consultants work under the terms of a model consultancy agreement prepared by the BPF and are responsible only for their own part of the work. The design leader (q.v.) is responsible for the co-ordination of the work of all consultants.

## Contingency

An unexpected event. The architect normally arranges for a contingency sum to be inserted in the bills of quantities (q.v.). The amount is usually about 3% of the expected contract sum. The purpose of the sum is to cover the cost of those small items which, in the best of jobs, tend to be overlooked.

If, unusually, there are no such items, the whole of

the sum is deducted from the contract sum and represents a saving to the employer. A contingency sum is not intended to cover additional work to that originally envisaged. In certain types of building, e.g., old or complex existing structures, the contingency sum may be increased to reflect the fact that there is more chance that unforeseen situations (hidden rainwater pipes, eccentric structure, rot) may arise.

**Contra proferentem**

A principle or rule of contract interpretation. 'If there is an ambiguity in a document which all the other methods of (interpretation) have failed to resolve so that there are two alternative meanings to certain words, the court may construe the words against the party seeking to rely on them and give effect to the meaning more favourable to the other party': D. Keating, *Building Contracts,* 4th edn., p.34. The rule does not seem to apply to 'negotiated' standard form contracts, such as JCT forms, where the document is prepared by representatives of actual and potential users: see: *Tersons Ltd v. Stevenage Development Corporation* (1963), a decision on the 4th edition of the ICE Conditions of Contract. Probably, however, the rule would apply where the employer makes *substantial* amendments to the printed text so that it ceases to be a 'negotiated document' and is put forward by him as his own. Probably, too, it applies to manuscript or typewritten insertions, e.g., in the appendix to the JCT forms, where these are inconsistent with the printed conditions: *Bramall & Ogden Ltd v. Sheffield City Council* (1985). The best known example of the application of the *contra proferentem* principle in the construction industry is the decision of the Court of Appeal in *Peak Construction (Liverpool) Ltd v. McKinney Foundations Ltd* (1971) which involved Liverpool Corporation's own form of contract. See also: *Unfair Contract Terms Act 1977.*

**Contract**

A binding agreement between two or more persons which creates mutual rights and duties and which is enforceable at law. There must be an intention to create a legal relationship. Thus, a simple promise to do something for a person is not legally binding. For example, if A agrees to give £5 to B and in return B agrees to clean A's car, a legally binding contract is in existence. If B simply promises to clean A's car, there is no contract and A can do nothing if B fails to keep his promise.

There are two basic types of contract:

— Specialty contracts (q.v.) or contracts under seal. This type of contract is often used by local authorities and corporations (q.v.).

— Simple contracts (q.v.) or contracts made in writing or orally. If written, these will be signed, not sealed, by the parties. This type of contract is the most common. Figure 11 illustrates the major differences between specialty and simple contracts. A number of features are essential in order to enter into a valid contract:

— There must be an *offer* (q.v.) by one party.

— There must be an unqualified *acceptance* (q.v.) by the other party.

— There must be *consideration* (q.v.) except in the case of contracts under seal.

— The parties must have *capacity to contract* (q.v.).

— There must be an *intention to create a legal relationship*.

— There must be *genuine consent*. For example: there must be no duress involved.

— The object of the contract must be *possible*.

— The object of the contract must be *legal*. For example: an agreement to defraud the Inland Revenue would not be a binding contract.

Contracts may be:

— Valid: they satisfy all the requirements for a legally binding contract.

— Void: they are not contracts at all because they are lacking in some important respect, e.g., lack of proper acceptance.

— Voidable: a contract which is not void but which can be made void at the instance of one of the parties.

# Figure 11

Simple and specialty contracts compared

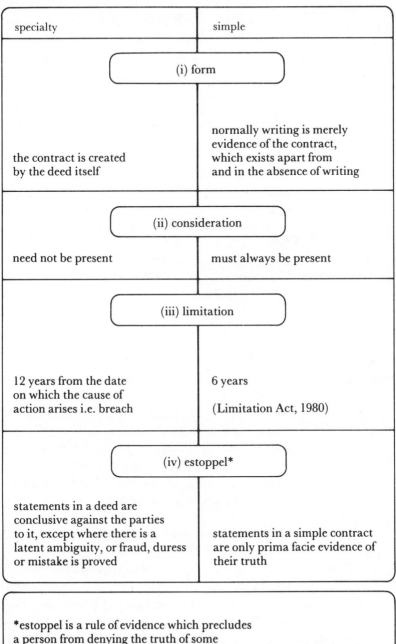

| specialty | simple |
|---|---|
| **(i) form** | |
| the contract is created by the deed itself | normally writing is merely evidence of the contract, which exists apart from and in the absence of writing |
| **(ii) consideration** | |
| need not be present | must always be present |
| **(iii) limitation** | |
| 12 years from the date on which the cause of action arises i.e. breach | 6 years<br><br>(Limitation Act, 1980) |
| **(iv) estoppel\*** | |
| statements in a deed are conclusive against the parties to it, except where there is a latent ambiguity, or fraud, duress or mistake is proved | statements in a simple contract are only prima facie evidence of their truth |

\*estoppel is a rule of evidence which precludes a person from denying the truth of some statement made by him, or the existence of facts which by words or conduct he has led others to believe in

— Unenforceable contracts: contracts which are valid but whose terms cannot be enforced because of some special reason, e.g., the operation of the Limitation Act 1980 (see also: *Limitation of actions*). Contracts for the erection of buildings are normally entered into by using one of the standard forms available. They have the following advantages:
— Designed specially for construction work.
— Comprehensive and continually updated in the light of experience and developments in the law.
— The contents are generally understood by the industry.
— Certain contracts are negotiated documents and, therefore, not to be construed *contra proferentem* (q.v.) against either party. See also: *ACA form of Building agreement; Agreement for minor building works; Anticipatory breach of contract; Breach of contract; Burden of a contract; Change of parties; Discharge of contract; Divisible contract; Entire contract;Essence of the contract; Formalities of contract; Fraudulent misrepresentation; GC/Works/1 contract; Illegal contract; Implied contract; Innocent misrepresentation; JCT contracts; Misrepresentation; Mistake; Performance; Privity of contract; Quasi-contract; Rectification; Repudiation; Rescission; Standard forms of contract.*

| | |
|---|---|
| **Contract documents** | A document is anything on which marks have been made with the intention of communicating information. Such things as writing, printing, typescript, drawings and photographs are documents. The documents which are brought together to form the evidence of a contract, agreed by the parties and signed as such, are termed the 'contract documents'. All the standard forms of contract define what are to be the contract documents: JCT 80, clause 2.1, ACA 2, recital C, GC/Works/1, clause 1(1), MW 80, 1st recital, IFC 84, 2nd recital. The printed form, drawings, specification (q.v.), bills of quantities (q.v.), schedules and schedules of rates (q.v.) are commonly included, depending on the type of contract desired. It is important, although rarely completely achieved in practice, that the documents |

are consistent with one another. In the case of inconsistencies, most standard forms provide that the printed conditions must override any other provisions if there is conflict. This reverses the general law that specially written terms take precedence over printed terms and sometimes leads to unwelcome results. Thus, under JCT terms, if the employer was given 21 days to honour the architect's certificates by a clause in the bills of quantities, it would have no effect unless the corresponding clause in the printed conditions had been properly amended and initialled by the parties.

All the contract documents must be signed by the parties and identified as being contract documents. Some such endorsement as 'This is one of the contract documents referred to in the Agreement dated...' and signed by the parties should suffice. See also: *Bills of quantities; Contract drawings; Priority of documents; Specification.*

---

**Contract drawings**

The drawings specifically referred to in the contract. They are usually identified by drawing number together with any revision number. The drawings must be signed by the parties and bound in with the rest of the contract documents (q.v.).

Although all the standard forms make provision for the architect to issue 'such further drawings or details as are reasonably necessary either to explain and amplify the contract drawings or to enable the contractor to carry out and complete the works in accordance with the conditions' (JCT 80, clause 5.4), such additional drawings cannot modify the contractor's obligations as contained in the contract documents. What that means is that the architect cannot, without a variation in cost to the contract, change anything contained in the contract drawings or contract bills. The contract drawings are usually small-scale drawings: plans, elevations, sections, site plan. It is important that they be as accurate as possible and they must be the same drawings on which the contractor submitted his tender. It is not unknown for drawings to be revised between the date of invitation to tender and the signing of the contract, but it must be the original tender drawings which are signed and bound into the contract. A fuller discussion of this point may be found in Chappell's *Contractual Correspondence for Architects*, p. 70. See also: *Contract documents*.

| | |
|---|---|
| **Contract sum** | The amount or consideration (q.v.) which the employer agrees to pay to the contractor for carrying out the works. It is written into the contract documents.<br>All the standard forms contain provision for adjusting the contract sum (see Tables 16 – 19) and, therefore, the amount of the final account (q.v.) may well be greater or less than the contract sum. The contract sum is generally stated to be exclusive of VAT. |
| **Contractor** | One who enters into a contract with another. The word is used to make the distinction between a person who enters into a contract to carry out work and services, often called an independent contractor, and a person who is a servant or employee of the person for whom he does the work. The contractor, unlike the employee, is not subject to detailed control.<br>In the construction industry, a contractor is invariably the person, partnership or company which carries out construction work. All the standard forms of contract refer to the contractor in this sense. |
| **Contractor's skill and care** | In the absence of any express term in the contract, the law will always imply that the contractor:<br>— Will carry out his work in a workmanlike manner.<br>— Will supply good and proper materials.<br>— Will ensure that the completed structure is reasonably fit for its intended purpose. In the case of a dwelling it must be reasonably fit for human habitation. This obligation may be excluded if an architect is employed.<br>These implied terms may be excluded (subject to the provisions of the Unfair Contract Terms Act 1977 (q.v.)) by an express term to that effect in the contract. |

# Table 16 JCT 80 clauses under which the Contract Sum may be adjusted

| Clause | Adjustment |
|---|---|
| 2.2.2.2 | Error in bills |
| 2.3 | Discrepancy in contract documents |
| 3 | Contract sum adjustments |
| 6.1.3 | Divergence between contract documents and requirements of statutory authorities |
| 6.1.4.3 | Emergency in complying with statutory requirements |
| 6.2 | Fees legally demandable under Act of Parliament, etc. |
| 7 | Levels and setting out |
| 8.3 | Opening up the works and testing |
| 9.2 | Royalties and patent rights |
| 13 | Variations |
| 17.2 and 17.3 | Defects, shrinkages and other faults |
| 21.2.3 | Insurance payments under clause 21.2 by the contractor |
| 22B.2.2 | Restoration and repair of damaged work |
| 26.5 | Loss and/or expense |
| 28.2.2.2 | Work begun but not completed at date of determination |
| 30.6 | Final adjustment of contract sum |
| 32.3 | Works required after outbreak of hostilities |
| 33.1.4 | Removal of debris and protective work after war damage |
| 34.3.3 | Loss and/or expense due to antiquities |
| 35.24.7 | Renomination of sub-contractor |
| 36.3.2 | Expense in obtaining goods from a nominated supplier |
| 38, 39 and 40 | Fluctuations |

## Table 17 ACA 2 clauses under which the Contract Sum may be adjusted

| Clause | Adjustment |
|---|---|
| 1.4 | Error in the bills |
| 1.7 | Fees in relation to statutory authorities, etc. |
| 6.4 (Alt. 2) | Repair and removal of debris |
| 6.9 | If the contractor fails to make an insurance claim |
| 6.10 | Claims by employer |
| 7.4 | Damage, loss and/or expense |
| 11.8 | Acceleration or postponement |
| 12.3 | Work required due to the default of the employer or architect |
| 12.4 | Contractor in breach of his obligations |
| 16.6 | Provisional sums |
| 17 | Variations |
| 18 | Fluctuations |
| 25.2 | Decisions of adjudicator |

## Table 18 GC/Works/1 clauses under which the Contract Sum may be adjusted

| Clause | Adjustment |
|---|---|
| 5(2) | Error in the bills |
| 9 | Variations |
| 11G(2) | Labour tax matters |
| 11G(3) | Sub-contract reductions or increases |
| 15 | Patent rights |
| 20(1) | Use of the authority's property |
| 23 | Suspension for frost, etc. |
| 26(2)(c) | Damage to the works |
| 38(3) | Prime cost sums |
| 38(4) | |
| 39 | Provisional sums |
| 44(3)(a) | After determination |
| 50 | Damage caused by the authority's works |
| 53 | Expense |

## Table 19  MW 80 clauses under which the Contract Sum may be adjusted

| Clause | Adjustment |
|--------|------------|
| **2.5** | Defects, etc., during the defects liability period |
| **3.6** | Variations |
| **3.7** | Provisional sums |
| **4.1** | Inconsistancies in the contract documents |
| **4.4** | Computation of the final amount |
| **4.5** | Contribution, levy and tax changes |
| **6.3A** | Insurance money |
| **6.3B** | Making good of loss or damage |

Other factors, also, may operate to reduce the liability of the contractor. For example, if the employer has the services of an architect on whose advice he relies. ACA 2 makes the position quite clear, so far as that contract is concerned, by including a special clause (1.2) which expressly refers to and preserves all implied warranties or conditions and puts on the contractor the duty to perform his obligations under the contract with 'all the skill, care and diligence to be expected of a properly qualified and competent contractor experienced in carrying out work of a similar scope nature and size to the Works'.

| **Contributory negligence** | Governed by the Law Reform (Contributory Negligence) Act 1945. An action for negligence (q.v.) against one party cannot be defeated merely by proving that the other party contributed to the damage by reason of his own negligence. In such circumstances, if the negligence of both parties is proved, the court will reduce the damage payable by the defendant (q.v.) by a proportion which has regard to the 'contributory negligence' of the plaintiff (q.v.). See also: *Civil Liability (Contribution) Act 1978.* |

| **Copyright** | Rights relating to creative work of an artistic, dramatic, literary or musical nature. They usually belong to the originator or creator. |

The rights are governed by a large body of legislation, notably the Copyright Act of 1956. Generally, copyright remains with the creator of the work for his lifetime and for fifty years thereafter. No one may produce, reproduce or copy his work without his express permission. Ownership of copyright may be transferred from the creator or a licence (q.v.) may be given to someone to reproduce the work while the creator retains the ownership of the right.

In published works it is usual, though not essential, to show that copyright is claimed thus: © V. Powell-Smith and D. M. Chappell (1985).

Architects have copyright in their designs. An architect commissioned to design a building retains

138

the copyright in his design but, normally, the client has a licence to reproduce that design as a building, provided the client has agreed the matter with the architect or paid a sufficient fee such that the architect's agreement to the use of his design is implied (*Stovin-Bradford v. Volpoint Properties Ltd and Another* (1971)). If the RIBA Architect's Appointment is used, the position is clearly set out:

— Copyright in all documents and drawings prepared by the architect and in work executed from them remains the property of the architect unless otherwise agreed.

— The client may reproduce the designs once only on the site for which they were intended if the architect has completed stage D or provided information in stages E, F and G and fees due have been paid or tendered.

— If stage D has not been completed, the client must obtain the architect's consent and pay any agreed fee before he may proceed to execute the work, provided that the architect shall not withhold his consent unreasonably.

If the architect suspects that a client, or anyone else, is about to use his designs without consent, express or implied, he can apply to the court for an injunction to restrain them. Note, however, that the courts will not grant an injunction if the work has been commenced because they consider that damages in the form of a suitable fee for reproduction will amply recompense the architect and stopping expensive building work is not justified in such circumstances. What constitutes commencement of building work may be a difficult matter to decide (*Hunter v. Fitzroy Robinson & Partners* (1978)).

It may also be difficult to prove infringement of copyright. It is easy to show that a design has been copied if every detail is exactly the same as the original, but the position is not so straightforward if portions only of the design have been copied. Small alterations to a design will not overcome the rights of the original designer. Similarly, if a substantial and recognizable feature of the original design is copied, the original architect will have a good case. The issue is a matter of degree and very uncertain in many instances. The architect should try and negotiate a suitable fee rather than resort to the courts in such instances.

| **Corporation** | An artificial legal person having a distinct legal existence, a name, a perpetual succession and a common seal. Corporations are classified as: |

—*Corporations sole*, which consist of only one member at a given time and are the successive holders of certain offices, e.g., the Bishop of Exeter. It is an office or function as opposed to its holder in his private capacity.

—*Corporations aggregate*, which consist of many members. They come into existence either by grant of a royal charter or by or under authority of an Act of Parliament, e.g., a limited liability company. The corporation is a separate legal entity distinct from the individuals who are its members for the time being.

Contracts made beyond the powers of the corporation, as laid down in its charter or limited by statute are *ultra vires* (q.v.) and void. This is not of great importance as regards building contracts. Today corporations can make contracts in the same form as is available to private individuals. The age-old requirement of the common law that corporations had to contract under seal (q.v.) was abolished by the Corporate Bodies Contracts Act 1960.

**Corporeal property**    Tangible property such as land or goods which has a physical existence in contrast with incorporeal property (q.v.) which consists of intangible legal rights. A *corporeal hereditament* is a tangible interest in land – the land itself and things which are annexed to or form a part of it ('fixtures' (q.v.)) while an *incorporeal hereditament* is a right over land, such as a right of way or other easement (q.v.). The word 'hereditament' denotes that the property is inheritable. See also: *Personal property; Real property.*

| | |
|---|---|
| **Corroboration** | Evidence (q.v.) which tends to strengthen other evidence. It is not strictly necessary in English law but it is always desirable. The court may act on the testimony of one witness alone, but in certain specified cases, e.g., perjury, corroboration is required. See also: *Hearsay; Parol evidence.* |
| **Corrupt practices** | Many standard form contracts contain clauses forbidding the contractor from indulging in corrupt practices, such as the giving of bribes or the taking of secret commissions. GC/Works/1, clause 55 is such a provision and entitles the Authority (the employer) to determine the contract and/or to recover from the contractor the amount or value of the bribe, etc. JCT 80, clause 27.3 ( JCT 63, clause 25(3)), in the local authority editions, confers a similar right to determine the contractor's employment 'under this or any other contract' for such practices, which are, in any case, a criminal offence under the Prevention of Corruption Acts 1889 to 1916.<br>Very strict legal rules at common law enable the employer to rescind a contract tainted by corrupt practices and to recover any secret bribes or commission in any case (see: *Salford Corporation v. Lever* (1891)). See also: *Bribery and corruption; Fraud.* |
| **Cost reimbursement contract** | A type of contract by which the contractor receives all his costs together with a fee. There are four common variations:<br>— Cost plus percentage: The contractor is paid the actual cost of the work reasonably incurred plus a fee, which is a percentage of the actual cost, to cover his overheads and profit. This form of contract is often used for maintenance work or for work where it is difficult to estimate the work to be done or for emergency work. It is possible to invite tenders on the basis of the percentage but there is no incentive for the contractor to make good progress or to save money because his fee rises with the total cost of the job.<br>— Cost plus fixed fee: Similar to the cost plus |

percentage contract and used for similar situations. The important difference is that, because the fee is a fixed lump sum, the contractor has more incentive to finish quickly and maximize his profit as a percentage of turnover. It is usual for some indication of the total cost to be given to tenderers. The Joint Contracts Tribunal (q.v.) has produced a suitable form of contract – Fixed Fee Form of Prime Cost Contract.

— Cost plus fluctuating fee: Similar to the fixed fee contract and used for similar situations. An estimate is made of the total cost. The amount of the fee received by the contractor varies inversely to the costs actually achieved. Thus, if the costs are less than the estimated costs, the contractor receives a greater fee calculated in accordance with an agreed sliding scale and vice versa. It is to the contractor's advantage to reduce costs and finish the work quickly.

— Target cost: Used in similar situations to the contracts previously discussed, it can also be used for a wide variety of conditions. Priced bills of quantities (q.v.) or a priced schedule are agreed and a target cost obtained for the project. The contractor's fee is usually quoted as a percentage of the target cost. Provision is made for the target cost to be adjusted to take account of variations and fluctuations. The contractor is paid the actual costs reasonably incurred. The total of these costs is compared with the adjusted target cost. If they show a saving, the fee is increased in accordance with a pre-agreed formula, and vice versa. The disadvantage of this type of contract lies in the complex measurement procedures involved and the difficulty of agreeing targets and percentages. See also: *Management contract; Target cost (contract) (BPF); Value cost contract.*

**Costs**

After litigation (q.v.) or arbitration (q.v.) the general rule is that the unsuccessful party has to pay the costs of the successful party. The awarding of costs is at the discretion of the court, however, and circumstances may be such that the judge decides that each party must pay his own costs or in exceptional cases (where the action is considered frivolous, for example) that the successful party must pay. The situation can also be influenced if one party has made a payment into court (q.v.). Even if a litigant is awarded costs, they are unlikely to cover all his expenses. This is a very good reason for achieving a settlement (q.v.) before the hearing. See also: *Commercial Court; Official referees; Sealed offer.*

## Counsel

A barrister or group of barristers.

## Counterclaim

In legal proceedings, a defendant may respond to a claim for damages by serving a defence and a claim for damages against the plaintiff (q.v.). This latter claim is termed a 'counterclaim' or 'crossclaim'. The counterclaim may not be part of the defence; it may, indeed, have no relevance to the original claim. It may simply be a claim which the defendant intended to pursue in any event. It is for the court to decide whether it is convenient to deal with both claim and counterclaim at the same time. If the court decides that it is not convenient, the counterclaim will be struck out and it is for the defendant then to bring a separate action, as plaintiff, on the substance of the counterclaim.

Architects will be familiar with the device of counterclaiming if they have been involved in suing for outstanding fees. In many cases, a client will counterclaim, alleging negligence, in order to prevent the architect obtaining summary judgment (q.v.). It is difficult to show that a counterclaim is entirely frivolous and the architect may drop his original claim or face long delays before, possibly, obtaining judgment. See also: *Pleadings.*

## Counter-offer

For a contract to come into existence there must be an offer (q.v.) by one party and an unqualified acceptance (q.v.) by the other. If the second party signifies 'acceptance' with qualifications, this is not true acceptance, but merely a counter-offer, which the first person is free to accept or reject. A counter-offer destroys the original offer and the second party may not subsequently purport to accept the original offer: *Hyde v. Wrench* (1840).

A counter-offer must be distinguished from a mere request for further information (*Stevenson v. McLean* (1880)). For example, if contractor A requests a quotation from supplier B, B's quotation is the offer. It may contain special terms of business. If A writes purporting to accept the offer subject to his own contract terms, this is a counter-offer. The process may continue and is known to lawyers as the 'battle of forms'.

In these circumstances, if there is a contract it is the set of terms last in time which are acted upon which is decisive. The correct approach is to see whether one party has accepted the other's terms by express words or conduct, e.g., by acting upon them: see: *Butler Machine Tool Co. Ltd v. Ex-cell-O Corporation (England) Ltd* (1979). However, in some cases there will be no contract at all because neither party has accepted the other's offer or counter-offer.

| | |
|---|---|
| **Courts** | *The Concise Oxford Dictionary* defines a court as an 'assembly of judges or other persons acting as tribunal' as well as a 'place or hall in which justice is administered'. |

Courts can be classified in several ways. Figure 12 represents diagrammatically the major Courts in England and Wales. They are divided into *superior* and *inferior* courts. Inferior courts are those which are subject to control by the High Court. Only the decisions of superior courts play any part in the development of judicial precedent and it is only decisions of superior courts which have any binding authority in later cases (see: *Judicial precedent*). Some courts have only criminal jurisdiction, while others hear civil matters only. Some are hybrid and can hear both types of case.

*Magistrates' courts* deal mostly with minor criminal matters and are normally staffed by Justices of the Peace who have no legal qualifications. Paid

**Figure 12**

Diagram showing the organisation of the English
court system

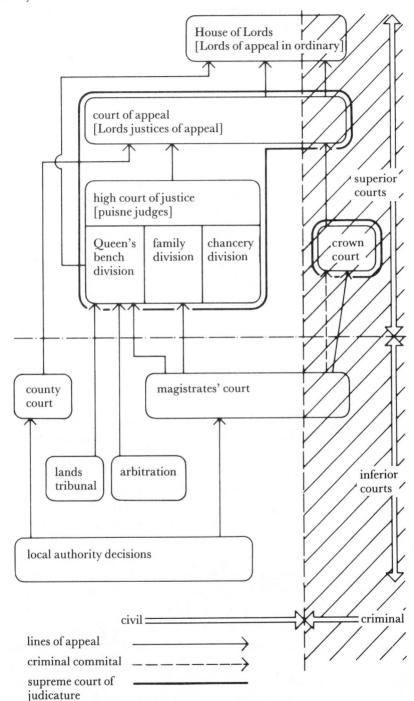

Stipendiary Magistrates – who have legal qualifications – are appointed in London and major centres. Magistrates' Courts have some limited jurisdiction, e.g., hearing certain appeals against local authority decisions.

*Crown Courts* deal with serious criminal matters and also hear appeals from decisions of magistrates' courts. They are part of the Supreme Court of Judicature and are served by High Court Judges and Circuit Judges.

*County Courts* deal with the bulk of civil litigation, but there is a monetary limit on the amount of the claim. They are staffed by Circuit Judges appointed by the Queen on the advice of the Lord Chancellor from among practising barristers and solicitors of experience. There is no jury.

*The High Court of Justice* (which is part of the Supreme Court of Judicature) is divided into three:
— Queen's Bench Division.
— Family Division.
— Chancery Division.

High Court Judges are appointed by the Crown on the advice of the Lord Chancellor from the ranks of eminent practising barristers of long-standing. Building contract disputes are normally dealt with in the Queen's Bench Division, often by the Official Referees (q.v.).

*The Court of Appeal* consists of a Criminal and a Civil Division, is presided over by the Master of the Rolls and consists of him and Lords Justices of Appeal, who are usually promoted from the High Court bench. They sit in Courts of three and hear appeals (q.v.) from both County Courts and the High Court. The Criminal Division hears appeals against conviction and sentence.

*The House of Lords* as a judicial body consists of Lords of Appeal in Ordinary, together with the Lord Chancellor. Appeals are heard by the Appellate Committee of the House of Lords, usually sitting as a committee of five. Before an appeal can be heard the appellant must obtain the permission of the Court of

Appeal or the Appeal Committee of the House of Lords itself. In practice, only matters of the greatest importance proceed this far.

The structure of the courts in Scotland is different. The House of Lords is the final appellate court for Scotland as well as for England and Wales. See also: *Commercial Court; Official referees.*

---

**Covenant**

A promise or an agreement made under seal. A covenant can also be implied by law, in certain cases, e.g., leases.

*Restrictive covenants* most directly affect the construction industry. They restrict the use of freehold land according to the original agreement. They are attached to the land not the person, so that a person buying land also takes on the benefit or burden of any covenant which applies to the land: s. 56, Law of Property Act 1925. This is an exception to the doctrine of privity of contract. Thus, a covenant may restrict the building of anything on land A for the benefit of the owner of land B. New owners may purchase the land but the restrictive covenant remains unless, of course, the two owners (who must be the only ones affected) agree that the covenant may be removed.

In the case of a restrictive covenant imposed on all the owners of land in a particular area for the benefit of that area (i.e., a 'building scheme'), such as a housing estate, the covenant can be enforced by any of the owners.

To enforce a restrictive covenant, the following conditions must be satisfied:

— The covenant must confer a benefit on the land or other land.

— The convenant must be preventive, i.e., to stop something occurring, and must not require the expenditure of money. A covenant to build and keep a boundary wall in good condition is not restrictive.

— The person seeking to enforce the covenant must show that he has been assigned the benefit of the covenant or that it attaches to his land.

Outmoded restrictive covenants may be modified or

discharged by the Lands Tribunal (q.v.).

An *express covenant* may be made, usually between landlord and tenant, in written form. It often covers such things as the tenant's duty to repair, insure against fire, pay the rent.

An *implied covenant* is one that is not written down but is implied by law. Common implied covenants relating to landlord and tenant, if not expressly stated, are that the tenant will have 'quiet enjoyment' of the land (no other party can question his right to the land) and that the tenant will pay the rent. See also: *Restrictive covenant*.

| | |
|---|---|
| **Criminal liability** | Liability which arises under the criminal law, as opposed to civil law. Conviction of a criminal offence may result in a fine, imprisonment or some other punishment. A crime is an offence against the State. The law has declared various kinds of conduct criminal. For the most part, criminal liability in the building industry will result from breach of some specific statutory provision or requirement of regulations, e.g., s. 4(1) of the Health & Safety at Work, etc., Act 1974 which imposes general duties on people in control of non-domestic premises being used as a place of work. |
| **Cross-examination** | The second stage in the examination of witnesses in judicial or arbitral proceedings when the witness is cross-examined by or on behalf of the opposing party. Leading questions may be put, and a very wide range of questions is allowed. The object of cross-examination is to shake the witness's testimony and establish matters which are favourable to the cross-examining party. The witness can be asked questions the answers to which tend to discredit him by showing that he is a person not to be believed. See also: *Examination-in-chief; Re-examination; Witness*. |
| **Crown** | The term 'the Crown' may mean the Queen acting as Head of State on the advice of her Ministers and is largely synonymous with the term 'the State'. |

In the context of building contracts the term means the various Government departments. In general, the Crown has the same power to make contracts as local authorities, companies in the private sector, or individuals, but the following should be noted:

— There are limits on the contractual capacity of the Crown, although their extent is not entirely clear. In practical terms, building and other contracts with Crown departments can be enforced by and against the Crown.

— There are special Crown contracting procedures which have been developed over the years. See also: *GC/Works/1 contract*.

---

**Crown privilege**

The Crown (q.v.) has a right to object to producing a document in court on the ground that it is contrary to the public interest to do so. The privilege (q.v.) is claimed by an affidavit (q.v.) sworn by the appropriate Minister which states that he has examined the document personally and objects to its being produced. The courts may, however, question a claim of Crown privilege.

---

**Custom**

Long-standing practice or usage is binding on those within its scope. It is a subsidiary source of law, though largely unimportant today.

Evidence of trade custom or usage may be given and proved to show that words in a contract are to be interpreted in a particular way, e.g., in *Myers v. Sarl* (1860) where evidence was allowed to show that 'weekly account' was a term of art well known in the building trade at that time. Implied terms (q.v.) may also be established by proving trade custom or usage, e.g., 'reduced brickwork' as meaning brickwork 9 inches thick (*Symonds v. Lloyd* (1859)).

It must be established, however, that the custom relied on is:

— Open and notorious, i.e., generally accepted and acted on.

— Not contrary to law (*Crowshaw v. Pritchard & Renwick* (1859)).

— Reasonable and certain in its operation.

In general, customs will only be implied if they are not expressly excluded and where they do not contradict any other terms implied by the general law. They are difficult to prove in practice.

| **Damage; Damages** | Damage is any harm suffered by a person. For an action (q.v.) to lie, it must be wrongful damage. Damages are the compensation awarded by the court or claimed by the plaintiff (q.v.). See also: *Consequential loss; Direct loss and/or expense; Remoteness of damage; Restitutio in integrum; Special damages.* |
|---|---|
| **Dangerous premises** | The local authority (q.v.) has the power to deal with premises which are in a dangerous or defective condition under ss. 76 to 81 of the Building Act 1984. The procedure is by way of complaint to the magistrate's court which may make an order requiring works to be carried out where any building or structure or part thereof is in such a condition as to be dangerous to a person in the street, in the premises themselves, or in adjoining premises. Section 78 in fact contains an emergency procedure which can be invoked where immediate action is necessary. The local authority may take any necessary action to abate the nuisance (q.v.) and recover expenses from the person in default. See also: *Abatement; Occupiers' liability.* |
| **Day** | A twenty-four hour period extending from midnight to midnight is called a natural day. The period between sunrise and sunset is called a civil day. Contracts commonly refer to day in the first sense; they may also refer to working days. In the absence of any special definition in the contract, a working day is any day other than Sundays, Good Friday, |

Christmas Day, a bank holiday or a day declared to be a non-working or non-business day. The term working day must be expressly stated in the contract if that is what is meant; it will not be implied unless to do otherwise would make nonsense of the particular provision.

ACA 2 refers throughout to 'working days' and defines this expression (article G) as meaning Monday to Friday inclusive but excluding any day which is a public holiday in the country in which the Works are to be executed and any day which is a holiday under the Building and Civil Engineering Annual and Public Holiday Agreements. The Model Conditions for the Hiring of Plant (1979) defines a day as being 8 hours unless otherwise specified in the contract (clause 1 (d)).

If the contract requires fourteen days' notice, the notice expires on the fifteenth day. However, if fourteen *clear* days' notice is required, the notice does not expire until the sixteenth day. See also: *Month; Notice; Week; Year.*

---

**Dayworks**

If works are carried out by the contractor and the works cannot properly be valued by measurement, they may be valued on a prime cost (q.v.) basis. The amount of work done and materials used are recorded and a percentage is added.

JCT 80 makes provision (clause 13.5.4), that vouchers (commonly called 'daywork sheets') must be delivered to the architect or his representative not later than the end of the week following that in which the work was carried out. The valuation must comprise *either* the prime cost of the work (as defined in the 'Definition of Prime Cost of Daywork carried out under a Building Contract', current at date of tender and issued by the RICS and BEC) plus percentage additions as set out by the contractor in the contract bills (q.v.) *or* if the work is of a specialist nature and the body representing the employers in that trade has issued a definition, the prime cost calculated in accordance with that definition plus the percentage additions as before.

GC/Works/1 provides for daywork (clause 9(1)(d)) to be valued by the value of materials used and plant and labour employed in accordance with the basis of charge for daywork described in the contract. Clause 24 requires the contractor to give the SO reasonable notice of the commencement of daywork and to deliver vouchers to the SO by the end of the week following each pay week.

Neither ACA 2 nor MW 80 expressly provides for daywork. Clauses 17 and 3.6 respectively provide instead for valuations to be agreed. In practice, daywork calculations in respect of work and materials will take place.

It is, of course, quite possible to carry out the whole of a contract using dayworks as a basis for valuation and payment.

---

**Death**

The death of a person may end some claims and liabilities. For example a contract for personal services ends on the death of the person contracted to give those services. This situation *may* occur in respect of individual architects or contractors and *would* apply, for example, if the employer had engaged a sculptor to embellish some part of the building and the sculptor died. In general, claims for negligence against a party do not lapse on the death of that party but may be pursued against his heirs. Death is important in respect of many situations, e.g., wills. A partnership ends with the death of any one partner although the terms of the partnership usually provide for the remaining partners immediately to form a new partnership to continue the business. See also: *Frustration*.

---

**Debenture**

A document, issued by a company, which acknowledges a loan and provides for repayment with interest. It usually contains a charge which is fixed on property which is definite or ascertainable and floating on property which is subject to change. A debenture holder has the right to make an immediate appointment, without notice, of a receiver (in the case of a floating charge – a receiver (q.v.) or receiver and manager) if:

— There has been a default in repayment of interest.

— The security is in jeopardy.

There is usually a provision in the debenture to the effect that the receiver or receiver and manager shall be deemed to be an agent of the company.

The company's assets do not vest in the receiver, but he has power to realize the assets by sale. The receiver does not become a party to contracts in existence with the company, and it follows that he cannot vary them (*Parsons v. Sovereign Bank of Canada* (1911)). Furthermore, the receiver 'must fulfil company trading contracts entered into before his appointment or he renders it liable to damages if he unwarrantably declines to do so': *George Barker Ltd v. Eynon* (1974). See also: *Insolvency; Liquidation.*

| | |
|---|---|
| **Debt** | A sum of money owed by one party to another, and recoverable by means of legal action. Liquidated damages due to the employer are often stated to be 'recoverable as a debt'. A speedy way to do this, if the debtor has no defence or counter-claim, may be to apply for summary judgment (q.v.).<br><br>If a party cannot pay his debts as they fall due, he is insolvent (q.v.) which may result in bankruptcy (q.v.) in the case of an individual, or liquidation (q.v.) in the case of a company registered under the Companies Acts. |
| **Deceit** | A tort (q.v.) consisting essentially of a fraudulent misrepresentation (q.v.) made with the intention that the other person should rely on it and which causes damage to him. See also: *Fraud.* |
| **Declared sub-contractors or suppliers** | A term used in the BPF System (q.v.) – but not in the BPF edition of the ACA Contract itself – in respect of sub-contractors listed in the contractor's tender submission. They are those sub-contractors he has used to prepare his tender and with whom he intends to place sub-contracts or orders. They are sub- |

contractors (q.v.) or suppliers (q.v.) in the ordinary legal sense, and any resulting contractual relationship will be between them and the contractor only, and the contractor is responsible for their acts and defaults under the general law. The contractor requires the prior consent of the Client's Representative (q.v.) before sub-letting in this way: ACA 2, clause 9.2. Under the BPF System, tenders must be submitted using BPF forms 7 and 8, and the latter document includes space for the contractor to declare his proposed sub-contractors, giving a definition of the work involved as well as the proposed sub-contractor's name and address.

| | |
|---|---|
| **Deed of Arrangement** | See: *Arrangement, deed of.* |
| **Deemed** | To be treated as. The word is used not only in statutes (q.v.) but also in building contracts. The 'deemed' thing must be treated for the purposes of the statute or contract as if it were the thing in question. For example, clause 10 of JCT 80 states that instructions given by the architect to the person-in-charge 'shall be deemed to have been issued to the Contractor ', i.e., such instructions shall be treated as though they have been issued to the contractor. |
| **Deemed variation** | Generally, an architect's instruction which is treated as being an instruction requiring a variation even though the instruction may not specifically state as much. Deemed variations are provided for in the standard forms, e.g., JCT 80, clause 6.1.3 in relation to divergences (q.v.) between statutory requirements and contract documents. See also: *Deemed.* |
| **Defamation** | A tort (q.v.) which consists of publishing to a third party false and derogatory statements about another person without lawful justification. A statement is defamatory if it exposes the person defamed to 'hatred, ridicule or contempt'. Defamation in a permanent form, e.g., in writing, is called *libel* (q.v.) while in an impermanent or intransitory form, e.g., the spoken word, it is called *slander*. |

Defamation is of little importance in the context of building contracts, save as regards 'reasonable objections' made to a proposed nominated sub-contractor (q.v.) under, e.g., clause 35 of JCT 80. Provided such objections are made reasonably, they will be given privilege (q.v.) unless the maker was actuated by malice (spite or ill-will) or published his objection beyond those who have an interest to receive it, i.e., the architect and (possibly) the employer. The same principle applies to references about the character and abilities of a former employee.

| | |
|---|---|
| **Default** | Failure to act, especially a failure to meet an obligation. The word is used frequently in building contracts, especially in indemnity (q.v.) clauses. JCT 80, clause 20.2 ( JCT 63, clause 18(2)) thus refers to '... negligence, omission or default of the contractor, his servants or agents...' An earlier version of that clause was considered by the High Court in *City of Manchester v. Fram Gerrard Ltd* (1974) where it was held that for there to be a 'default' does not necessarily require that the injured party should be able to sue the defaulter. The judge cited the decision of Parker J. in *Re Bayley-Worthington & Cohen's Contract* (1909) where it was said: 'Default must ... involve either not doing what you ought to do or doing what you ought not, having regard to your relations with the other parties concerned in the transaction; in other words, it involves breach of some duty you owe to another or others. It refers to personal conduct and is not the same thing as breach of contract.'<br>On the facts before him, Kerr J. held that 'default' is established 'if one of the persons covered by the clause either did not do what he ought to have done, or did what he ought not to have done in the circumstances, provided ... that the conduct in question involves something in the nature of a breach of duty...' On the facts he held that the conduct of sub-contractors in applying and using a water-proof coating which contained a phenolic substance and misinforming the plaintiffs about the curing period amounted to a 'default' in the context of the indemnity clause. |

**Defective Premises Act 1972**

The construction of dwellings is subject to the provisions of this Act which came into force on 1 January 1974. The Act does not apply to Scotland or Northern Ireland and is limited to dwellings (including blocks of flats). It excludes houses and flats sold under the National House Building Council Scheme.

Section 1 (1) provides: 'Any person taking on work for or in connection with the provision of a dwelling ... owes a duty to see that the work which he takes on is done in a workmanlike or, as the case may be, professional manner, with proper materials and so ... that ... the dwelling will be fit for human habitation when completed'.

This provision is 'in addition to any duty a person may owe apart' from the Act and extends the common law duties owed to the buyer of a house in the course of erection in a number of ways. It applies to 'conversions' and not just erection of a dwelling. It extends its benefits to every person acquiring an interest in the dwelling, i.e., subsequent purchasers, subject to the limitation period (q.v.) which arises 'at the time when the dwelling was completed' or, in the case of rectification work, 'at the time when the further work was finished'.

A builder who carries out work in compliance with instructions given by or on behalf of the person for whom the dwelling is being built, e.g., under JCT 80 or JCT Minor Works contracts, is given a defence. He has no liability under the Act 'to the extent that he does (the work) properly in accordance with those instructions ... except where he owes a duty to (the client) to warn him of any defects in the instructions and fails to discharge that duty': s. 1(2).

Section 6 (3) outlaws clauses excluding or restricting liability under the Act, and probably extends to such provisions as JCT 80, clause 30.9, which make an architect's certificate conclusive.

It is important to appreciate that the Act is very widely drawn. The duty imposed by s. 1(1) extends not only to builders and developers but also to architects and other designers. It also extends to local authorities, housing associations, etc., when exercising their powers under the Housing Acts: s.1(4)(b). See also: *NHBC Scheme.*

**Defective work**     In the context of all standard forms of building contract defective work is work which is not in accordance with the contract. The architect may have a degree of discretion in accepting or rejecting work, but he has no power to insist upon higher standards than those laid down in the contract documents. There is, of course, an implied term (q.v.) in every building contract to the effect that the contractor will use proper skill and care in executing the work. Thus, a contractor could not plead simply that the defective construction was specified and detailed and so escape all liability. The contractor who discovers that a particular detail, if constructed, would lead to what would be generally accepted as defective work has a duty to point out the defect to the architect and seek instructions.

JCT 80 deals with defective work, by implication, in many clauses requiring the contractor to carry out the work properly (notably clause 2) and, expressly, clauses 8.4, 17 and 27.1.3. These clauses give the architect power to have defective work removed from site and to have defects which appear during the defects liability period (q.v.) made good and give the employer power to determine the contractor's employment if the contractor persistently neglects to remove defective work and thereby the works as a whole are materially affected.

ACA 2 similarly carries the implication that the contractor will not produce defective work and provides for dealing with it in clauses 8.1 (a), 12 and 20.1 (d). These clauses give the architect similar powers to those in the JCT 80 and give the employer similar powers of termination if the contractor persistently neglects to remedy the defective work at the request of the architect.

GC/Works/1 empowers the SO, in clause 7 (1)(d), to

require the removal or re-execution of any work; in clause 32, to require defective work which may appear during the maintenance period (q.v.) to be made good and empowers the Authority, in clause 45, to determine the contract in respect of the contractor's 'inferior workmanship'.

The employer also has his common law rights in respect of defective work whether before or after completion. See also: *Contractor's skill and care; Latent defect; Patent defect.*

| | |
|---|---|
| **Defects clause** | A clause in a contract to permit the contractor, for a specified period, to return to the site in order to remedy defective work. Its purpose is to remove the necessity for the employer to bring an action for damages at common law in respect of defective work, though if work is defective he will be able to do this (within the limitation period) even though the defects liability period has expired. See also: *Defects liability period; Maintenance clause.* |
| **Defects liability period** | A period of time after the works are completed and during which the contractor must make good any patent or other defects. The start of the period is signalled by the date which the architect certifies the works:<br>— Have achieved practical completion ( JCT 80, clause 17.1; IFC 84, clause 2.9; MW 80, clause 2.5).<br>— Are completed to his satisfaction (GC/Works/1, clause 42 (1)).<br>— Are fit and ready for Taking-Over (ACA 2, clause 12).<br>GC/Works/1 and ACA 2 refer to it as the 'maintenance period'. Many contractors and architects use the same terminology which is misleading, maintenance (q.v.) having a rather different meaning to defects liability. The length of the period is a matter for the contracting parties. Usually a period of six months is inserted by the architect for general work and three months for minor works. There is nothing to prevent much longer periods being specified provided the contractor is |

aware at the time of tender. It is common for mechanical and engineering works to have a twelve months' period in order to allow defects to appear during the full range of seasonal variations of temperature and humidity.

All the main forms of contract incorporate the phrase 'which (may, shall) appear' during the period to indicate the extent of the contractor's liability. Some commentators are of the opinion that the defects which are present at the time of completion of the works are included. Although it seems reasonable and the contractor has, in any case, liability to carry out the work in accordance with the contract, it is wise to note any outstanding defects at the time of completion to avoid disputes. ACA 2 makes express provision to do this in clause 12.1.

All the forms make reference to 'defects, shrinkages and other faults' except G C/Works/1 which refers to defects only. The phrase must be interpreted *ejusdem generis* (q.v.) so that ' other faults' must be similar to defects and shrinkages (q.v.). The contractor's obligation is to make good defects arising from:
— Workmanship or materials not being in accordance with the contract documents (q.v.).
— Frost occurring before the date certified for completion.

The architect has the whole of the defects liability period and, in the case of the JCT 80 and ACA 2 forms, 14 days after the end of the period in which to notify the contractor of defects. The contractor has a reasonable time (q.v.) in which to make good the defects at his own cost. When all the defects have been made good, JCT 80, MW 80, IFC 84 and GC/Works/1 require the architect to issue a certificate to that effect.

The defects liability period is primarily for the contractor's benefit so that he can rectify defects and put the works in accordance with the contract. It does not remove the employer's common law rights to sue for breach of contract within the limitation period (q.v.).

| **Defence** | In pleadings (q.v.) it is a set of reasons put forward by the defendant (q.v.) to show why a claim made by the plaintiff (q.v.) should not succeed. They are carefully drafted and couched in formal language. They may range from a complete denial of the plaintiff's allegations, possibly coupled with a counterclaim (q.v.), to an admission of the claim while raising matters in justification. There are many variations in the form of defence, depending upon the ingenuity of the defendant's legal advisers. |
|---|---|
| **Defendant** | The person against whom legal proceedings are brought and called, in Scotland, the Defender. In arbitration, he is referred to as the Respondent. |
| **Delay** | In the context of building contracts the term 'delay' is used to indicate that the works are not progressing as quickly as intended and, specifically, that, as a result, completion may not be achieved by the completion date (q.v.) specified in the contract documents (q.v.). |

Most standard forms provide that the employer is entitled to deduct liquidated damages (q.v.) if the contractor does not achieve completion by the due date. In order to preserve the employer's right to deduct such damages, provision is also made for the contractor to be given extensions of time (q.v.) in certain circumstances. In the absence of an extension of time clause, there is no power to extend time. JCT 80, in clause 25.2.1.1, lays an obligation upon the contractor to notify the architect of *all* delays which may affect the progress of the work. ACA 2, in clause 11.5 (alternatives 1 and 2), is not absolutely clear on the point and it may well be that the contractor is obliged to notify only those delays for which he is seeking extension of time, although this was not the intention of the compilers. GC/Works/1, in clause 28(2)(i), makes it clear by reference to 'such delay' that the contractor is only obliged to notify delays for which he is seeking an extension of time. See also: *Acceleration of work; Extension of time.*

| **Delegated legislation** | Bye-laws, rules and regulations made by local authorities, Secretaries of State, etc., under powers delegated to them by Parliament. |
|---|---|
| | Today, Parliament tends to pass Acts (q.v.) of a general character and entrusts to particular Ministers the power of giving effect to these general provisions by means of specific regulations. The characteristic of all delegated or subordinate legislation is that power to make it must be derived from Parliament. Once validly made, however, these bye-laws and regulations have statutory force and effect, e.g., The Building Regulations 1976. |
| | Delegated legislation can be challenged in the courts on the ground that it is *ultra vires* (q.v.), i.e., that the person making it has acted beyond his powers. Regulations and bye-laws so made are void. |
| **Delegatus non potest delegare** | Literally, a delegate cannot delegate. A general principle that someone to whom powers have been delegated cannot delegate them to someone else. The same rule applies to duties. In general, an architect has no power whatever to delegate his duties to anyone unless his contract with the client expressly empowers him to do this: *Moresk Cleaners Ltd v. Thomas Henwood Hicks* (1966) where an architect, without his client's permission, employed a contractor to design a structure. |
| **Delict** | Broadly speaking, delict is the Scottish equivalent of the English law of tort (q.v.). Most actions in delict are based on negligence (q.v.). |
| **Deposition** | A statement on oath of a witness in judicial proceedings, duly signed by the maker. Depositions are common in criminal courts and statute allows them to be used in civil proceedings in certain circumstances. |
| **Derogation** | Taking away something which is already granted. Thus it also means prejudicing or evading what is already granted. For example, where a landlord has |

granted a lease and he later purports to create a right of way over the leased land in favour of a third party. The basic principle is that nobody can derogate from his own grant.

**Design**

A rather vague term denoting a scheme or plan of action. In the construction industry, it may be applied to the work of the architect in formulating the function, structure and appearance of a building or to a structural engineer in determining the sizes of structural members.

In general terms in relation to building contracts, the architect will be responsible for the design of the building and the contractor is responsible for the materials and workmanship in putting the design together on the site. This generality is often qualified in practice, however, depending upon the circumstances. The contractor may take some responsibility for design, for example in the BPF System (q.v.), or design responsibility may be thrust upon him, for example, where the architect does not undertake any supervision (*Brunswick Construction Ltd v. Nowlan* (1983)).

The professional designer such as an architect is under a duty to exercise reasonable care in his design. 'The test is the standard of the ordinary skilled man exercising and professing to have a special skill. A man need not possess the highest expert skill at the risk of being found negligent ... it is sufficient if he exercises the ordinary skill of an ordinary competent man exercising that particular art': *Bolam v. Friern Hospital Management Committee* (1957). However, by the terms of a particular contract the designer may in effect be guaranteeing the result and undertaking that the structure designed is reasonably fit for its intended purpose: *Greaves & Co. Ltd v. Baynham, Meikle & Partners* (1975).

For a discussion of the complex problems involved in design liability see *Design Liability in the Construction Industry*, by D.L.Cornes.

**Design and build contract**

Sometimes known as a 'package deal contract' (q.v.). In this type of building contract the contractor takes full responsibility for the whole of the design and

162

construction process from initial briefing to completion. The JCT have produced a standard form of contract to cover this kind of work where no architect is employed by the employer (Standard Form of Building Contract With Contractor's Design, 1981 Edition). It follows JCT 80 quite closely but omits all references to 'the architect' and inserts 'the employer' instead where necessary. The main headings are as follows:

Recitals.

Articles.

1 Contractor's obligations.

2 Contract sum.

3 Employer's agent.

4 Employer's requirements and contractor's proposals.

5 Settlement of disputes – arbitration.

Conditions.

1 Interpretation, definitions, etc.

2 Contractor's obligations.

3 Contract Sum – additions or deductions – adjustment – Interim Payments.

4 Employer's instructions.

5 Custody and supply of documents.

6 Statutory obligations, notices, fees and charges.

7 Site boundaries.

8 Materials, goods and workmanship to conform to description – testing and inspection.

9 Copyright, royalties and patent rights.

10 Person-in-charge.

11 Access for employer's agent, etc., to the Works.

12 Changes in the employer's requirements and provisional sums.

13 Contract sum.

14 Value Added Tax – supplemental provisions.

15 Unfixed materials and goods.

16 Practical completion and defects liability period.

17 Partial possession by employer.

18 Assignment and sub-contracts.

19 Fair wages.

20 Injury to persons and property and employer's indemnity.

21 Insurance against injury to persons and property.
22 Insurance of the works against clause 22 Perils.
23 Date of possession, completion and postponement.
24 Damages for non-completion.
25 Extension of time.
26 Loss and expense caused by matters affecting the regular progress of the Works.
27 Determination by employer.
28 Determination by contractor.
29 Execution of work not forming part of the contract.
30 Payments.
31 Finance (No. 2) Act 1975 – statutory tax deduction scheme.
32 Outbreak of hostilities.
33 War damage.
34 Antiquities.
35 Fluctuations.
36 Contributions, levy and tax fluctuations.
37 Labour and materials cost and tax fluctuations.
38 Use of price adjustment formula.
Appendices.
Supplemental provisions (VAT).
It is anticipated that the employer will normally nominate an architect or clerk of works to be his agent for contract purposes. ACA 2 may also be used as a design and build contract. See also: *Design*.

| **Design leader** | The term used under the BPF System (q.v.) to describe the person with overall responsibility for the pre-tender design and for sanctioning the contractor's design. He may be an employee of the client or an independent consultant and is usually, though not necessarily, an architect or an engineer. The design leader co-ordinates the work of all consultants and obtains statutory approvals, etc. He provides design advice on variations (q.v.) as the project proceeds, and the limits of his authority are clearly defined in the BPF *Manual*. He cannot issue orders to consultants which would vary the work from the brief or lead to |

increased cost or delay and he cannot give instructions to the contractor except in an emergency.

The design leader's duties may vary from project to project, but in essence he assumes total contractual responsibility for pre-tender architectural and engineering design for a fixed fee.

| **Details** | Small subordinate items. In building contracts, the term is used to denote the large-scale drawings of the architect or consultants (q.v.). It may also be used to refer to schedules giving minute particulars, e.g., a bar bending schedule could come under the general heading: steelwork details. |
|---|---|

| **Determination** | The bringing to an end of something, for example, the determination of a dispute. The word is most commonly used in the context of building contracts to refer to the ending of the contractor's employment. Both parties have a common law right to bring the contract to an end in certain circumstances (see: *Contract*), but most standard forms give the parties additional and express rights to determine upon the happening of specified events. Some of these rights are similar under different contracts and Table 20 shows a brief comparison. |
|---|---|

It should be noted that in some instances the giving of notice is required, while in others determination is automatic (e.g., bankruptcy). Some contracts distinguish between determination which is the fault of one party or the other or which is the fault of neither party. GC/Works/1 gives no contractual right to the contractor to determine. This contract also refers to determination of the *contract*, while others refer to the determination of the *contractor's employment* under the contract. In practice, it makes little difference, since all contracts make express provision for what is to happen after determination, although it may be argued that putting an end to a contract also removes any obligations under clauses purporting to deal with subsequent events.

In ACA 2, 'termination' is used instead of 'determination' but the effect is the same.

In all cases the procedure prescribed by the relevant clause should be followed exactly.

## Table 20  Comparison of determination clauses under JCT 80, IFC 84, MW 80, ACA 2 and GC/Works/1

| Cause | JCT | IFC | MW | ACA | GC/Works/1 |
|---|---|---|---|---|---|
| **By Employer** | | | | | |
| Contractor wholly suspends the work | √ | √ | √* | √ | |
| Contractor fails to proceed regularly and diligently | √ | √ | √* | √ | |
| Contractor does not comply with instruction re. defective work, etc. | √ | √ | | √~ | √ |
| Contractor assigns without consent | √ | √ | | √ | |
| Contractor fails to operate fair wages clause | √[2] | √ | | | |
| Contractor bankruptcy or liquidation, etc. | √● | √● | √* | | √* |
| Contractor corrupt | √[2]* | √[2]* | | | √* |
| Contractor otherwise in breach | | | | √ | |
| At the employer's discretion | | | | | √* |
| **By Contractor** | | | | | |
| Non-payment | √ | √ | √ | √ | |
| Obstruction by employer | √* | √ | √ | √ | |
| Delay in works for specified period due to: *Force majeure* | √* | | | | |
| Damage by insurance contingencies | √* | | | | |
| Civil commotion | √* | | | | |
| Certain A.I.s | √* | √· | | | |
| Late instructions | √* | √ | | | |
| Delay by employer's men | √* | √ | | | |
| Opening up and testing | √* | | | | |
| Failure to give access | | √ | | | |
| Employer's breach | | | √ | √ | |
| Employer bankruptcy or liquidation, etc. | √[1] | √* | √* | | |
| **By Either Party** | | | | | |
| Damage to existing works due to insurance contingencies | √* | | | | |
| Outbreak of hostilities | √* | | | | |
| Suspension of work for specified period due to: *Force majeure* | | √* | | √* | |
| Damage by insurance contingencies | | √* | | √* | |
| Civil commotion | | √* | | | |
| War, etc. | | | | √* | |

1 Not applicable to local authorities.   * Notice not required before determination.
2 Only applicable to local authorities.   ● Automatic determination.

| | |
|---|---|
| **Deviations** | Departures from prescribed contractual standards. See also: *Extra work*. |
| **Direct loss and/or expense** | The phrase used in JCT 80, clause 26 ( JCT 63, clause 24) to describe the reimbursement to which the contractor is entitled under the claims (q.v.) provisions of the contract in respect of both disruption (q.v.) and prolongation.<br><br>After a good deal of controversy, it is now clearly settled law that this phrase – or similar phrases such as 'direct loss and/or damage'– extends to those heads of claim which would be recoverable at common law as damages for breach of contract: *Wraight Ltd v. PH & T (Holdings) Ltd* (1968) and *F. G. Minter Ltd v. Welsh Health Technical Services Organisation* (1980).<br><br>In practice, this requires precise and exact calculation. Figures cannot be plucked out of the air and it is up to the contractor to prove that he has in fact suffered or incurred the loss or expense which he is claiming. See also: *Claims; Consequential loss*. |
| **Direct payments clause** | Where nominated sub-contractors (q.v.) are involved in the work, JCT 80, clause 35.13.5 provides that the employer may pay a nominated sub-contractor directly if the contractor has failed to discharge sums due on the previous certificate. The procedure is as follows:<br><br>1 Before the issue of each certificate, the contractor must furnish reasonable proof to the architect that any sums directed to be paid to the sub-contractor have been paid.<br><br>2 If the contractor fails to provide reasonable proof, the architect may issue a certificate to that effect stating the amount in question. (If the architect is satisfied that absence of proof stems solely from failure on the part of the sub-contractor, these provisions do not apply).<br><br>If the certificate is issued, the employer must pay the amount direct to the sub-contractor and deduct an equal sum from future payments due to the contractor (including VAT), provided that the employer is not |

obliged to pay more than is available to him by means of deduction from the contractor.

4 If two or more sub-contractors are to be paid and the sum available is insufficient, the employer is to divide the amounts pro rata owing or in some other fair way.

If the employer and nominated sub-contractor have entered into the agreement NSC/2 or NSC/2a, the above provisions are mandatory upon the employer.

**Directions**

A term used in construction contracts, particularly JCT 80, clause 12, usually to mark a distinction from 'instruction' (q.v.). The clerk of works's directions are said to be of no effect unless confirmed in writing by the architect. A direction might thus be defined as a provisional instruction pending confirmation. In ordinary language, the distinction between direction and instruction is not clear except that 'instruction' has more force.

In law, a judge may issue a direction to a jury. In this case he is clarifying a point of law. A summons for directions asks the court to decide various procedural matters, for example: the dates for exchange of particular documents.

**Discharge of contract**

Release from contractual obligations. This may occur in a number of ways:

— Agreement: where both parties agree to treat the contract as at an end.

— Performance: when both parties have fulfilled their obligations under the contract, e.g., the builder has completed the building and the employer has paid for it.

— Waiver: where one party agrees to waive his rights to have the other party fulfil some obligation.

— Frustration (q.v.).

— Breach (q.v.): the breach must be of some fundamental term of the contract in order to allow the injured party to treat it as repudiation (q.v.).

— Operation of law: examples are: the contract falling under the Limitation Act 1980, bankruptcy of one party or the object of the contract becoming illegal during its currency.

— Replacement of one contract by another (novation (q.v.)). In the case of a simple contract (q.v.) for a lump sum, if one party issues instructions to vary the contract, the other party is entitled to consider the original contract at an end and a new contract, incorporating the variation, in being. Severe financial repercussions may result. The effect is avoided in the standard forms of building contracts by the insertion of a variation clause to allow variations of the original contract works.

**Disclaimer**

A technical phrase referring to the power of a trustee in bankruptcy (q.v.) or the liquidator (q.v.) to renounce any kind of onerous property, including contracts. Thus, in the case of a liquidator, s. 323 (1) of the Companies Act 1948 confers this right on him in the case of unprofitable contracts (among other things). The court may allow the exercise of this right provided it does not prejudice other parties. 'Disclaimer' is also used colloquially to refer to notices or contract terms which purport to limit liability for breaches of contract, etc. See also: *Exemption clause; Unfair Contract Terms Act 1977.*

**Discovery/inspection of documents**

In both arbitration and litigation, discovery of documents is the procedure under which one party discloses to the other not only the documents which he will produce at the hearing but all other documents bearing on the issue. Each party serves on the other a list of *all* documents in his possession or control relating to the matters in dispute. All the documents listed must be made available for inspection by the other party who may take copies of them. This is so, no matter how prejudicial to the disclosing party's case the documents are, e.g., internal memoranda commenting on the validity of a claim, etc. The list is not confined to a selection. The only exception is that certain documents are privileged, e.g., Counsel's opinions, correspondence with one's own solicitor about the dispute, etc.

In the High Court discovery is automatic. In arbitration, an order for discovery is made at the preliminary meeting. If this fails to resolve any problems, the High Court has power to make an order requiring discovery: Arbitration Act 1950, s.12.

The list of documents is usually prepared in a standard form and includes two schedules:

Schedule 1

Part 1

Relevant documents which are listed numerically in date order and which the party has in his possession, custody or power and to the producing of which he has no objection.

For example, the contract documents, correspondence between the parties, etc.

Part 2

Relevant documents which he objects to produce, and which must contain a statement of the grounds on which privilege is claimed.

Schedule 2

Relevant documents listed as above which have been but are no longer in the possession, etc., of the party, e.g., originals of correspondence. He must say what has become of them and who has possession of them. Inspection of documents is usually followed by the preparation of an agreed 'bundle' of documents which both parties are prepared to admit as evidence without the need for strict proof. See also: *Arbitration; Pleadings; Privilege.*

---

**Discrepancies**    Differences or inconsistencies. Thus, if a contract drawing (q.v.) showed bricks for a particular situation to be rustic facings and the contract bills (q.v.) gave the bricks for the same situation to be smooth-faced engineering, there would be a discrepancy between the drawings and the bills. It is quite possible, in fact quite common, for there to be discrepancies of various kinds among the many constituent parts of the contract documents (q.v.). One drawing may not agree with the rest of the drawings or it may be in conflict with the information in the bills.

All the standard forms make provision for the treatment of discrepancies. JCT 80, clause 2.3, states that if the contractor finds any discrepancy in or divergence between two or more of the:

— Contract drawings.
— Contract bills.
— Architect's instructions requiring a variation.
— Any further drawings, etc., issued by the architect,

he must notify the architect in writing and the architect must issue an instruction resolving the difficulty. A similar provision, in clause 6.1, refers to the finding of a 'divergence' between statutory requirements and the contract documents.

There is some dispute as to the precise meaning of the word 'if' in these clauses, i.e., 'If the contractor shall find...' It is generally assumed among architects that the average contractor using normal skill and care should find discrepancies in good time so as to avoid costly mistakes, the word 'if' indicating that there might not be any discrepancies not that the contractor may not find them. Contractors usually take the clause to indicate that their obligation is only to report discrepancies *if* they find them; on balance it is suggested that the contractor's view is correct.

ACA 2 removes such disputes (clause 1.5) by expressly making the contractor responsible for using his 'skill, care and diligence' to ensure that there are no discrepancies at the date of the contract. If he subsequently finds a discrepancy, he must notify the architect who shall issue an instruction. Only if the contractor could not reasonably have found the discrepancy at the date of the contract will he be entitled to payment.

MW 80 provides, in clause 4.1, that inconsistencies shall be corrected and such corrections be treated as variations under clause 3.6. The contractor is not made specifically responsible for finding inconsistencies but, reading this clause in conjunction with clause 1.1, it seems probable that he would be. GC/Works/1 simply states (clause 4(1)) that in the case of any discrepancy, the printed condition shall prevail. That does not cover the situation if there is a discrepancy between drawings and bills of quantities. The point is covered by clause 7(1)(b) which empowers the SO to issue an instruction. It does not, however, resolve the question of responsibility for finding discrepancies.

**Discretion**

The ability to decide something in the light of what is fair and reasonable in all the circumstances. Discretionary power is vested in judges in certain cases and some contracts give the architect discretionary powers, e.g., JCT 80, clause 30.3, gives the architect discretion to include or exclude the value of materials off-site in the sums certified in the interim certificates.

**Disorder**

A rather loose term included in ACA 2, clause 11.5, alternative 2, as a ground for awarding an extension of time. It may be considered as a serious disturbance of public order, probably involving an element of violence, rather than the lesser sorts of disorder which can none the less amount to a breach of the peace. See also: *Civil commotion; Civil war; Commotion; Insurrection; Riot.*

**Disruption**

A term used in the ACA 2 and GC/Works/1 forms of contract, clauses 7.1 and 53(1) respectively, to describe severe breaking down of the orderly progress of the works. The ordinary meaning of disruption is 'violent destruction or dissolution'. Therefore, it cannot cover minor interferences with progress. A claim for disruption may be distinguished from a prolongation claim (q.v.) in that it does not depend upon the completion date being exceeded to be successful. An architect's instruction may cause the contractor severe disruption of his programme, but by efficient re-organization, he may be able to complete the contract on time. Despite having completed on time, he will have incurred considerable administrative costs for which he is entitled to be reimbursed over and above any value of the instruction. Labour, materials, plant and the contractor's planned sequence of operations may also be affected. In all cases it is for the contractor to prove the loss and/or expense incurred as a consequence of disruption. See also: *Acceleration of works; Claims; Extension of time; Loss and expense.*

**Distress**
A summary remedy under which someone may take possession of the personal goods of another person and hold them to compel performance of a duty or the satisfaction of a debt or demand. Distress is used by the Inland Revenue to enforce payment of income tax, and also by rating authorities in respect of local rates. The most common example of distress is the right of a landlord to distrain on his tenant's goods for non-payment of rent.

**Disturbance**
A word often used in connection with the regular progress (q.v.) of the works. It means an interruption or disruption (q.v.) and usually forms grounds for a contractual claim. See also: *Claims; Loss and expense.*

**Divergence**
A separating or differing. The word is found in clauses 2.3 and 6.1 of JCT 80. It is used in conjunction with the word 'discrepancy' (q.v.) in clause 2.3 and appears to add little to the meaning. In clause 6.1, it is used alone because it better expresses the sense that the requirements of the contract documents and statutory requirements may differ. See also: *Discrepancy.*

**Divisible contract**
One in which payment is due for partial performance, in contrast to an entire contract (q.v.). 'A divisible contract is one which is so framed that it permits one party to demand performance without tendering performance himself': Cheshire & Fifoot's *Law of Contract*, 10th edn., p.525. A common example is a sale of goods on credit where the obligation of the

seller to deliver the goods is independent of the obligation of the buyer to pay the price. Whether a contract is entire or divisible is a matter which depends upon the intentions of the parties as interpreted by the courts.

| **Documentary evidence** | Evidence in the form of written, printed or drawn documents. Examples are; letters, drawings, contract documents (q.v.), deeds, wills, books and reports. Before documentary evidence is admissible in court, it must be proved authentic. That is not to say that the contents of the document must be proved to be correct, but that the document must be what it is purported to be. For example, a document put forward as being a report on a specific topic written by one person for the benefit of another must be shown to be about the topic, written by that person for the benefit of another. The contents of the report may later prove to be in error. The burden of proving documentary evidence is removed if both parties to the dispute agree. In most building disputes, much of the documentary evidence can be agreed in advance, leaving only key documents or points of law to be decided by the court. See also: *Admissibility of evidence*. |
|---|---|
| **Domestic sub-contractor** | A term found in the JCT 80 contract, principally in clause 19.2. It refers to any person or firm, other than a nominated sub-contractor (q.v.), to whom the main contractor (q.v.) sub-lets any portion of the works. If the contractor wishes to sub-let the plastering work, he must first obtain the architect's written permission. The contractor does not have to obtain the architect's consent to the actual sub-contractor to be used (although it is good practice to do so) only to the fact of sub-letting. Of course, it might be reasonable for the architect to refuse consent until he is informed of the name of the sub-contractor. JCT 80 also enables the employer to specify domestic contractors by means of a list in the Contract Bills: clause 19.3. The employer details in the contract documents work which the contractor is to price, but |

which in fact is to be executed by a domestic sub-contractor chosen by the contractor from a list provided by the employer.

Provided that the contractor has the choice of at least three persons named in the contract bills (q.v.) by the employer, the chosen sub-contractor will be a domestic sub-contractor. See: *Named sub-contractors*. If the list falls below three for any reason and is not increased, the work is to be carried out by the contractor who may sub-let it to a domestic sub-contractor. There is no contractual relationship between the employer and the domestic sub-contractor. Claims between them must pass through the contractor. Thus, if the domestic sub-contractor's work is defective, the employer will seek redress from the contractor. It is then for the contractor to seek redress, in turn, from the domestic sub-contractor. See also: *Privity of contract; Sub-contractor; Vicarious performance.*

**Drawings and details**   The usual means of communicating information from the architect to the builder. Reference is made to both in the JCT 80 and ACA 2 forms of contract. No reference is made to 'details' in the GC/Works/1 form. In practice, it probably makes little difference because the provision of drawings and details would be covered in such references as 'further drawings' (clause 54(3)). Strictly, a drawing is not always a detail, neither is a detail always a drawing. A drawing might best be described, in this context, as a visual representation of a building or some part of a building usually drawn to a designated scale. A detail would normally be a drawing of some small part of a building so as to show, to a large scale, the important features of construction. 'Details', plural, may also mean a written description going into some depth. For example, the architect may furnish *details* of concrete lintels by providing the contractor with schedules giving bar lengths and diameters, lintel sizes and number, and describing the position of the bars in the lintels; but he would provide a *detail* of a concrete lintel by producing a drawing to full-size or half full-size. In general, when the architect or contractor refer to drawings they mean all the drawings irrespective of size of scale; when they refer to details they mean large-scale drawings. If reference to schedules is intended, the word 'schedule' is usually used. See also: *Contract drawings*.

**Due time**

The correct period of time. In building contracts, the due time for completion is the length of time between the date for commencement and the date for completion, i.e., the contract period. The *due date* is the correct date by which some action should be commenced or completed. Thus the due date for completion is the date stated in the contract documents (q.v.) by which the works must be complete.

The due time is not always set out precisely. For example, JCT 80, clause 25.4.6 gives as one of the grounds for extension of the contract period 'the Contractor not having received in due time necessary drawings ... ' The period of time will clearly depend upon the circumstances in the case. It must allow the contractor to place orders, organize work, etc., before it is necessary for him to begin the particular work, but there is scope for considerable dispute in deciding how long a period he requires.

**Duty of care**

The modern law of negligence (q.v.) is based on the concept of a duty of care and unless the injured person can establish that he was owed a duty of care by the defendant an action for negligence is doomed to failure. There are many general situations which the law recognizes as giving rise to such a duty and similar duties may arise under a contract.

The classic test is the so-called 'neighbour principle' set out by Lord Atkin in *Donoghue v. Stevenson* (1932) (see: *Negligence*), but it is clear that the category of duty situations is being altered. 'In accordance with changing social needs and standards new classes of persons legally bound or entitled to the exercise of care may from time to time emerge' (Asquith L.J. in

*Candler v. Crane, Christmas & Co.* (1951)).

*Examples* of duty situations are:

— Manufacturers, etc., towards the ultimate consumer (*Donogue v. Stevenson* (1932)).

— Employers to employees.

— Designer towards third parties.

— Builder/architect towards purchasers and subsequent occupiers.

— Designer/landlord towards tenants (*Rimmer v. Liverpool Corporation* (1984)).

— Sub-contractor towards employer (*Junior Books Ltd v. The Veitchi Co. Ltd* (1982)).

**Easements and profits**

An easement is a right, held by one person, to use the land belonging to another or to restrict the use by another. Examples are right of way (q.v.), right of drainage and right to discharge water on to neighbouring property. These are known as *positive easements* as compared to right of light (q.v.) and right of support, which are known as *negative easements*.

An easement is attached to land, not to a person. The land which enjoys the benefit is known as the *dominant tenement*; the land on which the easement is exercised is known as the *servient tenement*. For an easement to exist, the two pieces of land must have different owners.

A profit à prendre is the right to remove something from another's land, for example, turf or gravel and where several people enjoy the right communally it is known as 'a right of common' and must be registered under the Commons Registration Act 1965.

Both easements and profits may be created by:
— Act of Parliament.
— Express grant, normally by deed.
— Express reservation, when land is sold.
— Prescription (q.v.).
See also: *Wayleave*.

**Eichleay Formula**

A United States formula for calculating the 'head office overhead' percentage of a contractor's money claim for delay. It is widely used in Federal Government contracts but has also been adopted in non-government contract cases although it is not universally accepted even in the United States.

Recently this formula has appeared in this country as an alternative to the Hudson or Emden formulae (q.vv.). The Eichleay formula is a three-step calculation:

$$1. \quad \frac{\text{Contract billings}}{\substack{\text{Total contractor} \\ \text{billings for} \\ \text{contract period}}} \times \substack{\text{Total HO overhead for} \\ \text{contract period} =} \substack{\text{} \\ \text{allocable overhead}}$$

$$2. \quad \frac{\text{Allocable overhead}}{\text{Days of performance}} = \substack{\text{Daily contract HO} \\ \text{overhead}}$$

$$3. \quad \substack{\text{Daily contract HO} \\ \text{overhead}} \times \text{Days of compensable delay}$$
$$= \text{Amount of recovery}$$

The formula can be subjected to a number of criticisms and, at best, gives a rough approximation. In particular, the formula does not require the contractor to prove his actual increased overhead costs from the delay which is an essential requirement in English law, e.g., under JCT 80, clause 26. Moreover, as set out above there is the possibility of double-recovery, to allow for which it is at least necessary to deduct any head-office overhead recovery allowed under normal valuation rules in respect of variation orders. It is unusual, too, in applying daily rates. See also: *Emden Formula; Hudson Formula.*

---

**Ejusdem generis rule**  A rule used in the interpretation of contracts (q.v.) to the effect that where there are words of a particular class followed by general words, the general words must be treated as referring to matters of the same class as those listed. For example, in *Wells v. Army & Navy Co-operative Society Ltd* (1902) an extension of time clause in a building contract allowed the architect to grant an extension of time to the contractor if the works were 'delayed by reason of any alteration or addition ... or in case of combination or workmen, or strikes, or by default of sub-contractors ... *or other causes beyond the contractor's control*'. The 'other causes' were held to be limited to those *ejusdem generis* with the specific causes listed and therefore did not include the employer's own default in failing to give the contractor possession of the site.

The modern tendency of the courts is to restrict the operation of the rule (see: *Henry Boot Construction Ltd v. Central Lancashire New Town Development Corporation Ltd* (1980)). The rule will not apply if the parties establish that the words used are to be given an unrestricted meaning. In any event, as was remarked in the *Henry Boot* case, while the rule is ordinarily applied in the case of deeds (q.v.), wills and statutes (q.v.), 'it is of less force when one is dealing with a commercial contract'. (See also: *Chandris v. Isbrandtsen-Moller Co. Inc.* (1951).)

| | |
|---|---|
| **Elemental bills of quantities** | A system of classification of the contents of the bills of quantities (q.v.) into elements instead of the more usual trade or constructional section divisions. In practice, it means that the lists of work and materials are grouped under headings which reflect the parts of a building, for example: floors, roofs, windows, staircases, rather than carpentry, joinery, finishings, etc. |
| | The principal benefit of elemental bills is in cost analysis where the various parts of a building may be accurately costed and comparisons of costs made with the use of differing materials or with other similar buildings. A quantity surveying office which uses this method will, in time, build up a very useful set of comparative costs to aid cost estimating for new buildings. Some architects and contractors, used to traditional bills, find it difficult to locate items quickly in elemental bills and put up resistance to their use. On the other hand, many architects and contractors find them more logical than traditional bills. Work items are easy to locate once the principle has been grasped. |
| **Emden Formula** | Another formula approach to the controversial topic of overhead and profit recovery in a claims situation under standard form contracts. Unlike the Hudson formula (q.v.) this one takes a percentage from the contractor's overall organization, i.e., on costs and profit expressed as a percentage of annual turnover. |

It is so called because it appears in Emden's *Building Contracts & Practice*, 8th edn., vol. 2, p.N/46:
'When it is desired to claim extra head-office overheads for a period of delay a calculation is adopted as follows:

$$\frac{h}{100} \times \frac{c}{cp} \times pd$$

Where h = the head-office percentage, c = the contract sum, cp = the contract period and pd = the period of delay. (cp and pd should be calculated in the same units, e.g., weeks.)
The head-office percentage is normally arrived at by dividing the total overhead cost and profit of the organization as a whole by the total turnover ... The formula ... notionally ascribes to the contract in question an amount in respect of overheads and profit proportional to the relation which the value of the contract in question bears to the total turnover of the organization.'
Although this approach is more realistic than that of some other formulae it is of limited value in practice and is simply a rough and ready approximation of the situation. In principle, it is necessary for the contractor to prove that there was an increase in overhead costs attributable to the delay or disruption and this is something which any formula method of calculation ignores. See also: *Eichleay Formula; Hudson Formula.*

**Emergency powers**    Those powers which may be invoked by the Government in cases of emergency, national danger or other wholly exceptional circumstances, and now derived almost entirely from Act of Parliament, e.g., the Emergency Powers Acts 1920 and 1964, which give the Government a permanent reserve of power for use in peacetime emergencies, such as during a major strike. They are seldom invoked in practice. Many building contracts provide for what is to happen in the case of exercise of emergency powers. For example, JCT 80, clause 25.4.9 allows 'the exercise after the Date of Tender by the United Kingdom

Government of any statutory power directly affecting the execution of the works' by, e.g., restricting the availability or use of labour, as a ground for extension of time, and the exercise of such powers might well fall within the meaning of *force majeure* (q.v.). See also: *Government action*.

**Employer**

In building contracts, the word does not have the legal 'master and servant' connotation of employment law. It is used to refer to the building owner, the person or body which commissions building work and enters into a contract with the building contractor. The JCT 80, ACA 2, IFC 84 and MW 80 contracts use the word 'employer' throughout in this sense. The GC/Works/1 contract refers to the 'authority' (q.v.) which has, to all intents and purposes, the same meaning. See also: *Master*.

**Encroachment**

Intruding gradually or by stealth on to another person's land. Minor encroachments on neighbouring property are quite frequent when fences are erected or rebuilt, and boundaries are frequently varied in this way. The process is commonly called 'squatter's rights' or, more accurately, acquiring title by adverse possession (q.v.).

**Entire completion**

See: *Performance*.

**Entire contract**

A contract in which 'complete performance' by one party is a condition precedent (q.v.) to the liability of the other party (*Cutter v. Powell* (1795)). For example, where the carrying out and completion of work by one party is necessary before payment by the other party is due. Whether or not a contract is an entire one is a matter of interpretation of the contract; it depends on what the parties agreed. A lump sum contract (q.v.) is not necessarily an entire contract. The test for complete performance is in fact 'substantial performance' (q.v.). What is substantial is not determined by a comparison of cost of work done and work omitted or done badly (*Hoenig v. Isaacs* (1952)).

| **Equities** | The right to invoke equitable remedies for fraud, mistake, etc. Equities are the lowest kind of interest in property, etc. |
|---|---|

| **Equity** | Literally, fairness or natural justice. A body of rules which grew up alongside the common law as a supplement to it and formerly administered in separate courts. In time the principles became systematized and equity supplemented and sometimes prevailed over common law. Equity must not be confused with ethical or moral concepts. Originally there was a moral aspect to the system, but the modern attitude is summed up by a statement of Lord Justice Fry who, in dismissing a claim against a company director guilty of sharp practice, said, 'if we were sitting in a court of honour, our decision might be different': *Re Cawley & Co. Ltd* (1889). Towards the end of the last century, legislation fused the administration of law and equity and so both legal and equitable rules and remedies are now applied throughout the legal system. It is expressly laid down that whenever there is any conflict between common law (q.v.) and equity, the latter is to prevail. Such cases of conflict are rare. |
|---|---|

| **Errors** | Mistakes (q.v.). In the context of building contracts, errors are usually made in regard to fact or to law. Errors of fact may be sufficient to allow one party to apply to the court to have the contract put aside. Errors of law are irrelevant. Most forms of contract make some provision for the correction of errors. JCT 80 refers, in clause 2.2.2.2, to the correction of errors in the contract bills (q.v.); in clause 7, to the correction of errors arising from the contractor's inaccurate setting out; in clause 14.2, to the acceptance of errors in the computation of the contract sum (q.v.); in clause 30.9.1.2, to accidental inclusion or exclusion of any work, materials, goods or figure in any computation or any arithmetical error, all of which are excluded from the conclusiveness of the final certificate. ACA 2 refers (clause 1.4) to the correction of errors in the contract bills and, in clause 3.1, to mistakes, |
|---|---|

inaccuracies, discrepancies and omissions in drawings for which the contractor is responsible.

GC/Works/1 refers, in clause 5(2), to the correction of errors in the bills of quantities. All such references to errors are intended to prevent the contract being vitiated by providing an agreed remedy for them.

Errors in bills of quantities submitted in connection with tendering procedures are often dealt with by the codes of procedure for single and two-stage selective tendering (q.vv.).

Obvious *clerical* errors in a contract will be read by the courts as corrected when interpreting a contract, but this does not apply to mistakes made by the contractor in his tender price. Such mistakes are binding on the contractor unless, before the tender is accepted, the employer or the architect discovers the difference and realizes that it was not intentional. If the error is discovered the position is different: *Webster v. Cecil* (1861).

Mistakes in bills of quantities are not infrequent and give rise to problems. In lump sum contracts (q.v.) errors not discovered by the employer or architect before acceptance clearly bind the contractor in relation to the original work (*Riverlate Properties Ltd v. Paul* (1974)) and in valuing additional quantities, errors in rates are also included.

| | |
|---|---|
| **Essence of the contract** | A term, the breach of which by one party gives the other party a right to rescind the contract, is sometimes said to be of the essence of the contract. It must be a term so fundamental that its breach would render the contract valueless or nearly so to the other party. A term may be of the essence because it is stated to be so by the contract itself or it may be judged to be of the essence by the court. The phrase is often used in connection with time. In building contracts time will not normally be of the essence unless expressly stated to be so. See also: *Delay; Fundamental breach; Rescission.* |
| **Establishment charges** | Otherwise known as 'establishment costs' are the cost to the contractor of his site administration. They include such things as purely supervisory or |

administrative staff, site accommodation, water, light, heat, electricity charges, canteen, welfare, etc. The costs are important to a contractor who is framing a claim for loss and expense. See also: *Claim*.

**Estate**

A technical term used in connection with the ownership of land. It describes the extent of the proprietor's interest in the land, e.g., a freehold or leasehold estate. In common parlance it also refers to the land itself, e.g., 'the Whiteacre Estate'. The same term is also used as the equivalent of property, e.g., the estate of a deceased person.

**Estimate**

A term widely used in the building industry. It has two possible meanings.
— Colloquially and in the industry generally it means 'probable cost' and is then a judged amount, approximate rather than precise.
— A contractor's estimate, in contrast, may, dependent on its terms, amount to a firm offer, and if this is so, its acceptance by the employer will result in a binding contract: *Crowshaw v. Pritchard and Renwick* (1899).
As regards its first connotation, architects and quantity surveyors are frequently required to provide an estimate of cost to a client at an early stage of a project in order that he can decide whether to proceed. It is generally accepted that the estimate will be higher or lower than the final figure. An initial estimate may be as much as 15% astray and it is, therefore, essential that the architect or quantity surveyor inform the client of the possible margin of error. Other factors should be stated, such as whether inflation has been taken into account, exclusion of VAT and the currency of prices. The final cost estimates, produced before the tender stage, may have a very small margin of error, say 5%. Realistically, this is too small because variations in tender price may easily be in the order of 15%, excluding those prices which are clearly not intended to be competitive. Clients tend to expect accuracy and, therefore, architects will often err on the high side in order to avoid unpleasant surprises

when tenders are opened. It is certainly a mistake to pitch any estimate too low simply to 'sell' a scheme because subsequent failure to achieve the figure is unfair to the client and he may sue for the return of his fees – at the very least.

It is not unusual, on small works, for contractors to produce an estimate of the cost of carrying out work. In the absence of a professional adviser, the employer may not realize that the final figure may exceed the estimate. See also: *Offer; Quotation: Target cost; Tender.*

| | |
|---|---|
| **Estoppel** | A principle which precludes a person from denying the truth of a statement made by him or from alleging that a fact is otherwise than it appeared to be from the circumstances.<br><br>There are three kinds of estoppel:<br>— Estoppel by record: A man is not permitted to dispute the facts on which a judgment against him is based.<br>— Estoppel by deed: A statement of fact in a deed (q.v.) cannot be disputed by either party to it. Thus a party to a deed cannot deny the truth of the recitals (q.v.) it contains.<br>— Estoppel by representation: Where someone expressly or impliedly by conduct has made a factual statement or conducted himself so as to mislead another person he cannot afterwards go back on the representation. For example, allowing another person to appear to be one's agent or to have an authority wider than he in fact has. See also: *Agency.* |
| **Evasion** | See: *Avoidance.* |
| **Evidence** | Information tending to establish facts, the facts themselves or opinions based on the facts. In court, there are rules of evidence, which must be observed, as to what evidence may be produced. In civil cases the burden of proof lies with the person asserting the facts. The standard of proof is the balance of probability, i.e., it is more likely to be as the person asserting states than otherwise. See also: *Admissibility of evidence; Expert witness; Hearsay; Parol evidence.* |

| | |
|---|---|
| **Ex contractu** | Arising out of contract. The term is used to refer to claims which arise out of the *express* provisions of the particular contract in contrast to other types of claim (q.v.). For example, JCT 80, clause 26 confers on the contractor a right to claim for 'loss and expense caused by matters materially affecting regular progress of the works' and similar *ex contractu* claims arise under ACA 2, clause 7 (employer's liability) and GC/Works/1, clause 53 (prolongation and disruption expenses). The architect (or client's representative (q.v.) under BPF edition of ACA 2 ) has power under the terms of his appointment to quantify or agree *ex contractu* claims, but not other types of claim. |
| | All the current forms of contract allow additional or alternative claims for breach of contract based on the same facts, see, e.g., JCT 80, clause 26.6. The contractor can recover his loss or expense only once, but a claim for breach of contract may avoid some of the restrictions under the particular contract clause. For example, if the contractor has neglected to make application within a reasonable time in accordance with JCT 80, clause 26.1.1, it is probable that a late claim will be rejected by the architect. There is nothing to prevent the contractor making the same claim at common law for breach of contract, but he can only recover his loss once. |
| **Ex gratia claim or payment** | A claim or payment met or made 'as a matter of grace'. It is sometimes called a 'sympathetic' claim and the essential point is that the employer is under no legal obligation to meet it. *Ex gratia* payments are sometimes made to settle or compromise a claim rather than go to the expense of contesting it in litigation or arbitration. |
| | Under most standard form contracts the architect or his equivalent has no authority to settle such claims or to authorise *ex gratia* payments. He must be given express authority by the employer if he is to settle such claims, and none of the standard contracts endow him with that authority. |

GC/Works/1, clause 44(5) gives the *Authority* (employer) power to make 'such allowance, if any, as in [its] opinion is reasonable' where the Authority has exercised the special power of determination contained in the clause and where it is satisfied that the contractor has suffered *hardship* as a result. This provision in effect merely enables the employer to make an *ex gratia* allowance which it could do in any event. See also: *Claim*.

**Ex officio**   By virtue of one's office.

**Examination-in-chief**   The first stage in the examination of a witness (q.v.) in judicial or arbitral proceedings. It is carried out by the party calling the witness, generally through counsel or a solicitor. There are many strict rules which must be observed in examination-in-chief, e.g., leading questions may not be asked. A leading question is one which suggests its own answer, e.g., 'Did the site agent tell you that he could not care less?' However, a witness may be led in the introductory part of his testimony, e.g., 'Are you the project architect?' See also: *Cross-examination; Re-examination.*

**Examination of site**   Under the general law the employer does not warrant the suitability of the site for the works. The precise conditions of contract may emphasize the position or they may amend it so that the contractor is entitled to additional payment if the ground conditions are not as represented to him. It is quite common for a clause to be inserted in the bills of quantities (q.v.) requiring the contractor to satisfy himself regarding all matters in connection with the site. GC/Works/1, clause 2, is in similar vein, but it does contain a grain of comfort in that it refers to information given in the bills of quantities. If the bills have been prepared in accordance with the Standard Method of Measurement (q.v.) the contractor may well have a claim if the ground is not as described (*C.Bryant & Son Ltd v. Birmingham Hospital Saturday Fund* (1938)).

JCT 80 also refers to the SMM in clause 2.2.1 and the contractor is entitled to claim additional payment if he is put to more expense in excavation than he was led to expect. ACA 2 provides, where the contractor is responsible for the provision of drawings (clause 2.6), that ground conditions are his responsibility but he is entitled to receive payment for any measures he needs to take after encountering 'adverse ground conditions or artificial obstructions' unless he should have foreseen them or an adjustment is made to the contract sum (q.v.) under clause 1.4 (bills of quantities). Whether the contractor is able to claim for site conditions is a matter of interpretation of the contract (q.v.). See also: *Misrepresentation*.

| **Excepted risks** | The term used in JCT 63, clauses 20(b) and 20(c) (and now referred to in JCT 80 as 'the clause 22 perils') to describe those risks which are carried by the employer and which may affect the execution of the works although they are outside the contractor's control. The definition reflects the exceptions commonly to be found in 'All Risks' policies of insurance. In IFC 84, they are referred to as 'clause 6.3 perils'. |
|---|---|

The definition covers fire, lightning, explosion, storm, tempest, flood, bursting or overflowing watertanks, apparatus or pipes, earthquake, aircraft and other aerial devices or articles dropped from them, riot and civil commotion, but excluding any loss or damage caused by ionizing radiations or contamination by radioactivity from any nuclear fuel or from nuclear waste from the combustion of nuclear fuel, radioactive, toxic, explosive or other hazardous properties of any explosive nuclear assembly or nuclear component thereof, pressure waves caused by aircraft or other aerial devices travelling at sonic or supersonic speeds. See also: *Accepted risks*.

| **Exceptionally adverse weather** | See: *Adverse weather conditions*. |
|---|---|

| **Execution** | A word with several meanings in a legal context. 'To execute a contract' means to render it effective by |
|---|---|

signing it, or by signing, sealing and delivering it. It may also mean to carry out its terms.

Execution is also the process by which judgments of the court may be enforced, and hence 'Writ of Execution' or 'Warrant of Execution' which directs the sheriff (or county court bailiff) to seize the judgment debtor's personal property to satisfy the judgment, costs and interest.

| | |
|---|---|
| **Exemption (exception or exclusion) clause** | A clause in a contract which attempts to exclude liability or limit it in some way. See: *Unfair Contract Terms Act 1977*. |
| **Expert** | Someone with special skill, knowledge or professional qualifications. ACA 2, clause 25.3 , alternative 1 and 2, and 25.2, alternative 2, states that in giving a decision under the disputes procedure the adjudicator (q.v.) and architect respectively are 'deemed to be acting as expert and not as arbitrator'. The effect of this is:<br>— The provisions of the Arbitration Acts 1950 to 1979 are not applicable to their decisions.<br>— There is no requirement for the architect, etc., to hold a hearing.<br>— As experts, adjudicator and architect are liable for negligent decisions (*Sutcliffe v. Thackrah* (1974)) even though an arbitrator is probably immune from an action for negligence. See also: *Adjudication; Arbitration*. |
| **Expert witness** | A witness who appears for one party at an arbitration hearing or in court proceedings and who gives evidence based upon his expert knowledge of some facet of the case. His duty is to assist the court or tribunal. An expert witness may and usually does give his opinion. Expert evidence is given by a person with the requisite skill and experience about the opinion that he holds on the basis of facts related to and/or perceived by him. Under the Civil Evidence Act 1972 expert evidence can only be admitted by leave of the judge or arbitrator. Other witnesses may |

only give evidence as to facts, i.e, what they saw or heard. Thus, in a building case, a labourer may be called upon to give evidence as to what he saw before a brick wall collapsed – cracking, leaning, etc. He would not be asked what, in his opinion, caused the collapse. An experienced engineer, architect or surveyor, however, may be asked to give his expert opinion on the cause of the collapse. Anyone may be an expert witness provided only that he has the necessary expertise in the field in dispute. Thus a bricklayer would be entirely suitable, if properly experienced, to give an opinion on, say, standards of brickwork.

The expert witness is chosen to appear for one side or the other because his opinion favours them. His views, however, must be sincerely held. His principal duty is to assist the court or the arbitrator to get at the truth, and he must not attempt to conceal something which would benefit the other party. It sometimes happens that an expert witness changes his mind during the course of a hearing. In such a case he is under an obligation to notify his own party and to offer to withdraw. He is under no obligation to volunteer information which would assist the other party. To act as an expert witness is often a thankless task because he is clearly going to be subjected to a very searching cross-examination (q.v.) during which his reputation as an expert may be affected. Courses for persons specializing in this field are held by the Chartered Institute of Arbitrators. See also: *Arbitration; Evidence.*

---

**Express term**

Terms which are actually recorded in a written contract or which are expressed and agreed openly at the time the contract was made. Thus, JCT 80, clause 10 clearly states that the contractor 'shall constantly keep upon the Works a competent person-in-charge'. This provision leaves no room for doubt, as far as it goes. An express term will prevail over any term which would otherwise be implied on the same subject matter.

It is the function of the court to determine what the terms of the contract are and to evaluate their comparative importance and effect. Traditionally, contract terms are either *conditions* or *warranties*, the former being major terms and the latter subsidiary or minor terms. Breach of a condition entitles the innocent party to treat the contract as discharged if he so wishes. Breach of a warranty, in contrast, merely entitles him to claim damages (q.v.). Since the decision of the Court of Appeal in *Hong Kong Fir Shipping Co. Ltd v. Kawaski Kisen Kaisha Ltd* (1962) it has been recognized that this classification is not exclusive. Between conditions and warranties there is an intermediate class of 'innominate terms' the effect of whose breach depends not on classification of the term but upon the seriousness of the breach and its effects. In recent years, the concept of a 'fundamental term' (q.v.) has emerged, and differing terminology is used. See also: *Implied terms; Interpretation of contracts*.

| | |
|---|---|
| **Extension of preliminaries** | The term refers to a technique of valuation carried out by the quantity surveyor under certain circumstances.<br>The preliminaries section of the bills of quantities (q.v.) is priced by the contractor at tendering stage. He may choose to do this in various ways. For example, he may price every item individually having regard to his actual costs or he may simply allow a percentage to preliminaries of the total cost of the measured work; alternatively and rarely, he may simply pluck a figure from the air to serve as a total for all the preliminaries.<br>When the quantity surveyor is preparing his monthly valuations prior to the issue of interim certificates (q.v.) he must allow a sum of money to represent a reasonable proportion of the contractor's preliminaries price. If the contractor has priced individual items (erecting offices, insurance, etc.), the quantity surveyor will look carefully at each item to arrive at his figure. If the preliminaries figure is simply |

a lump sum, the quantity surveyor will often merely divide the sum by the expected number of valuations to arrive at a suitable figure.

If it seems likely that the contract period will be extended but no financial claim is involved, the quantity surveyor will reduce the monthly preliminary figure so as to extend the preliminaries to the end of the contract. The process is also known as 'adjustment of preliminaries'.

If a financial claim is made for delay, the process is rather more complex. Briefly, the monthly preliminary figure is not reduced and the same basis of calculation used to arrive at the monthly figure is used to calculate that element of loss and/or expense in both a prolongation and disruption situation. This is because items included in the preliminaries section are kept on site longer than is necessary or to carry out the variation. However, there is no automatic claim by way of extension of preliminaries; in each and every case the claimant contractor must prove his loss, preferably by reference to records. See also: *Claims; Loss and/or expense.*

---

**Extensions of time**

All the standard forms of contract contain provision for the insertion of a completion date (q.v.) and for the employer to deduct or receive liquidated damages (q.v.) in the event of late completion. However, the employer would forfeit his right to liquidated damages if he were wholly or partly the cause of the delay (*Holme v. Guppy* (1838)). There is no power to extend time unless the contract so provides. The standard forms provide for the architect to extend the time for completion for a variety of reasons (Table 21 shows a comparison between the forms). The grounds for extension divide into two groups:

— Those for which the employer or his agents (including his employees, etc.) are responsible.

— Those for which neither the employer nor the contractor are responsible, and which are outside the control of either party.

The first set of grounds are the most important. In

# Table 21 Comparison of extension of time clauses in standard forms

| Grounds for extension | JCT 80 25·4 | IFC 84 2·3 | MW 80 2·2 | ACA 2 Alt.1 11·5 | ACA 2 Alt.2 and BPF/ACA 11·5 | GC/Works/1 28(2) |
|---|---|---|---|---|---|---|
| *Force majeure* | ✓ | ✓ | ✓ | | ✓ | ✓ |
| Exceptionally adverse weather conditions | ✓ | ✓ | ✓ | | | |
| Weather conditions making continuance of work impracticable | | | ✓ | | | ✓ |
| Damage due to insured risks | ✓ | ✓ | ✓ | | ✓ | |
| Damage due to accepted risks | | | | | | ✓ |
| Civil commotion, riot, rebellion | ✓ | ✓ | ✓ | | ✓ | ✓ |
| Strikes and lock-outs | ✓ | ✓ | ✓ | | | ✓ |
| War, hostilities, invasion | ✓ | ✓ | ✓ | | ✓ | ✓ |
| Compliance with specified architect's instructions | ✓ | ✓ | | | | ✓ |
| Late instructions, etc. | ✓ | ✓ | ✓ | ✓ | ✓ | ✓ |
| Delay on the part of nominated sub-contractors or suppliers | ✓ | | | | | |
| Employer's direct work or supply | ✓ | ✓ | ✓ | ✓ | | |
| Exercise of governmental power | ✓ | | ✓ | | | |
| Contractor's unforseeable inability to obtain labour or materials | ✓ | ✓ | | | | |
| Work under statutory powers by statutory undertakers | ✓ | ✓ | ✓ | | ✓ | |
| Employer's failure to give ingress or egress | ✓ | ✓ | ✓ | ✓ | | |
| Deferment of possession | | ✓ | | | | |
| Act, omission or default of employer or architect | | | | ✓ | ✓ | ✓ |
| Any other reason beyond control of the contractor — Foreseen | | ✓ | | | | |
| Any other reason beyond control of the contractor — Unforeseen | | ✓ | | | ✓ | |

the absence of an express provision to extend time in the contract, the architect would be unable to extend time due to the employer's default (q.v.) and time would become 'at large' (*Astilleros Canarios SA v. Cape Hatteras Shipping* (1981)). The contractor would be under no other obligation in respect of the completion date than to complete within a reasonable time and the employer would lose his right to liquidated damages. The employer could try to prove his actual loss at common law, but it would not be easy. Time will also become at large if the architect does not exercise any power he may have to extend time because of the employer's default (*Peak Construction Ltd v. McKinney Foundations (Liverpool) Ltd* (1970)) or if he fails to exercise the power properly and at the right time.

It is often said that the extension of time clause in the standard forms are there for the benefit of the employer. That is correct as far as they concern the employer's default. However, it should not be overlooked that many of the grounds, i.e., those which provide for extensions due to events outside the control of both parties, mainly benefit the contractor. Without them, he would be obliged to stand the burden of liquidated damages. The employer may, of course, benefit indirectly by obtaining a lower tender figure than would otherwise be the case.

The provisions in respect of extensions of time are often complex. For a fuller discussion of the subject see Powell-Smith and Sims, *Building Contract Claims* and Chappell, *Contractor's Claims – An Architect's Guide*.

| | |
|---|---|
| **Extra work** | Very often simply referred to as 'extras'. Work which is required by the employer, to be carried out by the contractor and which is additional to the work described in the contract documents (q.v.). It is usually contained in an instruction (q.v.) of the architect and treated as a variation (q.v.) of the contract to be valued by the quantity surveyor according to the rules set out in the contract. |
| **Extrinsic evidence** | See: *Parol evidence*. |

**FASS/NFBTE forms of sub-contract**

Two standard forms of sub-contract were produced for use with the JCT 63 Standard Form of Building Contract, one for use where sub-contractors were nominated, the other for sub-contractors generally. The documents were both based on similar provisions in the JCT 63 form.

The form for use where the sub-contractor was nominated under JCT 63 was generally known as the 'green form', and is so referred to in many reported judgments. The other form for use where a sub-contractor was not nominated was known as the 'blue form' and notes to some of its clauses indicated that it was also intended to be used with other types of main contract, notably GC/Works/1. Both forms have now been withdrawn by the sponsoring bodies. In 1980 the Joint Contracts Tribunal issued a Standard Form of Nominated Sub-Contract (NSC/4 and NSC/4a) for use in conjunction with JCT 80, and its provisions neatly dovetail with those of the main contract.

In the same year the NFBTE/FASS/CASEC Standard Form of Sub-Contract for Domestic Sub-Contractors (DOM/1) was issued for use where the main contract is in one of the JCT editions either with or without quantities. A similar form (DOM/2) was published in 1981 for use in conjunction with the JCT Standard Form 'With Contractor's Design' (1981).

DOM/1 consists of 37 clauses, together with an Appendix and is the only sub-contract form suitable for use by domestic sub-contractors (q.v.) under JCT 80.

| | |
|---|---|
| **Fair valuation** | The JCT 80 and GC/Works/1 forms of contract set out rules for the valuation (q.v.) of architect's or superintending officer's instructions (clauses 13 and 9 respectively). JCT 80 allows the quantity surveyor to value work at fair rates and prices if the work is not of similar character to, or not executed under similar conditions of, the work set out in the contract bills (q.v.). GC/Works/1 allows valuation at fair rates and prices if the work is not similar to work set out in the bills of quantities (q.v.) or schedule of rates (q.v.) and it is not practicable to deduce rates and prices from them. MW 80, in clause 3.6, allows valuation on a fair and reasonable basis, using the relevant prices in the priced specification, schedules or schedule of rates, for all variations. The ACA 2 form has no equivalent provision. |

Much has been written about the meaning of the word 'similar' in the context of valuations. The ordinary meaning of 'similar' would be 'almost but not precisely the same' or 'identical save for some minor particular'. When dealing with variations, however, it is not safe to consider 'similar' as anything other than 'identical', for the simple reason that even a minor difference in the description of an item in the bills of quantities may cause the contractor to considerably amend his prices. A full discussion of the point is to be found in Powell-Smith and Sims, *Building Contract Claims*, pp. 87-9.

What is 'fair' will depend on the whole of the contractor's pricing. It has been suggested that if a contractor has priced keenly in the contract as a whole, a fair valuation will take account of the fact and vice versa. Some contractors, however, adopt a pricing strategy by which some items are keenly priced while others show a handsome profit margin. A fair valuation is solely the responsibility of the quantity surveyor under the standard forms. The contractor's remedy, if aggrieved is to go to arbitration.

| | |
|---|---|
| **Fair wages clause** | A clause sometimes found in local authority contracts which usually reproduces the terms of the House of Commons Fair Wages Resolution of 14 October 1946. This Resolution was rescinded from August 1983, but many local authorities still have this requirement in their standing orders, and fair wages clauses appear in JCT 80 (clause 19A), JCT 63 (clause 17A), GC/Works/1 (clause 51), IFC 84 (clause 5.7), and Minor Works (clause 5.4). |
| **Fees** | Generally a payment given or due to any professional person, public office or for entrance to museums, art galleries and the like. It is referred to in many contracts (e.g., JCT 80, clause 6.2) as a sum payable to a statutory or local authority. |
| | Fee also refers to the quality of inherited land. The highest is *fee simple* which is, to all intents and purposes, unfettered ownership. |
| **Fiduciary** | Where someone is in a position of trust in relation to another he is bound to exercise his rights and powers in good faith for the benefit of the other person and cannot make any profit or advantage from the relationship without full disclosure. A person in a fiduciary position must not put himself in a position where his duty and his interest conflict. Fiduciary relationships include trustee and beneficiary, and solicitor and client. |
| | A number of building contracts, e.g., JCT 80, clause 30.5.1 , provide that the employer's interest in the retention monies (q.v.) 'is fiduciary as trustee for the contractor and for any nominated sub-contractor'. The clause adds, contrary to the general law of trusts, that the employer has no obligation to invest the retention money, but the legal effect of this is doubtful because the Trustee Act 1925 and the Trustee Investments Act 1961 oblige a trustee to invest trust monies in prescribed investments. |
| **Final account** | The ACA 2 form of contract, clause 19.1, provides that the contractor shall submit within 60 working |

days of the expiry of the maintenance period (q.v.) a final account for the works. This will be a detailed summing up of the effects upon the contract sum (q.v.) of all additions, deductions and alterations. GC/Works/1 also refers to the final account, in clause 41(2), but in this instance it is to be prepared by the quantity surveyor. See also: *Bill of variations*.

---

**Final certificate**      The last certificate issued by the architect in connection with a contract. The effects of the final certificate vary according to the form of contract being used.

JCT 80, clause 30.8, stipulates that the final certificate must be issued in accordance with a particular time limit - before the end of a time period, usually three months, which is stated in the Appendix (q.v.) and which begins at the latest of the following events:

— The end of the defects liability period (DLP) (q.v.).

— The completion of making good of defects.

— The receipt by the architect or quantity surveyor of the documents necessary for the adjustment of the contract sum, including documents relating to the accounts of the nominated sub-contractors and nominated suppliers.

Failure to issue the final certificate in due time is a breach of contract for which the employer is liable: *Rees & Kirby Ltd v. Swansea City Council* (1983).

The contractor will often demand the final certificate during the earliest three months, i.e., from the end of the DLP. Because it is virtually unknown for there to be no defects during the DLP, the earliest possible period will be three months from the completion of making good of defects. In practice, the period often commences with receipt of the documentation. There is, however, no excuse for undue delay in the issue of a final certificate and if it can be accomplished towards the beginning, rather than the end of the period, so much the better for all concerned. It should be noted that architects have traditionally delayed issuing a final certificate until the last possible moment for fear of the effects noted below. The final certificate must state:

— The total amounts already stated as due (note: not *paid*) in previous interim certificates (q.v.).

— The contract sum (q.v.) adjusted as provided in the contract (clause 30.6.2).

— The difference between the above two sums shown as a balance due to the contractor from the employer or vice versa.

The balance will be a debt from one to the other as appropriate from the fourteenth day after the date of the final certificate. The conclusiveness of the final certificate is modified from the situation under the JCT 63 form. The final certificate is now conclusive evidence, in any proceedings arising out of the contract, that:

— where the quality of materials or the standard of workmanship are to be to the reasonable satisfaction of the architect, they are to his reasonable satisfaction. This means that the certificate is not conclusive evidence about workmanship and materials which are not stated to be to the architect's satisfaction. In general, the contractor still retains his obligation to have carried out the works in accordance with the contract documents (q.v.).

— the contract sum has been adjusted as necessary in accordance with the contract provisions except in the case of a mistake when the certificate shall be conclusive as far as the other computations are concerned.

If proceedings have already been commenced before the issue of the final certificate, it becomes conclusive, subject to terms of judgment or settlement, after the proceedings have finished or after twelve months have elapsed during which time neither party has taken any further step, whichever is earlier. If either party commence proceedings after the final certificate has been issued but before fourteen days have elapsed, the certificate is conclusive evidence in regard to everything except the matters in dispute.

The ACA 2 form, clause 19, stipulates that the final certificate must be issued within 60 working days:

— After the end of the maintenance period (q.v.).

– After the architect has received the contractor's final account (q.v.) together with all the documents necessary for computation of the final contract sum and all documents prepared by the contractor for the work.

The final certificate must state:

— The final contract sum.

— The total amount already paid under clause 16.3.

— The difference between the above two sums shown as a balance due to the contractor from the employer or vice versa.

The balance will be a debt from one to the other as appropriate from the 10th working day after the issue of the final certificate. The fact that it is the amount already *paid* which has to be stated, immediately raises the question: What is the position if the last interim certificate issued by the the architect has not been honoured by the employer by the time the architect is to issue the final certificate? In practice, the situation should never arise because the contractor will have invoked his termination powers under clause 20.2. If the contractor has not invoked his power to terminate, the architect will be obliged to certify only those sums already paid. The danger of the architect's overcertifying in such a situation is avoided by clause 19.5 which empowers the architect to delete, correct or modify any sum previously certified by him.

The final certificate is specifically stated to leave the contractor's liabilities, arising out of or in connection with the contract, intact (clause 19.5). Under the ACA 2 form, therefore, the final certificate is not to be regarded as conclusive. Clauses 7.5 and 17.6 make the final certificate the only time at which the architect is empowered to adjust the contract sum in regard to matters provided for in clauses 7.2 and 17.1 when the contractor has failed to comply with the appropriate provisions.

GC/Works/1, clause 41(3), provides that, if at the end of the maintenance period the SO has certified that the works are satisfactory and the final sum (q.v.) has been agreed (or determined by arbitration), the balance between the final sum and amounts previously paid to the contractor will be paid by the authority to the contractor or vice versa as appropriate. There is no particular time limit set on the issue of the final certificate although it clearly must be issued within a reasonable time of the contractor's completing all his work, including defects. Clause 42 provides for certificates to be issued. Unlike the JCT and ACA forms, GC/Works/1 is not specific in regard to what information must be included on the certificate. It would be advisable, in the interests of all parties, to indicate briefly the way in which the final amount on the certificate has been calculated. The final certificate is not stated to be conclusive and, therefore, it can be opened up and revised by the arbitrator.

MW 80, clause 4.4, lays down a time scale for the issue of the final certificate:

— The contractor has three months from the date of practical completion (q.v.) to supply the architect with all documentation reasonably required for the computation of the final amount to be certified.

— The architect has 28 days from the receipt of the documentation to issue the final certificate, provided that he has issued a certificate (under clause 2.5) that the contractor's obligations have been discharged. There is no suggestion that, if the architect is not in a position to issue a clause 2.5 certificate by the date of expiry of the 28 days, the 28-day period begins to run from the issue of the clause 2.5 certificate. In such circumstances, it is likely that the architect would simply hold the final certificate until the contractor had fulfilled his obligations and then issue the two certificates on consecutive days.

This form of contract makes no mention of the information to be contained in the final certificate other than that it must certify the sum remaining due to the contractor or the employer. A simple and clear calculation showing how the sum is derived would seem to be advisable. The sum certified becomes a debt from one party to the other 14 days after the date of the final certificate. An example of a final certificate is shown in Figure 13. See also: *Certificates; Interim Certificate.*

**Final sum**

The amount which represents the contract sum (q.v.) as adjusted to take into account all additions, deductions and alterations to the contract. It is the total sum payable to the contractor, inclusive of sums already paid after the issue of the final certificate (q.v.).

**Finance Act (No. 2) 1975**

This measure introduced the construction industry tax deduction scheme which came into operation on 6 April 1977. From that date, the position is that all payments under a contract for what the Inland Revenue define as 'construction operations' and made by 'contractors' to 'sub-contractors' are subject to a deduction by the payer on account of the payee's tax liability.

Because of the complexities of the legislation, a number of standard form contracts have introduced special clauses to deal with the requirements of the Act, e.g., JCT 80, clause 31 and ACA 2, clause 24. Minor amendments to the scheme were made by the Finance Act 1980 and details of the current scheme are found in the Inland Revenue booklet 'Construction Industry Tax Deduction Scheme' (IR 14/15 (1980)).

**Firm price contract**

A contract in which the price of labour and materials are not subject to fluctuations (q.v.); sometimes referred to as a fixed price contract (q.v.).

**Fit and ready**

A term used only in the ACA 2 contract. It is not defined in the contract, but it is clear that it is not the same as 'practical completion' (q.v.) in the JCT forms because clause 12.1 gives the architect the option of issuing his certificate that the works are fit and ready for Taking-Over (q.v.) provided that the contractor gives a written assurance to complete with all due diligence (q.v.) items contained on the architect's or

## Figure 13
Final certificate

**FINAL CERTIFICATE**

Architect's name:    A.W.Pugin

Address:    Gothic Buildings, St Chad's, Birmingham

To –

Employer's name:    The Duke of Omnium

Date 20 December '85

Job reference AWP/DO/1234

Address:    Trollope House, Belstead

And to –

Contractor's name:    Buildrite Contractors Ltd

Address:    The Crescent, Belstead

I/We certify in accordance with Clause 19.2 of the Agreement dated __1 August 1984__

for the Works __New Factory, Anytown, West Midlands__

that the balance due is as stated hereunder:

| | |
|---|---|
| The Final Contract Sum adjusted in accordance with Clause 15 of the Agreement | £ 75,242.00 |
| Less total amount paid to the Contractor under Clause 16.3 of the Agreement | £ 71,479.90 |
| Less any deduction made by the Employer under the Agreement | £ 452.00 |
| Balance due to the Contractor from the Employer/ Balance due to the Employer from the Contractor (delete whichever does not apply) | £ 3,310,10 |

Signed _____A.W.Pugin_____ Architect

| | | | | | |
|---|---|---|---|---|---|
| X | Employer | X | Q.S. | ☐ | |
| X | Contractor | ☐ | | ☐ | |
| X | Architect | ☐ | | ☐ | |

© Association of Consultant Architects 1982

204

the contractor's list. The architect can wait until the items are completed before issuing his certificate if he so desires.

| | |
|---|---|
| **Fitness for purpose** | Under the Sale of Goods Act 1979, s. 14, there is an implied condition (q.v.) that the goods (q.v.) are reasonably fit for the purpose required, if this has been made known to the seller, expressly or by implication. In business dealings – as opposed to consumer transactions – it is possible to contract out of this to a limited extent, provided the exemption clause (q.v.) is 'fair and reasonable'. This applies to goods supplied to a contractor by a merchant, and the seller is liable even if he has taken every care or did not know of the defect.<br><br>A similar term of reasonable fitness for purpose will be implied at common law in building contracts where the contractor undertakes design as regards the completed structure: *Independent Broadcasting Authority v. EMI Electronics Ltd and BICC Construction Ltd* (1980). 'It is now well recognized that in a building contract for work and materials a term is normally implied that the main contractor will accept responsibility to his employer for materials provided by nominated sub-contractors. The reason for the presumption is the practical convenience of having a chain of contractual liability from the employer to the main contractor and from the main contractor to the sub-contractor – see: *Young & Marten Ltd v. McManus Childs Ltd* (1969)': Lord Fraser.<br><br>The Supply of Goods and Services Act 1982 (q.v.), which applies to building contracts, is also of relevance. |
| **Fixed price contract** | A contract in which the contractor quotes a price for the whole of the work (see: *Contract sum*). In essence, the contractor takes the risk of judging how much work is involved and its cost. JCT 80 with and without quantities are fixed price contracts, but the 'with approximate quantities' variant is not; this is a remeasurement contract (q.v.). In practice, if the |

contract documents (q.v.) do not accurately reflect the work to be done, the contractor is entitled to a variation in the contract sum. See also: *Lump sum contract*.

| | |
|---|---|
| **Fixtures and fittings** | Fixtures are goods which have become so affixed to land as to have become in law part of the land. They are contrasted with fittings which are goods which retain their character as personal property (q.v.). The general rule is that fixtures installed by a tenant become the property of the landlord and may not be removed by the tenant when his tenancy comes to an end, but three groups of 'tenant's fixtures' can be removed: |

— Ornamental and domestic fixtures which can be removed provided no serious damage is caused to the fabric of the premises by the removal.
— Trade fixtures, e.g., fittings of a public house, including the beer pumps.
— Agricultural fixtures.
It is often difficult to decide whether a thing is a fixture or not. The word implies something fixed to the soil or attached in a substantial way. Whether an item is a fixture or not is a mixed question of law and fact to be determined by the judge in all the circumstances: see: *Holland v. Hodgson* (1872).
The rule relating to fixtures is largely important in building contracts in that once the contractor has affixed materials to the building, the property in them passes from him to the employer.
'Materials worked by one into the property of another become part of that property. This is equally true whether it be fixed or movable property. Bricks built into a wall become part of the house, thread stitched into a coat which is under repair, or planks and nails and pitch worked into a ship ... become part of the coat or the ship' (*Appleby v. Myers* (1867)).

| | |
|---|---|
| **Fluctuating price contract** | A contract in which adjustment is allowed for fluctuations in the prices of labour, materials, etc. Various degrees of fluctuation are allowed under the |

provisions of the standard forms. The extent to which fluctuations are allowed will have a significant effect upon the contractor's tender figure. See also: *Firm price contract; Fluctuations.*

| | |
|---|---|
| **Fluctuations** | The cost to the contractor of labour and materials, etc., used in the works will alter during the contract period. It may fall but, more usually, it will rise. In the absence of any provision in the contract, the contractor would have to take the risk. In order to cover himself, he would probably make an estimate of the likely rise in costs before inserting his prices in his tender (q.v.); higher tender figures result. It is often thought to be of overall advantage to the employer, as well as giving the contractor some guarantee of recovering his costs, to insert a clause in the contract allowing the contractor to recover some or all of the increases if and when they occur; rather than price the risk. Most standard forms allow for this to be done by providing clauses which may be included or deleted as the parties agree. JCT 80, for example, has a selection of three clauses: |

— 38, which allows contribution, levy and tax fluctuations – a bare minimum provision to take account of statutory adjustment to items such as national insurance contributions.

— 39, which allows labour, materials cost and tax fluctuations – the contractor can recover full fluctuations on the construction work, but not his preliminaries. This is calculated by reference to awards by the National Joint Council for the Building Industry, in the case of labour costs, and to the contractor's basic prices (q.v.) in respect of materials.

— 40, which allows fluctuations in accordance with price adjustment formulae rules issued by the Joint Contracts Tribunal. Details of price changes are issued monthly. There is usually provision for making part of the contract sum not subject to this formula (the non-adjustable element). With this exception, full fluctuations are recovered.

**Force majeure**

A French law term, found in many standard contracts as a ground for granting extension of time (q.v.). It is used 'with reference to all circumstances independent of the will of man, and which it is not in his power to control': *Lebeaupin v. Crispin* (1920). It is wider in its meaning than Act of God (q.v.) or *vis major* (q.v.) but in building contracts it generally has a limited and restricted meaning because such matters as war (q.v.), strikes (q.v.), fire and weather conditions are dealt with expressly.

The following events have been held to be within the definition of *force majeure* in varying types of contract:

— A strike.
— A breakdown of machinery.
— Supply shortages as a consequence of war.
— Refusal of an export licence.
— Fire caused by lightning.

*Force majeure* is referred to in JCT 80, clause 25.4.1 and 28.1.3.1 , IFC 84, clause 2.4.1, and ACA 2, clause 11.5 and 21.

**Forecast tender price**

This is the term used in the BPF System (q.v.) to describe the forecast by the Design Leader (q.v.) and agreed by the Client's Representative (q.v.) of the likely cost of constructing a project. It forms part of the master cost plan (q.v.).

**Foreseeability**

'Reasonable foreseeability' is the standard generally used by the law to determine whether a defendant is liable for his actions in tort (q.v.) and a somewhat similar test is applied in respect of remoteness of damage (q.v.) in contract (see: *Hadley v. Baxendale* (1854)).

'You must take reasonable care to avoid acts or omissions which you can reasonably foresee would be likely to injure your neighbour ... persons who are so closely and directly affected by my act that I ought reasonably to have them in contemplation as being so affected when I am directing my mind to the acts or omissions which are called in question' – Lord Atkin in *Donoghue v. Stevenson* (1932).

It is this principle on which the tort of negligence

(q.v.) is based, but the rule is not, it seems, of universal application, e.g., in tort you take your victim as you find him, so that if you injure someone who subsequently dies because he reacted abnormally to the injury, you will be liable for his death (*Smith v. Leech Brain & Co. Ltd* (1961)). In general, however, the defendant is liable only for the consequences of his act which a reasonable man could have foreseen. In claims for breach of contract or for loss and/or expense under the standard contract forms (e.g., JCT 80, clause 26) the damages or amount recoverable are subject to the test of foreseeability set out in *Hadley v. Baxendale* (1854) as explained in *Victoria Laundry (Windsor) Ltd v. Newman Industries Ltd* (1949) and in *The Heron II* (1967), i.e., damages are recoverable in respect of losses which the contracting parties might reasonably contemplate at the time the contract was made, as a not unlikely consequence of the breach or event relied on. See also: *Injury; Negligence; Remoteness of damage*.

| | |
|---|---|
| **Forfeiture** | The loss of some right or property as a result of specified conduct, but in building contracts usually referring to the employer's right to determine the contract or seize plant and materials, etc. See: *Forfeiture clause*. |
| **Forfeiture clause** | A clause in a building contract which gives one party, usually the employer, the right to determine the contract, turn the contractor off site, etc. In standard form building contracts it is usually referred to as 'determination of employment' or 'termination'. In this sense JCT 80, clause 27 and ACA 2, clause 22 are forfeiture clauses. Forfeiture clauses are strictly interpreted by the courts and any prescribed procedure must be followed. Wrongful forfeiture or determination will normally amount to a repudiation of the contract by the employer. See also: *Determination*. |
| **Formal contract** | An alternative description of a contract made by deed or specialty (q.v.). Sometimes the expression is |

used to describe simple contracts (q.v.) which are entered into in a formal way, e.g., in a standard printed form, duly signed by the parties.

**Formalities of contract**

In general, there are no formalities attached to the making of a contract. A contract (q.v.) may be made orally, in writing, or even implied from conduct. In some cases, however, the law requires the presence of additional formalities before a contract can be enforced. Some contracts must be made by deed (q.v.); others must be in writing and in a few cases there must be written evidence of the contract. If these formalities are not complied with the contract is unenforceable by legal action. Happily, these problems do not trouble the building industry. Transfers of British ships or shares therein must be entered into under seal, for example. An assignment of copyright (q.v.) must be in writing, otherwise it is void, as must a bill of exchange, e.g., a cheque. Contracts of guarantee (q.v.) must also be in writing, in contrast to contracts of indemnity (q.v.) which need not.

By s. 40 of the Law of Property Act 1925, contracts for the sale of land or of an interest in land are unenforceable unless there is written evidence of the contract, signed by the defendant or his agent, although the contract may be enforced if there is what is called 'part performance'– which is a doctrine of equity (q.v.).

**Formula price adjustment**

See: *Fluctuations*.

**Forthwith**

As soon as reasonably can be: *London Borough of Hillingdon v. Cutler* (1967). The word is used in most forms of building contract to convey the fact that the action required must not be delayed. For example, JCT 80, clause 4.1.1, 'The Contractor shall forthwith comply with all instructions ...'; ACA 2, clause 20.1, ' ... the Employer may by further notice ... forthwith terminate ...'; GC/Works/1, clause 7(3), '... the

Contractor shall forthwith comply ...'; MW 80, clause
7.1, ' ... forthwith determine the employment of the
Contractor ...'

## Fossils

'A relic or representation of a plant or animal that
existed in a past geological age, occurring in the form
of mineralized bones, shells, etc.': *The New Collins
Concise English Dictionary*. In the absence of a special
clause in the building contract the employer is entitled
to fossils found under or fixed in any way to his land,
but the legal position is unclear as to who has the
right to fossils found lying on the surface.

The standard form building contracts usually contain
an express clause covering the position. JCT 80, clause
34, provides that 'all fossils, antiquities and other
objects of interest or value' found on the site or during
excavation are the property of the employer. The
contractor must try not to disturb the object, ceasing
work if necessary, and inform the architect or clerk of
works. The contractor may claim any direct loss and/
or expense caused to him by compliance with this
provision and may also be entitled to an extension of
time.

GC/Works/1, clause 20(2) provides to similar effect
and gives rise to similar claims. ACA 2, clause 14 is
to the same effect. See also: *Antiquities*.

## Foundations

Broadly, anything which supports something else. In
building work, the term is generally used to describe
the lowest artificial works placed in contact with the
natural ground to support a structure, e.g.: piles,
concrete rafts, concrete strip footings, etc. More
rarely, it is applied to the ground itself. In *Worlock v.
SAWS & Rushmoor Borough Council* (1982), the
question whether a floor slab which supported
internal partition walls of a building was a foundation
for the purposes of the then current building
regulations was considered. The court held that it
was. A foundation is 'an object which is placed in
position on or in the ground in the course of
constructing a building, or for the purposes of a

building which is to be constructed, the function of which is to provide support for that building so that in fact it transmits load to the material beneath ... ': Woolf J.

GC/Works/1, clause 21 stipulates that the contractor must not lay foundations until the SO has examined and approved the excavations. This clause simply clarifies what is normal practice on most building contracts.

| **Fraud** | Fraud is deliberate deception and is a type of tort known as deceit. It is one of the torts affecting business relationships. Usually it takes the form of fraudulent misrepresentation (q.v.) which was defined (*Derry v. Peek* (1889)) as a 'false statement, or one which (the maker) did not believe to be true, or was recklessly careless whether what he stated was true or false'. Fraud always involves dishonesty, but the motive is irrelevant. Someone who is induced to enter into a contract by a fraudulent misrepresentation may repudiate the contract and also recover damages (q.v.). Alternatively, he can affirm the contract, and still recover damages for deceit. It should be noted that the fraudulent misrepresentation must be one of the inducing causes of the contract. It is not possible to contract out of liability for fraudulent misrepresentation: *S. Pearson & Son Ltd v. Dublin Corporation* (1907). See also: *Rescission*. |

| **Fraudulent misrepresentation** | A false statement of fact which the maker does not honestly believe to be true. The absence of 'honest belief' is essential. If a fraudulent misrepresentation induces one party to enter into a contract, on discovering the fraud he can void the contract and treat it as at an end. Alternatively, he can affirm the contract and go ahead. In either case he can recover damages for the tort of deceit. A contracting party cannot escape liability for fraudulent statements made by him or on his behalf by putting an exclusion clause in the contract: *S. Pearson & Son Ltd v. Dublin Corporation* (1907). See also: *Fraud; Misrepresentation*. |

**Frontager**

Someone who owns or occupies land which abuts a highway (q.v.), river or seashore. The Highways Act 1980 contains procedures whereby private streets, as defined in the Act, can be made-up at the expense of the frontagers and formally adopted by the highway authority so that for the future the highway (q.v.) becomes maintainable at the public expense. See also: *Boundaries*.

**Frost damage**

All the standard forms limit the contractor's liability to make good damage caused by frost. He is not required to make good such damage if it was caused by frost occurring after practical completion (q.v.). JCT 80 limits the contractor's liability in clauses 17.2, 17.3. Clause 17.5 states most emphatically that the contractor may only be required to make good frost damage which may appear after practical completion if the architect specifically certifies that such damage was due to injury which took place before practical completion.

ACA 2 does not mention frost damage specifically. In clause 12.2, it refers only to 'defects shrinkages or other faults which may appear during the Maintenance Period.' But 'other faults' must be interpreted *ejusdem generis* (q.v.) to mean other faults like defects or shrinkages (q.v.). Damage by frost before the works are fit and ready for taking-over will clearly create a defect because the contractor has an obligation to protect the works under clause 1.2. His obligation in this respect must cease after taking-over when he is no longer in possession of the works. Frost damage after taking-over becomes the responsibility of the employer.

GC/Works/1 provides (clause 23) for the SO to instruct the contractor to suspend the execution of the works if he is of the opinion that frost damage may result from continuation. The contractor retains his general obligations in respect of the works during and after such suspension. Clause 32(1) limits the contractor's liability to make good frost damage during the maintenance period. He is only required to make good such damage if the cause (i.e., frost) arose before completion of the works.

MW 80 provides, in clause 2.5, that the contractor is liable to make good defects, etc., caused by frost occurring before practical completion. He is not liable for the effects of frost after practical completion.

**Frustration**

The release from contractual obligations of the parties to a contract which as a result of events completely outside the control of the contracting parties is rendered fundamentally different from that contemplated by the parties at the time the contract was made. It is not sufficient that the contract has turned out more difficult and expensive for one party to perform than he expected (*Davis Contractors Ltd v. Fareham UDC* (1956)). There are very few cases in which a building contract has been held to be frustrated, although it is often put forward as an excuse for non-completion. The position was aptly summarized by Lord Radcliffe in *Davis Contractors Ltd v. Fareham UDC:* 'Frustration occurs whenever the law recognizes that without default of either party a contractual obligation has become incapable of being performed because the circumstances in which performance is called for would render it a thing radically different from that which was undertaken by the contract.' This is a question of law which must depend not only on the event relied on but also on the precise terms of the contract.

In *Wong Lai Ying v. Chinachem Investment Co. Ltd* (1979) a massive landslip took with it a thirteen-storey block of flats, the debris from which, together with many tons of earth, landed on a building site. The landslip was held to be a frustrating event as it made further performance uncertain. The character and duration of any further performance would be radically different from that contemplated by the original contract. The landslip was an unforeseen natural disaster and a clause in the contract referring in general terms to what was to happen 'should any unforeseen circumstances beyond the vendor's control arise' could not be interpreted so as to cover the landslip.

A building contract may be frustrated if Government order prohibits or restricts the work (*Metropolitan Water Board v. Dick, Kerr & Co. Ltd* (1918)) and the total destruction of premises by fire has been held to frustrate an installation contract (*Appleby v. Myers* (1867)). Extreme delay through circumstances outside the control of the parties may frustrate a building contract, but only if the delay is of a character entirely different from anything contemplated by the contract.

Where a contract is discharged by frustration, both parties are excused from further performance and the position is governed by the Law Reform (Frustrated Contracts) Act 1943. Money paid under the contract is recoverable, but if the party to whom sums were paid or payable has incurred expenses, or has acquired a valuable benefit, the court has a discretion as to what should be paid or be recoverable.

The various standard form contracts often make provision for what is to happen should certain events occur, and in principle those express provisions prevail. JCT 80, clause 32, deals with the effect of an outbreak of hostilities (q.v.), war (q.v.) being a frustrating event. Clause 28 entitles the contractor to determine employment under the contract, inter alia for *force majeure* (q.v.) and certain other matters, some of which would be capable of being frustrating events provided the works are suspended for a stated period as a result. ACA 2, clause 21, is a special clause dealing with termination resulting from causes outside the control of the parties, and includes frustrating events such as *force majeure*, war and allied events. See also: *Discharge of contract; Illness.*

| | |
|---|---|
| **Functus officio** | Having discharged his duty or performed his function. The term is used of an architect who has discharged his duties under a building contract and has exhausted his authority. In *H. Fairweather Ltd v. Asden Securities Ltd* (1979) it was held, under JCT 63 terms, that |

once the architect had issued the final certificate (q.v.) under the contract then, if no notice of arbitration had been given under the contract conditions, the architect was thereupon *functus officio*, with the result that he could not thereafter issue any valid certificate under the contract. It is also used of an arbitrator who makes a valid award. His authority as arbitrator then comes to an end and with it his powers and duties. See also: *Arbitrator; Certificates.*

**Fundamental term**
An expression used to describe a term in a contract, breach of which entitles the innocent party to treat the contract as discharged. It is a vitally important term going to the very basis of the contract. The expression is sometimes used in respect of a contract term, breach of which cannot be avoided by an exemption clause (q.v.).

The phrase 'fundamental breach of contract' is sometimes used interchangeably. It has two different senses:

— A breach of contract so serious that the other party may treat the contract as at an end.

— A so-called principle of law that some breaches of contract are so destructive of the parties' obligations that liability for such a breach cannot be limited by an exemption clause. Recent case law states that there is no such principle of law; it is merely a rule of interpretation based on the presumed intention of the contracting parties (*UGS Finance Ltd v. National Mortgage Bank of Greece* (1964), the *Suisse Atlantique case* (1966) and *Photo Production Ltd v. Securicor Transport Ltd* (1980)). See also: *Condition; Express term; Implied term.*

**GC/Works/1 contract**

The full title is: The General Conditions of Government Contracts for Building and Civil Engineering Works. The second edition was published in 1977. A form for minor works is available (GC/Works/2). The contract has been prepared by and for government departments. An important feature of the contract is the 'Abstract of Particulars', (q.v.), which is similar to the Appendix (q.v.) in other forms of contract, and contains important terms and details. The contract may be used either with quantities or specification. The clauses are:

1. Definitions, etc.
2. Contractor deemed to have satisfied himself as to conditions affecting execution of the Works.
3. Vesting of Works, etc., in the Authority. Things not to be removed.
4. Specifications, Bills of Quantities and Drawings.
5. Bills of Quantities (applicable if so stated in the tender).
5A. The Authority's Schedule of Rates (applicable if so stated in the tender).
5B. The Contractor's Schedule of Rates.
6. Progress of the Works.
7. SO's instructions.
8. Failure of Contractor to comply with SO's instructions.
9. Valuation of the SO's instructions.
10. Valuation by measurement.
11. Variation of price (labour-tax matters).
12. Setting out Works.
13. Things for incorporation and workmanship to conform to description.

50. Facilities for other works.

51. Fair wages, etc.

52. Racial discrimination.

53. Prolongation and disruption expenses.

55. Corrupt gifts and payments of commission.

56. Admission to site.

57. Passes.

58. Photographs.

59. Secrecy.

61. Arbitration.

---

**Garnishee order**

A method of enforcing a judgment debt (q.v.). It is an order of the High Court requiring a third party, who owes money in the ordinary course of business to a judgment debtor, to pay the amount direct to the judgment creditor. A garnishee order is usually made in respect of a credit balance at the judgment debtor's bank (*Rogers v. Whitely* (1892)).

For example, A has obtained a judgment in the sum of £5000 against B. B will not pay although B has £10,000 standing to his credit at the bank. A garnishee order can be made requiring the bank to pay £5000 from B's account directly to A. Alternatively, the garnishee order could be made requiring any third party, owing £5000 to B, to pay it directly to A.

A garnishee order cannot be made unless there is a legal debt currently owing to the judgment debtor. Under the JCT and most other standard form building contracts, payments to the contractor are not existing debts until the architect's certificate has been issued (see: JCT 80, clause 30.1.1). In *Dunlop & Ranken Ltd v. Hendall Steel Structures Ltd* (1957) the High Court held that a garnishee order made before the issue of the architect's certificate was invalid, because there was no debt to be garnished.

---

**General damages**

Damages which the law presumes to have resulted from the act of the defendant (q.v.) which need not be specifically pleaded. They are recoverable as compensation for such loss as the parties may reasonably foresee as a natural consequence of the breach or act complained of. In *Franks & Collingwood v. Gates* (1985) it was a term of a building contract for alteration works that the contractor should maintain continuity of work until completion. This he failed to do. Judge Newey QC allowed the employer £500 as substantial general damages for this breach in respect of disappointment or the like resulting from the contractor's delay which meant that the employer was unable to occupy the premises as a holiday home. The judge said that it was settled law that foreseeable mental consequences of a breach of contract – unhappiness, frustration, disappointment and so on – may be taken into account in assessing general damages. 'These principles obviously apply to claims against builders as much as to claims against anyone else. The amount of general damages awarded for unhappiness must obviously depend upon its severity, but because of the impossibility of compensating effectively for feelings in money, he for his part would expect them always to be low ...' See also: *Damages; Special damages*.

**Good faith**

A person acts in good faith if he acts honestly, even though he may be negligent. In general, there is no duty to disclose prejudicial information to the other party during the course of contractual negotiations, except in the case of certain confidential relationships, e.g., solicitor and client, principal and agent, or in the case of contracts *uberrimae fidei*, e.g., contracts of insurance. See also: *Confidentiality; Misrepresentation; Uberrimae fidei*.

**Goods**

Personal tangible property, but not land. Building contracts usually refer to 'goods and materials' (e.g., JCT, clause 8.1). All items which are to be incorporated into the works will be classified as *goods* for purposes of the Sale of Goods Act 1979 (q.v.). In general building terms, goods are normally considered to be items which have already had some work done to them, e.g., doors, windows, electrical fittings, etc., as opposed to raw *materials* (q.v.).

| | |
|---|---|
| **Government action** | An express ground for extension of time under several forms of contract, e.g., JCT 80, clause 25.4.9, and ACA 2, clause 11.5(d). The action must, of course, interfere with the execution of the works. If it is not expressly referred to in the contract, government action probably falls under *force majeure* (q.v.). |
| **Government contracts** | See: *GC/Works/1 contract*. |
| **Guarantee and indemnity** | A contract whereby one party agrees to be responsible for the debts, defaults, etc., of another party in circumstances where the second party is liable to a third party is a guarantee contract. The responsibilities of the first party (the surety) take effect when the second party defaults. The precise extent of liability depends upon the terms of the contract. After default, the surety acquires any rights which the second party may have in respect of the default. A guarantee must be in writing if it is to be enforced. In contrast, an indemnity need not be in writing. An indemnity contract is where one party agrees to keep another safe from damage or loss. It is particularly applicable to insurance. Many contracts contain indemnity clauses for particular circumstances, e.g., JCT 80, clause 20, whereby the contractor undertakes to indemnify the employer against loss, etc., in respect of personal injury or death or damage to property arising out of or caused by the carrying out of the works. See also: *Bond*. |
| **Guaranteed cost contract** | A contract under which the employer agrees to pay the contractor his costs of labour, materials and overheads plus a sum of money which may be calculated in various ways. For a detailed consideration of this type of contract see: *Cost reimbursement contract*. |

| | |
|---|---|
| **Handover** | A term in common use in the building industry to denote the stage at which work is complete and the contractor hands over to the employer the keys and any useful documentation and the employer takes over the building. In the standard forms, the stage is variously described as 'practical completion', 'taking-over' and 'completion'. 'Handover' is slightly misleading, suggesting that the contractor hands over the building when he considers that it is ready, but it continues in popular use probably because it is easier to refer to a 'handover meeting' than a 'meeting to carry out an inspection prior to the issue of a certificate of practical completion'. See also: *Completion; Practical completion; Taking-over.* |
| **Hearing** | A general term referring to an occasion on which a person or persons may produce arguments or evidence to a court, arbitrator or other tribunal. Certain kinds of hearing have technical names such as trial, appeal, etc. See also: *Appeal; Natural justice; Reference; Trial.* |
| **Hearsay** | Hearsay is something which a witness (q.v.) has heard others say, e.g., 'John Smith told me that ...' As a general rule, hearsay evidence is not admissible. Hearsay is not confined to oral statements but can extend to documents. The general position has been stated in a leading case in this way: 'Evidence of a statement made to a witness by a person who is not himself called as a witness may or may not |

be hearsay. It is hearsay and inadmissible when the object of the evidence is to establish the truth of what is contained in the statement. It is not hearsay and is admissible when it is proposed to establish by the evidence, not the truth of the statement, but the fact that it was made': *Subraniam v. Public Prosecutor* (1956).

There are many exceptions to the rule against hearsay. The Civil Evidence Act 1968 enlarged the categories of evidence which are admissible in civil proceedings and prescribes a procedure for the admission in evidence of statements in documents which are otherwise hearsay. In arbitration the strict rules of evidence are not necessarily complied with. See also: *Admissibility of evidence.*

## Highway

A public right of way for vehicular or other traffic, including a way for pedestrians only. A very comprehensive definition is contained in the Highways Act 1980, which is a consolidating Act drawing together earlier enactments.

Local authorities have wide powers in regard to highways. At common law the owner of property adjoining a highway is entitled to access to it at any point, but there are many statutory modifications of this right, e.g., the formation or laying-out of a means of access to a highway is development for which planning permission is required.

## Hindrance or prevention

At common law it is an implied term of every building contract that the employer will not himself, or through his employees or agents, hinder or prevent the contractor from performing the contract. If there are acts of hindrance or prevention which cause delay, the employer cannot enforce any liquidated damages (q.v.) clause and the contractor may have a claim for damages against him (*Lawson v. Wallsey Local Board* (1882)).

In extreme cases, the contractor may treat the contract as having been repudiated by the employer (*Holme v. Guppy* (1838)). Generally, standard form contracts allow acts of hindrance and prevention by the employer or others for whom he is responsible as grounds for both extension of time and for money, e.g., JCT 80, clauses 25 and 26, but they are not necessarily – or even usually – exhaustive. See also: *Claims; Extension of time.*

**Hire**

A type of bailment (q.v.) whereby an agreement is made under which a person, called the hirer, obtains the use of goods for a specified or indeterminate period in return for payment.

It is a type of contract and the rights and liabilities of the parties will be governed by the express and implied terms of the contract. Legislation now affects the position, e.g., the Unfair Contract Terms Act 1977 (q.v.) and the Supply of Goods and Services Act 1982 (q.v.).

Because most construction industry plant is hired in, there are important implications should the contract be determined by the employer, who will have no rights in the hired plant, whatever the contract conditions between him and the contractor may provide.

Most plant in the construction industry is let in standard form terms called 'The Model Conditions for the Hiring of Plant' (1979), published by the Construction Plant-Hire Association, or a variant of those terms. These modify the common law position in several respects. Reference may usefully be made to V. Powell-Smith's *Model Conditions for the Hiring of Plant* (1981) which is the only available treatment of these conditions.

**Hire-purchase**

A hire-purchase agreement is one 'under which an owner lets chattels (q.v.) of any description out on hire and further agrees that the hirer may either return the goods and terminate the hiring or elect to purchase the goods when the payments for hire have reached a sum equal to the amount of the purchase price stated in the agreement or upon payment of a stated sum': Chitty, *Contracts,* 25th edn., vol. 2, para. 3212. It is in effect a means of buying goods on long-term credit and is today largely regulated by complex legislation, largely designed to protect private individuals.

Goods which are subject to a hire-purchase agreement do not belong to the purchaser (hirer) until he has exercised his right to purchase. This has implications where a building contract contains, for example, a vesting clause (q.v.) or forfeiture clause (q.v.). Such clauses are ineffective as regards third parties, including the owner of the goods let on hire-purchase.

**Hoardings**

The erection of hoardings is governed by the Highways Act 1980. Among other things, the local authority may require:

— A close boarded fence to its satisfaction.
— A convenient covered platform and handrail outside the hoarding for the benefit of pedestrians.
— Sufficient lighting.
— Maintenance.
— Removal when directed.

The erection of a suitable hoarding is the contractor's responsibility. It is covered under most forms of contract, e.g., JCT 80, clause 6.1.

**Hostilities**

A state of armed conflict between two or more States during which war (q.v.) may or may not be declared. JCT 80, clause 32 refers to hostilities as a ground for determination of the contractor's employment by either party.

ACA 2, clause 11.5, alternative 2 refers to hostilities as a ground for extension of time and, in clause 21(c) a ground for termination of the contractor's employment by either party. See also: *Force majeure; Frustration; Vis major.*

**Hudson Formula**

A method of calculating the 'head office overheads and profit' element in a contractor's claim for direct loss and/or expense arising under standard forms of contract, and in particular under JCT 80, clause 26. The formula is based on the percentage to cover profit and head office on-costs as built into the tender (q.v.). It is so-called because it appears in Hudson's *Building and Engineering Contracts*, 10th edn., p. 599. The formula is as follows:

$$\frac{HO/Profits\%}{100} \times \frac{Contract\ Sum}{Contract\ Period} \times Period\ of\ Delay$$
$$(e.g.\ in\ weeks) \quad\quad (in\ weeks)$$

The formula has been much criticized and does not appear to have received judicial approval in any reported case. It must be used with caution and the warning given by the author should not be overlooked. This emphasizes that the 'formula assumes that the profit budgeted for by the contractor in his prices was in fact capable of being earned by him elsewhere had the contractor been free to leave the delayed contract at the proper time'. Moreover, the formula is related entirely to an overrun of contract time, which can lead architects and contractors wrongly to associate financial claims solely with extensions of time. The formula can be subjected to several specific criticisms:

— It is based upon the contractor's allowances in his tender, which may never have been achievable.
— At best it requires adjustment to be made for the various factors for which recovery is not permitted, e.g., the contractor's own inefficiency.
— It ignores the contractor's duty to make realistic attempts to deploy his resources elsewhere during any period of delay (*Peak Construction (Liverpool) Ltd v. McKinney Foundations Ltd* (1970)).
— The value of the final account may well exceed the Contract Sum and any proper valuation of variations will have included an element of reimbursement for overheads and profit.
— The use of the formula as it stands results in profit being added to the profit already in the Contract Sum so that at the very least the formula as printed should read 'Contract Sum less overheads and profit' rather than 'Contract Sum'.

— The formula can also produce under-recovery for the contractor where inflation during the period of delay increases the overhead costs envisaged at the time of tender.

The formula approach to contract claims should be avoided if possible because *ex contractu* claims (q.v.) for 'direct loss and/or expense' or its equivalent must be equated with claims for damages for breach of contract at common law where a formula approach is not an acceptable method of quantifying damages. Other formulae sometimes used by contractors include the Emden formula (q.v.) – which is based on a percentage taken from the contractor's organization as a whole – and more recently the Eichleay formula (q.v.) which is of trans-Atlantic origin. Doubt is cast on the use of such formulae by such cases as *Tate & Lyle Distribution Ltd v. Greater London Council* (1982), and there is no reported English case in which such formulae have been approved.

**Illegal contract**  A contract which contravenes statute or common law. An illegal contract is void (q.v.) and a party to such a contract will not succeed in any action he may bring in the courts based upon the contract. Thus a party who is paid money on the basis of an illegal contract but then refuses to carry out his side of the bargain cannot be made to refund the money as a general rule. The money can only be recovered if the other party can show that some fraud or duress was used to induce him to enter into the contract. A building contract which, for example, had as its primary objective the contravention of the planning laws would be an illegal contract. Such a case might arise if the parties made an agreement to build in a green belt area.

The courts sometimes extend the concept to embrace contracts which are considered to be against public policy, e.g., restraint of trade. A contract may be illegal in its formation or a change in the law may make further performance illegal, in which case it is discharged by frustration. See also: *Contract; Frustration.*

**Illness**  Illness may result in frustration of contracts for personal services, such as contracts of employment (*Marshall v. Harland & Wolff Ltd* (1972)), but a great many factors need to be taken into account including the terms of the contract, the nature of the employment, the nature and duration of the illness, and the prospects of recovery. Where a contract is 'personal' in character, e.g., a well-known sculptor producing a work of art, grave and lengthy illness may also frustrate the contract. As the personality of an architect is generally of vital importance to the employer, the same principle will apply. Conceivably, if a builder is an individual and his personality is of importance to the completed work, serious illness could also result in frustration, but there appear to be no reported cases. See also: *Frustration*.

| | |
|---|---|
| **Implied contract** | A contract may be implied from the conduct of the parties, e.g., by the contractor starting work on receipt of an order (*A. Davies & Co. (Shopfitters) Ltd v. William Old Ltd* (1969)). See also: *Contract; Simple contract*. |
| **Implied term** | A term which is not written down in a contract or openly expressed at the time the contract is made but which the law implies. The expression is used in several different senses and implied terms may be included by:<br>— Statute, e.g., the Sale of Goods Act 1979 and the Supply of Goods & Services Act 1982.<br>— To give 'business efficacy' to a contract: *The Moorcock* (1889).<br>— Common law: often called implied warranties, e.g., that a contractor will supply good and proper materials (*Young & Marten Ltd v. McManus Childs Ltd* (1968)) and will provide completed work which is constructed in a good and workmanlike manner and of materials which are of good quality (*Test Valley Borough Council v. Greater London Council* (1979)).<br>— Trade usage or local custom: *Symonds v. Lloyd* (1859). Few contracts cover every eventuality by means of express terms (q.v.), but there are limits to when terms will be implied. A term will not be implied at common law merely because the court thinks it would have been reasonable to insert it into the contract and terms will be implied only under certain conditions:<br>— An implied term must not be in conflict with or |

inconsistent with an express term.

— It must be based on the imputed or presumed intention of the parties.

Contractors' claims (q.v.) may be based on breach of some implied term, e.g., by the employer not to prevent completion and to do all that is necessary on his part to bring about completion of the contract. See also: *Express term.*

**Impossibility**

A contract which is impossible to perform is void (q.v.) and cannot be enforced. A contract which is possible at the time it is made, but subsequently becomes impossible because of some intervening event is said to be frustrated. It was originally valid but may be declared void. In cases of impossibility of performance from the outset, the parties are left to bear their own losses unless one of them can show that he was induced to enter into the contract by fraud (q.v.) or misrepresentation (q.v.). See also: *Frustration.*

**Improper materials**

Materials which are not in accordance with the contract. The architect may instruct that such materials are to be removed from site, e.g., JCT 80, clause 8.4.

**Incorporation**

A word with several meanings in law. It may refer to the process by which a corporation (q.v.) is constituted, i.e., to form an organization with a separate personality in law. It is also used when referring to the inclusion of specific contract terms or conditions in a contract (cf. *Incorporation of terms*).

A further use of the word is found in many building contracts with reference to the passing of property or risk (q.v.), the general rule being that when building materials are actually built-in to a structure or building they become part of the building. The maxim of the law is *quicquid plantatur solo, solo cedit* ('whatever is affixed to the soil becomes part of the soil') and this basic principle will defeat any retention of title (q.v.) clause.

It is a question of fact when goods and materials become 'fully, finally and properly incorporated' into the works. The JCT Standard Forms say nothing expressly about where the risk lies once the goods are incorporated, but on general principle incorporated goods are at the contractor's risk, because of the wording of the appropriate contract clauses.

| | |
|---|---|
| **Incorporation of documents** | Extrinsic evidence of the intentions of the parties is not usually admitted (see: *Admissibility of evidence*) to assist the court in the case of a dispute. It is, therefore, crucial that all documents (drawings, bills of quantities, specification, etc.) are incorporated and become part of the contract documents (q.v.). This is normally achieved by inserting a reference to the documents in the printed conditions and clearly identifying each document to which reference is made. For example, each document may bear the written inscription: 'This is one of the contract documents referred to in the agreement dated ... ', signed and dated by the parties. |
| | It should be noted that it is possible to incorporate the terms of a standard form of contract by referring to it in an exchange of letters which form part of the contract. For example, a request to a contractor to quote for a job on the basis of the JCT 80 form of agreement for minor building works will incorporate those terms in the future contract (*Killby & Gayford Ltd v. Selincourt Ltd* (1973)), assuming, of course, that the contractor's tender does not attempt to impose conflicting terms. |
| **Incorporation of terms** | Terms (q.v.) may be incorporated into a contract by reference, e.g., in an exchange of letters referring to a particular set of standard terms. If a contracting party wishes to rely upon this he must show that the standard terms were incorporated. In order to do this he must prove that the parties intended the document in question to form part of the contract. This can be shown either by proving that the party alleged to be bound by the terms *signed* the form, etc., |

or that he entered into the contract having been given notice, or fully aware of it.

If a party has signed the document in question then in principle he will be bound by its terms even though he did not read it or understand its contents. The exception to this rule is where the person who put forward the document has misrepresented its contents (see: *Misrepresentation*): *Curtis v. Chemical Cleaning Co. Ltd* (1951). See also: *Unfair Contract Terms Act 1977*. The term relied on must, of course, be brought to the attention of the other party at or before the time the contract was entered into : *Olley v. Marlborough Court Ltd* (1949).

A reference in a contractual document to the contract being subject to general conditions 'available on request' is sufficient to incorporate into the contract the current edition of those conditions: *Smith v. South Wales Switchgear Ltd* (1978). This principle is of importance in the construction industry where, for example, an invitation to tender (q.v.) may refer to the contract conditions 'being available for inspection at the architect's office' – a common though bad practice.

The incorporation of terms by reference was discussed by the Court of Appeal in *Modern Buildings (Wales) Ltd v. Limmer & Trinidad Co. Ltd* (1975). The words 'in accordance with the appropriate form for nominated sub-contractors' were used in an exchange of correspondence between a main contractor and a nominated sub-contractor (q.v.). This was held sufficient to incorporate the terms of the then current FASS/NFBTE form of nominated sub-contract.

| | |
|---|---|
| **Incorporeal hereditament** | A right over land, such as a right of way (q.v.). See also: *Chattels; Goods.* |
| **Indemnity** | See: *Guarantee and indemnity.* |
| **Indemnity clauses** | All the standard form building contracts contain indemnity clauses under which one party – usually the contractor – promises to indemnify the other party |

against specified liabilities. For example, JCT 80, clause 20, ACA 2, clause 6 and GC/Works/1, clause 47.

Indemnity clauses are not favoured by the courts and are strictly construed against the person seeking to rely on them. 'If a person obtains an indemnity against a consequence of certain acts, the indemnity is not to be construed so as to include the consequences of his own negligence unless those consequences are covered either expressly or by necessary implication': Lord Devlin in *Walters v. Whessoe Ltd* (1960)

However, for the purposes of the Limitation Act 1980, under an indemnity clause time does not begin to run until the party indemnified has suffered loss, i.e., had judgment entered against him (*County & District Properties Ltd v. C. Jenner & Son Ltd* (1976)) and this effectively extends the period of liability and is important in a sub-contract situation. See also: *Contra proferentem; Insurance; Limitation of actions.*

| | |
|---|---|
| **Independent contractor** | A person (q.v.) who works under a contract for services as opposed to a contract of service, i.e., an employee (see: *Master*). It is often difficult to distinguish between the two. The most realistic test is that proposed by Denning L.J. in *Stevenson Jordan & Harrison v. Macdonald & Evans* (1952). There will be a contract for services 'if the work, although done for the business, is not integrated into it, but is only accessory to it', e.g., the normal architect-client relationship. The contractor under the normal building contract is an independent contractor. |

In general, a person is not liable for the negligence of his independent contractors or agents (see: *Agency*) to the same extent as he is liable for the negligence of his employees, and it is principally for this reason that the distinction between employees and independent contractors is important, although in many instances under building contracts the architect will be acting as the agent of the employer so as to make him vicariously responsible.

In *Rees & Kirby Ltd v. Swansea City Council* (1983) the

general position was aptly summarized:
'An architect is usually and for the most part a specialist exercising his special skills independently of his employer. If he is in breach of his professional duties he may be sued personally. There may, however, be instances where the exercise of his professional duties is sufficiently linked to the conduct and attitude of the employers so as to make them liable for his default.' See also: *Vicarious liability*.

**Industrial property**   A generic term applied to kinds of property rights of an intangible nature which are valuable in industry, e.g., patents (q.v.), trade marks and industrial 'know-how'.

**Inevitable accident**   An accident 'not avoidable by any such precautions as a reasonable man, doing such an act then and there, could be expected to take' (Sir Frederick Pollock), e.g., a fire caused by lightning. Inevitable accident is sometimes said to be a defence to certain kinds of actions in tort (q.v.) but modern writers consider that 'the conception of inevitable accident has no longer any useful function and it is doubtful whether much advantage is gained by the continued use of the phrase' (Winfield & Jolowicz).
As regards damage caused by fire, the Fires Prevention (Metropolis) Act 1774 – which applies to the whole country – provides that no action is maintainable against anyone on whose land a fire begins *accidentally* (*Collingwood v. Home & Colonial Stores Ltd* (1936)). The Act gives no protection where the fire begins accidentally but the owner is negligent in letting it spread (*Goldman v. Hargrave* (1967)). The burden of proving negligence is on the plaintiff: the defendant does not have to prove that the fire was accidental.

**Information**   In the context of building contracts it refers to drawings (q.v.), schedules, instructions (q.v.) which are generally the responsibility of the architect to produce. If information is not provided when it is needed, it is a breach of contract by the employer, but whether the contractor can claim under the provisions of the particular contract will usually depend upon whether he applied for the information at the right time, i.e., neither too early nor too late. The contractor's common law rights are unaffected by the timing of the application.

| | |
|---|---|
| **Injury** | Harm done to persons or property. Injury need not be physical, it may be purely economic loss. It is generally actionable either in contract (q.v.) or in tort (q.v.). See also: *Action; Damage; Damages; Insurance.* |
| **Innocent misrepresentation** | An untrue statement of fact made in the course of contractual negotiations which is one of the causes which induced the other party to enter into the contract when its maker is innocent of its untruth. It is contrasted with a fraudulent misrepresentation (q.v.) and a negligent misrepresentation (q.v). The test is whether the statement would have affected the judgment of a reasonable man in deciding whether to enter into the contract. <br><br> An innocent misrepresentation entitles the innocent party to rescind the contract provided he acts promptly. Damages can be granted at the discretion of the court for innocent misrepresentation under s. 2(2) of the Misrepresentation Act 1967. See also: *Misrepresentation; Rescission.* |
| **Innominate term** | See: *Express term.* |
| **Insolvency** | The state of being unable to meet one's debts when they are due and a creditor is pressing for payment. In such a situation: <br>— An individual may become or may be made bankrupt. <br>— A company registered under the Companies Acts may opt or may be forced to commence winding-up proceedings known as liquidation (q.v.). <br>See also: *Bankruptcy.* |

| | |
|---|---|
| **Inspection of documents** | A clause in the bills of quantities (q.v.) sent out with an invitation to tender, may refer to the drawings not included in the set sent to the contractor but available for inspection at the office of the architect. Depending upon the precise wording, such a clause may be sufficient to incorporate the documents in any subsequent contract. See also: *Incorporation of documents*. |
| **Inspection of the works** | Where constant inspection is required, a clerk of works should be appointed as inspector (q.v.). The architect is not required to make constant inspections. RIBA Architect's Appointment states in paragraph 3.10: |

'The architect will visit the site at intervals appropriate to the stage of construction to inspect the progress and quality of the works and to determine that they are being executed generally in accordance with the contract documents. The architect will not be required to make frequent or constant inspections.'

The position of the building control officer with regard to inspections has exercised several judicial minds and it is now established (*Anns v. London Borough of Merton* (1977)) that the building control officer (formerly known as the 'building inspector'), and through him the local authority, has a duty of care when carrying out inspections. Further cases have reinforced the position. This is the case whether or not an architect is employed on the work although, if an architect is employed, he will have the primary duty, but he can look to the local authority to take some part of his liability if the work complained of is not in accordance with the building regulations (q.v.) and the local authority, through its inspector, inspected the work.

The nature and extent of the local authority's duty of care towards building owners must be considered in light of their statutory responsibilities for public health and it seems that there must be 'present or imminent danger to the health or safety of' the occupiers for the local authority to be liable. In *Peabody Donation Fund v. Sir Lindsay Parkinson & Co. Ltd* (1984), where the House of Lords considered and explained its earlier decision in *Anns v. London Borough of Merton*, it was emphasized that local authorities, in the exercise of their building control functions, do not thereby owe a duty of care to a building developer to see that his property does not suffer damage, and the emphasis appears to be on the duty owed to the occupiers in relation to health and safety: *Ketteman v. Hansel Properties Ltd* (1985).

| | |
|---|---|
| **Inspector** | Someone who inspects, examines and checks. Many organizations have inspectors to ensure that work or duties are being carried out correctly. In the context of building contracts the architect, resident engineer or clerk of works have the role of inspector to varying degrees. JCT 80, clause 12 defines the role of the clerk of works as solely that of inspector on behalf of the employer under the direction of the architect. The RIBA Architect's Appointment lays down the limits of the architect's role in clauses 3.10, 3.11 and 3.12. He is to visit the site at intervals appropriate to the stage of construction to inspect the progress and quality of the works and to determine that they are being executed generally in accordance with the contract documents. He is not required to make frequent or constant inspections. Where such inspections are required a clerk of works or a resident architect will be employed. The architect's duty to inspect is often misunderstood by the employer. In *East Ham Corporation v. Bernard Sunley & Sons Ltd* (1965), Lord Upjohn said: 'The architect is not permanently on the site but appears at intervals, it may be of a week or a fortnight ... It is the contractor who is responsible for progressing the work in accordance with the requirements of the contract and the architect's instructions.' Other types of inspector who have relevance to the construction industry are inspectors appointed under |

237

the provisions of the Health and Safety at Work, etc.,
Act 1974.

For a fuller discussion of the duties involved in
inspection and supervision and the position of the
local authority with regard to the building regulations
see: *Inspection of works; Supervision of works.*

| | |
|---|---|
| **Instructions** | Directions or orders. In the standard forms of contract the word is normally used to refer to orders to the contractor from the architect. Instructions may or may not have a financial implication. For example, if the architect instructs the contractor to use more coats of paint than specified in the contract documents (q.v.) the employer will have to pay extra, or if the architect instructs the contractor to use fewer coats of paint, the employer will pay less. If, on the other hand, the architect merely issues an instruction requiring the use of a different colour (and issues it in good time) there should be no financial change. Instructions may be said to fall into six categories: |

— Additions to the work.

— Deductions from the work.

— Substitutions to the work.

— Procedural or clarifying instructions.

— Changes in standards.

— Changes in the method of working.

JCT 80, clause 4 deals specifically with instructions.
The contractor must comply immediately with any
instruction issued by the architect, provided:

— The contract expressly empowers the issue of the
instruction.

— The instruction is in writing.

— The contractor does not make reasonable objection
to the issue of an instruction requiring a clause 13.1.2
variation.

Empowering clauses are listed in Table 22. Although
the contract specifies that all instructions must be
issued in writing (clause 4.3.1), the following clause
(4.3.2) contains detailed provisions regarding what is
to happen if the architect purports to issue an
instruction which is not in writing. This is a necessary

# Table 22  Clauses under JCT 80 which empower the architect to issue an Instruction

| Clause | Instruction |
| --- | --- |
| 2.2.2.2 | To correct errors in the contract bills |
| 2.3 | In regard to discrepancies in or divergence between two or more of: contract drawings, contract bills, architect's instructions (except in relation to 13.2), any drawings, etc., issued by the architect |
| 4 | General power |
| 6.1.3 | In regard to divergence between statutory requirements and clause 2.3 documents or instructions requiring a variation in accordance with clause 13.2 |
| 7 | If the contractor has inaccurately set out the works and the amendment is not to be at his own cost |
| 8.3. | Requiring opening up or testing |
| 8.4 | In regard to the removal from site of work, materials or goods not in accordance with the contract |
| 8.5 | Requiring the exclusion of any person employed thereon from the works |
| 13.2 | Requiring or sanctioning a variation |
| 13.3.1 | In regard to provisional sums included in the bills |
| 13.3.2 | In regard to provisional sums included in a sub-contract |
| 17.2 | For schedule of defects after defects liability period and if the cost of making good defects is not to be entirely the cost of the contractor |
| 17.3 | Requiring defects to be made good during the defects liability period and if the cost of making good defects is not to be entirely the cost of the contractor |
| 22C.2.3.2 | In regard to the removal and disposal of any debris |
| 23.2 | In regard to postponement |
| 32.2 | Requiring protective work after determination due to outbreak of hostilities |
| 33.1.2 | To remove and dispose of debris and/or execute protective work after war damage |
| 34.2 | In regard to antiquities |
| 35.5.2 | Substituting NSC/1 and NSC/2 for the application of clauses 35.11 and 35.12 or vice versa |
| 35.8 | If the contractor informs the architect that he is unable to reach agreement with the proposed sub-contractor, so that necessary instructions may be issued |
| 35.9 | If the contractor informs the architect that the proposed sub-contractor is withdrawing his offer, so that necessary instructions may be issued |
| 35.10.2 | To nominate a sub-contractor after NSC/1 and 2 procedures |
| 35.11.2 | To nominate a sub-contractor where NSC/1 and 2 not used |
| 35.18.1.1 | To nominate a 'substituted sub-contractor' to carry out rectification work |
| 35.23 | If the proposed nomination does not proceed |
| 35.24.4.1 | To give to the sub-contractor notice specifying default |
| 36.2 | To nominate a supplier |

provision and recognizes the common situation where the architect visits the site and gives an oral instruction. If the architect confirms it, the instruction takes effect from the date of the confirmation. The contractor may confirm and it will take effect after the expiry of seven days if the architect does not dissent. If neither architect nor contractor confirm, the architect may confirm at any time prior to the issue of the final certificate (q.v.) and the instruction takes effect retrospectively from the date it was originally issued. If the contractor asks the architect to specify in writing the clause empowering the issue of an instruction, the architect must do so immediately. The contractor may then:

— Carry out the instruction when it will be deemed to be empowered by the provision specified by the architect (whether the architect is correct or not).

— Seek immediate arbitration.

If the contractor fails to carry out an instruction within seven days of receipt of a notice from the architect requiring compliance, the employer may employ and pay other people to execute the work and deduct the costs from monies due to the contractor. Note that the employer is entitled to deduct all extra costs and not just the money he pays to the third party he engages to do the work. Therefore, architect's and quantity surveyor's fees in connection with the additional work resulting from contractor's default become the contractor's liability. The employer would be wise to obtain competitive tenders for the work of others, if time allows, so that the contractor has little chance of succeeding in any claim that the employer could have had the work carried out at a cheaper rate.

The ACA 2 form gives the architect wide powers to issue instructions. Clause 1.1 states that the contractor must comply with and adhere strictly to the architect's instructions issued under the agreement. A full list of the matters on which the architect is empowered to issue instructions is contained in clause 8 (see Table 23).

## Table 23  Clauses under ACA 2 which empower the architect to issue an Instruction

| Clause | Instruction |
|---|---|
| 8.1(a) | For the removal from site of work or goods not in accordance with the contract |
| 8.1(b) | For the dismissal of incompetent or negligent persons employed upon the works |
| 8.1(c) | For the opening up and inspection or testing of goods or the work |
| 8.1(d) | For the amendment of obligations in respect of working space, hours, access or use of the site |
| 8.1(e) | For the alteration of design or quality or quantity of the works including removal from site of any materials brought onto the site |
| 8.1(f) | For any matter connected with the works |
| 8.1(g) | Discrepancies (clause 1.5)<br>Infringement of statutory requirements (clause 1.6)<br>Not to give statutory notices (clause 1.7)<br>Ground conditions and artificial obstructions (clause 2.6)<br>To provide samples (clause 3.5)<br>With regard to named sub-contractors (clause 9.4)<br>With regard to sub-letting (clause 9.5)<br>Requiring the contractor to permit work by others (clause 10.2)<br>Regarding acceleration or postponement (clause 11.8)<br>Regarding defective work during or immediately after the maintenance period (clause 12.2)<br>Regarding antiquities (clause 14) |

## Table 24  Clauses under GC/Works/1 which empower the S.O. to issue an Instruction

| Clause | Instruction |
|---|---|
| 7(1)(a) | Regarding the variation of the design, quality or quantity of work |
| 7(1)(b) | Regarding discrepancies between specification and/or bills of quantities and/or drawings |
| 7(1)(c) | For the removal from site of things for incorporation brought by the contractor and the substitution of other things |
| 7(1)(d) | For the removal and re-execution of contractor's work |
| 7(1)(e) | For the carrying out of work |
| 7(1)(f) | For working hours, overtime and nightwork |
| 7(1)(g) | For the suspension of the work |
| 7(1)(h) | Regarding the replacement of men graded foreman or below |
| 7(1)(i) | For opening up the work for inspection |
| 7(1)(j) | To make good defects under clause 32 |
| 7(1)(k) | To carry out emergency work |
| 7(1)(l) | To use excavated material |
| 7(1)(m) | Regarding any other necessary or expedient matter |

Clause 8.1 gives the architect authority to issue instructions at any time up to the date of Taking-Over and to issue instructions about removal from site of defective work, dismissal from the works of incompetent people, opening up of work for inspection and testing, altering obligations or restrictions as regards working hours, space or site access or use at any time during the maintenance period (q.v.) or within 10 working days of its expiry.

All instructions must be given in writing (clause 23.1) except in the case of an emergency (clause 8.3) when the architect may give an oral instruction and confirm it in writing within 5 working days. Since the contractor must immediately comply with an oral instruction under clause 8.3, he will be in a difficult position if the architect forgets to, or will not, later confirm such an instruction. There seems to be no good reason why the architect cannot issue a written instruction on site or, if the oral instruction is given by telephone, by the same day's post. If the contractor neglects to carry out instructions, the employer's remedy is to employ someone else to carry out the work (clause 12.4) and/or to invoke his right of termination (clause 20.1(d)).

GC/Works/1 refers to instructions in clauses 7 and 8. Clause 7(1) lists the instructions which the SO is empowered to issue (see Table 24). All instructions are intended to be issued in writing, but if any instructions are issued orally, clause 7(2) stipulates that the SO must confirm, if the contractor so requests, within 14 days of the issue of the instruction. The contractor must immediately comply with all instructions and the SO's decision regarding necessity is final and conclusive, i.e., not subject to review at arbitration. The SO may issue the contractor with a notice requiring compliance with an instruction within a specified period. If the contractor does not comply, the authority may engage others to carry out the work and recover additional expenses from the contractor. This provision is similar to JCT 80, clause 4.1.2.

MW 80 enables the architect to issue written instructions. The extent of his authority is not precisely set out, but there must be an implication that the instructions will be in connection with the contract. Oral instructions must be confirmed in writing within 2 days (clause 3.5). The clause contains a similar provision to JCT 80, clause 4.1.2.

In order to qualify as a written instruction, there must be evidence in writing together with an unmistakable intention to order something. An instruction may be implied from what is written down, but it is safer from the contractor's point of view to ensure that the words clearly instruct. For example, a drawing sent to a contractor with a compliments slip is not an instruction to carry out the work shown thereon. It may be deemed to be an invitation to carry out the work at no cost to the employer. The same comment applies to copy letters sent under cover of a compliments slip. An instruction on a printed 'Architect's Instruction' form is valid if signed by the architect. An ordinary letter is a valid instruction. The minutes of a site meeting may be a valid instruction if the contents are expressed clearly and unequivocally and particularly if the architect is responsible for the production of the minutes. Figure 14 is an example of an instruction.

| | |
|---|---|
| **Instrument** | A word with several meanings, but for the purpose of this book an instrument is a formal legal document, e.g., a statutory instrument (q.v.). The word is also used in a legal context to indicate an important factor in something, e.g., 'her evidence was an instrument in his arrest' (*Collins English Dictionary*). |
| **Insurance** | Contracts of insurance are a very specialized field and the advice of a broker should always be sought. All forms of contract contain insurance provisions except GC/Works/1; clause 25 deals with 'precautions against fire and other risks' and clause 26 deals with 'damage to works or other things', but there is no requirement for insurance to be taken out. |

## Figure 14
Architect's instruction

**ARCHITECT'S INSTRUCTION**

Architect's name:   A.W.Pugin

Address:   Gothic Buildings, St Chad's, Birmingham

To –

No. _____3_____

Contractor's name:   Buildrite Contractors Ltd

Date _4 October 1984_

Address:   The Crescent, Belstead

Job reference _AWP/DO/1234_

Works:   New Factory, Anytown, West Midlands

---

Instructions

Clause 8.1(e)

OMIT:   Bill of Quantities item 35F (MS Brackets)     600 No.

ADD:    Stainless Steel Curvilinear Brackets
        450 x 450 x 100 mm obtained from Fancy
        Fixings Ltd    Cat.No. FF 1851/c     600 No.

Signed ____A.W.Pugin____ Architect

| ☒ Employer | ☒ Q.S. | ☐ | ☐ |
| ☒ Contractor | ☒ C.W. | ☐ | ☐ |
| ☒ Architect | ☐ | ☐ | ☐ |

© Association of Consultant Architects 1982

This is because the government is its own insurer. It is, of course, open to the contractor to take out insurance for those things which are stated to be his risk. JCT 80, clauses 21 and 22, refers to the arrangements for insuring against injury to persons and property, and the works against what are termed 'Clause 22 perils' (fire, lightning, etc.). There are alternatives to suit the kind of development being insured and who is to bear the cost of premiums. IFC 84 has very similar provisions in clause 6. MW 80 has similar but less detailed provisions in clause 6.0. ACA 2 deals with insurance against injury to persons and property in clause 6.3 and there are alternative provisions for insurance of the works in clause 6.4. Clause 6.5 deals with insurance against injury to other property not caused by negligence, etc., and clause 6.6 is a deletable clause to be used if the contractor is responsible for drawings. It provides for professional indemnity cover. Clauses 6.7 to 6.10 (inclusive) deal with premiums, breach and claims. See also: *Uberrimae fidei.*

| | |
|---|---|
| **Insurrection** | A term meaning an uprising against State authority, rather less in ramification than outright revolution. It is expressly referred to in ACA 2, clause 11.5, alternative 2, as a ground for awarding an extension of time (q.v.). It is a ground for extending time in other forms of contract, usually under the head of *force majeure* (q.v.). See also: *Civil commotion; Civil war; Commotion; Disorder; Riot.* |
| **Interest on money** | Interest or financing charges cannot be claimed as general damages (q.v.) resulting from breach of contract so that in the absence of a contractual agreement to pay interest, late payment of a debt does not attract interest: *London, Chatham & Dover Railway Co. v. South Eastern Railway Co.* (1893). This rule, although much criticized, has recently been re-affirmed by the House of Lords in *President of India v. La Pintada Compania Navegacion SA* (1984). This rule, however, applies only to claims for interest |

by way of general damages and does not extend to claims for special damage (q.v.). 'If a plaintiff pleads and can prove that he has suffered special damage as a result of the defendant's failure to perform his obligation under a contract, and such damage is not too remote, on the principle of *Hadley v. Baxendale, ...*' it is recoverable: *Wadsworth v. Lydall* (1981).

The courts and arbitrators have statutory power to award *simple* interest in specified circumstances, but there is no power to award compound interest. The position under statute is as follows:

— Section 3 of the Law Reform (Miscellaneous Provisions) Act 1934 allows interest to be included in the sum for which judgment is given or an award is made, the interest to run from the date of the judgment or award.

— Section 35A of the Supreme Court Act 1981 (inserted by the Administration of Justice Act 1982) empowers a court or arbitrator to award interest alone where payment is made of an agreed debt after commencement of proceedings, but before judgment or award.

The contract itself may provide for the payment of interest on amounts overdue, and this is commonly done in contracts for the sale of goods, by inserting an express term to that effect.

Following the decision of the Court of Appeal in *F.G. Minter Ltd v. Welsh Health Technical Services Organisation* (1980) it is beyond doubt that under the 'direct loss and/or expense' provisions of the JCT contracts ( JCT 63, clause 24(1), 11(6), and 34(3); JCT 80, clause 26.1 and 34.3; IFC 84, clause 4.11) interest or financing charges must be included by the architect or quantity surveyor in an ascertainment of loss and/or expense. It is a constituent part of the debt. The same principle applies to similar wording in other standard form contracts. Under ACA 2, clause 7.1, the phrase used is 'damage, loss and/or expense', and clause 7.5 (dealing with the contractor's failure to submit estimates) refers specifically to interest or financing charges and debars the contractor from recovering them between the date of the contractor's failure to submit the estimates required by clause 7 and the date of the Final Certificate. In general, interest is to be calculated from the date when the loss, etc., was incurred. The actual wording of the clause must always be considered. The wording in JCT 80, for example, has been revised so that the ascertainment must relate to loss and/or expense incurred or likely to be incurred – and thus covers future losses – whereas under JCT 63 the wording referred only to losses in the past.

So far as the rate of interest is concerned, if the contract documents do not provide a rate, it is suggested that the correct thing to do is to take the rate at which contractors in general could borrow, disregarding the special circumstances of the particular claimant: *Tate & Lyle Food Distribution Ltd v. Greater London Council* (1981).

The whole position regarding interest is complex and reference may usefully be made to Powell-Smith and Sims, *Building Contract Claims*, pp. 117-23. See also: *Claims; Direct loss and/or expense.*

---

**Interference**

There is an implied term (q.v.) in all building contracts that the employer will not interfere with or prevent the carrying out of the works. If the employer is guilty of interference, the contractor may be able to repudiate the contract or claim damages at common law, depending upon the circumstances. The employer will also be liable for the interference of third parties for whom he is responsible unless provision is made in the contract. The employer will not be liable if the wrongful interference is caused by a third person for whom the employer is not responsible in law: *Porter v. Tottenham Urban District Council* (1915)).

JCT 80, clause 28.1.2, expressly states that if the employer interferes with or obstructs the issue of *any* certificate (not only financial certificates), the contractor has grounds for determining his own employment under the contract. Proving that the employer has interfered may not be easy. Clause 29 allows the employer to engage others to do work on site and any problems which the contractor may have can be dealt with by extension of time (clause 25.4.8.1) and/or by financial recompense (clause 26.2.4.1). Dictating the order in which the contractor is to carry out the work would normally amount to interference, but clause 13.1.2.4 allows the architect to vary such requirements albeit with financial implications.

ACA 2, clause 20.2(b) allows the contractor to terminate his own employment if the employer obstructs the issue of *any* certificate. Clause 10 permits the employer to engage others to carry out work on site and there is provision (clause 10.4) for the contractor to be paid damage, loss and/or expense if such other persons cause disruption (q.v.) to the regular progress of the works. The architect may issue instructions amending limitations of working space, working hours, access to the site or use of any part of the site (clause 8.1(d)).

Under GC/Works/1 there is no express provision for the contractor to determine his employment due to the interference of the authority in the issue of a certificate, but he has his common law right to do so (*Hickman & Co. v. Roberts* (1913)). Clause 50 allows the authority to execute other works on the site and if any damage is done to the contractor's works thereby, the authority must take financial responsibility.

MW 80, clause 7.2.2 gives the contractor the contractual right to determine his employment if the employer interferes with or obstructs the carrying out of the works.

The provisions in the various standard forms are intended to avoid the danger of the contractor seeking to repudiate the contract in the event of what may be considered to be some fairly normal occurrences, e.g., the employer bringing specialists onto the site to carry out certain works and thereby causing the contractor some delay or loss. Contractual provisions for the contractor to determine his own employment in the event of certain specified kinds of interference are in addition to the contractor's normal rights at common law. Many employers do not appreciate the legal position and it is something which architects should be careful to clarify at the beginning of the contract. See also: *Hindrance or prevention.*

| **Interim certificates** | A term, found in most standard forms, referring to the periodic certification of money due to the contractor. |

JCT 80, clause 30.1 requires the architect to issue interim certificates stating the amount due to the contractor from the employer. The amount is to be:

*Subject to retention:*

— Value of properly executed work.

— Fluctuations due under clause 40.

— Value of materials and goods delivered to site.

— Value of off-site materials if the architect so agrees.

— Value of nominated sub-contract works and materials.

— Contractor's profit on nominated sub-contract items.

*Not subject to retention:*

— Payments or costs incurred by the contractor related to statutory charges, setting out, opening up and testing, royalties, defects liability, insurance under clause 21.

— Loss and/or expense.

— Final payments to nominated sub-contractors.

— Fluctuations due under clauses 38 or 39.

— Certain specified nominated sub-contract costs.

*Less* fluctuations due to the employer (not subject to retention) and previous amounts certified.

The contractor is entitled to payment (q.v.) within 14 days of the date of issue of each certificate. The certificate is to be issued monthly or at such intervals as is stated in the Appendix (q.v.). The issue of regular interim certificates ends at practical completion (q.v.). After that, they may be issued:

— As and when further amounts are ascertained (q.v.) as payable.

— After the end of the defects liability period (q.v.) or when the certificate of making good defects is issued ( whichever is the later).

This is subject to the proviso that the architect shall not be required to issue an interim certificate within one calendar month (q.v.) of having issued a previous interim certificate. The provisions of IFC 84 are somewhat shorter, but very similar to the provisions of JCT 80. ACA 2, clause 16 sets out the procedure for the issue of interim certificates. On the last working day (q.v.) of each calendar month, the contractor must present to the architect an interim application stating the total amount due in accordance with clause 16.1 together with supporting documentation. Within 10 working days of receipt, the architect must issue an interim certificate stating the amount due to the contractor. Clause 16 and clause 18 (if used) state what must be included and what may be deducted in calculating the amount. The contractor is entitled to payment within 10 working days of the date of each interim certificate.

GC/Works/1 provides for what it terms 'Advances on account' under clause 40. The contractor may submit a claim at intervals of not less than one month. Supporting documentation must be provided. When the SO has agreed the valuation, he must issue an interim certificate (clause 40(3)). If the contract sum exceeds £100,000 and the contractor applies, he is entitled to a further payment (called an 'interim advance') which is to be estimated by the SO. Clause 40 specifies what must be included and what may be deducted from interim certificates. There is no period specified for the authority (employer) to honour certificates.

MW 80 provides for 'progress payments' under clause 4.2. The architect must certify the payments, if requested by the contractor, at intervals of not less than 4 weeks. The clause specifies what must be included and what must be deducted from the certificate. The employer must pay the amount within 14 days of the date of the certificate.

The amounts included in interim certificates under all the above-mentioned forms are subject to revision in the next certificate. This means that if the amount certified is too much, the next certificate can reduce it and vice versa. The process is usually simple because the value of work done is cumulative. That does not mean that the architect should not take great care in certifying interim certificates (see: *Sutcliffe v. Thackrah* (1974)) because there is always the danger that the contractor may go into liquidation (q.v.) or otherwise leave the site before completion (q.v.). In *Townsend v. Stone Toms & Partners* (1985) it was held to be a clear breach of contractual duty for the architect to certify work which he knows has not been done properly.

Figure 15 is an example of an interim certificate. See also: *Certificates; Final certificate.*

| | |
|---|---|
| **Interim payment** | A phrase referring to the periodic payments made during the progress of a contract; more commonly called 'interim certificates' (q.v.). |
| **Interlocutory** | Interim. A word used to describe the various applications, hearings, etc., which are stages in litigation or arbitration. An *interlocutory judgment* is one which is not final or which disposes only of part of the matter at issue. |
| **Intermediate Form of Contract (IFC 84)** | Produced by the Joint Contracts Tribunal in 1984 in response to a general demand for a form that was less complex than JCT 80 and more comprehensive than MW 80. The form is suitable for use where the proposed building works are: <br>— Of simple content involving the normally recognized basic trades and skills of the industry. <br>— Without any building service installations of a complex nature, or other specialist work of a complex nature. <br>— Adequately specified, or specified and billed, as appropriate prior to the invitation of tenders. <br>The form is normally most suitable for use if the |

## Figure 15
Interim certificate

**INTERIM CERTIFICATE**

Architect's name:  A.W.Pugin

Address:  Gothic Buildings, St Chad's, Birmingham

No. ___2___

Date  2 October 1984

To –

Employer's name:  The Duke of Omnium

Job reference  AWP/DO/1234

Address:  Trollope House, Belstead

And to –

Contractor's name:  Buildrite Contractors Ltd

Address:  The Crescent, Belstead

I/We certify in accordance with Clause 16 of the Agreement dated ___1 August 1984___
for the Works ___New Factory, Anytown, West Midlands___

that the amount stated below is due to the Contractor:

Total Value of work properly executed
in accordance with Clause 16.2 (a) of the Agreement
adjusted in accordance with Clause 18.1
of the Agreement, if applicable

£ 30,585.00

Amount of any adjustments to the Contract sum
in accordance with Clause 16.2 (b) of the Agreement
adjusted in accordance with Clause 18.1
of the Agreement, if applicable

Add/deduct £ _1,500.00_

£ 32,085.00

Less amounts previously stated as due

£ 19,485.00

Amount due to the Contractor £ 12,600.00   (1)

The Contractor is entitled to payment of 95% of the
amount stated as due at (1) above, namely

£ 11,970.00

Less liquidated and ascertained damages calculated
in accordance with Clause 11.3 Alternative 1, if applicable

£ _____

Net amount payable to the Contractor £ 11,970.00

Signed _____A.W.Pugin_____ Architect

| X | Employer | X | Q.S. | ☐ |
| X | Contractor | ☐ | | ☐ |
| X | Architect | ☐ | | ☐ |

contract period is not more than twelve months and the value of work not more than £250,000 (1984 prices). It may be suitable for rather larger or longer contracts but it should be borne in mind that the provisions are less detailed than the JCT 80 Standard Form and, if used for unsuitable works, there may be cases where the equitable treatment of the parties could be prejudiced. Contracts to the value of £50,000 (1981 prices) would normally be carried out under MW 80. Guidance on the use of the form is provided in Practice Note 20 (revised 1984).

The form may be used with drawings and either specification (q.v.), or schedules of work, or bills of quantities (q.v.). It is a lump sum contract with provision for interim payments (q.v.). The clauses are as follows:

— Recitals.
— Articles of Agreement.
— Conditions.
1. Intentions of the parties
2. Possession and completion
3. Control of the Works.
4. Payment.
5. Statutory obligations, etc.
6. Injury, damage and insurance.
7. Determination.
8. Interpretation, etc.
— Appendix.
Supplemental Conditions:
A. Value Added Tax.
B. Statutory tax deduction scheme.
C. Contributions, levy and tax fluctuations.
D. Use of price adjustment formulae.
E. Fair wages.

Two further forms are produced by the JCT for use with IFC 84:

— JCT Form of Tender and Agreement (NAM/T) for use between the contractor and a sub-contractor named by the employer.
— Sub-contract Conditions (NAM/SC).

The RIBA has produced an RIBA/CASEC Form of

Agreement to be used by the employer when inviting tenders or approximate estimates for the sub-contract works.

| | |
|---|---|
| **Interpretation clauses** | To assist in the interpretation of the intentions of the parties, many standard forms include a clause defining particular words and phrases used in the contract. Examples are JCT 80, clause 1; IFC 84, clause 8; MW 80, clause 8.0; GC/Works/1, clause 1; ACA 2, clause 23. See also: *Interpretation of contracts*. |
| **Interpretation of contracts** | Technically, the process of interpreting what the words in a written contract mean is called 'construing a contract'.<br>It is the expressed intention of the parties which is important and this is to be found by ascertaining the meaning of the words actually used and the courts have no power to modify the contract in any way. Extrinsic ('parol') evidence is not normally admissible, although there are well-defined exceptions to this rule. The first source of reference to discover the meaning of a word is a dictionary, but both courts and arbitrators must give effect to any special, technical, trade or customary meaning which the parties intended the word to bear. The contract itself may contain a definitions clause, e.g., JCT 80, clause 1, which may be looked at.<br>The main basic rule of interpretation is that the contract must be read as a whole – a particular clause must be seen in context and cannot be read in isolation. 'The contract must be construed as a whole, effect being given, so far as practicable, to each of its provisions': *Brodie v. Cardiff Corporation* (1919). This point is often overlooked by those without formal legal training who will seize on a particular word or phrase out of context.<br>In the building industry, the definition of the 'contract documents' (q.v.) is important. All well-drafted contracts will give a clear definition of them. Thus, JCT 80, clause 2.1, and ACA 2, Article C, give a comprehensive definition and in interpreting the |

contract it is to these documents that one looks. The wording of the contract may also attempt to introduce interpretative rules of its own. So it is with JCT 80, clause 2.2.1, which has the effect of making the printed conditions prevail over typed or handwritten documents. This reverses the normal and logical rule. The validity of this provision has been upheld time and time again (e.g., *M. J. Gleeson (Contractors) Ltd v. London Borough of Hillingdon* (1970)) and the printed conditions will prevail over any typed provisions in the Bills or Specifications. At the best, the Bills, etc., may be used 'not in the interpretation of the contract ... but in order to follow exactly what is going on ...' and presumably as part of the surrounding circumstances.

ACA 2 overcomes this difficulty by providing (clause 1.3) for 'priority of documents' (q.v.).

The court will disregard completely meaningless words and phrases. But the judicial task is to interpret the intentions of the parties and not to write a contract for them. Apparent inconsistencies between contract clauses will be reconciled if it is possible to do so, otherwise the court will give effect to the clause which, in its view, expresses the true intention of the parties.

| | |
|---|---|
| **Intervening cause** | A happening or event which breaks the chain of causation (q.v.). |
| **Invalidate** | To put an end to the validity of something. The word is used in GC/Works/1 (clause 7(4)) and MW 80 (clause 3.6). No instruction of the architect (or SO) requiring additions, omissions or alterations to the works will invalidate the contract. It is merely a statement of the position at common law since variations (q.v.) are provided for in the contract and complying with a provision can never alone invalidate the contract. ACA 2, therefore, makes no reference to the point. JCT 80 and IFC 84 refer to 'vitiate' (q.v.) which amounts to the same thing. |
| **Invitation to tender** | A preliminary procedure to the formation of a building contract. The architect or project manager (the Client's Representative in the BPF System (q.v.)) |

are normally responsible for inviting tenders from interested contractors. An invitation to tender does not amount to an offer (q.v.) in contractual terms. It is merely an invitation to the contractor to make an offer. See also: *Code of Procedure for Single Stage Selective Tendering 1977; Code of Procedure for Two Stage Selective Tendering 1983; Tender.*

**Invitation to treat**
An invitation by one party to another to make an offer (q.v.) which, if accepted, becomes the basis of a binding contract (q.v.). The most common example is the display of goods in a shop window. Even if price tags are attached to the goods, it is not an offer by the shop but an invitation to treat, i.e., an invitation to the passer-by to go into the shop and offer to buy the goods at the price shown (or indeed at any price). The shop may refuse to accept the offer and no contract results in that case. See also: *Contract.*

**Invitee**
A person who is invited onto an occupier's premises with the occupier's consent, express or implied, and to whom a common duty of care is owed under the Occupiers' Liability Act 1957, which defines the occupier's duty towards his 'visitors'. Everyday examples of an invitee are the milkman, postman and newspaper boy, as well as guests and tradesmen See also: *Occupiers' liability.*

**JCLI Form for Landscape Works**

A form of contract suitable for landscape works produced by the Joint Council for Landscape Industries. The current edition is dated April 1982 and it is almost identical in both content and format with the Agreement for Minor Building Works (MW 80) (q.v.) published by the Joint Contracts Tribunal (q.v.). It contains some additional provisions appropriate for landscape works, notably:
— Partial possession (2.6).
— Plant failures (2.7).
— Objections to nomination (3.8).
— Disturbance to regular progress (3.9).
— Retention (4.3).
— Fluctuations (4.6B).
— Malicious damage and theft (6.5A) or (6.5B).
The form refers throughout to the 'Landscape Architect' – a designation which is not protected by the Architects Registration Acts. See also: *Architects Registration Council*.

**JCT contracts**

The first form of building contract agreed between architects and builders was published in 1903. By 1931, after several editions of the form, a body known as the Joint Contracts Tribunal (q.v.) was set up to keep the form under constant review. Revised editions were published in 1939, 1963 and 1980. One of the main advantages claimed for the JCT contracts is that they are negotiated documents, agreed by representatives of all sides of the construction industry. Thus, a contract in JCT form is not an employer's 'standard form of contract' for purposes of s.3 of the Unfair Contract Terms Act 1977 and ambiguities will not be construed *contra proferentem* (q.v.) by the courts. This comment is only true of the latest edition of the contracts, however, and employers who use the 1963 edition of the contracts may find themselves caught by the provisions of the Act, because the JCT has withdrawn its sanction to that edition.

The range of contracts published on behalf of the JCT is being increased constantly. At the time of writing, they are as follows:

— Local Authorities With Quantities.
— Local Authorities Without Quantities.
— Local Authorities With Approximate Quantities.
— Private With Quantities.
— Private Without Quantities.
— Private With Approximate Quantities.
— Intermediate Form of Building Contract (IFC 84).
— Agreement for Minor Building Works.
— Fixed Fee form of Prime Cost contract.
— Agreement for Renovation Grant Works (where an architect is employed).
— Agreement for Renovation Grant Works (where no architect is employed).
— Standard Form With Contractor's Design.

A large number of tender documents, agreements, supplements and sub-contracts have been produced for use with the main forms of contract as follows:

— Fluctuations Supplement for Local Authority editions.
— Fluctuations Supplement for Private editions.
— Standard Form of Building Contract 1980 Formula Rules.
— Sectional Completion Supplement 1980.
— Minor Works Supplement 1980.
— Standard Form With Contractor's Design Formula Rules.
— Contractor's Designed Portion Supplement.
— NSC/1 Nominated Sub-Contract Tender and Agreement.

— NSC/2 and NSC/2a Employer/Nominated Sub-Contractor Agreement.
— NSC/3 Standard Form for Nomination of a Sub-Contractor.
— NSC/4 and NSC/4a Sub-Contract.
— FS NSC 80 Fluctuations Supplement (for both sub-contracts).
— Standard Form of Sub-Contract 1980 Formula Rules.
— TNS/1 JCT Tender for Nominated Suppliers 1980.
— TNS/2 JCT Warranty for Nominated Suppliers 1980.
— Fluctuations Clauses and Formula Rules (Supp/IFC 84).
— Tender and Agreement for Named Sub-Contractors under IFC 84 (NAM/T).
— Sub-Contract Conditions for Named Sub-Contractors under IFC 84 (NAM/SC).
— Sub-Contract Formula Rules for Named Sub-Contractors under IFC 84 (NAM/SC/FR).
A comprehensive set of practice notes is available and is updated on a regular basis. Standard Contract administration forms are also available. All JCT contract and supporting documents are published by RIBA Publications Ltd, Finsbury Mission, Moreland Street, London EC1V 8VB.
In Scotland, special supplements are published by the Scottish Building Contracts Committee.
A comparison of the principal features of common forms of contract is given in Table 25. See also: *ACA Form of Building Agreement; Government contracts.*

---

**Joint Contracts Tribunal (JCT)**

The tribunal (which is not strictly a tribunal but a committee) was formed in 1931. The constituent bodies now are:
— Royal Institute of British Architects.
— Building Employers Confederation (formerly National Federation of Building Trades Employers).
— Royal Institution of Chartered Surveyors.
— Association of County Councils.

# Table 25 Alternative standard contract forms

| Name | Upper cost limits | Contract documents | Advantages | Disadvantages |
|---|---|---|---|---|
| **The ACA Form of Building Agreement 1984** | No | Drawings<br>Schedules of Rates *or*<br>Bills of Quantities<br>Specification | • Adjudication during contract period<br>• Simple scheme of payment<br>• Provision for design responsibility by contractor with professonal indemnity cover<br>• Useful range of alternative clauses | • Not yet widely accepted<br>• Time periods not always realistic |
| **The JCT Standard Form of Building Contract 1980** | No | Drawings<br>Bill of Quantities (variants with approximate quantities or specification) | • Comprehensive<br>• Widely accepted negotiated document<br>• Comprehensive selection of ancillary forms | • Complex nominated sub-contract provisions<br>• Unrealistic fluctuations<br>• Printed conditions prevail over specially drafted ones<br>• Broad provisions for extensions of time<br>• Determination by contractor contains onerous provisions |
| **The JCT Standard Form of Building Contract 'with Contractor's Design' 1981** | No | Employer's Requirements<br>Contractor's Proposals (including contract sum analysis) | • Flexible<br>• May be used with or without architect's assistance<br>• May save time | • Good inspection procedures essential<br>• Contractor's obligations may be badly defined<br>• Likely to be increases in cost to achieve requirements<br>• Only limited responsibility for design on contractor |
| **The JCT Agreement for Minor Building Works** | Yes | Drawings<br>Specification *or*<br>Schedules | • Simple and easy to understand | • No provision for financial claims<br>• No nominated sub-contractors<br>• Minimal fluctuations<br>• Liquidated damages cannot be deducted<br>• No insurance for non-negligent damage to other works |
| **The JCT Intermediate Form of Building Contract for Works of Simple Content 1984** | Yes | Drawings<br>Bills of Quantities *or*<br>Schedules of Work *or*<br>Specification | • Provision for deferment of possession<br>• Flexible use<br>• Wide arbitration clause<br>• Wide testing provisions | • Not suitable where specialists employed<br>• Not suitable for long or complex contracts |
| **GC/Works/1 Government Conditions of Contract** | No | Drawings<br>Bills of Quantities *or*<br>Schedule of Rates<br>Specification | • Clear<br>• Rarely the subject of dispute<br>• May be used for building or civil engineering works | • Complex in parts<br>• Not a negotiated contract<br>• Unpopular with contractors |

— Association of Metropolitan Authorities.
— Association of District Councils.
— Greater London Council.
— Committee of Associations of Specialist Engineering Contractors.
— Federation of Associations of Specialists and Sub-Contractors.
— Association of Consulting Engineers.
— British Property Federation.
— Scottish Building Contract Committee.

The terms of reference under which the tribunal functions are, briefly, to review and update the Standard Forms of Building Contract, to produce, approve and update as necessary other ancillary forms and agreements, issue practice notes and liaise with other bodies. An important part of its constitution is the power of any of the constituent bodies to veto amendments, etc. This ensures that all JCT publications are published with the agreement of *all* members.

**Joint liability**

In some cases liability for a tort (q.v.) may be shared jointly between two or more defendants, e.g., in the law of employment where an employer is vicariously responsible for the torts of his employees or under the rules of agency (q.v.).

Under the Civil Liability (Contribution) Act 1978 the courts may apportion liability. Section 1(1) of the Act provides that 'any person liable in respect of any damage suffered by another person may recover contribution from any other person liable in respect of the same damage (whether jointly with him or otherwise)'. In other words, in the case of joint liability where only one wrongdoer is sued, he may bring in a co-defendant who is jointly liable. The amount of the contribution is to be such as the court finds 'just and equitable having regard to the extent of that person's liability for the damage in question'.

**Joint tortfeasor**

A joint wrongdoer. Certain torts may be committed jointly and the tortfeasors are jointly liable, e.g., directors with a limited liability company. See also: *Joint liability*.

| | |
|---|---|
| **Joint venture contracting** | A form of contracting where a general building contractor forms a joint company with a major sub-contractor (usually one specialising in mechanical and electrical services installation) for the purpose of undertaking a building contract jointly. Each of the parties is normally supported by a guarantee (q.v.) given by a parent or holding company. It avoids a conflict of interest between the two but can limit competition. |
| **Judgment** | The decision of a court in legal proceedings which determines the rights of the parties. It is also the reasoning of the judge in arriving at his decision. This may be reported and cited as an authority. The judgment is based on:<br>— The judge's decisions as to what are the important and relevant facts of the case *and*<br>— statements of the applicable rules of law.<br>The judgment prevents the parties from re-opening the dispute, except that they may have the right of appeal. See also: *Appeal; Judicial precedent; Law reports.* |
| **Judgment debt** | The sum of money which a judgment debtor has been ordered to pay as the result of court proceedings. A judgment debt bears interest (q.v.) at a statutory rate, which varies, from the date of judgment. Unless the judgment debtor has obtained from the court a stay of execution pending an appeal or trial of a counterclaim (q.v.) the judgment creditor may proceed to enforce the judgment in various ways. |
| **Judicial notice** | Notorious facts which are recognized by the courts without the need for proof, e.g., that the streets of London are full of traffic: *Dennis v. White & Co.* (1916). |
| **Judicial precedent** | The doctrine of judicial precedent is an important feature of the common law system. In general terms, a judge is bound to follow the decision of a previous judge in similar circumstances.<br>Not all the judgment is of binding force in subsequent |

cases, but only the legal principle which is necessary for the actual decision. This is known as *ratio decidendi* (the reason for decision): it is the legal principle upon which the decision rests. Judges often make general statements about the principles involved which are not germane to the facts before them. Such remarks are called *obiter dicta* and are not binding on another court, although they may be of persuasive authority in a subsequent case.

There may be several *rationes decidendi* in a judgment, in which case all are binding unless they are inconsistent with each other. The judges have limited power to distinguish cases they do not wish to follow. Sometimes they exercise considerable ingenuity in doing so. By distinguishing a case a judge finds, for example, that the facts of the earlier case are not sufficiently similar to those before him for the *ratio decidendi* to be applied.

The general rule is that every court in the judicial hierarchy binds all lower courts by its decisions; some courts bind themselves as well. A decision of the House of Lords is binding on all other courts. The Court of Appeal binds itself and the courts below it. In general, the decisions of the House of Lords are binding upon the House itself but, in rare cases, the House of Lords is free to depart from its own decisions if there is sufficient reason.

A higher court has power to *overrule* an earlier decision of a lower court and thus declare that it does not in fact represent the law.

The rules about judicial precedent are very complex, and too rigid adherence to precedent may lead to injustice in a particular case and sometimes restrict the proper development of the law. However, judicial precedent provides some degree of certainty and a basis for the orderly development of legal rules. See also: *Courts; Law Reports; Obiter dictum; Ratio decidendi; Stare decisis.*

**Jurisdiction**     (1) The power or authority of a court or tribunal to take cognizance of and to decide matters put before it. In the United Kingdom, the jurisdiction of the courts derives from the Queen, in whose name and by whose authority the judges exercise jurisdiction. (2) The territorial limits within which the judgments or orders of a court, etc., can be enforced.

**King's enemies**      See: *Queen's enemies.*

**Labour**

In the context of building contracts, it is given its ordinary meaning – workpeople or operatives, skilled or unskilled. JCT 80 makes the contractor's inability to secure essential labour to properly carry out the works a ground for extension of time provided the inability was outside the control of the contractor.

**Laches**

Negligence or unreasonable delay in asserting or enforcing a right. In rare cases it may be pleaded as a defence (q.v.), but only where there is no statutory time-bar. In the case of performance bonds (q.v.) conduct of the employer which prejudices the surety's position may discharge the obligation (*Kingston-upon-Hull Corporation v. Harding* (1892)) and this is another type of laches. It has been said that the validity of the defence 'must be tried upon principles substantially equitable. Two circumstances always important in such cases are the length of the delay, and the nature of the acts done during the interval, which might affect either party and cause a balance of justice or injustice in taking the one course or the other, so far as relates to the remedy': Lord Selborne in *Lindsay Petroleum Co. v. Hurd* (1874).

For example, if an adjoining owner (A) waited until building work was almost complete before seeking an injunction to prevent the contractor (B) from gaining access over part of A's land, B may be able to plead laches successfully on the grounds that A had delayed unreasonably and was acting with malice.

**Lands tribunal**

A tribunal created by the Lands Tribunal Act 1949 to deal with the following matters:
— Questions relating to compensation for the

266

compulsory acquisition of land. If the acquiring authority's offer is unacceptable to the expropriated owner, either party may refer the case to the Lands Tribunal, the decision of which is final as to the merits of the case.

— The discharge or modification of restrictive covenants (q.v.) affecting land. In some cases such covenants are outmoded in modern conditions, but this power can only be exercised on very limited grounds.

— Appeals from decisions of local valuation courts relating to rating assessments.

Procedure and practice before the tribunal is governed by special procedural rules. Its membership consists of a president and several nominated members, who usually sit singly. They are either lawyers or chartered surveyors. The tribunal gives a written and reasoned decision, and appeal on point of law (q.v.) lies only direct to the Court of Appeal. See also: *Courts; Sealed offer.*

| | |
|---|---|
| **Latent defect** | A defect which is not discoverable during the course of ordinary and reasonable examination but which manifests itself after a period of time. In building work the most common application is defects becoming apparent after the making good of defects certificate has been issued. If the contractor refuses to rectify such latent defects, the architect will often withhold his satisfaction with the work, and hence the final certificate (q.v.), until the defects have been corrected. The situation is more complicated if the final certificate has been issued. If the contractor refuses to rectify latent defects, the employer's only remedy is to sue for damages. The Limitation Act 1980 lays down a six-year period, for simple contracts (q.v.), and twelve years, for contracts under seal (q.v), from the date that the cause of action accrues, during which proceedings must be commenced. If, for example, defective foundations gave rise to severe settlement some seven years after a contract (under hand) was completed, the employer would be statute- |

barred from bringing an action against the builder under the contract. He could, however, bring an action for negligence in tort (q.v.) because the time period would not begin to run until the damage occurred: *Pirelli Cable Works Ltd v. Oscar Faber and Partners (A Firm)* (1983). However, not every breach of contract amounts to negligence.

If the defects could have been discovered by a reasonable examination by the architect, they will not be latent defects and the employer may be prevented from taking any action against the contractor, depending upon the precise contract provisions, after the issue of the final certificate.

In the case of sale of goods, there are implied terms that the goods will be in conformity with the description and with the sample, if any. If the goods supplied appear to, but do not in fact, conform, the defects will be latent and the supplier will be liable. This principle applies even if the goods conform to the sample and the sample itself contains hidden defects. It is the 'apparent sample', i.e., one without hidden defects which is to be taken as the true sample: *Adcock's Trustee v. Bridge R.D.C.* (1911). See also: *Patent defect*.

---

**Law reports**

Reports of decided cases are essential for the operation of the doctrine of judicial precedent (q.v.). From the time of Edward 1 (1272-1306) until today we have had law reports in some form, although their quality and reliability varies.

Law reporting rests on private initiative. There are no 'official' law reports, although since 1865 the Incorporated Council of Law Reporting has published a continuous series of reports known simply as 'The Law Reports', divided for convenience into volumes to cover the divisions of the High Court (see: *Courts*). Cases in the Court of Appeal are reported in the volume containing reports of cases in the Division in which the case was first heard. Decisions of the House of Lords are reported in a separate volume.

The Council is a private body but has semi-official

status and if a case is reported in the Law Reports that report will be cited to the court in preference to any other. The transcripts of the judgments are revised by the judge concerned.

There are many other series of reports, e.g., the All England Law Reports, but until recently many decisions of importance to the building industry went unreported and specialist building contract lawyers had to rely on privately circulated transcripts. Since 1976, however, a series of *Building Law Reports* has been published at the rate of three volumes a year. This series contains reports of all the major cases of interest to the building industry – including a number of decisions from the Commonwealth – and has the added benefit of a commentary on the issues involved. Decisions of the Official Referees (q.v.) of relevance to the building industry are fully reported in *Construction Law Reports*, published by The Architectural Press Ltd.

References to law reports are given by standardized abbreviations which indicate the volume and the series of reports wherein the case is reported. So, *British Steel Corporation v. Cleveland Bridge & Engineering Co. Ltd* (1981), 24 BLR 94, means that the case will be found in the twenty-fourth volume of *Building Law Reports* at page 94. Where a date is given within round brackets this refers to the year of the judgment, which is not necessarily the year of the report. Square brackets around the date refer to the year of the report. This is a legal convention.

---

**Legal tender**

A creditor is entitled to demand payment of a debt in legal tender, i.e., money. Legal tender consists of Bank of England notes for payment of any amount in England and Wales, gold coin of the realm to any amount, cupro-nickel or silver coins of more than 10p for any amount up to £10, cupro-nickel or silver coins of 10p or less up to £5, and bronze coins to an amount not exceeding 20p.

Scottish bank notes are not legal tender in England and Wales and only Bank of England notes of less than £5 are legal tender in Scotland.

A court would in practice require little evidence to be satisfied that a creditor had waived his legal right to payment in legal tender, e.g., past dealings where payment by cheque (q.v.) had been made and accepted.

| | |
|---|---|
| **Letters of intent** | A document sent before entering into a contract. It often expresses a firm intention to enter into a contract, sometimes requiring work to be put in hand. Usually, a letter of intent merely expressess an intention to enter into a contract in the future. |

Such letters are usually sent by the employer to a prospective contractor, nominated sub-contractor or nominated supplier. If sent by the architect, the letter must clearly state that it is sent on behalf of his client; otherwise the architect may find himself financially accountable if the contract does not proceed. The client must see the letter and agree its contents, preferably in writing. Legal scrutiny of each letter of intent is advisable because each case has its own peculiarities.

The whole process is fraught with difficulties:

— The main contractor, when appointed, may object to a nominated sub-contractor who has been given a letter of intent unless he is named in the contract tender documents.

— The employer will have to pay costs even if the contract does not proceed.

— The courts sometimes consider that a full binding contract has been created.

Letters of intent should be avoided if at all possible. The object of a letter of intent is to ensure that there is a limited or no contractual liability, but whether or not the sender has attracted liability depends upon the facts and surrounding circumstances of each case.

The difficulties arising from the use of letters of intent are avoided, so far as nominated sub-contractors are concerned, if the JCT Standard Form of Employer/ Nominated Sub-Contractor Agreement (NSC/2 or

NSC/2a) is used in conjunction with the JCT 80 main contract nomination procedure, since the matter of preliminary design, fabrication and allied work, and payment for it, is dealt with by clause 2.2. (In Scotland, clause 3 in NSC/2/Scot. applies.)

The case law is conflicting. In general, the courts look at the substance of each transaction rather than its form. In *Turriff Construction Ltd v. Regalia Knitting Mills Ltd* (1971), the contractors undertook pre-contract design work provided they were given 'an early letter of intent ... to cover (them) for the work they will now be undertaking'. The employer sent the letter requested, and it concluded that 'the whole to be subject to an agreement on an acceptable contract'. Judge Edgar Fay held that the employer was liable for the work carried out, ruling that the proviso applied only to the full main contract and not to the preliminary work carried out by the contractor which was done pending the conclusion of a formal contract.

In contrast, in *British Steel Corporation v. Cleveland Bridge & Engineering Co. Ltd* (1981), a letter of intent was held to negative *contractual* liability but to give rise to liability in restitution or quasi-contract (q.v.). The judgment of Robert Goff J. should be studied carefully, but in general it seems that the sender of such a letter is likely to be under a measure of liability, save in exceptional circumstances. Figures 16 and 17 illustrate letters of intent.

| | |
|---|---|
| **Levels and setting out** | The architect is responsible for showing accurately all necessary levels on the drawings and all dimensions to set out the building on the site. The contractor is responsible for transferring the levels and setting out the building on site. For a fuller discussion of the implications see also: *Setting out*. |
| **Liability** | A person is said to be liable when he is under a legal obligation to act or to suffer an action of another. Liability may be criminal (where a person may suffer fines or imprisonment) or civil (where a person may |

**Figure 16**
Letter from architect to contractor – letter
of intent

Dear Sir,

My Client *(insert name)* has instructed me to inform you that your tender of the *(insert date)* in the sum of *(insert amount in figures and words)* for the above project is acceptable and that I intend to prepare the Main Contract documents for signature subject to my Client *(insert the provisos appropriate to the particular situation)*.

It is not my Client's intention that this letter, taken alone or in conjunction with your tender, should form a binding contract. However, my Client is prepared to instruct you to *(insert the limited nature of the work required)*.

If, for any reason whatsoever, the project does not proceed, my Client's commitment will be strictly limited to payment for *(insert the limited nature of the work required)* at the cost reasonably and properly incurred. No other work included in your tender must be carried out without a further written order. No further obligation is placed upon my Client and no obligation whatever, under any circumstances, is placed upon me.

Yours faithfully.

**Figure 17**

Letter from architect to sub-contractor or
supplier – letter of intent

Dear Sir,

My Client *(insert name)* has instructed me to inform you that your
tender of the *(insert date)* in the sum of *(insert amount in figures and words)*
for *(insert the nature of the works)* is acceptable and that I intend to
instruct the Main Contractor to*enter into a Sub-Contract* with you
after the main contract has been signed.

It is not my Client's intention that this letter, taken alone or in
conjunction with your tender, should form a binding contract.
However, my Client is prepared to instruct you to undertake the
following limited work, namely *(insert the limited nature of the work
required)*. If, for any reason whatsoever, the project does not proceed,
my Client's commitment will be strictly limited to payment at cost
reasonably and properly incurred for the limited works described
above.

No other work† included in your tender must be carried out without a
further written order. No further obligation is placed upon my Client
and no obligation whatever, under any circumstances, is placed upon
me.

Yours faithfully.

*Substitute 'place an order' in the case of a Supplier.
†Substitute 'work or materials' in the case of a Supplier.

suffer various sanctions, e.g., pay damages). Civil liability may arise by the operation of statute (q.v.) or because parties have entered into a contract or in tort by virtue of common law. Thus, in building contract, the parties incur liabilities which they have decided upon themselves. The principal ones are that the contractor must carry out the work in accordance with the contract documents (q.v.) and the employer must pay the contractor for doing the work. Common law will also imply certain liabilities into contracts, such as that the contractor must use the kind of skill and care which the average contractor would use in the same circumstances. An architect will be liable for the consequences of his negligence. If he is proved negligent he will be required to pay damages. Liability may be *strict* – a person may be liable even though he is not negligent and has no intention to commit a tort: *Rylands v. Fletcher* (1868). Liabilities under certain Acts of Parliament fall into this category and sometimes also into the category of *absolute liability* where failure to carry out a duty imposed will render the person responsible liable quite irrespective of the amount of care taken or intention. See also: *Absolute liability; Duty of care; Strict liability.*

| **Libel** | Defamation (q.v.) in permanent form, e.g., in writing. Libel is actionable without proof of actual damage in contrast to slander (q.v.) which, in general, requires the plaintiff to prove loss. |

| **Licence** | Permission or authority to do something, e.g., to enter on land. The law on the subject is complex. Under the ordinary building contract, the contractor has a licence to occupy the site for the purposes of the contract, i.e., a contractual licence: *London Borough of Hounslow v. Twickenham Garden Developments Ltd* (1971). In general the employer is not entitled to revoke the contractor's licence before completion, although all well-drafted building contracts deal with the situation should the contract be determined. See also: *Forfeiture clause.* |

| | |
|---|---|
| **Licensee** | A person who enters land under licence (q.v.), e.g., the contractor under a building contract. ACA 2, clause 10 refers specifically to 'Employer's Licencees' while JCT 80, clause 29 contains a similar provision referring, *inter alia*, to work being carried out by 'persons employed or otherwise engaged by' the employer during the currency of the contract. Such clauses normally permit the employer's licensees to enter upon the site of which the contractor has been given possession and, normally, the contractor will have a contractual claim for any loss and/or expense which he suffers or incurs as a result and/or a right to extension of time (q.v.). |
| **Lien** | A right to hold someone else's property as security for the performance of an obligation. It is a right of retention which exists as a matter of law in connection with certain types of commercial relationship. A *possessory lien* is a creditor's right to retain possession of a debtor's property until the debt secured is discharged. A special lien – which is the most common type – is security for the payment of a particular debt connected with the property over which the lien is claimed. For example, a mechanic has a lien over a piece of plant he has repaired for the cost of the repairs. A general lien, which is very rare, is for the general balance owed, e.g., a stockbroker has a general lien over documents in his possession relating to shares owned by his client for all amounts due to him. An architect has a particular lien over drawings, specifications, etc., which he has produced, until his fees in connection with them have been paid. |
| **Life cycle cost analysis (LCCA)** | A technique deriving from the research of the Quantity Surveyors' Research and Development Committee and published by the Royal Institution of Chartered Surveyors in July 1983. It seeks to examine the total costs of a building throughout its useful life in order to evaluate and compare alternatives to achieve optimum long-term cost benefits. Two specific applications are: |

— To embrace construction and running costs at the design stage.
— To evaluate the running costs of existing premises.

The idea has been in circulation in the field of building maintenance for some time. LCCA refines and codifies it by providing a sophisticated methodology to arrive at a system of cost comparisons. A fundamental part of the system employs a form of cost discounting to present current and future costs on a comparable basis. The process is complicated and four distinct categories of information should be assembled:
— Costs in use or running costs, including fuel, maintenance and management.
— Physical information regarding the construction and fittings of the building.
— Quality of finishes and fittings.
— Performance of the building.

LCCA can be used to plan the cost management for the entire life of a building or for any shorter period desired. Tax implications can also be assessed. Properly applied, the system should transform the building owner's approach to new building and in particular the relationship between initial building design costs and costs in use (see Figure 18). The capital cost of a building has been found to be, on average, about one third of the total cost of the building throughout its life. That does not mean that a cheaper capital cost will give a reduced total of running costs. Generally, the reverse is true. Careful, comprehensive cost planning at design stage is the essence of the system.

**Limitation clause**     See: *Exemption clause.*

**Limitation of actions**     This term covers the rules prescribing the periods of time within which actions to enforce legal rights must be started, either by the issue of a writ (q.v.) or by serving notice of arbitration (q.v.).
In England and Wales the position is governed by the Limitation Act 1980, which prescribes the

## Figure 18

Relationship between initial building design
costs and costs in use

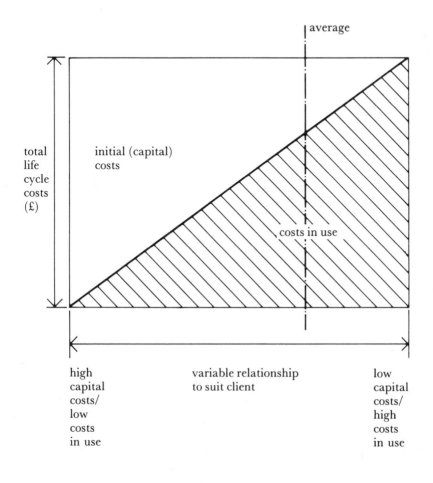

following periods:

— The time limit for actions founded on a simple contract is 6 years from the date of the breach of contract: s. 5.

— The time limit for actions founded on a specialty contract (q.v.) is 12 years.

— The time limit for actions founded on tort (q.v.) such as negligence, is 6 years, except in the case of actions for damages for personal injuries when it is 3 years.

It is not always easy to establish the date 'on which the cause of action accrued' in the case of claims in tort, particularly where defective building work is covered up. The leading modern case is the decision of the House of Lords in *Pirelli General Cable Works Ltd v. Oscar Faber & Partners* (1983) which establishes that in actions alleging negligence in regard to the erection of a building, time ordinarily begins to run not from the date of the alleged negligence, nor from when it ought to have been discovered, but from the date when the damage occurred.

This is the general rule, but Lord Fraser indicated a possible exception: 'Except perhaps where the advice of an architect or consulting engineer leads to the erection of a building which is so defective as to be doomed from the start.' Such cases are likely to be rare.

It must be noted that the Limitation Act 1980 does not extinguish the right to sue. It merely sets the time limits within which the plaintiff must begin his action, and so if a defendant pays up after the limitation period has expired, the payment is valid. This is in contrast to the situation in Scotland where the right to sue is completely extinguished: Prescription and Limitation (Scotland) Act 1973, which prescribes a limitation period of 5 years in respect of actions for breach of contract, delict (tort) or breach of statutory duty. This period runs from the time when the plaintiff first knew, or ought reasonably to have discovered, the loss or damage. In England, in cases of fraudulent concealment, i.e., deliberately concealing defects, time does not begin to run until the fraud is discovered or could have been discovered with reasonable diligence: 1980 Act, s. 32.

**Limited company**    A company in which liability (q.v.) of the shareholders is limited to the nominal value of the shareholding. Characteristics of a limited company are:

— It can only be formed under the rules laid down by the Companies Act 1985.

— A limited company comes into existence when it has been registered with the Registrar of Companies. Transactions carried out before registration may be taken to be the transactions of a partnership with unlimited liability.

— The powers of a limited company are constrained by the 'objects' clause of the Memorandum of Association.

— Accounts must be filed with the Registrar of Companies and they may be inspected by the public.

— There are certain statutory constraints on the running of the company, e.g., at least one Annual General Meeting must be held for all shareholders each year.

— A company normally comes to an end by being liquidated (q.v.) in accordance with the Companies Act 1985. It is a formal and possibly lengthy process.

— A·shareholder cannot bind the company by his actions.

— Dividends must be apportioned strictly in accordance with the shareholding.

— Changes in shareholding do not bring the company to an end.

— The company is run by a board of directors. They may or may not be shareholders. Normally, they will carry no personal liability for the actions of the company.

— A private limited company must put the word 'Limited' or the abbreviation 'Ltd' after the company name. Public limited companies must put the words 'Public Limited Company' or the initials 'PLC' after the company name.

— The minimum number of members in each case is two. See also: *Corporation; Ultra vires.*

**Liquidated damages**   A sum of money stated in a contract as the damages payable in the event of a specified breach. The sum must be a genuine pre-estimate of the loss likely to be caused by the breach or a lesser sum. There is no need to prove actual damage after the event and it does not matter that the actual loss is greater or less than the stated sum.

All the common forms of building contract include a liquidated damages clause to calculate the amount payable if the contractor fails to complete by the completion date (q.v.) or any extended date. A sum is included to represent the damages on a weekly or daily basis as appropriate. If no figure were stated, the employer would need to prove his actual loss and recover it by way of 'unliquidated damages' through court action.

The advantages of liquidated damages are:

— They do not require proof after the event.

— They can be simply deducted by the employer under the contractual mechanism.

— They are agreed in advance and stated in the contract so that the contractor knows the extent of his potential liability.

Liquidated damages clauses are likely to be construed *contra proferentem* (q.v.): *Peak Construction (Liverpool) Ltd v. McKinney Foundations Ltd* (1970), although this is probably not the case if the contract is in a negotiated form, e.g., the JCT Contracts: *Tersons Ltd v. Stevenage Development Corporation* (1963). But hand-written or typewritten insertions which are inconsistent with the printed provisions will, it seems, be so construed: *Bramall & Ogden Ltd v. Sheffield City Council* (1985).

It is essential that a careful calculation be made at pre-tender stage taking the relevant factors on the particular job into account. Figure 19 shows a possible format for such a calculation. In the public sector, where it is difficult to estimate the loss, it is usual to make use of a formula calculation, and it is thought that this is an acceptable method of approach.

There is some confusion among members of the construction industry regarding what constitutes a penalty. A penalty is not enforceable. It is either a predetermined sum which is not a realistic pre-estimate of damage or a sum which is payable on the occurrence of any one of a number of different kinds of events. It is of no consequence whether the sum is described as a penalty or not. It is the real nature of the sum which matters. Even if a sum is held to be a penalty, the employer may still pursue an action for his actual (unliquidated) damages at common law.

In *Dunlop Ltd v. New Garage Co. Ltd* (1915), Lord Dunedin noted the principles by which the court decides whether a clause provides for liquidated damages or a penalty:

'(i) Though the parties to a contract who use the words penalty or liquidated damages may *prima facie* be supposed to mean what they say, yet the expression used is not conclusive. The court must find out whether the payment stipulated is in truth a penalty or liquidated damages ...

(ii) The essence of a penalty is a payment of money stipulated as *in terrorem* of the offending party; the essence of liquidated damages is a genuine covenanted pre-estimate of damage.

(iii) The question whether a sum stipulated is penalty or liquidated damages is a question of construction to be decided upon the terms and inherent circumstances of each particular contract, judged as at the time of the making of the contract, not as at the time of the breach.

(iv) To assist this task of construction various tests have been suggested, which, if applicable to the case under consideration, may prove helpful or even conclusive. Such are: (a) It will be held to be a penalty if the sum stipulated for is extravagant and unconscionable in amount in comparison with the greatest loss which could conceivably be proved to have followed from the breach ... (b) It will be held to

**Figure 19**

Calculation of liquidated and ascertained
damages: typical format

Contract.............................................................................................................................

Client ...............................................................................................................................

Architect .........................................................................................................................

---

1. *Supervisory Staff (current rates)*            *Costs/Week*

    Architect: Estim. hrs/wk............ × time charge
              of £.......... per hour.                  £

    Quantity Surveyor: Estim. hrs/wk............ × time
                    charge of £.......... per hour       £

    Consultants: (as above for each one)         £

    Clerk of Works: Weekly salary (yearly)      £

                              52

                             TOTAL (1)      £

---

2. *Additional Costs\* (current rates)*

    Rent and/or rates and/or charges for present
    premises                                £

    Rent and/or rates and/or charges for alternative
    premises                                £

    Charges for equipment                 £

    Movement of equipment               £

    Additional and/or continuing and/or substitute
    staff                                     £

    Movement of staff (include travel expenses)   £

    Any site charges which are the responsibility
    of the client                           £

    Extra payments to directly employed trades   £

    Insurance                             £

    Additional administrative costs          £

                             TOTAL (2)      £

---

\*It is essential that all costs noted are additional, i.e: they would not be incurred if the
contract was completed on the Contract Completion Date. The headings given are
examples only. Every job is different.

†Professional fees are taken as 90% of total because some professional work remains to
be done after practical completion.

### 3. *Interest*

Interest payable on estimated capital expended
up to the Contract Completion Date, but from
which no benefit is derived. Estimated
expenditure taken as 80% of contract sum and
fees

| | |
|---|---|
| Contract sum: | £ |
| Architect's fees (90%)† | £ |
| Quantity surveyor's fees (90%)† | £ |
| Consultant's fees (90%)† | £ |
| Salary of Clerk of Works | £ |
| (£/wk × contract period) | |

Total    £ _____

Interest charges at current rate of ........%

$$\frac{\text{Interest/wk (80\% capital expended} \times \text{interest)}}{52}$$

TOTAL (3)    £

### 4. *Inflation*

Current rate of inflation........%/year

| | |
|---|---|
| TOTAL (1) × ........% × contract period (years) | £ |
| TOTAL (2) × ........% × contract period (years) | £ |

TOTAL (4)    £

### 5. *Total Liquidated and Ascertained damages/week*

| | |
|---|---|
| TOTAL (1) | £ |
| TOTAL (2) | £ |
| TOTAL (3) | £ |
| TOTAL (4) | £ |
| FINAL TOTAL | £ |

The FINAL TOTAL should be examined to see if it appears reasonable in all the circumstances. It should be appreciated that the calculation can only be approximate. If in doubt about the figure, reduce it. It is sound procedure for the architect to calculate the totals with the client, have the calculations typed out and send it to him for signature.

If sectional completion is to be used, the amounts of liquidated damages should be apportioned bearing in mind:
- The value of each section.
- The implications in cost to the client of each section. For example, the Clerk of Works may be required to stay on site until the last section is completed or his attendance may be reduced, at some stage, to half time.

be a penalty if the breach consists only in not paying a sum of money, and the sum stipulated is a sum greater than the sum which ought to have been paid ... (c) There is a presumption (but no more) that it is a penalty when "a single lump sum is made payable by way of compensation, on the occurrence of one or more or all of several events, some of which may occasion serious and others but trifling damages". On the other hand (d) it is no obstacle to the sum stipulated being a genuine pre-estimate of damage that the consequences of the breach are such as to make precise pre-estimation almost an impossibility. On the contrary, that is just the situation when it is probable that the pre-estimated damage was the true bargain between the parties.'

Liquidated damages clauses are usually linked with an extension of time (q.v.) clause and the position was clearly stated by the House of Lords in *Percy Bilton Ltd v. Greater London Council* (1982):

— The general rule is that the contractor is bound to complete the work by the date for completion stated in the contract, as extended. If he fails to do so, the employer is entitled to recover liquidated damages.

— The employer is not entitled to liquidated damages if he by his acts or omissions has prevented the contractor from completing by the due date, and if this occurs time may become 'at large'.

— These general rules may be amended by the express terms of the contract and are so amended by the common standard forms. These provide for extensions of time to be granted in appropriate cases.

— Failure by the architect properly to extend time or acts etc. of the employer not covered by the events listed in the extension of time clause will result in time being at large and liquidated damages being irrecoverable. The contractor's obligation is then to complete within a reasonable time and the employer is left to sue for unliquidated damages at common law. See also: *Damages; Extension of time; Penalty.*

**Liquidation**     Also known as 'winding-up'. The legal process for terminating the existence of a company which is registered under the Companies Act 1985.

There are three types of winding-up:
— Winding-up by order of the Court.
— Creditors, voluntary winding-up.
— Members, voluntary winding-up.
The first two apply to insolvent companies.
A 'winding-up by order of the Court' of an insolvent company may be commenced by the company, a creditor or the receiver (q.v.) presenting a petition to the Court to wind-up the company. If the Court makes a compulsory winding-up order, the official receiver becomes a provisional liquidator and he may apply to the Court for the appointment of a special manager. A meeting of the creditors called by the provisional liquidator decides whether or not to apply to the Court for the appointment of both a liquidator and a committee of inspection.

A 'creditors' voluntary winding up' has the advantage that the creditors can settle matters without recourse to the Court, but they may apply to the Court if they deem it necessary. The procedure starts with the company passing an extraordinary resolution that it cannot, by reason of its liabilities, carry on its business and that it is expedient that it be wound up. A meeting of creditors must be called on the same or the following day to appoint a liquidator and a committee of inspection.

A liquidator may only carry on the business if it is beneficial to the winding-up, for example, if the overall capital available is likely to be increased. The object of liquidation and the law governing it is to ensure equal distribution of the company's assets among the creditors, subject to the following order of preference:
— Fixed charges.
— Costs of the liquidation.
— Preferential creditors (e.g., rates, taxes, national insurance, etc., for a fixed period and wages for the previous four months to a statutory maximum per employee).
— Floating charges.
— Unsecured creditors (they may well be the creditors who force the winding-up).

If a company transfers the whole of its interests to a new company, it is known as 'reconstruction'. See also: *Insolvency*.

| | |
|---|---|
| **Liquidator** | A person who is appointed by a company or by the court to carry out the liquidation (q.v.) of the company's assets for the benefit of creditors. |

**Litigation**

The process of resolving a legal dispute before a court. The term is used in contrast to 'arbitration' (q.v.) which is the settlement of disputes before a private judge of the parties' choosing. The great jurist Sir Frederick Pollock defined litigation as a game in which the court is an umpire.

**Local authority**

Local authorities are statutory corporations charged with a range of functions over a limited geographical area. They are subject to the doctrine of *ultra vires* (q.v.).

There are special local authority editions of some standard form building contracts, e.g., JCT 80, but this has no legal significance. Outside London, *District Councils* are responsible for building control (q.v.) and are also responsible for most planning functions. Reference may usefully be made to *The AJ Legal Handbook*, Chapters 9 and 10, which deal with statutory authorities in England and Wales and in Scotland respectively.

**Lock-out**

When an employer excludes his employees from their place of work, thus denying them the opportunity to work. It is usually the result of an industrial dispute. JCT 80 (clause 25.4.4), IFC 84 (clause 2.4.4) and GC/Works/1 (clause 28(2)(d)) expressly refer to a lock-out as one of the grounds for extension of time (q.v.).

**Locus sigilli**

The place of the seal. This latin expression is often abbreviated to L. S. and is sometimes printed beside the attestation clause (q.v.) of a document requiring to be sealed.

A document is legally capable of being a deed (q.v.) provided it is presented as being a deed and it bears an indication of where the seal (q.v.) should be. It is not strictly necessary for a physical seal to be attached to or impressed on the document.

In *First National Securities Ltd v. Jones* (1978) a bank's printed mortgage form bore the printed letters L. S. in a circle. The defendant had signed his signature across the circle and there was an attestation clause (q.v.) signed by a witness. The Court of Appeal ruled that the document had been properly executed as a deed.

It is clearly preferable that any document, intended to be under seal, should have a seal attached, stamped or impressed to remove any possibility of later dispute on the matter.

| | |
|---|---|
| **Loss and expense** | A phrase used loosely to refer to the damage suffered by the contractor and for which he might be expected to bring a claim (q.v.). GC/Works/1 refers only to 'expense'. It is clear that the contractor may not claim under clause 53 of this contract for loss of profit (q.v.), i.e., he may claim for any expense over and above that which he might have expected; he cannot claim for money he expected to receive but, because of the event cited, did not receive. Most other contracts allow loss and expense. Although the phrase has been the subject of much discussion, it is clear that it means 'damages' as generally understood at common law. See also: *Direct loss and/or expense*. |
| **Loss of productivity** | Loss of productivity is a permissible part of a claim under the money claims clauses of most standard form building contracts. Thus, JCT 80, clause 26 entitles the contractor to recover 'direct loss and/or expense' if 'regular progress of the Works' has been or is likely to be affected by the matters listed in the clause. |

Some authorities have argued that this must involve *delay* (q.v.) in progress and that the contractor's entitlement is limited to the effects of delayed completion. A careful reading of the clause (and similar provisions in other contracts) does not support this view.

In principle the contractor is entitled to recover for loss of productivity, i.e., the effect of the event upon the cost of the work, by labour, plant and other resources having been used less efficiently during the original contract period, even if no extension of time (q.v.) is involved. Regular progress of the works can be 'materially affected' without there being any delay at all to completion (q.v.) and the additional cost (if proven) falls within the rule in *Hadley v. Baxendale* (1854) – as being foreseeable. It is the natural consequence of the specified act and must be something which the parties had, or should have had, in mind.

In broad principle, loss of productivity is easy to establish, but it is difficult to prove and quantify in detail, and at the very least the contractor must be able to isolate the various items of cost which have been affected by the particular disruptive events on which he relies. See also: *Claims; Foreseeability.*

| **Loss of profit** | Loss of profit is a recoverable part of a claim under the money claims clauses of the various standard forms of contract in common use, as well as being recoverable as a head of damages for breach of contract at common law, assuming of course that the contractor would have earned it had it not been for the event giving rise to the claim: *Hadley v. Baxendale* (1854); *Wraight Ltd v. P. H. & T. (Holdings) Ltd* (1968). It is, however, only the 'normal' profit which is recoverable – because such a loss is within the contemplation of the parties – and not an exceptionally high profit which the contractor might otherwise have earned unless the other party to the contract knew, at the time of the contract, facts which would bring the abnormal profit within his contemplation: *Victoria Laundry (Windsor) Ltd v. Newman Industries Ltd* (1949). |

There is no *automatic* right to recover lost profit: The

better view is that such a claim is allowable only where the contractor is able to demonstrate that he has been prevented from earning profit elsewhere in the normal course of his business as a direct result of the disruption or prolongation ... ' Powell-Smith and Sims, *Building Contract Claims,* p.111, referring to *Peak Construction (Liverpool) Ltd v. McKinney Foundations Ltd* (1970). See also: *Claims; Damages.*

---

**Lump Sum contract**　　When one party carries out work for a stated and fixed amount of money payable by the other. All the main forms of building contract are considered to be lump sum contracts even though they contain provisions for the adjustment of the contract sum (q.v.) for such things as fluctuations and variations. The important point is that the original contract sum is stated for a given amount of work. Some contracts are expressly not lump sum contracts, e.g., JCT 80 Private edition, With Approximate Quantities. If the contract expressly provides for remeasurement, it is not a lump sum contract. See also: *Firm price contract; Fixed price contract.*

**Main contract**    A term sometimes given to the contract between employer and contractor to distinguish if from the contracts (sub-contracts) between the contractor and his sub-contractors. Thus the contractor (q.v.) is also referred to as the 'main contractor', or 'principal contractor'. See also: *ACA Form of Building Agreement; BPF System; JCT contracts.*

**Maintenance**    The carrying on of or keeping up to a particular standard. In relation to building, the word is used to refer to the carrying out of regular work and repairs including replacement as necessary over a period of time, possibly the life of the building.

The word is used by GC/Works/1 to denote the defects liability period. It is regrettable because to use the word in this way does violence to its ordinary meaning. If the contractor were indeed required to 'maintain' a building for a period of six months after completion, it would involve his keeping it in pristine condition despite occupation and the passage of time. In fact, GC/Works/1 defines the contractor's responsibility more narrowly. See also: *Defects liability period; Maintenance clause; Maintenance period.*

**Maintenance clause**    A clause included in the ACA 2 and GC/Works/1 forms of contract, clauses 12.2 and 32 respectively, designating a period of time after the works are completed during which the contractor is to make good defects. See also: *Defects liability period.*

**Maintenance period**    A misleading phrase in some contracts referring to the period of time after the works are completed during which the contractor is to make good defects.

For example, ACA 2, clause 12.2 refers to the maintenance period. See also: *Defects liability period; Maintenance clause.*

**Management contract**

A loose term which can cover a wide variety of contractual situations. It is commonly used to refer to a type of contract where the main contractor is selected at a very early stage and appointed to manage the construction process and input his own expertise during the pre-contract stages. The contractor receives a fee for his services which is agreed between the parties before the contractor is appointed. Competitive tendering is usual for the various sub-contract elements. Points to note are:
— The contractor is responsible to the employer for the construction process.
— The system is most useful for large and complex contracts when a considerable degree of co-ordination of specialists is required and where early completion is vital.
— Accurate programming and cost planning is essential for success.
— The selection of a suitable contractor to undertake the management work is not an easy process.
See also: *BPF System; Cost reimbursement contract; Design and build contract; Project management.*

**Master**

1. The traditional legal term for an employer of labour, i.e., the relationship of employer and employee. The major distinction between the relationship of master and servant and that of employer and independent contractor (q.v.) appears to be that in the former case the employer has the power to direct and control how, when and what work is to be done. An employer is vicariously responsible for acts done by his employee in the course of his employment. See also: *Vicarious liability.*
2. Masters of the Supreme Court are officers of the High Court in England. They perform certain judicial work and issue directions on matters of practice and procedure. Taxing Masters are responsible for the taxation of costs (q.v.).

**Master cost plan**

Under the BPF System (q.v.) this is a schedule prepared by the Client's Representative (q.v.) of the total expenditure required to complete the project. 'At all times it should provide the best possible estimate of the final cost of the project, of the future cash flow, and of the future cost of the building.' The BPF *Manual* contains, in Appendix A2.3, a checklist of the information which the master cost plan should include, arranged under the following headings:
— Description of project.
— Basis of cost plan.
— Forecast tender price.
— Other costs.
— Target cost.
— Development cost.

**Master programme**

1. A term to be found in JCT 80, clause 5.3, and referring to the contractor's overall programme for the execution of the works. The reference in the contract merely formalizes what has long been the practice in most contracts through an appropriate clause in the bills of quantities (q.v.) or specification (q.v.). The clause does not state the form the programme should take. The type of programme required should be specified in the bills of quantities or specification as appropriate, e.g., bar chart, network analysis, line of balance, etc. Except for the smallest jobs, it is advisable to request a network analysis to be prepared, because it clearly highlights delay and disruption. Note that, if no programme is specified, it is probable that the contractor is under no obligation to supply one. The footnote to the clause points out that the provision may be deleted, but this is an unwise practice because, although the master programme is not a contract document (q.v.) it is an invaluable aid to monitoring contract progress for both architect and contractor. Not only should a good programme show the start and finish dates and relationships of the key operations, but also the way in which sub-contractors of all kinds will be integrated into the work. It is good practice for the contractor to

# Figure 20

Example of master programme

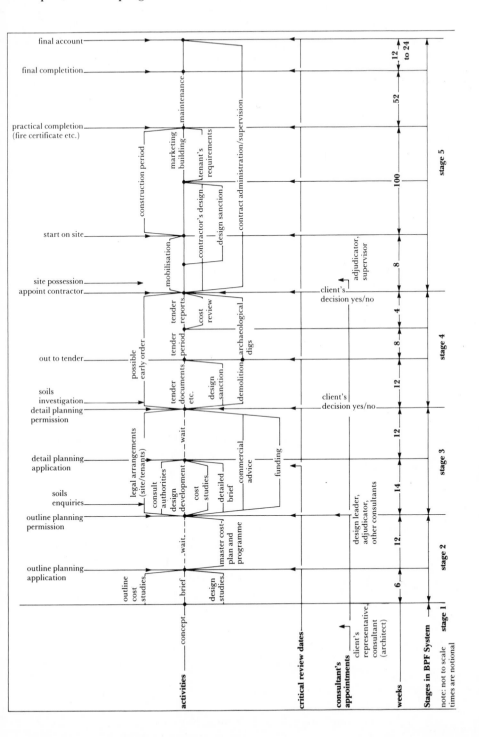

293

note (realistic) dates for receipt of information –
drawings, schedules, nominations, etc., from the
architect. The architect should not 'approve' the
contractor's master programme. He must treat it as
mere information from the contractor of what he
intends to do and when he intends to do it.
2. Under the BPF System (q.v.) for building design
and construction the same term is used to describe
the schedule prepared by the Client's Representative
(q.v.) of the main activities required to complete the
project. An example is shown in Figure 20. This
master programme is produced at an early stage in the
development of the project, and is updated by the
Client's Representative as the project progresses to
tender stage. See also: *Regularly and diligently; Time
schedule.*

**Materially affected**

A phrase used in the JCT 80 and IFC 84 forms of
contract. Clause 26 of JCT 80 refers to regular
progress of the works being 'materially affected'. It is
a condition precedent to the contractor being able to
claim loss and/or expense. Clause 27.1.3 refers to the
works being 'materially affected' by the contractor's
refusal or neglect to comply with the architect's
instructions requiring him to remove defective work
or materials. It is a ground for the employer to
determine the contractor's employment.
The addition of the word 'materially' makes clear
that it is not sufficient if it can be said that the works
or progress (as the case may be) are *affected*. They
must be affected in some important or significant
way or to a substantial extent. The word is not
precisely defined in the contract. It is clear that trivial
disruptions are excluded and whether progress can
be said to be materially affected will depend upon the
exact circumstances of each case.
GC/Works/1 refers to 'materially' disrupted, clause
53(1), to the same effect.

**Materials**

Although most building contracts draw a distinction
between 'goods' and 'materials' there is no distinction

in law. Both are 'goods' for the purposes of the Sale of Goods Act 1979. In building practice, the things used to construct the building, e.g., bricks, sand and cement, timber, screws, etc., which are the raw elements of the building before any work has been done, are called 'materials' in contrast to such things as door furniture and sanitary fittings which are normally described as 'goods'.

The Supply of Goods and Services Act 1982 (q.v.) which applies, inter alia, to building contracts implies certain conditions and warranties in regard to materials and goods supplied under a building contract. These implied terms (q.v.) parallel those implied by the Sale of Goods Act 1979 in respect of sales of goods, e.g., that the goods are to be of merchantable quality.

Under some forms of contract, e.g., JCT 80, clause 25.4.10.2, 'the contractor's inability for reasons beyond his control and which could not reasonably have been foreseen at the date of tender to secure such goods and materials as are essential to the proper carrying out of the Works', shortage of materials may be a ground for extension of time. It would not excuse late completion at common law. See also: *Sale of goods*.

| | |
|---|---|
| **Measure and value contract** | A general name given to any contract where there is no fixed contract sum (lump sum contract) but where the work is measured and valued by the quantity surveyor as it proceeds in order to arrive at the price to be paid to the contractor. See also: *Measurement contract*. |
| **Measure of damages** | See: *Damages*. |
| **Measurement** | Generally, the ascertaining of length, breadth or height, volume or area of objects, buildings, land etc., in terms of a particular system of measurement, e.g., metric.<br>In building contracts, measurement of the work is |

carried out by the quantity surveyor either before work begins, from the drawings prepared by the architect, or during the progress and after the completion of the work. The quantity surveyor works to a set of rules embodied in the Standard Method of Measurement (q.v.). See also: *Bills of quantities; Measurement contract.*

**Measurement contract**

Normally used where the precise quantity (and sometimes type) of work cannot be accurately determined at the time of tender. A basis is provided for tendering purposes and the completed work is measured and payment made in accordance with the tender rates. Two main types of measurement contract are:
— Where approximate quantities are used. This type is suitable where the type of work is known but the quantity is unknown (see also: *Bills of quantities*).
— Where a schedule of prices (q.v.)·is used. This type is suitable where even the type of work is not known for certain.

**Merchantable quality**

Under s.14 of the Sale of Goods Act 1979 there is an implied term (q.v.) that the goods are of 'merchantable quality'. 'Merchantable quality' is defined as meaning that the goods 'are as fit for the purpose...for which goods of that kind are commonly bought as it is reasonable to expect having regard to any description applied to them, the price (if relevant) and all the other circumstances...' The term 'merchantable' is a relative one, but the goods must remain 'merchantable' for a reasonable time. If the buyer examines the goods he will not be protected against defect that examination ought to have revealed, i.e., patent defects (q.v.). A similar provision is made by the Supply of Goods and Services Act 1982 (q.v.). In business transactions – which includes sales of building materials – the term can be excluded so far as it is reasonable to do so. See also: the *Unfair Contract Terms Act 1977.*

**Minutes of meeting**

The official record of a meeting. It is essential that all meetings, even of the most informal kind, which have any relevance to a contract, should be recorded in some way. Short meetings, meetings between two people or telephone calls may be recorded by means of a brief note of all the important points being put into the file. Meetings on a more formal basis, such as pre-contract, design team or site meetings, should be minuted.

The meetings should have an agenda to ensure that necessary points are discussed and, if possible, a time limit so as to concentrate minds. The minutes of such meetings should be the responsibility of one person, often the architect or project manager (q.v.). They must record only the important items which, in practice, may mean recording only decisions made. A format for a typical site meeting is shown in Figure 21.

It is essential to circulate minutes to all participants as soon as possible after the meeting. Any disagreements as to the accuracy of the minutes should be recorded at the next meeting, if there is to be a series of meetings, or circulated. Otherwise, some note must be put at the beginning of each meeting recording that the minutes are agreed as a true record. Where a contract calls for a certificate to be issued, a notice given or an application made, it is not thought that a note in any minutes will suffice, and certainly a note in the minutes about information supply cannot amount to a 'specific application' for that information by the contractor.

| **Misconduct** | Conduct falling below the standards required in the circumstances. It is particularly serious in the case of professional persons who have a duty to conduct themselves with complete integrity. Thus an arbitrator (q.v.) who misconducts himself by hearing one party in the absence of the other without good reason would be guilty of misconduct and liable to be replaced if the absent party made application to the court.

Section 23 (1) of the Arbitration Act 1950 empowers the court to remove an arbitrator where he has 'misconducted himself or the proceedings' and the provision is cast in very wide terms. It does not

**Figure 21**

Typical format of minutes of a site meeting

Job Title:                                                    Ref. No:
Location:
Site Meeting No:
Present:

1.0  The minutes of Site Meeting No. ..................... held on the .....................
     are agreed as a true record
2.0  Matters arising from the minutes of the last meeting
3.0  Contractor's progress report
4.0  Clerk of Works' report
5.0  Consultants' reports:
     5.1  Structural Engineer
     5.2  Heating and Ventilating Engineer
     5.3  Mechanical Engineer
     5.4  Electrical Engineer
     5.5  Landscape Architect
6.0  Financial report by Quantity Surveyor
7.0  Any other business
8.0  Date and time of next meeting

Circulation of Minutes to:

| | | | |
|---|---|---|---|
| Employer | _ Cps | Mechanical Engineer | _ Cps |
| Contractor | _ Cps | Electrical Engineer | _ Cps |
| Quantity Surveyor | _ Cps | Landscape Architect | _ Cps |
| Structural Engineer | _ Cps | Clerk of Works | _ Cps |
| Heating & Vent. Engineer | _ Cps | File | _ Cps |

necessarily involve moral turpitude, and the best
definition is that it is 'such mishandling of the
arbitration as is likely to amount to some substantial
miscarriage of justice': *Williams v. Wallis & Cox*
(1914).

An architect could be guilty of misconduct by
favouring one contractor during the tendering
process.

---

**Misrepresentation**

A misrepresentation is an untrue statement of fact
made during the course of pre-contractual
negotiations and which is one of the factors which
induces the other party to contract.

If the misrepresentation becomes a term of the
contract, then liability depends on whether it is a
condition (q.v.), or a warranty (q.v.), but in either
case the innocent party will have a remedy for breach
of contract (q.v.).

Misrepresentations which do not become part of the
contract – which is the normal situation – may also
give rise to liability at common law and under the
Misrepresentation Act 1967, as amended.

A misrepresentation may be:

— Fraudulent (q.v.) when it is made without honest
belief in its truth.

— Innocent (q.v.) where it is made without fault.

— Negligent (q.v.) (see also: *Negligent misstatement*).

In all cases the innocent party may rescind the
contract (see: *Rescission*) or, alternatively, claim
damages (q.v.). By s.2 (2) of the Misrepresentations
Act 1967, damages can only be granted as an
alternative to rescission in the case of *innocent
misrepresentations*. The award of damages in that case
is discretionary, e.g., *Howard Marine & Dredging Co
Ltd v. A. Ogden & Sons (Excavations) Ltd* (1977) where
damages were awarded for an innocent
misrepresentation about the dead-weight of barges to
be used in connection with excavation work.

---

**Mistake**

Where the contracting parties are at cross-purposes
about some material fact this may make the purported
contract void (q.v.). Lawyers call this an 'operative

mistake' and it must be distinguished from 'mistake' in the popular sense.

Operative mistake is classified as:

— Common mistake – where both parties make the same mistake.

— Mutual mistake – where the parties are at cross-purposes about some essential fact.

— Unilateral Mistake – where only one party is mistaken.

An operative mistake may either nullify or preclude consent, but the cases establish that this is extremely limited in scope, although in some cases the courts have intervened to prevent hardship by giving equitable relief: *Solle v. Butcher* (1950).

Operative mistake has not proved important in the field of building contracts, its main application being that the employer could not accept the contractor's tender if he knew that its terms were not intended by the contractor: *McMaster University v. Wilchar Construction Ltd* (1971) where the employer 'accepted' a tender in the knowledge that the contractor had omitted its first page, which contained a fluctuations clause. See also: *Contract; Equity.*

**Mitigation of loss**

Someone seeking to recover damages for breach of contract (or any other reason) should do everything reasonably possible to reduce the amount of his loss. He is not entitled simply to sit back and wait. For example, if a builder constructs a roof badly and there are defects which allow water to enter the building, the architect will ask him to put the matter right. If the builder refuses, the employer will, no doubt, take whatever steps are open to him, either within the contract or at common law to recover damages (q.v.). The employer should also take whatever steps are reasonable to reduce the amount of damage suffered. In the example, the necessary steps might well be to pay others to do the work in order to avoid extensive internal damage to the building by the water. The employer would be unable to recover through the courts the loss which he could have avoided by taking reasonable steps. In some cases it would be reasonable to postpone remedial work until damages were recovered. Mitigation of loss does not cover the situation where the employer or his architect might, by minute and careful inspection, have *discovered* defects at an earlier date than they did: *East Ham B. C. v. Bernard Sunley Ltd* (1966). In that case Lord Upjohn said: 'I am at a loss to understand why the negligent builder should be able to limit his liability by reason of the fact that at some earlier stage the architect failed to notice some defective work.' See also: *Inspections; Supervision.*

**Mobilization**

A term found in JCT 80, clause 32 (Outbreak of hostilities), referring to the readying of armed forces for war.

**Moiety**

A legal term meaning a half or one of two equal parts. It is found in some forms of contract, particularly in relation to retention money and its release.

**Monopoly**

Where the supply of certain goods or services is controlled by one or a group of manufacturers and traders. There are statutory restrictions on monopoly situations, but this is of little importance in the construction industry. See also: *Restrictive trade practices.*

**Month**

A *lunar month* is a period of 28 days in contrast to a *calendar month*, which is a period of 30 or 31 days (28 days in February, or in a leap year, 29 days). In statutes, contracts and deeds 'a month' means a calendar month unless the contrary is indicated: Interpretation Act 1978, s.3; Law of Property Act 1925, s.61.

**Mutual dealings**

Section 31 of the Bankruptcy Act 1914 and section 317 of the Companies Act 1985 apply certain rules regarding set-off to insolvent limited companies. They apply to a situation 'where there have been mutual credits, mutual debts or other mutual dealings...' In such a situation 'an account shall be taken of what is due from one party to the other in respect of such mutual dealings...' and that only the balance due on the taking of such an account shall be claimed. The rules embrace debts and credits arising out of any number of contracts between the same parties. Sums owing on one contract may be set-off against sums due on another.

This is of great importance in the construction industry where such dealings take place between main contractors and their sub-contractors or suppliers (see: *Rolls Razor Ltd v. Cox* (1967)) and as between employers and their contractors. In the normal course of things, each party would be liable to pay money owing to the other and any set-off would be by agreement only. This would mean that, if liquidation occurred, the solvent party would be liable to pay his debts to the party in liquidation and, in turn, could only expect to receive whatever dividend was finally declared. For example, A owes £100 to B; B owes £80 to A. A becomes insolvent. If B pays the £80 he owes, he may then have to wait until A's affairs are settled when he may receive 1p in the pound, i.e., £1. When mutual dealings are taken into account, however, B would owe nothing and expect to receive, eventually, 1p in the pound of £20 (the balance), i.e., 20p. B's loss in the first instance would be £99, in the second instance £19.80. The procedure is a protection for the solvent party. In *Willment Brothers Ltd v. North-West Thames Regional Health Authority*, (1984) the operation of a building contract between employer and contractor was held sufficient to establish that there had been 'mutual dealings' between them for the purposes of section 31 of the 1914 Act.

| **Named sub-contractors and suppliers** | A term used in the BPF System (q.v.) to refer to specialists whose advice has been sought during the design stages. They are named in the invitation to tender to the main contractor with an indication of whether the client requires that they be invited to tender for their part of the work. Provision for named sub-contractors is made in clause 9 of ACA 2.<br>IFC 84 refers to 'named persons as sub-contractors' in clauses 3.3.1 to 3.3.7 inclusive. The provisions are closer to the JCT 80 than to the ACA provisions, but such sub-contractors must be distinguished from the nominated sub-contractors (q.v.) in the JCT 80 Standard Form for which clause 35 makes detailed provision.<br>JCT 80, clause 19.3, provides a similar mechanism under which the architect may detail in the main contract documents work which the contractor is to price but which is to be executed by a sub-contractor chosen by the main contractor from a list provided by the employer. The Bills (q.v.) must provide to this effect and the contractor's right to select from the list is by and at his sole discretion. |
| **National House-Building Council** | The NHBC is a non-profit making insurance company recognized under Statute. Its Chairman is appointed by the Secretary of State for the Environment. Its principal aim is to improve the private house-building industry in the United Kingdom.<br>To achieve this end, the NHBC:<br>— Undertakes research into housing and construction |

in order to improve its standard building specification (called 'the Council's Requirements') with which all builders registered with it must comply.

— Carries out a spot check system of inspection of all dwellings registered with it.

— Operates an insurance scheme which guarantees the performance of the builder or developer to complete dwellings to satisfactory standards and to remedy all defects which occur within, broadly, the first 2 years and thereafter to insure the property for a further 8 years against major damage caused by structural defects.

Houses built by registered builders are exempt from the provisions of s.1 of the Defective Premises Act 1972 (q.v.). The contractual arrangements between the builder and the house purchaser are set out in a 'House Purchaser's Agreement' (HB 5) and there is provision for arbitration (q.v.) in respect of disputes arising under the scheme. The NHBC has more than 250 Field Staff responsible for inspecting dwellings and investigating claims. The Ten Year Insurance Scheme has been in operation since 1967 and currently it pays 3,000 claimants, on average, more than £6 million a year.

By careful monitoring of the cause of insurance claims, the NHBC is then able to amend its standard building specification in order to prevent such claims from arising in the future. In 1975, for instance, it was established that over 50% of claims related to defective infill which caused sinking floor slabs. The NHBC introduced a requirement in 1975 which specified that if more than 600 mm of infill were used, the builder must put in a suspended floor construction. As a result of this change, claims for foundation failures are now less than half of what they would otherwise have been.

The NHBC publishes an extensive list of both technical publications and information booklets for purchasers, builders and the professions generally. They are all available, most of them without charge, from the Information Office, NHBC, 58 Portland Place, London W1N 4BU.

**National Schedule of Rates**

First introduced in 1982 for the benefit of local authorities engaged in maintenance and repair work and certain other minor building work, it was revised and updated in March 1984 to take account of altered circumstances and conditions.

The National Schedule of Rates is intended for use with term contracts (q.v.) and consists of the following:

— Introduction and general information.

— Model tender forms and contract documents.

— Model preliminaries (q.v.) and standard preambles.

A separate schedule of descriptions and up to date prices is issued quarterly to subscribers.

The intention is to make available a standard and generally acceptable set of documents to assist mainly public sector organizations in carrying out their maintenance obligations and to meet the competitive tendering requirements of the Local Government Planning and Land Act 1980. Principal characteristics are:

— Each rate is broken down to form the basis for bonus measurement or material allocation.

— The only cost to local authorities is the annual subscription.

— Save only in minor matters, it complies with the Standard Method of Measurement, 6th Edition (SMM6) (q.v.).

— It can be used with contractors as well as direct labour organizations.

— Computer-based with a rationalized system of numbering.

— Comprehensive but mainly designed for housing maintenance.

— Simple to use.

— Generally acceptable to industry.

— Adaptable.

— Constantly monitored.

— Sponsored by the Building Employers Confederation and the Society of Chief Quantity Surveyors in Local Government.

See also: *Schedule of prices*.

**Negligence**

A category or branch of the law of tort (q.v.) and which is a rapidly developing area of the law. Negligence is not the same as carelessness or mistake: it is conduct and not a state of mind. It is the omission to do something that a reasonable man would do, or the doing of something that a prudent and reasonable man would not do.

A plaintiff (q.v.) suing in negligence must show:
— The defendant (q.v.) was under a duty of care (q.v.) to him.
— The defendant was in breach of that duty.
— As a result of the breach the plaintiff suffered damage (q.v.), which may be purely economic or financial ( *Junior Books Ltd v. The Veitchi Co. Ltd* (1982)).

The situations in which negligence may arise are endless. In *Donoghue v. Stevenson* (1932) Lord Macmillan said: 'The categories of negligence are never closed' and the boundaries of negligence are being extended constantly.

In relation to building contracts the most usual situations are:
— Negligent misstatements (q.v.).
— Negligent actions.

Negligence liability is important in the field of sub-contracting. Because of the doctrine of privity of contract (q.v.) the employer cannot sue the sub-contractor direct for bad work, unless there is a collateral contract (q.v.). The principle applies only to claims in contract and it is now clear (*Batty v. Metropolitan Property Realizations Ltd* (1978)) that there may be dual liability in contract and in tort. This means in this context that if the sub-contractor is guilty of negligent work which results in damage he is liable to be sued by the person who has suffered loss or damage. It is not all work which is not up to contract standard which is negligent and the plaintiff would have to establish negligence. Pure financial loss is covered and it is no longer necessary to establish personal injury or property damage.

The architect may be negligent in designing a building or in his supervision; the quantity surveyor may be negligent in preparing estimates of cost; and the contractor may be negligent in carrying out the work.

There is a large and, unfortunately, fast growing body of case law dealing with the negligence of architects, contractors and local authorities. Some of the more important cases are shown in Table 26. See also: *Care, standard of; Duty of care; Reasonable foreseeability.*

**Negligent misstatement/ misrepresentation**

Since 1963 it has been the law that a negligent misstatement which is acted upon can give rise to liability in tort (q.v.): *Hedley Byrne & Co. Ltd v. Heller & Partners Ltd* (1963). This is so even if only economic or financial loss results, as opposed to physical damage to person or property, though it appears that there must be some 'special relationship' between the maker of the statement and the recipient. Liability under the *Hedley Byrne* principle is not confined to factual statements, but extends to all forms of negligent advice, legal and financial, even if these are matters of opinion, e.g., advice as to probable building costs.

There can also be liability for negligent misrepresentation under s.2 (1) of the Misrepresentation Act 1967, which imposes liability in damages for negligent misrepresentations made in a pre-contractual situation. Under the Act, it is for the person making the representation to disprove his negligence, in contrast to the position at common law where the plaintiff bears the burden of proving negligence (q.v.). See also: *Misrepresentation.*

**Negotiated contract**

A contract which is not put out to tender, but where the price is agreed by negotiation between the parties. See also: *Code of Procedure for Two-Stage Selective Tendering.*

**Nemo dat quod non habet**

One cannot give what he has not got. A fundamental principle of law which is of great importance so far as the ownership of goods and materials is concerned.

# Table 26  Some major cases on negligence

| Name of case | Comment |
| --- | --- |
| **Anns v. Merton London Borough Council (1977)** | Defective foundations – local authorities under a duty of care to ensure buildings constructed in accordance with building regulations. Owners or occupiers may sue for breach of this duty |
| **Batty v. Metropolitan Property Realizations Ltd (1978)** | Builders and developers are people possessed of special skill. Dual liability in contract and tort. Liability to purchaser for negligent site survey |
| **Greaves & Co. (Contractors) Ltd v. Baynham, Meikle & Partners (1974)** | Liability of consultant engineers – liability for failure to meet higher standard imposed by contract even though reasonable care taken |
| **Hedley Byrne & Co. Ltd v. Heller & Partners Ltd (1963)** | Liability for negligent advice resulting in purely economic loss |
| **Junior Books Ltd v. The Veitchi Co. Ltd (1982)** | Liability of nominated sub-contractor to employer for consequential financial loss arising from defective work |
| **Pirelli General Cable Works Ltd v. Oscar Faber & Partners (1983)** | Limitation period begins to run when actual damage occurs, whether discoverable or not |
| **Sutcliffe v. Thackrah (1974)** | Architect liable for negligent certification – not quasi-arbitrator – potential liability to contractor |
| **William Hill Organisation Ltd v. Bernard Sunley & Sons Ltd (1982)** | Plaintiffs cannot claim a remedy in tort which is more than the contractual obligations assumed by the defendants |
| **Worlock v. SAWS & Rushmoor Borough Council** | Contractor's skill and care – liability of local authority for negligent inspection of foundations |

Although most standard contracts provide for ownership in goods and materials to pass when their value is included in interim certificates (q.v.) this is effective only in so far as the contractor owns the goods and materials. If they are sold to him subject to a retention of title (q.v.) clause, for example, ownership will not pass.

JCT 80, clause 16.1 and ACA 2, clause 6.1, are typical vesting clauses (q.v.) which provide for the property in goods and materials intended for the works to pass to the employer when the contractor has received payment. Such clauses are not binding on those who are not parties to the contract because of the doctrine of privity of contract (q.v.) and will not defeat the maxim *nemo dat quod non habet*. See also: *Retention of title*.

| | |
|---|---|
| **Nominal** | Less than the actual amount, small or trivial. Generally encountered in relation to money. A nominal sum of money is a sum so small as to be virtually worthless having regard to the circumstances. |

A court may award nominal damages to a plaintiff (q.v.), even though he has technically proved his case, because it considers that, by his conduct, he deserves no more; or nominal damages (usually £2) may be awarded for a technical breach of contract. An architect might charge only nominal fees, perhaps because he is hopeful of further commissions from the same client or because the client is a charity which he wishes to support. See also: *Copyright; Damages.*

| | |
|---|---|
| **Nominated sub-contractors** | Sub-contractors (q.v.) named by the employer. Architects often find it convenient to include sums in the contracts to be expended on nominated sub-contractors. However, the practice can give rise to considerable problems. JCT 80, clause 35, contains the most comprehensive provisions for nomination of sub-contractors. A special series of forms is available for tendering and sub-contract purposes (NSC/1, NSC/3, NSC/4 and NSC/4a). A form of Employer/ |

Nominated sub-contractor Agreement (NSC/2 or NSC/2a) is to be completed to form a contractual link between employer and nominated sub-contractor; the purpose is to give the employer redress direct against the nominated sub-contractor in certain specified instances. This agreement in no way affects the contractual relationships between the nominated sub-contractor and main contractor: *George E. Taylor & Co. Ltd v. G. Percy Trentham Ltd* (1980)). The nominated sub-contractor is responsible to the contractor for his work and the contractor is responsible to the employer for the whole of the work. Recent cases have shown that the nominated sub-contractor can be liable to the employer in tort for negligence, irrespective of any contractual relationship, or lack of it, between them (*Independent Broadcasting Authority v. EMI Electronics and BICC Construction Ltd* (1980) and *Junior Books Ltd v. The Veitchi Co Ltd* (1982)). Considerable difficulties may arise where a nominated sub-contractor fails and renomination is necessary (clause 35.24). The employer has a duty to renominate in such circumstances and the contractor has neither the duty nor the right to carry out the work himself: *North-West Metropolitan Regional Hospital Board v. T. A. Bickerton & Son Ltd* (1970).

---

**Nominated suppliers**  Provisions for the nomination of suppliers are found in JCT 80, clause 36. A nominated supplier can arise in one of four ways:
— If a prime cost sum is included in the contract bills (q.v.) and the supplier is named in the bills or by an instruction.
— If a provisional sum is included in the contract bills and in its expenditure the supply of goods or materials is made the subject of a prime cost sum in an instruction.
— If a provisional sum is included in the contract bills and the supply of goods and materials is from a single supplier by virtue of an instruction, the supply shall be made the subject of a prime cost sum and the

supplier is deemed to have been nominated.

— If a variation arises for supply of goods and materials for which there is a single supplier by virtue of an instruction, the supply shall be made the subject of a prime cost sum and the supplier deemed to have been nominated.

The clause provides that the architect shall only nominate (unless otherwise agreed) a supplier who will enter into a contract of sale with the contractor containing extensive provisions detailed in clause 36.4. A form of tender (TNS/1) is available. If the nominated sub-contractor limits, restricts or excludes his liability to the contractor, it in no way affects the operation of clause 36.4 unless the architect has approved the restrictions, etc., in writing.

**Nomination**

In general, the naming of a person or firm to undertake a particular task or office. In building contracts, nomination refers to the naming of a person or firm to undertake part of the work or to supply goods. Such nomination is done by the employer. Certain contracts, e.g., MW 80, make no provision for nomination. See also: *Nominated sub-contractors; Nominated suppliers.*

**Notices**

To give notice to a person means that the matter referred to in that notice has been brought to his attention. A person given notice cannot thereafter deny knowledge of the matter.

Notices may be of three kinds:

— Actual: The most usual kind of notice associated with building contracts is communicated from one party to another preferably in writing (q.v.) but sometimes orally. The difficulty about oral notices, of course, is in proving that they were ever given. A witness to an oral notice would be necessary.

— Imputed: Where an agent and principal are involved, a notice given to the agent is deemed (q.v.) to be given to the principal. Thus, a notice given by the contractor to the architect would be deemed to have been given to the employer provided the notice concerned something for which the architect was empowered to act as agent for the employer and provided there were no express terms in the contract to the contrary. In JCT clause 28.1.1, for example, the contractor is required to give the initial notice of default to the employer. It is thought that it would not be sufficient to give the notice to the architect. However, in clause 28.1.3, the contractor is allowed to give the determination notice to the employer *or* the architect.

— Constructive: Notice is deemed to have been given to a party if that party could have been aware of the notice by reasonable enquiry. An example is a notice posted on a site where development is to take place under the Town and Country Planning Act 1971, section 26.

Some contracts make express provision for notice to be given in a particular form or in a particular way. GC/Works/1, clause 1 (6) requires notice to be in writing, typescript or printed. A particularly important provision of the clause states that if a notice is sent by registered post or recorded delivery to the contractor's last known place of abode or business, it will be deemed to have been served on the date when, in the ordinary course of the post, it would have been delivered. Thus, the contractor will be deemed to have received it even if it is delayed for a day or two in the post. A similar provision in clause 23.1 of the ACA 2 form deems delivery two working days after pre-paid first-class posting.

It is important to comply precisely with contractual provisions with regard to notices. A party in default whose notice has expired may try to plead an irregularity in service if the matter comes before an arbitrator or the court. If the contract requires a notice to be sent by registered post, for example, and it was in fact delivered by hand, the court may judge that it was improperly served (but see: *Goodwin & Sons Ltd v. Fawcett* (1965)).

| | |
|---|---|
| **Notional** | Imaginary or speculative, not known for certain. In a building context, it is generally used with regard to sums of money. An architect, working on a percentage |

312

fee basis, may make a calculation of the likely total fee based on a notional figure for the contract sum (q.v.). If the quantity surveyor knows that he will be delayed in arriving at a final sum to represent loss and/or expense (q.v.) in a particular case, he may quickly arrive at a notional sum, i.e., what he expects the final sum will be, for the purposes of informing the architect what amount can, with safety, be paid to the contractor as an interim measure.

**Novation**

The substitution of a new contract for an existing one. It can only be done with the consent of all the parties concerned. Unlike assignment (q.v.) which involves a transfer of rights, novation consists of cancelling an existing obligation and then creating a new obligation in its place.

Clause 22.7 of ACA 2 refers expressly to novation. If the contractor's employment under the contract is terminated and the employer so requires, the contractor agrees and consents to the novation to the employer of the contractor's interest in and under any sub-contracts and to take all necessary steps to make the novation effective. This, of course, requires the sub-contractor's consent.

**Nuisance**

A category of the law of tort (q.v.). There are three types of nuisance:

— *Public Nuisance.*

An act or omission without lawful justification which causes damage, injury or inconvenience to the public at large. It is a crime as well as a tort. Examples are: obstructing the highway or keeping an immoral house. A private individual has a private remedy for public nuisance only if he suffers damage or inconvenience over and above that being caused to the public at large, e.g., where a builder's skip obstructs the highway and the access to private property. Prosecutions for public nuisance are rare.

— *Private Nuisance.*

An unlawful interference or annoyance which causes damage or annoyance to an owner or occupier of land in respect of his enjoyment of his land. Examples are: smell, smoke, noise, encroaching tree-roots, etc. A person wishing to sue for nuisance must prove actual damage. He may adopt self-help and abate the nuisance (see: *Abatement*), e.g., by cutting off the branches of overhanging trees, or he may sue for an injunction or damages or both. An action for nuisance can only be brought by a person with an interest in the land.

It is no defence to show that the nuisance existed before the plaintiff came to his land, but something that was originally a nuisance can be legalized by the passage of time. In *Sturges v. Bridgman* (1879), both principles are illustrated. The defendant had used some noisy machinery for more than 20 years, but the vibrations caused by it only became a nuisance when the plaintiff erected a consulting room at the end of his garden near the noise. It was held that time only begins to run when the act in fact became a nuisance and that in the circumstances the defendant could not rely on prescriptive right.

— *Statutory Nuisance*.

Something declared to be a nuisance by statute, e.g., by ss. 91 and 92 of the Public Health Act 1936, which among other things lists 'any premises in such a state as to be prejudicial to health or a nuisance'. The remedy is by way of an abatement notice served by the local authority (q.v.) on the person responsible. If an abatement notice is not complied with, or the nuisance is likely to re-occur, the offender can be taken before the magistrates' court which may make a nuisance order and/or impose a fine.

**Null**  Invalid. Devoid of legal effect. See also: *Void*.

**Oaths and affirmations**

The general rule is that all witnesses must give evidence (q.v.) on oath or affirmation in proceedings before a Court and this is often followed in arbitration. Section 12(2) of the Arbitration Act 1950 gives the arbitrator a discretion whether or not to examine the witnesses on oath or affirmation and section 12(3) gives him the power to do so.

The current general rules about oaths and affirmations are found in the Oaths Act 1978. A false statement on oath or affirmation amounts to the criminal offence of perjury.

The usual form of oath in civil proceedings is: 'I swear by Almighty God that the evidence I shall give shall be the truth, the whole truth, and nothing but the truth.'

The person taking the oath holds the New Testament or, in the case of a Jew, the Old Testament, in his uplifted hand, and says or repeats this formula after the person administering the oath.

Witnesses not of the Christian or Jewish faith may take the oath with the appropriate ceremonies which are binding on them but, if this would cause delay or inconvenience, they may be required to affirm instead. This also applies to any person who objects to being sworn, e.g., a Quaker. Such people solemnly affirm by repeating after the administrator: 'I, ABC, do solemnly, sincerely and truly declare and affirm that the evidence I shall give shall be the truth, the whole truth, and nothing but the truth.'

In Scotland the oath is administered in a slightly

different way, with uplifted hand but without either Testament, by repeating the words of the oath after the judge or arbitrator, who stands up and holds up his right hand similarly, while saying the words to be repeated. Anyone who wishes to take the oath in the Scottish manner may do so in any part of the United Kingdom.

| **Obiter Dictum** | Part of a judgment (q.v.) which is not the *ratio decidendi* (q.v.) or reason for the decision. It is a statement of law made by the judge in the course of a judgment (q.v.) which is not necessary to the decision or based upon the facts as found. A statement is *obiter* if: |

— It is based on facts which were not found to exist or which, if so found, were not material.

— It is a statement of law which, although it may be based on facts as found, is not material to the decision.

For example, in *Rondel v. Worsley* (1969) the House of Lords expressed certain opinions that a barrister might be liable for negligence (q.v.) when acting other than as an advocate and that immunity extended to solicitors when acting as advocates. The case was concerned only with a barrister's liability when acting as advocate and so these opinions were *obiter*.

It is often difficult to decide what is and what is not *obiter dictum* until a later court considers a previous case and isolates the basis of the previous decision. Thus, statements long thought to be part of the *ratio* are sometimes put to one side.

Words said *obiter* may be persuasive in future cases, depending upon the circumstances and the standing of the judge. In the absence of direct authority, they may form the basis of future actions.

| **Obscurities** | Things which are not clear. See: *Ambiguity*. |

| **Obstruction** | JCT 80, clause 28.1.1, specifies interference with or obstruction by the employer of the issue of any certificate due under the contract as a ground on which |

the contractor may determine his employment under the contract. Other standard form contracts contain similar provisions, e.g., ACA 2, clause 20.2 (b), IFC 84, clause 7.5.2, etc.

There is a considerable body of case law on what constitutes interference or obstruction, but for the most part it deals with the contractor's right to recover money without a certificate where the employer has interfered with the independent exercise of the architect's powers as certifier. In such a case the contractor can sue without a certificate: *Hickman & Co. v. Roberts* (1913).

In *R.B. Burden Ltd v. Swansea Corporation* (1957), it was said that 'the clause is designed to meet such conduct of the employer as refusing to allow the architect to go on site for the purpose of giving his certificate, or directing the architect as to the amount for which he is to give his certificate or as to the decision which he should arrive at on some matter within the sphere of his independent duty. I do not think that negligence or omissions by someone who, at the request or with the consent, of the architect, is appointed to assist him in arriving at the correct figure to insert in his certificate can amount to interference ...': Lord Tucker. It seems, therefore, that in this context, obstruction is used in the sense of impeding. In a different context, obstruction by the employer with the contractor's carrying out of the works, etc., amounts to prevention or hindrance which will be a breach of an implied term of the contract.

| **Occupation** | This term refers to the actual physical control or use of land. Title to certain personal property (q.v.) may be acquired by occupation, e.g., taking physical control of it, as is the case with such things as fish, game, etc. See also: *Occupier; Occupiers' liability.* |

| **Occupier** | Someone who owns and occupies land or other premises and who has actual use of that land, etc. An occupier owes a duty of care (q.v.) to third parties under the Occupiers' Liability Act 1957, as amended. |

In *Wheat v. E. Lacon & Co. Ltd* (1966), Lord Denning MR said: 'Wherever a person has sufficient degree of control over premises that he ought to realize that any failure on his part to use care may result in injury to a person coming lawfully there, then he is an "occupier" and the person coming lawfully there is his "visitor" and thus is under a duty to his visitor to use reasonable care.' See also: *Dangerous premises; Occupiers' liability*.

**Occupiers' liability**

The Occupiers' Liability Act 1957 provides (s. 2) that an occupier of premises owes 'the common duty of care' to his 'visitors', who are those invited or permitted by him to be there, including those who enter under legal authority, e.g., a police officer. The occupier in this context means the person who has physical control or possession of the premises, and may include the landlord: *Wheat v. E. Lacon & Co. Ltd* (1966). A trespasser is not a 'visitor' for the purposes of the Act, the duty to trespassers being contained in the Occupiers' Liability Act 1984, which replaced the rather complex common law rules. The common duty of care is defined as being a duty to take such care as in all the circumstances is reasonable in order to ensure that the visitor will be reasonably safe in using the premises for the purposes for which the occupier invited or permitted him to be there. It does not impose on the occupier any obligation in respect of risks willingly accepted by the visitor as his. The occupier must be prepared for children to be less careful than adults, and may expect that a person, in the exercise of his trade or calling, will appreciate and guard against risks ordinarily incident to it so far as the occupier leaves him free to do so.

The duty can be discharged by a reasonable warning of any known danger, but it should be noted that as a result of s. 2(1) of the Unfair Contract Terms Act 1977 (q.v.) it is not possible by means of a notice to exclude or restrict liability for death or personal injury resulting from *negligence* (q.v.).

The obligations imposed by the Act apply to all those occupying or having control over any fixed or movable structure or any premises or structure, e.g., scaffolding, and so a sub-contractor may be an 'occupier' in respect of his part of the works. Trespassers are owed a lesser duty under the 1984 Act, which also affords some protection to people exercising rights of access to the countryside or using private rights of way. Section 1 (3) of the 1984 Act says that an occupier owes a duty to a trespasser, etc., only if '(a) he is aware of the danger or has reasonable grounds to believe that it exists; (b) he knows or has reasonable grounds to believe that the other is in (or may come into) the vicinity of the danger ...; and (c) the risk is one against which, in all the circumstances of the case, he may reasonably be expected to offer the other some protection'.

The lesser duty is to take such care as is reasonable in all the circumstances of the case to see that the entrant does not suffer *injury* (not property damage) on the premises by reason of the danger concerned' s.1 (4). This duty can be excluded altogether by an appropriately worded notice.

---

**Offer**

An expression by one party of willingness to be bound by some obligation to another. If the offer is accepted, a binding contract results.

An offer may be made in writing or orally or by conduct. It may be made to an individual or group or to the whole world (*Carlill v. Carbolic Smoke Ball Co.* (1893)). An offer terminates:

— If rejected by the offeree.
— If revoked by the offeror before acceptance.
— If either party dies before acceptance.
— If a time limit is stipulated and it expires before acceptance.
— By lapse of time, if not accepted within a reasonable time, and no time limit has been specified.

It is important to note that if one party rejects the offer by another and subsequently decides to accept the offer after all, the offer is no longer available for acceptance unless the offeror agrees. If an offer is made by post, it is only revoked when the offeree receives the revocation. If he has already posted his acceptance (q.v.) the revocation is of no effect and a full binding contract is formed.

A tender (q.v.) is an offer. An invitation to tender (q.v.) is not an offer but what is known as an 'invitation to treat' or an invitation to make an offer.

| | |
|---|---|
| **Official Referees** | Specialist circuit judges who deal with construction industry business. Although they have the status of Circuit Judges, they are High Court Judges in function. There are six Official Referees, the senior of whom is usually styled the Senior Official Referee. They are based at the High Court in the Strand, although if the majority of witnesses live at a distance from London or in other special cases they will sit at a location which is convenient to the parties. |

The Official Referees are not concerned exclusively with the construction industry, but form in effect a Construction Industry Court because the industry is the major user of their services. The main types of action dealt with by the Official Referees are:

– Claims by and against architects, engineers, surveyors and other professionals in contract and in tort.

– Claims relating to building, civil engineering and construction generally. These include a great many cases involving the interpretation of the standard form contracts such as JCT 80.

– Claims by and against local authorities in respect of their statutory duties, especially those relating to the building regulations, public health and building legislation generally.

– Claims relating to work done and materials supplied or services rendered.

Many of the cases are lengthy and complex and involve highly technical issues as well as difficult points of law. Long cases are often divided into sub-trials. Under the Rules of the Supreme Court, Order 58, there is a limited right of appeal direct to the Court of Appeal from a decision of an Official Referee on a point of law and on a question of fact relevant to a charge of fraud or breach of professional duty, but not otherwise. In consequence, many cases of importance are finally disposed of by the Official Referees.

The majority of construction industry disputes which proceed to litigation are listed as 'Official Referee's business' and the initial proceedings may now be specially marked in this way.

An important but little-known aspect of their functions is the duty imposed on them to sit as arbitrators to decide any matter referred to them by agreement between the parties: Arbitration Act 1950, s.11. This service is little used in practice.

The more important judgments of the Official Referees are now reported regularly in *Construction Law Reports*, published by The Architectural Press Ltd. See also: *Courts; Scott schedule.*

---

**Off-site materials**

Materials which are intended to be used on the works but which, for convenience or safety, are not stored on site. Whether the contractor is to receive payment for such materials is generally left to the discretion of the architect. (MW 80 and GC/Works/1 make no provision for payment for off-site materials.) The problem is twofold. On the one hand the contractor may be seriously financially embarrassed if he has paid for large quantities of materials and he may be tempted to bring them on to site and risk damage to obtain payment; however, the JCT forms of contract do not permit interim payments for materials brought on to site prematurely. On the other hand, the employer must be certain that he becomes the owner of goods for which he has paid and that no other party retains an interest in the materials or goods (see: *Retention of title*). It is generally not in the employer's interest to pay for materials off-site because of the difficulty which may be experienced in proving ownership if, for example, the contractor becomes insolvent (q.v.). However, the architect may, in some instances, judge it expedient to do so and the forms which allow it lay down stringent conditions.

ACA 2 makes payment subject to whatever conditions the contract documents (q.v.) may provide.

JCT 80, clause 30.3 provides:

— Materials must be intended for incorporation.

— Nothing must remain to be done to the materials before incorporation.

— They have been set apart and marked to identify the employer and the works.

— The contract for supply between contractor and supplier is in writing and expressly provides that property (ownership) shall pass to the contractor or sub-contractor not later than the time at which they are set aside and marked as above.

— Any sub-contractor concerned shall provide similar guarantees.

— The materials are in accordance with the contract.

— The contractor provides reasonable proof that he owns the materials.

— The contractor provides reasonable proof as regards insurance against loss.

See also: *Ownership of goods and materials*.

**Omissions**

In the context of building contracts, 'omissions' refer to work or materials which have been priced by the contractor and included in the contract sum, but which the employer no longer requires. The architect issues an instruction to omit the work or materials and the omitted work is valued and an appropriate adjustment made in the next financial certificate.

An omission may also refer, if so provided by the contract, to the removal of obligations or restrictions imposed by the contract documents on the contractor in respect of working space, working hours, etc., e.g., JCT 80, clause 13.1.2. See also: *Variation*.

**Omitted work**

All the standard forms contain provision for the architect to omit work from the contract. Without such a provision, an instruction to omit work would amount to a breach of contract. In general, the value of omitted work is ascertained by reference to the rates in the bills of quantities (q.v.) or the priced specification (q.v.) or priced schedule of rates (q.v.). ACA 2, however, contains provisions (clause 17) for the contractor to submit estimates which are to be agreed. The principal clauses relating to the valuation of omitted work are: JCT 80, clause 13.5.2; GC/Works/1, clause 9 (1); IFC 84, clause 3.7.2; MW 80, clause 3.6. See also: *Variations*.

**Operational bills of quantities**

A system of setting out bills of quantities (q.v.) with regard to operations rather than the more usual trade bills.

The series of operations are predetermined as is the order in which they are carried out. The materials only are measured by the quantity surveyor; it is the contractor's responsibility when pricing to allow for the labour required for each operation. Individual prices are totalled to obtain the total tender sum.

The system has not found great favour, probably because it is not usual for the contractor to be informed of the order in which he is to carry out the work. He may well be able to carry out the total work at a cheaper overall price if left to his own order of working. The system probably works best when the tender is to be negotiated, so that the contractor can discuss the order of work before bills are prepared.

**Order**

A direction of a court. All directions of a court in any proceedings are termed 'orders' unless they amount to a decree of judgment.

The term is also used to refer to the procedural rules of the courts, e.g., the Rules of the Supreme Court (contained in the 'White Book') which are sub-divided into orders.

A typical Court Order is shown as Figure 22.

**Order 14 procedure**

See: *Summary judgment*.

**Overheads**

Generally, the costs of head office administration proportioned to each contract. Included are staff working on the individual contracts and general support staff, rates, electricity, heating, telephones,

# Figure 22

## Typical court order

IN THE     BLANKSHIRE     **COUNTY COURT.**

BETWEEN    J.A.CREDITOR LTD     PLAINTIFF

AND

⌐                        ¬

A.DEBTOR        DEFENDANT

L                        ⌐     CASE No.     84 00295

ON THE APPLICATION OF    the Defendant

and the court being satisfied that the defendant is unable to pay and discharge the sum payable by

him in this action [or the instalments due under the judgment or order in this action].

(1) Delete as necessary

IT IS ORDERED ~~that the judgment or order be suspended(¹)~~

the warrant of execution issued in this action be suspended(¹)

~~the warrant of committal issued in this action be suspended for(¹) (²)~~

(2) State time.

upon the following terms, namely:-

that the defendant, do pay into the office of this court [~~or to the office of~~

~~the~~ _____ ~~County Court]~~ the sum of £ 2,586.14p.

[by instalments of £ 150         for every calendar month, the first instalment to be paid] on

or before the   27 July 1984

~~OR~~

~~that the defendant be discharged from custody under the warrant of committal~~(³)

(3) State terms including liability to re-arrest if so ordered.

DATED    3 July 1984

---

**METHOD OF PAYMENT**

*By calling at the Court Office* Payment may be made in cash or by BANKER'S DRAFT, GIROBANK DRAFT (if a Girobank account holder) or by CHEQUE SUPPORTED BY A CHEQUE CARD SUBJECT TO THE CURRENT CONDITIONS FOR ITS USE. Drafts and cheques must be made payable to H.M. PAYMASTER GENERAL and crossed.

PAYMENT OTHERWISE THAN AT THE COURT OFFICE COUNTER DURING OFFICE OPENING HOURS IS AT THE PAYER'S OWN RISK.

Remittances to the court by post must be by POSTAL ORDER, BANKER'S DRAFT OR GIROBANK DRAFT (if a Girobank account holder) only, made payable to H.M. PAYMASTER GENERAL and crossed. Cheques, giro cheques and stamps are not accepted. Payment cannot be received by bank or giro credit transfer.

This form should be enclosed and postage must be prepaid. A stamped addressed envelope must be enclosed to enable this form, with a receipt, to be returned to you.

---

Address all communications to the Chief Clerk AND QUOTE THE ABOVE CASE NUMBER

THE COURT OFFICE at   The Castle, Blanktown, Blankshire

is open from 10 a.m. to 4 p.m. Monday to Friday

**N.41**   Order suspending judgment, order, execution or committal.
Order 25, Rule 8(1)

S5689 (25268) Dd.8332666 75m 1/83 G.W.B.Ltd. Gp.870

office equipment, etc. There is often much dispute, when a claim arises, as to the proportion of overheads to be allowed. Formulae are sometimes used to arrive at overheads, but they are not universally accepted. See also: *Eichleay Formula; Emden Formula; Hudson Formula.*

**Ownership of goods and materials**

If goods and materials are unfixed, the employer must take care that he does not pay for them unless he is sure that, on payment, ownership passes to him. The situation was highlighted in *Dawber Williamson Roofing Ltd v. Humberside County Council* (1979). The contract was on JCT 63. The contractor had sub-contracted the roofing to the plaintiffs on the 'blue form'. The blue form provided that the sub-contractor should be deemed to 'have knowledge' of the terms of the main contract. JCT 63 provided that ownership of materials was to pass to the employer when their value had been paid to the main contractor by the employer. The main contractor went into liquidation (q.v.) after the employer had paid him for slates delivered to site by the plaintiffs, but before the main contractor had paid the plaintiffs. It was held that the plaintiffs were entitled to recover the slates and damages or the value of the slates. In effect, the employer was put into the position of paying twice for the same goods because the contractor had no title in the slates to pass on to the employer and there was no privity of contract (q.v.) between employer and sub-contractor. JCT 80 and NSC/4 and NSC/4a have been amended in an attempt to rectify the situation. The situation is complex and architects should check that title has passed to the contractor (in so far as that is possible) before certifying unfixed materials. See also: *Retention of title; Vesting clause.*

| | |
|---|---|
| **PC** | Initials representing Prime Cost (q.v.). |
| **Package deal contracts** | Sometimes known as 'design and build contracts' because they incorporate both elements in one package (hence 'package deal'). Figure 23 compares this type of contract with the traditional form. The main benefit, from the employer's point of view, is that the package deal places all the responsibility for the work, from taking the initial brief to completion of the work, in one place – with the contractor. If something goes wrong or there are defects, the employer is not faced with the usual problem of sorting out design from constructional responsibilities. On the other hand, the employer has no independent advice on which to call if he is in doubt since the contractor, however kindly motivated, will have his own financial interests at heart. An unscrupulous contractor could take advantage of the employer's lack of expertise. It is up to the employer to weigh the pros and cons before deciding which system to adopt or else appoint a professional to supervise the work on his behalf. See also: *Design and build contract; Turnkey contract*. |
| **Parol evidence** | Once a contract has been reduced to writing 'verbal evidence is not allowed to be given ... so as to add to or subtract from, or in any manner to vary or qualify the written contract': *Goss v. Nugent* (1833). This basic rule of interpretation is called the parol evidence rule. It covers not only oral evidence but other extrinsic evidence as well: drafts, pre-contract letters. |

## Figure 23
Package deal contract

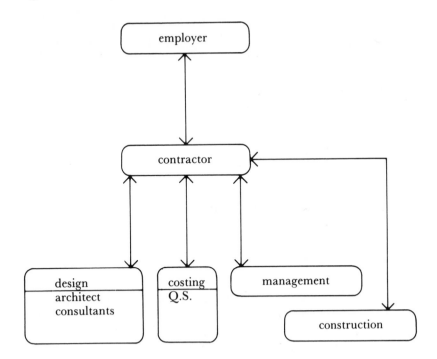

Traditional contract

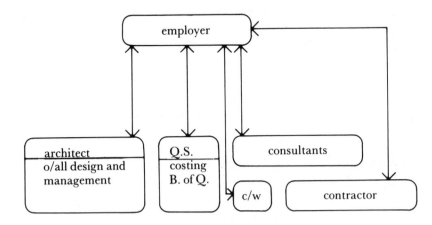

⟵————⟶ lines of contractual relationship

etc., are all excluded. It also prevents evidence being given of preliminary negotiations between the contracting parties.

It is subject to exceptions. Thus, it does not apply where misrepresentation (q.v.) is alleged or where one party claims that there is a collateral contract (q.v.). However, it remains a basic rule when interpreting written or printed contracts.

Since most building contracts are in standard form, various optional clauses may be deleted and there may be typewritten or manuscript amendments. Logically the rule would exclude a court or arbitrator from looking at the deletions. In fact the House of Lords has ruled that one is entitled to look at the deleted words 'as part of the surrounding circumstances in the light of which one must construe what [the parties] have chosen to leave in': *Mottram Consultants Ltd v. Bernard Sunley & Sons, Ltd* (1974). 'Surrounding circumstances' is an imprecise phrase which can be illustrated but hardly defined. 'In a commercial contract it is certainly right that the court should know the commercial purpose of the contract and this in turn presupposes knowledge of the genesis of the transaction, the background, the context, the market in which the parties are operating' and so on: Lord Wilberforce.

Extrinsic evidence will also be admitted to explain the written agreement, and in particular to show the meaning of individual words and phrases used by the parties. The starting point is the ordinary English usage as defined in a standard dictionary, but both courts and arbitrators must give effect to any special technical, trade or customary meaning which the parties intended the word to bear. See also: *Interpretation of contracts*.

| | |
|---|---|
| **Partial possession** | All the standard forms (except MW 80 and IFC 84) make provision for the employer to take possession of part of the works before completion. If partial possession is required under IFC 84, a special clause (2.11) must be inserted in the printed form. The text |

of the clause is given in Practice Note IN/1. Under GC/Works/1 (clause 28A) the SO can instruct the contractor to allow partial possession. In other forms, the contractor's agreement is required. On partial possession:

— The architect must issue a certificate to that effect.

— The certificate must state the value of the work taken over. (This is for the purposes of the contract only.)

— Half the retention in respect of the part taken over must be released.

— The amount of liquidated damages must be reduced in proportion to the value of the work taken over to the total contract sum.

— The contractor's liability, if any, for the insurance of the part is removed.

For partial possession to have contractual significance, it requires a formal act such as the issue of a certificate stating the date on which possession took place. Partial possession will not be implied if the employer simply moves items of furniture into the part in question: *English Industrial Estates Corporation v. George Wimpey & Co. Ltd* (1972).

Partial possession is not the same thing as *Sectional completion* (q.v.). Where it is known at the outset that completion is required in sections the contract must be amended accordingly. JCT 80 has a special supplement for the purpose.

| | |
|---|---|
| **Partnership** | A way of carrying on business which is governed by the Partnership Act 1890. It is defined as 'The relation which subsists between persons carrying on business in common with a view of profit.' It is the most common type of professional business arrangement. The characteristics of a partnership are that the partners share profits and losses (not necessarily equally) and they carry on the business together. Each partner carries unlimited liability for partnership debts. It is known as 'joint and several liability' because they are liable together and independently. Thus, a creditor may sue the |

partnership or an individual partner to recover a debt. For example, if a partnership runs into debt which the assets of the firm will not cover and one partner removes himself from the jurisdiction (q.v.), the other partner or partners will be liable for the whole of the debt to the full extent of their personal assets.

Unlike a limited company (q.v.), a partnership has no independent existence beyond the partners themselves. If a partner dies or becomes bankrupt (q.v.), the partnership comes to an end. It also ends when a partner retires or a new partner is taken into the firm. The maximum number of partners is normally twenty, but certain professional partnerships are allowed to have an unlimited number of partners, e.g., architects, surveyors, estate agents, solicitors, accountants, etc.

Each partner has the power to bind the others in regard to any matter concerning the partnership. Partners may be bound even though a partner acts beyond his authority if the general public has reason to believe that he is acting on behalf of the partnership. For this reason, all partners must show the utmost good faith in their dealings with one another. That means revealing all matters to one another which may effect the partnership. It is not necessary, although desirable, to draw a deed of partnership; a simple written or oral agreement will suffice. Whether or not a partnership exists is a matter of fact. A court will look at all the circumstances. Sharing of profit and loss suggests a partnership, but the situation, particularly in small firms, may be confused. Frequently, employees share in the profits by way of bonuses. Therefore, some indication that a person has a more fundamental interest is required, e.g., involvement in the making of policy decisions. A person may be deemed to be a partner if he is represented on office stationery as such, whatever the internal arrangements of the firm may be. Where some members of a firm are named as 'associates' or 'executives', it is desirable that their names are separated from the names of the partners on the firm's notepaper or they may well find themselves becoming liable in the event of the firm becoming insolvent (q.v.). See also: *Liability*.

**Party wall**
A technical term used to describe a particular type of wall between properties. There are three categories of party wall. First, and most commonly, where the wall is divided vertically, the whole wall being subject to reciprocal easements (q.v.). Secondly, where the wall is divided vertically into strips, one belonging to each adjoining owner. Thirdly, where the wall belongs entirely to one owner, subject to his neighbour's rights to have it maintained as a dividing wall (*Watson v. Gray* (1880)). See Figure 24. The basic rights are those of support and user over the structure, and there is nothing to prevent one owner demolishing his half of the wall so long as he does not disturb his neighbour's right of support (*Kempston v. Butler* (1861)). Where one person owns the whole of the wall, he may do as he likes with it subject to resulting damage in negligence or other statutory controls if he demolishes his building.

The position in London is governed by the London Building Act 1930 and Part V of the London Building Acts (Amendment) Act 1939, as amended, the effect of which is to override some of the common law rules. The provisions are too detailed to be dealt with here and reference may usefully be made to V. Powell-Smith's *Boundaries and Fences* (2nd edn, 1975), pp. 155-64.

**Passing of risk**
Goods and materials are said to be at someone's risk when he is liable for the accidental loss of or damage to them.

The basic presumption in sales of goods is that the initial presumption as to risk will move to the buyer at the same time as ownership is transferred to him (Sale of Goods Act 1979, s. 20), but the parties to a contract can always provide otherwise, and this is almost invariably the case under the standard forms

**Figure 24**
Party wall categories (plan views)

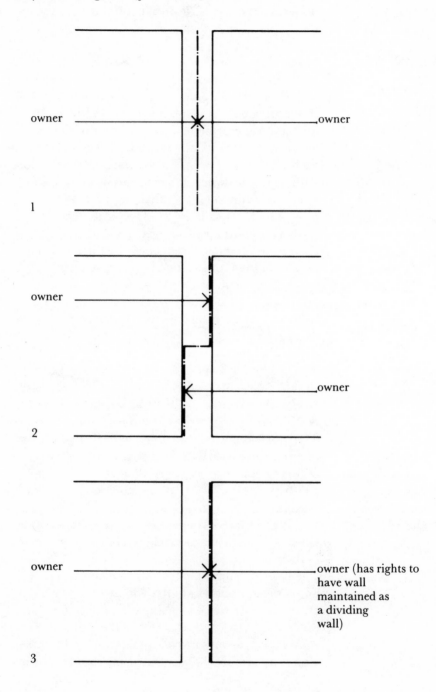

owner           owner

1

owner

owner

2

owner           owner (has rights to
have wall
maintained as
a dividing
wall)

3

of building contract in common use where, although ownership may pass to the employer, e.g., on incorporation (q.v.), into the works or on payment, the risk remains with the contractor. For example, under JCT 80, the contractor's obligation (clause 2.1) is to 'carry out and complete the Works ...' He does not fulfil that obligation until the architect certifies practical completion. The passing of property does not, in this instance, transfer the risk. ACA 2, clause 6.2, is an explicit clause to the same effect: 'The risk of loss or damage to any Section or to the Works shall remain with the contractor until the taking-over of such Section or of the Works, as the case may be.' See also: *Sale of goods*.

**Patent**

A Crown grant of sole rights with regard to an invention. The grant is normally valid for a period of twenty years from the date the specification is filed. Payment in respect of patent rights (i.e., the right to use a patented article or process belonging to another) is generally the responsibility of the contractor. JCT 80, clause 9, deems such sums to have been included in the contract sum (q.v.) and provides that the contractor shall indemnify the employer against any claims arising from the infringement of patent rights by the contractor (clause 9.1). The contractor is not liable to indemnify the employer and moneys payable shall be added to the contract sum where the contractor is complying with architect's instructions. GC/Works/1, clause 15, is a broadly similar provision.

**Patent defect**

A defect which is discoverable by reasonable inspection. In the context of the building contract, the term embraces all the items which the architect or the clerk of works might be expected to find and bring to the contractor's attention so that remedial work can be carried out. Patent defects are plain to see, or, at least, that is the theory. Whether the architect could or should have seen defects on site during site visits has exercised more than one judicial mind. Where the final certificate (q.v.) is conclusive or partially so, its issue may preclude the employer from bringing any proceedings against the contractor for patent defects. See also: *Inspector; Latent defects; Supervision.*

**Payment into court**

In any action for debt or damages the defendant may pay money into court in satisfaction of all or any of the plaintiff's claims. He may do this at any time after acknowledging service of the writ (q.v.) – even after the trial of the action has begun. The payment in may be made with or without a denial of liability. If the plaintiff accepts the amount paid in, he can discontinue the action by taking the money out of court. He is then entitled to his costs to the date of payment in. Alternatively, he can leave the money in court and continue with his action. The judge will not be told of the payment in until all questions of liability and damages have been determined.

If, in the event, the plaintiff recovers less or no more than the amount paid in then in the majority of cases he will have to pay the whole costs of the action, including the defendant's costs, from the date of payment in. See also: *Costs; Sealed offer.*

**Payments**

Usually made by the employer to the contractor as the work progresses. On very small jobs, the payment may be one lump sum when the contract is finished. All the standard forms provide for interim certificates (q.v.) to be issued by the architect before payment is made. See also: *Advances; Certificates; Performance; Stage payments.*

**Penalty**

Sums of money inserted in a contract which is extravagant and unconscionable, the purpose being to coerce a party to performance. A 'penalty clause' is invalid and the sum is irrecoverable in contrast to liquidated damages (q.v.).

Although many contractors think otherwise, sums inserted in the usual 'liquidated and ascertained damages' clauses in standard form building contracts are moderate, and there appears to be no reported case in which a sum has been disallowed as a 'penalty' because of its amount under a building contract. It is wrong to speak of liquidated damages clauses as 'penalty clauses'.

| | |
|---|---|
| **Performance** | The carrying out of an obligation imposed by contract or statute. In building contracts *complete performance*, where the contractor carries out the whole of the works in accordance with the contract documents and the employer pays the contract sum (q.v.), will discharge the contract. *Partial performance* by one party may be sufficient evidence of his intention to be bound by the terms of a contract if he has not made formal acceptance. Whether or not performance is complete is a matter for the courts to decide in each particular case. The point is particularly important where payment depends upon the whole of the work being completed. The courts will, however, grant relief to the contractor who can show, in such a case, that he has achieved *substantial performance,* i.e., the work is complete save for some minor omissions or defects. In *Hoenig v. Isaacs* (1952), Denning L. J. said: 'Where a contract provides for a specific sum to be paid on completion of specified work, the courts lean against a construction of the contract which would deprive the contractor of any payment at all simply because there are some defects or omissions.' See also: *Entire contract; Specific performance.* |

| | |
|---|---|
| **Performance bonds** | See: *Bonds.* |

| | |
|---|---|
| **Performance specification** | An alternative to the specification (q.v.) as traditionally understood. Instead of describing precisely all the work and all materials required in a building, the performance specification sets out criteria which must be met by the contractor. The idea is to give the contractor maximum scope for initiative and price competition. For example, a traditional specification might describe an external wall in terms of type of brick, number of courses to a given height, thickness of wall, size of cavity, material |

for the internal leaf, insulation type and thickness, wall ties, DPC, etc. A performance specification would require that the wall would last a given number of years, be waterproof, have a given $U$-value, have a certain colour range, have certain maintenance characteristics, etc. The criteria may be very precise or very broad and commonly contain the overall requirement of compliance with building regulations (q.v.) and British Standards.

The writing of a performance specification is a skilled task and may take longer than a traditional specification. It is a mistake, therefore, to use a performance specification to attempt to overcome pressing deadlines. It is important to make a clear distinction, in the specification, between those criteria which are mandatory and those which are at the contractor's discretion. Outline dimensioned drawings are usually provided with the specification and form part of the contract. The other essential part of the contract documentation is the contractor's proposals. JCT Design and Build Contract (q.v.) provides a list of the contract documents in clause 2.1. Very often, the architect will prepare a performance specification for work for which he intends to invite tenders with a view to nomination (q.v.). A lift installation is a good example of work which requires a performance specification in order that a proper comparison of prices can be made.

| **Period of delay** | A term used in JCT 80 (Appendix) to refer to the continuous period of time for which the works can be suspended as a result of outside causes before the contractor is entitled to determine his employment under clause 28.1.3. Two periods are provided for:<br>— Delay by reason of loss or damage caused by any one of the Clause 22 perils (usually three months).<br>— Delay for any other reason (usually one month).<br>See also: *Determination; Frustration.* |
|---|---|
| **Persistent neglect** | A term used in JCT 80 (clause 27.1.3) and IFC 84 (clause 7.1(c)). If the contractor refuses or *persistently neglects* to comply with a written notice from the architect requiring him to remove defective work or |

improper materials or goods and, in consequence, the works are materially affected (q.v.), the employer will have grounds for determination of the contractor's employment. The written notice would be one given under clause 8.4 of the JCT 80 form (clause 3.1.4 of the IFC 84 form). For the contractor to 'persistently neglect' to comply it would not be enough if he did not comply immediately. The employer would have to show that the neglect had carried on over a period of time. What the period of time would be would depend upon individual circumstances and whether the works were materially affected thereby. In practice, it is usually quite clear if persistent neglect is taking place.

| **Personal injury** | See: *Injury to persons.* |
|---|---|

| **Personal property** | Also called personalty. All forms of property other than freehold estates and interests in land. It is contrasted with real property (q.v.) and covers everything (other than freehold estates and interests) which is capable of being owned. Some things are incapable of being owned, e.g., the air or running water. Such an item is known as *res nullius* – a thing belonging to nobody. Personal property is not confined to tangible objects, which are known as *chattels*, but includes intangible rights such as debts and copyright. Rights of this sort are called *choses in action* (q.v.) as opposed to *choses in possession*. For example, a lender of money has a present right to repayment from the borrower – a chose in action. That right is a property right enforceable by means of legal action and may, subject to conditions, be transferred to a third party by assignment (q.v.). Leasehold interests are, for historical reasons, classified as personal property and are called *chattels real* in contrast to *chattels personal*. Figure 28 shows the position in diagram form. |
|---|---|

| **Personal representative** | An executor or administrator of the estate of a deceased person. He is a trustee and stands in the |
|---|---|

shoes of the deceased. In contractual terms, a personal representative is a named person acting as agent for one of the parties with full authority. The architect is not the personal representative of the employer. See also: *Agency; Representative; Trust.*

**Person-in-charge**

Clause 10 of JCT 80 and clause 3.4 of IFC 84 provide for the contractor to keep a competent person-in-charge constantly upon the works. The person is clearly intended to be the site agent or foreman and he is to be capable of receiving instructions from the architect, such instructions being deemed (q.v.) to have been given to the contractor himself. The term is also mentioned in MW 80, in clause 3.3. The difference, however, is that he need not be constantly upon the works, but only at all reasonable times. What is reasonable will depend upon the size and complexity of the work and, if known, the dates of the architect's visits. See also: *Competent; Site manager.*

**Plaintiff**

The party who complains and brings proceedings in the High Court or the County Court. The party against whom the proceedings are brought is called the Defendant. In arbitration (q.v.) the parties are called Claimant and Respondent respectively. Procedure in the courts is governed by delegated legislation (q.v.) made by special committees under statutory authority. In arbitration, the arbitrator is under no obligation to follow the procedure of the High Court, and the procedural rules should be agreed at the preliminary meeting. In Scotland the parties to litigation are called the Pursuer and Defender.

**Planning consent**

The Town and Country Planning Act 1971 is the principal Act dealing with the control of development. A multitude of supplementary Acts, General Development Orders and Regulations have modified and amended the original Act. Control is exercised by local planning authorities and, except in a few clearly defined instances, application must be made to the planning authority if it is desired to carry out development which is defined in section 22 of the Act. It is often prudent to obtain *outline permission* before making a detailed application. It involves a minimum of drawings and information being submitted and the authority will either give or refuse consent to the principle of the development, for example, whether an office block would be permitted in a particular area. The obtaining of *detailed permission* will involve full details being submitted. Development must begin within five years of the date of the planning permission or the permission lapses. If outline permission has been obtained, application must be made for detailed permission within three years. The authority have wide powers to make conditions on the permission and to reserve matters for further approval. Appeal may be made to the Secretary of State for the Environment against refusal of planning permission.

Planning regulations are exceedingly complex and the advice of the local planning officer should always be sought when any development is contemplated. See also: *Building line; Notice.*

**Plans**

A very general word of imprecise meaning. It is usually taken to mean the drawings to a small scale showing work to be carried out. A 'plan' is, strictly, a horizontal section through a portion or the whole of the work to any scale as opposed to a vertical section or cut. In broad terms, it may refer to any idea or scheme of action.

**Plant**

A rather broad term referring to the equipment used by the contractor. Its meaning may be restricted by the wording of the contract. Thus, JCT 80, clause 27.4.3, refers to 'any temporary buildings, plant, tools, equipment, goods and materials ...' In that instance it is clear that plant refers to something other than equipment, tools or temporary buildings. Mechanical diggers, mixers and vehicles are indicated. In general terms, however, 'plant' might be used to describe any kind of mechanical or non-mechanical equipment, including scaffolding and huts. Plant can be either temporary – such as dumpers, cranes and the like – or permanent and built into the works – such as boilers, fans and the like.

**Pleadings**

The formal documents in civil litigation (q.v.) or arbitration. They are served by each party on his opponent and contain allegations of fact on which the party is relying. They are usually expressed in very formal language and must be carefully drafted. They should enable the court or arbitrator to ascertain precisely the issues between the parties and serve to establish any common ground.

**Point of law**

A question of law as opposed to one of fact and usually referred to in connection with the former case stated (q.v.) procedure under the Arbitration Act 1950. Statute may confer a right to appeal to a higher court on point of law only.

**Possession**

In the absence of an express term (q.v.) in the building contract, a term will be implied that the contractor must have possession of the site in sufficient time to allow him to complete the works by the contract completion date (q.v.): *Freeman & Son v. Hensler* (1900)).

Most standard forms state the date on which possession must be given ( JCT 80, clause 23.1; IFC 84, clause 2.1; ACA 2, clause 11.1). MW 80 does not give a date for possession, but does give a date for commencement of the works (clause 2.1). In practice and in law, this must also be the latest date for possession. GC/Works/1, clause 6, makes provision for the SO to give possession or the order to commence. Although no period of time or date is specified, the order must be given within a reasonable time after acceptance of the contractor's tender. The contract period, and hence the date for completion, is to be stated in the Abstract of Particulars (q.v.).

If the employer fails to give possession on the due date, the contractor is entitled to sue for damages

and the date for completion may become at large
(see: *Time at large*). It is not possible to overcome the
problem by issuing an instruction to postpone the
work and, subsequently, awarding an extension of
time to cover postponement. Possession of the site
and the carrying out of work are two entirely different
things. The contractor will need to do a number of
things which are not strictly carrying out the works
and for which he must have possession of the site.
ACA 2, however, is drafted broadly enough to allow
the architect to defer possession and award an
extension under clause 11.5, alternative 1 or 11.5(e),
alternative 2, relating to the employer's default.
IFC 84, makes provision for the deferment of possession
for up to six weeks under clause 2.2; and an extension
of time can then be awarded under clause 2.4.14.

| | |
|---|---|
| **Possessory title** | Title to land acquired by occupying it for 12 years without paying rent or otherwise acknowledging the rights of the true owner. The period is 30 years in the case of Crown land. See also: *Adverse possession*. |
| **Postponement** | All the common forms of contract allow the architect to postpone the whole or any part of the works. There is usually an express term to that effect. Postponement is a serious step because the contractor will be entitled to: |

— An extension of time.
— Financial reimbursement for loss and expense.
— Determine his employment if the works are
postponed for a longer period than allowed by the
contract or, if no period is stipulated, a reasonable
period.
The employer, in the absence of an express term, has
no implied right to postpone the work. There is an
implied term in every building contract that the
employer will allow the contractor to begin work on
the date fixed for commencement and continue
working so as to complete the works by the contract
completion date (q.v.). Without the express term,
therefore, the contractor may be able to treat

postponement as an act of repudiation on the part of the employer and sue for damages. In general, the wording of the clause does not extend to deferring the giving of *possession* (q.v.) of the site.

JCT 80 allows postponement under clause 23.2, extension of time under clause 25.4.5.1, loss and/or expense under clause 26.2.5 and determination under clause 28.1.3.4.

IFC 84 allows postponement under clause 3.15, extension of time under clause 2.4.5, loss and/or expense under clause 4.12.5 and determination under clause 7.5.3.

GC/Works/1 allows suspension of the works under clause 7(1)(g), extension of time under clause 28(2)(c) and expense under clause 9(2)(a)(i) provided that the work has not been suspended under clause 23 to avoid the risk of damage by frost, inclement weather or the like. There is no contractual provision for the contractor to determine his own employment, for any reason, under this contract. If the suspension continued for a lengthy period, however, the contractor could use his common law rights.

ACA 2 allows suspension of the works under clause 11.8, extension of time under the same clause (which involves stating a new date for completion), payment under clause 17.1. Clause 11.8 is essentially a provision for postponing the date of Taking-Over. Some degree of suspension is implied. It is likely that the architect has wider powers of suspension under clause 8.1(f) which enables him to issue instructions 'on any matter connected with the Works'. In that case, an extension of time would be awarded under clause 17 which also provides for payment. There is no provision for termination of the contractor's employment due to suspension of the works unless the delay lasts for 66 consecutive days and is due to:

— *Force majeure* (q.v.).

— Clause 6.4 contingencies.

— War, etc.

Therefore, if a suspension is ordered by the architect, the contractor is thrown upon his common law rights if the delay lasts for an unreasonable period (which might well be considered to be 66 consecutive days). MW 80 probably gives the architect power to postpone under clause 3.5; extension of time would fall under clause 2.2 but there is no provision for reimbursement of loss and/or expense which would have to be agreed by the employer or become the subject of an action by the contractor at common law. The contract expressly allows the contractor to determine his employment if the employer suspends the carrying out of the works for a continuous period of at least one month.

It has been held that an instruction to postpone will be implied if the architect issues an instruction to the contractor which necessarily entails postponement of the work, even though the instruction is not issued under the appropriate clause and does not specifically instruct postponement (*M Harrison & Co. (Leeds) Ltd v. Leeds City Council* (1980) and *Holland, Hannen & Cubitt (Northern) Ltd v. Welsh Health Technical Services Organisation and others* (1981)). See also: *Suspension*.

| | |
|---|---|
| **Practicable steps** | A phrase found in JCT 80, clause 25.4.7, and which refers to 'delay on the part of Nominated Sub-Contractors or Nominated Suppliers which the Contractor has taken all *practicable steps* to avoid or reduce' (our italics). The steps which the contractor is required to take are all those which, in practice, he can take. In order to decide whether the contractor has taken all practicable steps, all the circumstances must be considered. Therefore, practicable may be taken to mean not *possible* but possible in all the circumstances. |

| | |
|---|---|
| **Practical completion** | A phrase found in JCT 80, principally in clause 17. It marks the date at which:<br>— The defects liability period (q.v.) begins (clause 17.2).<br>— The contractor's liability for insurance (q.v.) under clause 22A ends.<br>— Liability for liquidated damages (q.v.) under |

clause 24 ends.

— Liability for damage caused by frost occurring thereafter ends (clause 17.2).

— The employer's right to deduct full retention ends. Half the retention percentage becomes due for release (clause 30.4.1.3).

— The period of final measurement and valuation begins (clause 30.6.1.2).

— Regular interim certificates (q.v.) cease to be issued (clause 30.1.3).

— The period for the architect's final review begins under clause 23.3.3.

— Any reference to arbitration can be opened (Article 5. 2).

Despite the enormous importance of the date, the contract does not define 'practical completion'. Under clause 17.1 the architect must issue a certificate forthwith (q.v.) when, in his opinion, 'practical completion' is achieved. It is generally agreed that it does not mean 'nearly complete'. Some commentators refer to it as complete for all the practical purposes of the contract, but it is not the same thing as substantial completion (q.v.).

Some architects insist that all work is totally complete before issuing a certificate of practical completion; others certify when a considerable amount of work is complete save only that which can be finished without inconveniencing the employer. It would appear to be going too far to insist on total completion before issuing a certificate, otherwise the contract could have referred merely to 'completion'. The addition of the word 'practical' must have some relevance.

From a legal point of view, the phrase is ambiguous. The question is whether it covers the situation where the works are substantially finished but there are defects. This is an important matter since the architect's power to order the remedying of defects during the defects liability period is limited to defects 'which shall appear' during that period.

There is conflicting case law. In *J. Jarvis & Sons Ltd v. Westminster Corporation* (1970) Viscount Dilhorne took the view that 'pracitical completion' meant that there must be no defects apparent in the works at the date on which the architect issues the certificate. 'The defects liability period is provided in order to enable defects not apparent at the date of practical completion to be remedied. If they had been apparent, no such certificate would have been issued.' In other words, the architect can issue his certificate even if he knows that some latent defects (q.v.) are present.

In contrast, in *P. & M. Kaye Ltd v. Hosier & Dickinson, Ltd* (1972) it was suggested that the architect could withhold his certificate until all known defects, except trifling ones, were corrected. In the most recent case – *H.W. Nevill (Sunblest) Ltd v. Wm. Press & Son Ltd* (1981) – the High Court favoured the view expressed in *Jarvis*. The judge said 'I think that the word "practically" ... gave the architect a discretion to certify that (the contractor) had fulfilled its obligation ... where very minor *de minimis* works had not been carried out, but if there were any patent defects in what (the contractor) had done the architect could not have given a certificate of practical completion.' It seems on balance that the architect is justified in issuing his certificate if he is reasonably satisfied that the works accord with the contract, notwithstanding that there are *very minor* defects which can be remedied during the defects liability period (q.v.).

ACA 2 uses the phrase 'fit and ready for Taking-Over' (clause 12). 'Taking-Over' may be considered to be loosely equivalent to 'practical completion' but there are some important differences. The contractor must notify the architect when he considers that the Works are or will be fit and ready for Taking-Over. The architect is expressly given discretion to issue a 'Taking-Over' certificate upon receipt of the contractor's written undertaking to complete with all due diligence (q.v.) any work contained in the architect's or contractor's list. If the architect opts to wait until all the outstanding listed items are complete, he must then issue his certificate forthwith (q.v.) when the items are completed.

His certificate marks the date at which:

— The contractor's liability for loss or damage to the works and to goods intended for the works ends (clause 6.2).

— The contractor's liability for insurance under clause 6.4, Alternative 1, ends.

— Liability for liquidated or unliquidated damages, under clause 11.3, alternatives 1 or 2 respectively, ends.

— The maintenance period begins (clause 12.2).

—The regular calculation of fluctuations (if applicable) on interim certificates ends (clause 18.1).

— No further reference may be made to the Adjudicator (q.v.) under clause 25.1, Alternative 1.

— Any reference to arbitration can be opened under clause 25.6, Alternative 1 or 25.5, Alternative 2.

— The period for review of extensions of time granted begins (clause 11.7).

GC/Works/1 makes reference, at clause 28(1), to the Works being 'completed' to the satisfaction of the SO (q.v.). The wording indicates that this is equivalent to 'practical completion'. The SO is not specifically required by this clause to issue a certificate although he must certify completion, under clause 42(1). His certificate marks the date at which:

— The contractor's liability for liquidated damages ends (clause 29(1)).

— The SO can require all copies of the Specification, Bills of Quantities and Drawings to be returned (clause 4(4)).

— The contractor's liability for frost damage ends (clause 32(2)).

— The contractor is entitled to receive the estimated Final Sum less one half of the reserve (clause 41(1)).

— Reference to arbitration can be opened under clause 61(1).

— The maintenance period begins (Abstract of Particulars).

See also: *Completion.*

---

**Precedent**          See: *Judicial precedent.*

**Preliminaries**　　　That part of the Bills of Quantities (q.v.) which describes the Works in general terms and lists the contractor's general obligations, the restrictions imposed by the employer and the contractual terms.

**Prescription**　　　The vesting of a right by reason of lapse of time. Prescription is the most important method of acquiring easements (q.v.) over property such as rights of light and rights of way. It is based on long enjoyment as of right.

At common law it was necessary to prove that the right had been enjoyed since 1189 – the beginning of legal memory – but because of the difficulty of proving enjoyment for so long a period, evidence of use for a period of 20 years raised a presumption that the right had existed in 1189.

A prescriptive claim could be defeated by showing that the right must have arisen at a later date, and to make matters easier the courts evolved the doctrine of 'lost modern grant', under which if user could be proved for 20 years, a lawful grant would be presumed. That presumption could be defeated by proof that during the period when the grant could have been made there was nobody who could lawfully have made it.

The Prescription Act 1832 was passed to simplify these difficulties so that claims to easements generally cannot be defeated by showing that user commenced after 1189 if 20 years' uninterrupted enjoyment as of right is shown. If 40 years of enjoyment without interruption is proved, the right becomes absolute unless it has been enjoyed by written agreement or consent. In the case of rights of light (q.v.) there is only one period, 20 years, and the actual enjoyment need not be as of right.

The Act makes no change in the common law requirements as to prescription itself: the right claimed must have been exercised *nec vi, nec clam, nec precario* – it must not have been exercised forcibly (*vi*), secretly (*clam*) or with consent ( *precario*).

**Presumption**　　　A conclusion or inference of fact which may or must be drawn from other established facts. Presumptions are important in the law of evidence (q.v.).

| | |
|---|---|
| **Pre-tender design** | Under the BPF System (q.v.) this is the term used to refer to the design and specification carried out by the Design Leader (q.v.) and Consultants (q.v.) before tenders are invited. |
| **Pre-tender information** | The information, in the form of drawings, schedules or reports, which the employer or his architect provide for the contractor to consider when preparing his tender. Some information will be provided and sent to the contractor. Other pieces of information may be retained by the architect, and the contractor will be notified of their existence and availability. It is important that all pre-tender information be accurate. Inaccurate or misleading information can lead to an action for damages or the contract being set aside on the grounds of misrepresentation (q.v.). |
| **Price** | The monetary value of something. The price at which a builder is prepared to carry out work will include the cost of labour, materials and overheads together with an addition for profit. 'Prices' is a word often used to refer to the sums which the builder inserts against the items in bills of quantities (q.v.). See also: *Schedule of prices*. |
| **Priced programme** | Under the BPF System (q.v.) the Design Leader must produce a priced programme. This consists of a priced schedule of his design activities and a programme showing how they will be carried out. Where separate Consultants (q.v.) are appointed they must undertake a similar exercise. Priced programmes become part of the BPF master programme (q.v.) and master cost plan (q.v.).<br>The priced programme is used as a plan of work and a basis for reporting progress. Payment to the Design Leader and Consultants is based on completed activities shown in the priced programme. See also: *Schedule of activities*. |
| **Prime cost** | The actual cost to the contractor of undertaking work, e.g., the wages paid, the cost of supervision, the |

price of materials and of sub-contract work. In contracts let on the basis of reimbursing the contractor his prime cost, it is important to have a precise definition of what prime cost is to be reimbursed.

| **Prime cost (PC) sums** | A term found in many standard forms of contract. Its meaning is subject to some variation, depending upon the contract or the person using the phrase. It is often confused with the term 'provisional sums' (q.v.) and the phrases 'PC sums' and 'provisional sums' are used indiscriminately. A prime cost sum is a sum of money included in a contract, usually by means of an item in the bills of quantities (q.v.). The sum is to be expended on materials or goods from suppliers or on work to be carried out by sub-contractors nominated by the employer. The contractor has to add his required profit to this sum at tender stage. By description a prime cost sum should be a specific and accurately known amount and should be obtained as a result of a direct quotation or tender from the supplier or sub-contractor concerned. The reason for confusion with a provisional sum becomes clear when it is appreciated that, in practice, a PC sum is seldom put in the bills as a precise amount. Thus a figure of £468.50 is obtained from the supplier and a figure of £500.00 is put in the bills 'to allow for increases for various reasons.' The additional £31.50 is, in effect, a small contingency sum. Alternatively, a PC sum is inserted before quotations have been invited. The contractor's profit is calculated on the bill sum (i.e., £500.00) and must be adjusted when the final supply sum is known. Where Bills of Quantities are based upon the Standard Method of Measurement (q.v.), 6th edn., the term 'prime cost sum' is defined at item A.8.1(b). GC/Works/1 mentions PC sums in clause 38. JCT 80 mentions PC sums principally in clause 30.6.2. |
|---|---|
| **Priority of documents** | Standard form contracts often contain an express term dealing with the priority to be given to the various contract documents. In the absence of such a |

term, where there is a contract in printed form with handwritten or typewritten insertions, additions or amendments which are inconsistent with the printed words, the written words prevail: *Robertson v. French* (1803).

This sensible rule can be overridden as is done in JCT 80, clause 2.2.1 which states that 'nothing contained in the Contract Bills shall override or modify the application or interpretation of that which is contained in the Articles of Agreement, the Conditions or the Appendix'. This clear wording means that specially written clauses in the Bills, e.g., dealing with insurance, will not prevail if they conflict with the wording of the printed form: see, e.g., *M.J. Gleeson (Contractors) Ltd v. London Borough of Hillingdon* (1970).

More sensibly, ACA 2, clause 1.3, provides that 'the provisions of this Form of Agreement shall prevail over the provisions contained in any other of the Contract Documents save only the following provisions which shall prevail over anything contained in this Form of Agreement...' See also: *Interpretation of contracts*.

| **Privilege** | In the law of evidence (q.v.) the rule which enables a witness to refuse to answer certain questions or to produce a document. |

In the law of evidence (q.v.) the rule which enables a witness to refuse to answer certain questions or to produce a document.

In the law of defamation (q.v.) privilege refers to a defence, e.g. statements made by witnesses in judicial proceedings are absolutely privileged so that the person making them is not liable in defamation. Other statements may be privileged to a lesser extent (generally termed 'qualified privilege') provided that the contents are honestly believed to be true by the writer and there is an absence of malice, for example, communications between client and professional adviser. It is generally accepted that communications between a client and his solicitor enjoy absolute privilege for obvious reasons. If a defendant (q.v.) seeks to use some part of his own privileged document in evidence, he will be deemed to have waived his privilege in the whole document so far as it relates to the same subject matter: *Great Atlantic Insurance Co. v. Home Insurance Co.* (1981).

A letter sent from one employer to another, in response to a request regarding the suitability of an applicant for a job, will usually enjoy qualified privilege. See also: *Without prejudice.*

---

**Privity of contract**     A rule of English law which means that only the actual parties to a contract can acquire rights and liabilities under it (*Dunlop v. Selfridge* (1915)). This rule applies even though the contract itself provides that a third-party shall be entitled to sue (*Tweddle v. Atkinson* (1861)).

The doctrine of privity of contract is subject to several exceptions. For example:

— The covenants (q.v.) in a lease are normally binding not only on the original parties but on their successors in title.

— A husband who insures his life in favour of his wife or children may, under statute, create enforceable rights in them.

— Agency(q.v.).

Privity of contract is an inconvenient notion in modern commercial practice because in the common situation of a series of linked transactions, the law normally treats each link as a totally separate relationship.

In building contracts the practical consequences are two-fold:

— The main contractor carries responsibility for a sub-contractor's work, etc., so far as the employer is concerned. The employer cannot sue the sub-contractor direct in contract, unless there is a separate direct contract between them, e.g., as where JCT Agreement NSC/2 is signed.

— As there is no direct contractual relationship between sub-contractor and employer, neither can sue the other in contract, although a breach of the sub-contract may, at the same time, amount to a tort (q.v.). In that case the employer can sue the sub-contractor in tort, e.g., for negligence:

*Junior Books Ltd v. The Veitchi Co. Ltd* (1982).
Figure 9 is a diagram showing the operation of the
doctrine.

| | |
|---|---|
| **Procurable** | The normal meaning is 'obtainable'. Clause 8.1 of the JCT 80 form provides an important qualification of the contractor's obligations under 2.1. It provides that materials, goods and workmanship must be of the respective kinds and standards described in the contract bills (q.v.) only *so far as procurable*. Therefore, if he is unable to obtain goods, etc., of the required kinds or standards, his obligation appears to end. On what is to happen then, the contract is silent. In practical terms, much will depend upon circumstances. If, for example, the contractor cannot obtain the kind of materials for which he tendered because he was late in placing his order, the onus is probably on him to offer an alternative of at least equal standard. Similarly, if the materials were unobtainable at the time he offered to provide them. If, however, the materials become unobtainable through no fault of the contractor, it is suggested that the architect will be obliged to issue an instruction (q.v.) varying the materials, with consequent adjustment to the contract sum (q.v.). |

Architects will be prudent to make full enquiries
before accepting that materials are not procurable. It
is not unknown for a contractor to plead this clause
because the materials are either more expensive than
he anticipated or more difficult to obtain. Neither
situation falls under clause 8.1.

| | |
|---|---|
| **Productivity payments** | Sometimes known as 'bonus payments' or 'incentive schemes'. They are paid to operatives by contractors to encourage rapid completion of work. In practice, every operative on site expects to receive a bonus and haggling over payments is a major source of grievance. Many contractors agree special bonus schemes with their men, but schemes which are in accordance with the rules of the National Joint Council for the Building Industry rank for inclusion in fluctuations payments |

under JCT 80, clause 39.1.1.4. Under JCT 63, such payments did not rank as eligible fluctuations in wages: (*William Sindall Ltd v. North West Thames Regional Health Authority* (1977).

**Programme**    A schedule or chart showing stages in a scheme of work. JCT 80, clause 5.3.1.2  makes reference to a master programme (q.v.) but it is not a contract document (q.v.). The contractor may produce many subsidiary programmes during the course of a contract to assist him to plan the work efficiently. The architect will also produce programmes, particularly at the commencement of the design stage, to help him organize the design team. Popular forms of programme are:
— Network analysis and critical path.
— Precedence diagrams.
— Bar (Gantt) charts.
— Line of balance.
— Advancing fronts.
Each method has its own particular advantages depending upon the type of job and the people for whom it is intended. See also: *Master programme*.

**Project management**    A very loose term referring to the management of a building project.
A project manager may be appointed by the employer to co-ordinate the entire job from its inception to its completion. His relationship with the other professionals must be clearly set out and respective powers and responsibilities established. Since practice varies from contract to contract, it is impossible to define his role precisely. He could be appointed to take over the whole of the architect's traditional management and co-ordinating functions together with those of the main contractor. The concept is still in the process of evolution.
The supporters of project management suggest that it provides an efficient and cost effective method of producing a building. Opponents believe that it fragments existing responsibilities and fails to achieve

any improvement in timing and cost.

Project managers can be architects, engineers, quantity surveyors, surveyors or managers specializing in the building field. Diagrams showing the relationships of project managers to other members of the building team are at Figures 25 and 26. See also: *Client's representative (BPF)*.

| | |
|---|---|
| **Prolongation claim** | A claim made by the contractor for financial reimbursement because the contract period has been extended as a result of the default of the employer. It is expressly mentioned in clause 53 of GC/Works/1, but not in other standard forms. Contractors commonly refer to all claims for loss and/or expense (q.v.) as 'prolongation claims', which is misleading because it implies that either every extension of the contract period carries an automatic claim for reimbursement or that a financial claim cannot be made unless an overrun of the contract period has occurred. Both of these implications are wrong. See also: *Claims*. |
| **Proof of evidence** | A written statement of what a witness (q.v.) will say. It is produced mainly for the benefit of counsel who will use it to examine a witness before a court or arbitration hearing and to assist in cross-examining witnesses for the other party. In Scotland it is referred to as a 'precognition'. |

The proof is usually written after discussion with counsel so that he can decide what is and what is not important. Proofs may be prepared by counsel after discussion but, in the case of an expert witness, it is better prepared by the witness himself. This is because the witness will indicate most accurately the opinions he holds and how he intends to express them. A sample of the typical layout of a proof of evidence is shown in Figure 27.

High Court procedure forbids the taking of a proof of evidence into the witness-box. The procedure may vary in arbitrations (q.v.), depending upon what is agreed between the parties. Note that if a witness is allowed to read his answers from a proof, the arbitrator and the other side must have copies.

**Figure 25**
Project management 1

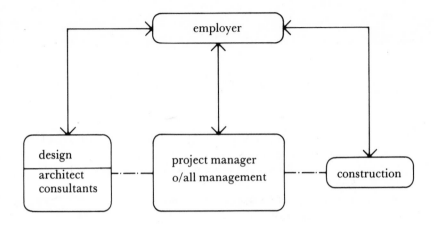

**Figure 26**
Project management 2

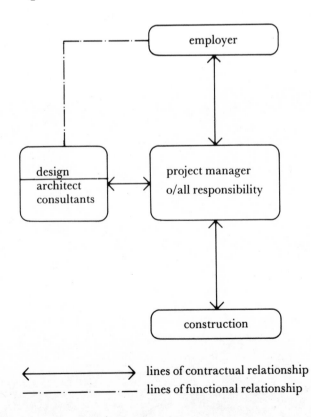

**Figure 27**

Sample proof of evidence for use by an
expert witness

Proof of Evidence

Case name
Witness's name in full $\Big\}$ (should appear at the top of each page)

---

Table of contents (Witnesses who object to taking the oath should
   state that they will 'affirm')
1. Qualifications (qualifications, membership of professional bodies,
   name and address of firm)
2. Experience (description of *relevant* experience)
3. Previous involvement (if any)
4. Investigations (Investigations and examinations undertaken by the
   witness personally)
5. History (of the disputed matters, if applicable)
6. Other relevant factors (anything else which the witness has considered)
7. Opinion (together with clear and concise reasons. This is the most
   important part)
8. Signature and date

| **Property** | In legal terms, 'property' denotes something capable of being owned. Property is divided into two sorts (see Figure 28): real and personal, very roughly land and movable goods respectively. See also: *Bailment; Chattels; Corporeal property; Hire; Incorporeal hereditaments; Lien; Personal property; Real property.* |
|---|---|
| **Provisional quantities** | In otherwise accurately measured bills of quantities (q.v.) it is common to find some quantities noted as 'provisional'. They usually refer to items which are unknown or uncertain in extent at the billing stage. For example, with regard to substructure or drainage works, it is not uncommon for the quantity surveyor to include items for excavating in rock, or running sand or below the water table. The quantity is only an estimate; as the work proceeds it is re-measured at the rate the contractor has inserted against the bill of quantities item. |
|  | Provisional quantities are also taken for such things as cutting holes through walls and floors for plumbing and other services. They are often taken from a schedule supplied by the specialist concerned and are commonly referred to as 'builder's work'. |
| **Provisional sum** | A term used to denote a sum of money included in the contract by the employer, normally as an amount in the bills of quantities (q.v.). It is provided to cover the cost of something which cannot be foreseen or detailed accurately at the time tenders are invited. (Contractor's profit is not added to this sum.) It may be expended as the architect instructs, upon which a prime cost sum (q.v.) may arise. |
|  | For example: the architect may know that he requires a retaining wall to be constructed, but he does not know accurate dimensions or details. He may ask the quantity surveyor to make an estimate (q.v.) of the likely cost and insert that sum in the bills at tender stage. During the progress of the contract, the architect may issue an instruction, together with full details of the wall, to the contractor. At Final Account (q.v.) stage, the quantity surveyor deducts the |

**Figure 28**

Division of property

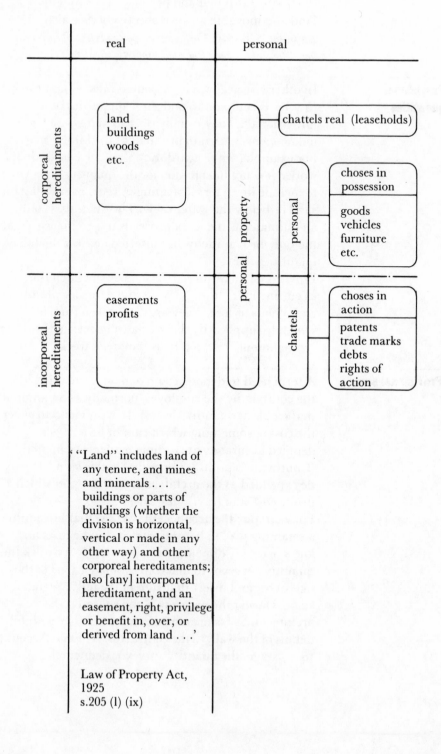

' "Land" includes land of
any tenure, and mines
and minerals . . .
buildings or parts of
buildings (whether the
division is horizontal,
vertical or made in any
other way) and other
corporeal hereditaments;
also [any] incorporeal
hereditament, and an
easement, right, privilege
or benefit in, over, or
derived from land . . .'

Law of Property Act,
1925
s.205 (l) (ix)

provisional sum from the contract sum (q.v.) and adds back the value of the retaining wall ascertained in accordance with the contract provisions for the valuation of variations (q.v.). Where bills of quantities are based upon the Standard Method of Measurement (q.v.), 6th edn., the term 'provisional sum' is defined at item A.8.1(a). See also: *Prime cost sums*.

| | |
|---|---|
| **Proxy** | (1) A lawfully appointed agent.<br>(2) In company law, the term refers to a person appointed to represent and vote for another at meetings as well as the formal document of appointment. |

**Quality of work**

Standard or degree of excellence. The term is used in IFC 84, clause 1.2. The quality of work is usually set out in the specification (q.v.) or bills of quantities (q.v.) or on the contract drawing (q.v.). IFC 84 provides that, in the case of inconsistency of description between documents, the contract drawings will prevail. The quality of work is the subject of much argument on site and it is notoriously difficult to specify quality to any fine degree. The use of British Standards, Codes of Practice, standard specification clauses and the definition of tolerances is all helpful, but the contractor will usually base his pricing on his knowledge of the architect and employer. Where quality is specified precisely, the contractor is bound to provide materials and workmanship to that quality, but not, it should be noted, above the quality described.

**Quantity surveyor**

A professional person whose expertise lies mainly in the fields of the measurement and valuation of building and civil engineering work and cost advice. Most standard forms of building contract make reference to the quantity surveyor, generally with regard to the valuation of work in progress, variations, financial claims and the preparation of the final account. ACA 2 contains an optional provision in clause 15.2 for the appointment of a quantity surveyor. MW 80, unusually, refers only to the appointment of a quantity surveyor, but not to any specific duty. Long before a contract is placed, the quantity surveyor will be involved in advising the employer and the architect on probable costs of the completed building. He can produce a cost plan which is a highly sophisticated method of controlling costs throughout the design and development stage. If the work is of sufficient size, he will also produce bills of quantities (q.v.) or such other document for pricing which he will advise in the particular circumstances. He will generally carry out all the negotiations with the contractor which have a cost implication. The quantity surveyor is normally appointed by the employer sometimes on the advice of the architect. The quantity surveyor is usually a member of the Royal Institution of Chartered Surveyors (12 Great George Street, Parliament Square, London SW1P 3AD) which issues a code of conduct and recommended fee scales.

Quantity surveyors are also employed within contractors' firms where they may specialize in estimating, claims preparation and measurement of work in progress.

| | |
|---|---|
| **Quantum meruit** | As much as he has deserved – a reasonable sum. This Latin phrase is often used as a synonym for *quantum valebant* which means 'as much as it is worth'. It is the measure of payment where the contract has not fixed a price or where, for some reason or another, the contract price is no longer applicable. |

There are four situations in which a *quantum meruit* claim is applicable:

— Where work has been done under a contract without any express agreement as to price.

— Where there is an express agreement to pay a 'reasonable price' or a 'reasonable sum'.

— Where work is done under a contract which both parties believed to be valid at the time but which is in fact void (q.v.).

— Where work is done at the request of one party but without an express contract, e.g., work done pursuant to a Letter of Intent (q.v.). This is a claim in quasi-contract (q.v.) or restitution. 'In most cases where work is done pursuant to a request contained in a letter of intent, it will not matter whether a contract did or did not come into existence; because if the party who has acted on the request is simply claiming payment, his claim will usually be based upon a *quantum meruit*, and it will make no difference whether that claim is contractual or quasi-contractual. A *quantum meruit* claim... straddles the boundaries of what we now call contract and restitution...': *British Steel Corporation v. Cleveland Bridge & Engineering Co. Ltd* (1981).

If extra work is done completely outside the contract, then payment on a *quantum meruit* may be implied (*Sir Lindsay Parkinson & Co. Ltd v. Commissioner of Works* (1950)), but this is very rare. Many contractors erroneously assume that they are entitled to claim on a *quantum meruit* basis merely because they are losing money but in fact such a claim will only lie, if at all, where what the contractor does is substantially different from what he undertook to do.

---

**Quasi-contract**

Restitution or quasi-contract is the term used to cover those cases where money is paid at another's request, or money is received for the use of someone else, as *quantum meruit* claims (q.v.). The common feature is that the category covers cases of unjust enrichment or unjust benefit, and aims 'to prevent a man from retaining the money of, or some benefit derived from, another which it is against conscience that he should keep' (*The Fibrosa case* (1943)).

In the context of the construction industry, the most common instance is that of a *quantum meruit* (q.v.) claim for work done or services rendered. Similarly, if money is paid under a mistake of fact (not law), it is recoverable in this way. Under the provisions of the Law Reform (Frustrated Contracts) Act 1943, where a contract is frustrated, money paid under the contract may be recovered, subject to a claim for set-off (q.v.) for expenses incurred by the recipient of the payment. If a partnership (q.v.) is determined prematurely, the court has power to order the full or partial return of any premium paid by a partner for admission to the firm: s.40, Partnership Act 1890. See also: *Frustration*.

**Queen's (King's) enemies**

A traditional term used in contracts to refer to enemies of the State. GC/Works/1, clause 1 (2)(f) lists 'King's enemy risks' among the 'accepted risks' for insurance purposes. It defines that expression by reference to s.15(1)(a) of the War Risks Insurance Act 1939 where the definition is 'risks arising from the action taken by an enemy or in repelling an imagined attack by an enemy, as the Board of Trade may by order define'. Clause 25 (1) imposes on the contractor an obligation to take all reasonable precautions to prevent loss or damage from any of the accepted risks while under clause 26(1) the Authority (employer) is to pay the contractor for making good any loss or damage to the works which is wholly caused by the accepted risks. GC/Works/1, clause 28 (1)(e) lists accepted risks as a ground for extension of time.

**Quotation**

A price given usually in the form of an offer (q.v.) for the carrying out of work or the supply of materials or both. It is normally expected to be a precise figure, capable of acceptance (q.v.) so as to form a binding contract. See also: *Estimate; Offer; Tender*.

**RIBA contracts**

An incorrect and outdated method of referring to the standard forms of contract published by the Joint Contracts Tribunal (q.v.). The title was correct until 1977, when the Royal Institute of British Architects (q.v.) withdrew its name from the documents, which are now correctly referred to as the JCT Forms. Despite the fact that these contracts are prepared and issued by the Joint Contracts Tribunal, the copyright (q.v.) is said to be vested in RIBA Publications Ltd. By item B 586 of Court Business (5 August 1977) the judiciary and legal profession were instructed to refer to what is now JCT 80 as 'the JCT Contract' or 'the Standard Form of Building Contract' but this direction is widely ignored in practice.

The current (1980) JCT Contract derives from a form agreed as long ago as 1893 and agreed by various representative national bodies in 1909. Further editions were issued in 1931, 1939 and 1963, all of which were known as 'the RIBA Contract' and are so referred to in the law reports (q.v.) and textbooks, largely because they were published by the RIBA.

**Rates**

A local tax assessed on and made payable by a person in respect of his occupation of land or buildings. JCT 80, clause 6.2 requires the contractor to pay 'any fees or charges (including any rates or taxes) legally demandable' and these are to be added to the contract sum.

In general, site huts and buildings are not rateable (*London County Council v. Wilkins* (1957)) while the work is in progress. However, if there is a sufficient degree of permanency rates may become payable, but this will be rare: *Ravenseft Properties v. London Borough of Newham* (1976).

**Ratio decidendi**

The principle of law on which a judicial decision is based. It is the reason or ground for the decision and makes a precedent (q.v.) for the future. For the purpose of the doctrine of precedent it is the *ratio* which is the vital element in the decision. Not every statement of law made by a judge in the course of his judgment is part of the *ratio*. It must be distinguished from *obiter dictum* (q.v.) which is a statement made 'by the way' and not necessary for the decision.
In general, the *ratio* of a case will be the statement of the principles of law which apply to the legal problem disclosed by the facts before the court. The area is fraught with difficulty because:
— A judge does not usually state that a particular statement is the *ratio*.
— A judge may give what may appear to be alternative *rationes decidendi*.
— A later court may distinguish the precedent.
— Even if the facts found in an earlier case appear identical with those in a later case the judge in the later case may draw a different inference from them: *Qualcast (Wolverhampton) Ltd v. Haynes* (1959).

**Real property**

Most legal systems recognize a distinction between land, which is immovable and as a general rule indestructible, and other pieces of property such as cars, books or clothes. In England, for historical reasons, ownership may exist in respect of both real and personal property (q.v.). Real property (realty) is broadly speaking a freehold estate or interest in land. In law, 'land' has a very wide definition; it includes not only the actual soil itself but all the things growing upon it or permanently attached to it, as well as rights over it. This has important consequences in building contracts because as goods and materials are incorporated into the building they cease to be personal property and become part of the land. Real property is a term which is applied solely to interests in land. Interests under leases – leaseholds – are 'interests in land' in one sense, but for historical reasons are classed as personal property (q.v.). They occupy an anomalous position and are technically known as *chattels real*.

Figure 28 shows the position in diagram form.

| | |
|---|---|
| **Reasonable** | A term which is virtually impossible to define satisfactorily. What is reasonable in one case will most certainly be found to be unreasonable in another. 'Reasonable' used to be taken to mean whatever the man in the street (or the man on the top of the Clapham omnibus) thought of as reasonable. Guidelines have been set out in the Unfair Contract Terms Act 1977 (q.v.), which are valid for that Act only, but may be found useful as an indication of the statutory position in a particular case. It is for the courts to decide whether any particular action or inaction is reasonable in all the circumstances. |
| **Reasonable time** | What is reasonable time will depend upon the circumstances of each particular case. It is a favourite expression in contracts when it is impossible to set down exactly how much time is intended. It might well be equated with 'appropriate time' in some cases. JCT 80, clause 17.2 lays down that defects, etc., shall be made good by the contractor 'within a reasonable time after receipt of such schedule...' In fact a reasonable time could be a week, in the case of a very small job with few defects, or many months if the job is large. What is clearly intended is that the contractor will organize so as to make steady progress in completing the work. He should not, for example, start work on the defects, then stop for a week, then start again, etc. ACA 2 attempts to clarify the matter by stating precise times as often as possible. It does not state that the times are reasonable and, indeed, in some cases they appear to be unreasonable, e.g., 5 working days to agree to the contractor's estimates (clause 17.3). See also: *Reasonable*. |

**Receiver; Official Receiver**

A person appointed by the court or by creditors for the purpose of gathering assets and protecting them usually for the benefit of creditors. He is usually an officer of the court.

An official receiver is an officer of the Board of Trade appointed as an interim measure, in bankruptcy, until a trustee in bankruptcy has been appointed. See also: *Bankruptcy; Insolvency; Liquidation.*

**Receiving order**

In bankruptcy proceedings a receiving order is made by the court on presentation of a bankruptcy petition unless the debtor is able to establish a valid reason against so doing. As soon as the order is made, the Official Receiver (q.v.) becomes the receiver of the debtor's property. This protects the property from both the debtor and his creditors and puts an end to all legal proceedings against the bankrupt and his property in respect of any debt which is provable in the bankruptcy. See also: *Bankruptcy; Insolvency.*

**Recitals**

Statements in a deed (q.v.) which are introductory of its operative clauses. Their purpose is to set out the facts on which the deed is based ('narrative recitals') and to give reasons for the subsequent clauses ('introductory recitals'). The operative clauses of the deed prevail over the recitals, but if the operative clauses of the deed are ambiguous, the recitals may be an aid to interpretation (q.v.) of the operative clauses. Recitals usually begin *'Whereas ... '*

In standard form building contracts they may be of very great importance, particularly as regards description of the works or the site (q.v.). For example, in JCT 80, and the Agreement for Minor Building Works (MW 80), the recitals are the only place in the contract where the exact nature of the work to be undertaken by the contractor is specified.

**Rectification**

A discretionary remedy (q.v.) whereby the court can order the correction of errors in a written contract. It is rarely granted.

The House of Lords described the remedy as one

available 'where parties to a contract, intending to reproduce in a more formal document the terms of an agreement upon which they are already *ad idem,* use, in that document, words which are inapt to record the true agreement reached between them. The formal document may then be rectified so as to conform with the true agreement which it was intended to reproduce, and enforced in its rectified form': *American Airlines Ltd v. Hope* (1974).

Rectification will only be ordered where the written document fails to represent what the parties agreed. It will not be ordered where the document fails to represent what they intended to agree. It must be shown that the parties were in complete agreement on the terms of the contract, but by an error wrote them down wrongly. See also: *Clerical errors; Errors.*

**Re-examination**

The final stage in the examination of witnesses in judicial or arbitral proceedings. Following cross-examination (q.v.) the witness may be re-examined by or on behalf of the party calling him with the object of reinstating any of the witness's testimony that has been shaken in cross-examination. Leading questions may not be asked and new matters cannot generally be raised. See also: *Examination-in-chief; Witness.*

**Reference**

The proceedings before an arbitrator (q.v.) and so the 'costs of the reference' means the costs incurred by the parties in the conduct of the proceedings as opposed to the costs of the award (q.v.) which are the arbitrator's fees and expenses.

The same term is used for a written testimonial about someone's character and abilities.

**Registered office**

Every company, private or public, must have an office registered with the Registrar of Companies. The office need not, often is not, the normal place at which the company does business. It is often the address of the company's solicitors or accountants. The important thing is that members of the public must have an address, not subject to overnight change, to which correspondence may be sent or where writs may be served. Service at the registered office is deemed (q.v.) to be service on the company.

**Registrar**

County Court Registrars exercise both judicial and administrative functions. They deal with interlocutory matters and costs, including questions of taxation of costs (q.v.). There are also various District Registrars of the High Court and a writ (q.v.) may be issued out of the appropriate District Registry. District Registrars carry out similar functions. See also: *Courts*.

**Regular progress**

A term used in many standard forms of contract to indicate the way in which the work is to be carried out. The progress of the work must bear a relationship to the contractual completion date (q.v.). What is regular progress will depend upon the precise terms and circumstances of the contract. See also: *Regularly and diligently*.

**Regularly and diligently**

The phrase used in JCT 80, clause 23 ( JCT 63, clause 21(1)) to describe the contractor's obligation as to progress. Breach of this obligation is a ground for determination under JCT 80, clause 27.1 ( JCT 63, clause 25(1)). This phrase probably means more than an express restatement of the contractor's common law obligation as to progress, i.e., it must bear some relationship to the specified date of completion. Whether or not the contractual standard is achieved is probably to be judged by the usage of the construction industry, and in light of related express terms of the contract.

In *London Borough of Hounslow v. Twickenham Garden Developments Ltd* (1970), Megarry J. said that the question of whether or not the contractor has proceeded 'regularly and diligently' with the works must be decided in light of the facts. He remarked that 'the words convey a sense of activity, of orderly progress, of industry and perseverance: but such words provide little help on the question of how much activity, progress and so on is to be expected ... it may be that there is evidence that could be given, whether of usage among architects, builders and building owners or otherwise, that would be helpful in construing the words.'

The number of workers on site and the amount of plant and equipment there are relevant factors in considering whether or not the contractor is making regular and diligent progress. The architect must look at the master programme (q.v.), the work done and to be done, the time available, the labour, and the contractor's capacity or ability to do the work. A slow rate of progress judged against the performance of other contractors is an indicator that the contractor is not proceeding 'regularly and diligently' although low productivity on site may well be explained by other factors which are outside the contractor's control, and comparison of contracts is notoriously difficult.

In GC/Works/1, clause 6 the contractor's progress obligation is to 'proceed with due diligence and expedition in regular progression', while ACA 2, clause 10 requires him to proceed 'regularly and diligently and in accordance with the Time Schedule'.

The contractor's obligation as to progress is important in relation to claims for extension of time(q.v.) as well as determination (q.v.) of employment.

| | |
|---|---|
| **Regulations** | Restrictions and/or directions. The word is found in GC/Works/1, clause 35, which compels the contractor to comply with the rules and regulations of any government establishment within whose boundaries he is executing work. |
| **Reinstatement** | A word used normally in connection with the insurance provisions of the standard forms (see: e.g., JCT 80, clause 22A.1). Reinstatement means the putting back of materials or workmanship in the same state and to the same standard as they were before the need for reinstatement arose. The |

reinstatement value may well be greater than the straightforward value of works because reinstatement will include all necessary demolition and ancillary work. It is, therefore, important that insurance covers the full cost of all work, including a percentage for professional fees.

**Relevant event**    A term used in the JCT 80 form of contract, clause 25, to indicate grounds for the awarding of an extension of time (q.v.). There are twelve such relevant events listed in clause 25.4.

**Remedies**    See: *Rights and remedies*.

**Remoteness of damage**    A contract breaker is not liable for all the damage which ensues from his breach of contract, nor is a tortfeasor (q.v.) responsible for all the damage which flows from his wrongful act. Some damage is said to be too remote and is therefore irrecoverable.
In contract, the basic rule was stated in *Hadley v. Baxendale* (1854):
'Where two parties have made a contract which one of them has broken, the damages which the other party ought to receive in respect of such breach of contract should be such as may fairly and reasonably be considered *either* as arising naturally, i.e., according to the usual course of things, from such breach of contract itself, *or* such as may reasonably be supposed to have been in the contemplation of both parties, at the time they made the contract, as the probable result of the breach of it.'
There are two branches of this rule (indicated by the italicised either/or in the quotation) and it should be noted that under the second rule the contract breaker is only liable if he knew of the special circumstances at the time the contract was made: *Victoria Laundry (Windsor) Ltd v. Newman Industries Ltd* (1949).
A similar test is applied in tort where the phrase 'reasonably foreseeable' is used as opposed to 'reasonably contemplated'. See also: *Damages*.

**Removal of defective work**    JCT 80, clause 8.4 gives the architect power to order removal from site of work, materials or goods which are not in accordance with the contract. The architect is not empowered merely to order that defective work should be corrected; he must order removal from site in order for the instruction to be valid. In *Holland, Hannen & Cubitt (Northern) Ltd v. Welsh Health Technical Services Organization and others* (1981), a case on JCT 63 (in which clause 6(4) had the same wording as clause 8.4 of JCT 80), Judge John Newey QC said: 'In my opinion, an architect's power under clause 6(4) is simply to instruct the removal of work or materials from the site on the ground that they are not in accordance with the contract. A notice which does not require removal of anything at all is not a valid notice under clause 6(4).'

| **Re-nomination** | Many standard forms of building contract provide a mechanism whereby the architect, on behalf of the employer, may nominate specialists as sub-contractors. Problems may arise where the nominated sub-contractor defaults or fails. |

Many standard forms of building contract provide a mechanism whereby the architect, on behalf of the employer, may nominate specialists as sub-contractors. Problems may arise where the nominated sub-contractor defaults or fails.

This problem was considered by the House of Lords under JCT 63 in the well-known case of *North-West Metropolitan Regional Hospital Board v. T.A. Bickerton & Son Ltd* (1970), where a sub-contractor nominated under a PC sum went into liquidation. The liquidator (q.v.) refused to complete the sub-contract. It was held that in these circumstances the employer, through the architect, was bound to make a fresh nomination. The main contractor was neither bound nor entitled to take over the nominated sub-contractor's work.

Under the JCT Standard Form, the problem has been overcome in JCT 80, clause 35, which now provides expressly (clause 35.24) for the architect to re-nominate where the original sub-contractor fails for any reason. The *Bickerton* principle appears to be of general application in the sense that where the original contract provides for work to be done by a nominated sub-contractor, if the nominated sub-contractor defaults or otherwise fails, the employer must provide a substitute. This general position may be affected by the particular wording of the contract, e.g., ACA 2, clause 9.7, dealing with 'named sub-contractors' (q.v.) provides that in such circumstances the main contractor 'shall select another person to carry out and complete the work ...'

It seems, therefore, that in the absence of some express term to the contrary the main contractor is neither bound nor entitled to do the nominated sub-contract work himself. Later cases have developed the position further. The immediate loss arising from the nominated sub-contractor's withdrawal or failure falls on the main contractor (*Percy Bilton Ltd v. Greater London Council* (1981)) since the nominated sub-contractor's failure is not a default or breach of contract on the part of the employer. However, the architect is bound to re-nominate and the employer is responsible for any loss arising from a delay in re-nomination. The architect has a reasonable time (q.v.) in which to make the re-nomination (which runs from the date of receipt of the contractor's request for a re-nomination instruction) and it has been held that:

— Any apparent delay in re-nomination does not of itself make the period of time involved unreasonable unless the delay is caused by the fault of the architect or employer.

— The architect is entitled to have regard to the interests of the employer by seeking lump sum tenders from proposed re-nominees.

However, the same case suggests that (unless the contract wording provides otherwise) the main contractor is not bound to remedy defects in the work of the original nominated sub-contractor where these arise before completion of the sub-contract works, and such loss falls on the employer. To be valid, the re-nomination must cover both existing defective sub-contract work and completion work, otherwise the main contractor is entitled to reject the re-nomination (*Fairclough Building Ltd v. Rhuddlan Borough Council* (1985)).

---

**Repair**

The word is found in the insurance clauses of contracts. It has its ordinary meaning – to restore to the same condition as obtained before the event which necessitated a repair being carried out.

**Representative**  One who stands in the place of another. JCT 80 makes provision, clause 11, for the architect's representative to be allowed access to the site and, clause 13.5.4, for vouchers to be signed by the architect's authorized representative. The rules of agency (q.v.) govern a representative. It is, therefore, important that the architect specifies:
— Who is to be his representative.
— The extent of the representative's authority.
The architect must put the information in writing and communicate it to anyone who may have dealings with his representative. The contractor should do likewise in respect of his representatives. The information is commonly exchanged and minuted in the first contract meeting.

**Repudiation**  This is the term used to describe those breaches of contract which consist of one party clearly indicating, at a time before the contract has been fully performed, that he no longer intends to fulfill his contractual obligations: *Mersey Steel & Iron Co. v. Naylor, Benzon & Co.* (1884).
In general, the innocent party is not bound to accept the repudiation; he may affirm the contract if he wishes. If he accepts the repudiation, the contract is discharged and the innocent party may sue for damages.
Although the concept of repudiation is simple in theory, there are considerable difficulties in practice. It is not always clear whether there has been a wrongful repudiation and it is for this reason that most standard form building contracts contain clauses entitling one party to terminate on the happening of specified events. See also: *Anticipatory breach of contract; Breach of contract; Damages; Determination.*

**Reputed ownership**  Section 38(1)(c) of the Bankruptcy Act 1914 provides for the vesting in a bankrupt's trustee in bankruptcy 'all goods being, at the commencement of the bankruptcy, in the possession, order or disposition of the bankrupt, in his trade or business, by the consent and permission of the true owner, under such circumstances that he is the reputed owner thereof'. This is known as the 'reputed ownership' or 'order and disposition' clause and authorizes the use of one man's property to pay another's debts provided the conditions laid down in the section are met. The doctrine of reputed ownership does not apply in the winding-up of companies but only in the case of bankruptcy.

Where building materials are stored for convenience in the contractor's premises with the consent of the employer to whom they belong, in the event of the contractor's bankruptcy, they would probably be in the reputed ownership of the contractor (*Re Fox, ex parte Oundle & Thrapston RDC* (1948)) and, therefore, available to help pay his debts. It is, however, a question of fact as to how far materials and plant belonging to the employer are in the contractor's reputed ownership and the case law is conflicting and inconsistent. In *Re Fox, ex parte Oundle & Thrapston RDC* (1948) it was held that mere proof of possession might in some cases raise a *prima facie* case of reputed ownership but this could be rebutted by proof, or judicially recognized custom (q.v.). The primary question is always whether the bankrupt's possession of the goods was such that the inference was that he was the reputed owner. In that case, building materials stored in the contractor's yard were held to be in his reputed ownership, but materials lying loose on the site and tiles belonging to a sub-contractor also lying loose on site were not. The bankrupt's possession of the materials on site was 'ambiguous' and not therefore within s. 38.

It is in order to avoid the operation of s. 38 (1)(c) that most building contracts provide that where off-site materials or goods are included in interim certificates they must be separately stored and marked – see JCT 80, clause 30.3. Care must be taken, however, if it is desired to certify materials off-site because given an unscrupulous contractor, the procedure is open to abuse and the employer could quite easily be deceived.

The only justification for this out-moded and unfair rule which has been advanced is that of James L.J. in *Ex parte Wingfield* (1879): 'If goods are in a man's possession, order or disposition, under such circumstances as to enable him by means of them to obtain false credit, then the owner of the goods who permitted him to obtain that false credit is to suffer the penalty of losing his goods for the benefit of those who have given him credit.'

A *retention of title clause* (q.v.) in a contract of sale to an individual (or partnership) may be defeated by the operation of s. 38 (1)(c).

| **Rescission** | The termination or abrogation of a contract by one of the parties. |

The termination or abrogation of a contract by one of the parties.

A contract may be rescinded on grounds of misrepresentation, mistake, or fraud and also where the other party repudiates the contract by committing a serious breach of contract.

Rescission is effected by taking proceedings to have the contract set aside by the court (as in the case of misrepresentation) or by giving notice to the other party of one's intention to treat the contract as at an end.

*Restitutio in integrum* (q.v.) is an essential pre-condition to the right to rescind. If it is impossible, the parties are left to their other remedies, e.g., damages. In practical terms, the defendant must indemnify the plaintiff against the obligations created by the contract: *Boyd & Forrest v. Glasgow Railway* (1915).

**Resident architect**

If frequent or constant inspection by the architect is agreed to be necessary, an architect is sometimes appointed to be resident on the site. The possibility is specifically referred to in the RIBA Architect's Appointment, paragraph 3.12, and in GC/Works/1, clause 16. A resident architect will be deemed to have all the powers of the architect under the contract, being his representative, unless his authority is specifically defined. GC/Works/1 limits his authority to 'all the powers of the SO under condition 13(1) and (2) and such other powers of the SO under the contract as the SO may give notice of to the contractor'. The resident architect must be distinguished from the clerk of works (except under GC/Works/1, clause 16) who has no power to issue instructions, etc., but only the duty to inspect the work.

**Respondent**

The person against whom an appeal (q.v.) is brought (in litigation) or against whom a claim (q.v.) is made in arbitration (q.v.) proceedings. See also: *Arbitration; Plaintiff*.

**Restitutio in integrum**

Restoration to the original position. Before a contract can be rescinded (see: *Rescission*) this principle must be satisfied. 'The principle of *restitutio in integrum* does not require that a person should be put back into the same position as before; it means that he should be put into as good a position as before, e.g., if property has been delivered, it must be restored, and the party seeking rescission must be compensated for the money, etc., which he has expended as a result of obligations imposed on him by the contract. The court must do what is practically just, even though it cannot restore the parties *precisely* to the state they were in before the contract' (*Erlanger v. New Sombrero Phosphate Co.* (1878)).

**Restitution**

An obligation on one party to restore goods, property or money to another. It arises in situations where goods, etc., have been transferred by virtue of mistake (q.v.), illegality or other lack of legal authority, and is intended to avert injustice. See also: *Letter of Intent; Quantum meruit*.

**Restrictive covenant**

A negative obligation affecting freehold land and restraining the doing of some act on or in relation to the land in question, e.g., a prohibition in the title deeds against using the premises other than as a private dwelling. A restrictive covenant is enforceable not merely between the original parties to the agreement but also as between the successors in title to both parties. A restrictive covenant 'runs with the land' provided that it exists for the benefit or protection of the land. The burden or liability to be sued on a restrictive covenant binds a subsequent purchaser: *Tulk v. Moxhay* (1848).

Restrictive covenants are registrable as land charges under s. 10 of the Land Charges Act 1925, and registration amounts to actual notice (q.v.) of the existence of the covenant to every prospective purchaser. Such covenants remain enforceable indefinitely and may in practice hinder conversion and development. In some cases outmoded restrictive covenants may be modified by the Lands Tribunal (q.v.). See also: *Covenant*.

| | |
|---|---|
| **Restrictive trade practices** | Very complex statutory provisions govern restrictive trading agreements which must be registered with the Director-General of Fair Trading if they are to be enforceable. The legislation catches restrictive tendering agreements between contractors or others, whether they are formal or informal. The specified restrictions include those relating to prices, terms and contract conditions: *Re Birmingham Association of Building Trades Employers' Agreement* (1963). It is possible that an employer who entered into a contract which was against his interests because of such an agreement which ought to have been registered would have a claim for damages. |
| **Retention fund; Retention monies** | A sum or sums of money held by the employer as a safeguard against defective or non-performance (q.v.) by the contractor. It is a safeguard for the employer against latent defects or defects which may subsequently develop and the contractor's possible failure to complete the contract. It is provided for the general protection of the employer: *Townsend v. Stone Toms & Partners* (1985). The fund is a percentage (normally 5%) of the work properly executed by the contractor. It is built up by deducting the appropriate percentage from the quantity surveyor's valuation of work in progress at each certificate. |

JCT 80, clause 30.5.1, IFC, clause 4.4 (if the employer is not a local authority) and ACA 2, clause 16.4 state the employer's interest as trustee (without obligation to invest). ACA 2 and the private edition of JCT 80 provide for the employer to set the money aside in a separate bank account. (This is a requirement of the general law – *Rayack Construction Ltd v. Lampeter Meat Co. Ltd* (1979) – whenever the contract provides that the retention money is to be held in trust). The purpose is to safeguard the contractor's money in the event of the employer becoming insolvent. See also: *Fiduciary*.

| **Retention of title** | Many supply contracts contain a clause whereby the seller retains title in the goods until he has been paid for them. The right to retain title is recognized by s.19 (1) of the Sale of Goods Act 1979 but such clauses have only become common in the building industry in the last ten years. The purpose of such a clause is to protect the seller in case of the buyer's insolvency (q.v.). |

A typical retention of title clause provides that the seller retains ownership of the goods sold notwithstanding delivery until the goods have been paid for, or sometimes until all debts due by the buyer to the seller have been paid. A retention of title clause is of no real value once the goods have been incorporated into the building, because ownership passes to the employer as soon as they are actually built into the works: *Reynolds v. Ashby* (1904). It seems that the clause is also worthless where the materials have been admixed with other materials to form a new material, e.g., sand mixed with cement and water.

The effectiveness of such was upheld by the Court of Appeal in the *Romalpa* case (1976) and more recently in: *Clough Mill Ltd v. Geoffrey Martin* (1984).

The latter case concerned the supply of yarn on credit terms, the contract of sale providing that the ownership of the yarn was to remain with the sellers, who reserved the right to dispose of it 'until payment in full for all the [yarn] has been received ... in accordance with the terms of this contract or until such time as the buyer sells the [yarn] to its customers by way of bona fide resale'. Payment was stated to become due immediately on the buyer's insolvency, and various other rights were reserved by the sellers, all of which were upheld by the Court of Appeal. The clause did not require to be registered as a charge under section 95 of the Companies Act 1948.

Similarly, in *Archivent Sales & Developments Ltd v. Strathclyde Regional Council* (1984), builders' merchants supplied ventilators to a contractor and delivered them to site. The sale was on terms that 'until payment of the price in full is received by the company the property and the goods supplied by the company shall not pass to the customer'. A Scottish judge upheld the validity of the clause.

Retention of title clauses cause many problems in building contracts and in 1978 Joint Contracts Tribunal (q.v.) issued a formal notice entitled 'Retention of title (ownership) by suppliers of building materials and goods.' The JCT thought that there was no justification for any change in the wording of JCT 63, clauses 30(2) and 14(1) ( JCT 80, clauses 30.2 and 16.1) for the following reasons:

'1. A requirement on the contractor to prove ownership of on-site materials and goods could raise serious legal problems, both for the contractor, any relevant sub-contractors and for the employer (and his professional advisers). Such a requirement would, therefore, be difficult to meet and so might mean, in practice, that payment machinery for on-site goods and materials would not be operated. Moreover, the obtaining of proof of ownership would probably add to administrative costs as would the checking of such proof by, or on behalf of, the employer ...

2. The degree of risk to the employer from not obtaining proof of ownership before paying for on-site goods and materials was not considered sufficiently great to justify the possible additonal costs ...
[because]:

(a) The period of risk runs only until such time as the on-site goods and materials are incorporated in the works; from the time of incorporation they cease to be chattels, and any right to repossess by a supplier would be lost. The period of risk is, therefore, from the date of payment by the employer of the relevant interim certificates to the time at which the relevant goods and materials are incorporated in the works. This is unlikely to be more than a relatively short period.

(b) During the limited period referred to in (a), the risk of re-possession by the supplier would only, in practice, arise if the main contractor became insolvent ...

(c) The tribunal understands that in many cases the supply contract permits the contractor or sub-contractor to re-sell the goods and materials. In such cases the supplier's rights are against the proceeds of sale and the supplier has no right to re-possess the goods and materials. This reduces the risk to the employer still further.'

However, the architect is unwise to include goods brought on site in interim certificates without proof of ownership, and none of the provisions in the JCT standard forms appear effective to defeat a retention of title clause in a supplier's sale contract.

Clause 16.2 (b) of ACA 2 enables the value of goods and materials intended for but not incorporated in the works to be included in interim certificates where the contract documents expressly provide for such payment, but this is to exclude 'the value of any such goods and materials where the Architect is not satisfied ... that the property' in them is vested in the contractor. GC/Works/1 makes no specific provision for the effect of retention of title clauses. See also: *Ownership of goods and materials*.

---

**Revocation**    The withdrawal of an act already done or promised. For example, the revocation of an offer may be made at any time before acceptance (q.v.) or the revocation of a will. It may be done by an individual or company or it may occur through the operation of law, by death or by order of the court.

**Right of light**     A negative easement (q.v.) which entitles one owner
to prevent his neighbour building so as to obstruct
the flow of light through particular windows. The
property enjoys the privilege of 'ancient lights'. In
determining whether there has been an actionable
interference with a flow of light the test is: How much
light is left, and is that sufficient for the comfortable
use and enjoyment of the house according to the
ordinary requirements of mankind? It is a right to
receive a reasonable amount of light and nothing
more: *Colls v. Home & Colonial Stores* (1904).
The test most commonly applied is the 'forty-five
degree' test, i.e., the interference will not be
considered a nuisance (q.v.) if the light can still flow
to the window at an angle of 45° from the horizontal.
Under the Rights of Light Act 1959 the owner of
land over which a right of light might be acquired by
user (q.v.) may now register as a land charge a notice
identifying the properties and specifying the size and
position of a notional screen. This prevents any right
of light being acquired by the adjoining property and
circumvents the cumbersome common law necessity
of erecting an actual screen. While the notice is in
force the other party may seek cancellation or
variation of the registration.

**Right of way**     The right to pass across land belonging to another.
The right may be public, in which case any member of
the public has the right to use it, or private, when it
is an easement (q.v.) for the benefit of adjoining land.
In the latter case, only the owner of the land and
such people as he permits may use it. A public right
of way is usually created by Act of Parliament or by
custom (q.v.) as access from one public place to
another. Figure 29 shows examples of public and
private rights of way. See also: *Highway; Prescription.*

**Rights and remedies**     A phrase found, for example, in JCT 80, clauses 26.6,
27.1 and 28.1. It is provided that the clause is without
prejudice (q.v.) to any other *rights and remedies* which
the contractor (or employer) may possess. That is to

**Figure 29**

Rights of way

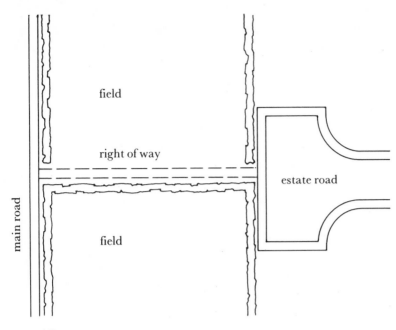

public

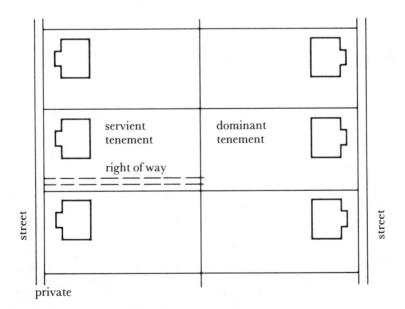

private

say, the parties' common law rights are unaffected. That would be the position anyway if the sub-clause were left out, in the absence of anything to the contrary (see also: *Unfair Contract Terms Act 1977* ). The rights are the parties' rights at common law; the remedies are the remedies available to satisfy those rights.

**Riot**

An unlawful assembly of at least three people with a common purpose, with intent to assist one another, by force if necessary, against anyone who opposes them, and who have begun to execute that purpose in a violent manner so as to alarm at least one person of reasonable firmness and courage: *Field v. Metropolitan Police Receiver* (1917). People taking part in a riot are guilty of an offence at common law. The term is used in JCT 80, clause 1.3, under the general head of 'Clause 22 perils' (q.v.) and in ACA 2, clause 11.5, Alternative 2, as a ground for awarding an extension of time. See also: *Civil commotion; Civil war; Commotion; Disorder; Insurrection.*

| | |
|---|---|
| **SI** | An abbreviatation for Statutory Instrument (q.v.). |
| **SIAD Works Agreement** | A standard form of contract published by the Society of Industrial Artists and Designers in 1983. It is supported by various administrative forms for interim certificates, etc., and is intended for work such as shop-fitting, etc. |

The Agreement consists of 12 clauses, the contract documents being the specification, schedules, agreement and conditions. Bills of quantities (q.v.) are not used. The contractor's obligation is 'to carry out and complete the Works in accordance with the Programme', though the programme (q.v.) is not a contract document.

There are the usual provisions for possession, completion and liquidated damages, but there is no VAT agreement. The contract provides for a bonus for early completion. The contract is a fixed price one although provision is made for payment for ordered variations and extra cost caused by statutory requirements.

Extensions of time and claims for loss and expense are linked. Subject to written notice, the contractor may be entitled to an extension of time if, in the opinion of the Supervising Officer (q.v.), completion of the works is delayed for causes 'beyond the control of the contractor or which could not reasonably have been foreseen and being foreseen avoided by the contractor'. Should the Supervising Officer fail to grant an extension of time within 7 days of receipt of

the contractor's notice, he must give written notice
stating his reasons for not so doing.

Whatever the reason for extension of time, e.g.,
adverse weather conditions (q.v.), the contractor is
entitled to any 'proven loss or expense', which seems
to confer on the contractor wider claims than is the
case under other standard forms.

The contract also makes provision for nominated
sub-contractors and suppliers, and there are common
form clauses dealing with certificates and payment,
insurance liabilities, determination, and arbitration.
Copies of the SIAD Works Agreement are available
from SIAD, Nash House, 12 Carlton House Terrace,
London SW1Y 5AH.

| | |
|---|---|
| **SR & O** | An abbreviation for Statutory Rules and Orders (q.v.). |

| | |
|---|---|
| **Sale of goods** | Comprehensive statutory provisions regulating the sale of goods are contained in the Sale of Goods Act 1979, which applies throughout the United Kingdom. |

The Act applies only to sales of goods, and so has no
application to building contracts as such, for they are
contracts for work and materials. However, sales of
building materials to the contractor, and similar
transactions, are within the Act, which implies certain
conditions and warranties as to fitness for purpose
(q.v.), merchantable quality (q.v.), etc.

Under the Act, property in the goods passes at the
time when the parties intend it to pass. Section 18 of
the Act sets out certain presumptions about the
intentions of the parties. It must be noted that the
fact that the price remains unpaid does not affect the
position as to the transfer of ownership unless the
contract provides that property is to pass when the
price is paid. In practice it is now common for the
seller to contract on terms which include a retention
of title (q.v.) clause. Similarly, the parties may agree
that property is to pass before the goods are delivered
and indeed in the case of specific goods, the

presumption is that the parties intend property to pass at the time the contract is made.

In general, a non-owner cannot transfer title to goods, and nobody can give a better title than he himself possesses (*Bishopsgate Motor Finance Co. Ltd v. Transport Brakes Ltd* (1949)) and this principle has caused practical problems under building contracts, especially as regards off-site goods and materials which have been paid for under the contract by the employer and the contractor is not the owner of the goods: *Dawber Williamson Roofing Ltd v. Humberside County Council* (1979). See also: *Ownership of goods and materials; Transfer of risk.*

| | |
|---|---|
| **Sanction** | (i) Under BPF System (q.v.) this is the process by which the Client's Representative successively agrees the work of the design team to ensure that it meets the requirements of the brief. There is a similar process whereby the contractor's design is sanctioned to ensure that it complies with the contract documents (q.v.). Contractually, the latter aspect is dealt with by clauses 2.2-2.4 of the BPF/ACA Contract where the mechanism is laid down. The BPF *Manual* describes the concept of sanctioning as *nihil obstat* (nothing hinders) because, once satisfied, the sanctioned material is returned endorsed 'returned with no comment', the object being to ensure that design responsibility is not diminished. See also: *Approval.* |
| | (ii) Generally, a reaction which indicates approval or disapproval of something – usually conduct – tending to induce conformity with required standards. The word may be used in the sense of authorization or alternatively for the penalty laid down for contravention of some legal requirement. |
| **Schedule contract** | A contract based upon a schedule of prices (q.v.). |
| **Schedule of activities** | The document prepared by the contractor which, under one of the options in the BPF System for building design and construction (q.v.) and which replaces the priced Bill of Quantities (q.v.). It is a |

priced list of separate activities within the contractor's total programme and sets out his design and management intentions, as well as the various construction activities. It is used as part of the tender documents, serves as a programme and for monitoring progress. The Schedule of Activities is one of the contract documents (q.v.) under the BPF/ACA contract and forms the basis of payment to the contractor, who is paid as each specified activity is completed.
Preliminary and recurring items in the Schedule, e.g., site offices, telephone, scaffolding, etc., are paid pro rata as the work proceeds.
The Schedule can also be used by the contractor for monitoring costs and progress during construction. Examples are given in Figures 30 and 31. See also: *BPF System; Schedule of rates.*

| | |
|---|---|
| **Schedule of basic prices of materials** | A list of the basic prices of materials from which the contractor has produced his tender. If a fluctuation clause is contained in the contract, the contractor will be required to submit a schedule of basic rates of materials so that adjustment of prices can be carried out. The contractor is usually asked to present estimates to support his rates. Careful checking is necessary because certain materials have standard prices and prices vary with the amount required. |
| **Schedule of prices** | Where time is very short or it is not practicable for some other reason to prepare even bills of approximate quantities (q.v.), a schedule may be produced giving descriptions only of the work to be carried out and the materials to be used. The employer may put prices against each item and require tenderers to state the percentage above or below the given prices for which they would be prepared to carry out the work. Alternatively, the tenderers may be asked to put their own prices against the items. It is extremely difficult to prepare a tender by this method or to compare tenders received, because contractors normally balance their rates in accordance with the amounts of work and materials |

**Tender submission schedule of activities**

Project:

Contractor:                                                                 Schedule/Sheet No.

| No. | Activity description | Quantity | Resources | Start time (week no.) | Duration (weeks) | Price £ |
|---|---|---|---|---|---|---|
| 1.0 | Site set-up | | | 1 | 5 | 27,000 |
| 2.0 | Demolition/site clearance | | | 2 | 5 | 55,000 |
| 3.0 | Piling | | | 7 | 6 | 63,600 |
| 4.0 | Substructure to ground slab | | | 11 | 16 | 360,600 |
| 5.0 | Superstructure to roof | | | 17 | 26 | 470,000 |
| 6.0 | Brickwork/blockwork | Breakdown of quantities to be listed in developed schedule | (See schedule of activities for prelims and plant). Other details to be listed in developed schedule | 17 | 22 | 311,500 |
| 7.0 | Granite cladding | | | 30 | 18 | 204,000 |
| 8.0 | Windows | | | 25 | 16 | 80,000 |
| 9.0 | Roof timbers & leadwork | | | 43 | 12 | 135,400 |
| 10.0 | Mechanical & electrical | | | 30 | 70 | 1,275,000 |
| 11.0 | Lift installation | | | 55 | 20 | 84,000 |
| 12.0 | Plaster & screed | | | 40 | 17 | 140,000 |
| 13.0 | Carpentry | | | 40 | 30 | 240,400 |

**Figure 30**

Minimum information on schedule of activities submitted with a tender

**Tender submission schedule of activities**

Project:    Tender date:
Contractor:    Schedule/Sheet No.

# Figure 31
Schedule of activities used in tender submission showing preliminary cost activities

| No. | Activity description | Quantity | Resources | Start time (week no.) | Duration time (weeks) | Price £ |
|---|---|---|---|---|---|---|
| | Preliminaries | | | | | |
| 1 | Site offices | 60m² | | 1 | 65 | 6,000.00 |
| 2 | Telephone | 2 | | 1 | 68 | 950.00 |
| 3 | Gantry | – | | 1 | 68 | 2,000.00 |
| 4 | Hoardings & scaffolding | – | | varies | varies | 22,5000.00 |
| 5 | Site electrics | – | | varies | varies | 2,600.00 |
| 6 | Insurance | – | as per specification | duration of contract | | 5,500.00 |
| 7 | Water & rates | – | | duration of contract | | 2,750.00 |
| 8 | Staff | 1 | site agent | 2 | 68 | |
| | | 1 | general foreman | 1 | 78 | |
| | | 2 | engineers | 2 | 6 / 10 | 53,400.00 |
| | | 1 | storekeeper | 6 | 60 | |
| | | 1 | timekeeper | 2 | 66 | |
| | | 1 | quantity surveyor | 10 | 68 (inc. final A/C) | |
| 9 | Tower crane (inc. driver banksman( | 1 | G280 | 5 | 30 | 30,000.00 |
| | | 1 | | 5 | 30 | 925.00 |
| 10 | Compressors | 2 | | 1 | 68 | 9,400.00 |
| 11 | Dumpers (inc. drivers) | 2 | 4 tool | 30 | 30 | 750,00 |
| 12 | Vibrator pokers | 3 | | – | – | 68,000.00 |
| 13 | Non-mechanical plant | – | | – | – | 8,500.00 |
| 14 | Site electrician/fitter | 1(½ time) | | 1 | 68 | |
| | | | | | Add to total | £213,275.00 |

390

required. The system is most commonly used for small contracts or for contracts for maintenance work and is also referred to as a Schedule of Rates. See also: *Term contracts*.

**Schedule of rates**　Contracts which do not include bills of quantities (q.v.) but rely on drawings and specifications, require the contractor to submit a schedule of his rates used to arrive at the tender figure in order that variations can be accurately and fairly valued.

The schedule of rates is an optional contract document under ACA 2 (see Recital C ) and under GC/Works/1 (see clause 1).

**Scott Schedule**　A 'Scott' or 'Official Referee's' Schedule is a formal document used in litigation or arbitration, which sets out the issues in dispute in tabular form, with the contentions of the opposing parties. There is no set form prescribed but the object is to present the issues in dispute as clearly as possible. It is common for some of the issues to be resolved at this stage, leaving only minor items, thus simplifying and shortening the hearing. It is good practice to agree the headings for the various columns at the hearing of the summons for direction before the Official Referee (q.v.) or at the preliminary meeting before the arbitrator.

The Scott Schedule was invented by Mr G.A.Scott QC about 60 years ago, and can be used in cases involving a multiplicity of claims to require each party to set out his case positively item by item and to answer each other party's case in the same way. The Schedule can be extended to claims between defendants and to third and subsequent parties. From the completed Schedule representative items are selected for trial, so avoiding the necessity of trying all. Various examples of a Scott Schedule are set out in Emden's *Building Contracts*, 4th edn., vol. 1, pp. 556-7; Keating's *Building Contracts*, 4th edn., pp. 262-7 and Powell-Smith and Sims, *Building Contract Claims*, pp. 274-6.

The judge or arbitrator has power to order the preparation of such a schedule.

**Scott v. Avery clause**   A provision in an arbitration clause which has the object of preventing the court from interfering with the arbitration agreement by allowing the parties to bring an action in the courts. Its validity was upheld by the House of Lords in the case of this name in 1856, holding that a party had no right to sue until arbitration had taken place and that it was not contrary to public policy to enforce such a clause. The usual wording is:

'Arbitration shall be a condition precedent to the commencement of any action at law' or

'The obligation shall be to pay such a sum as may be awarded upon arbitration under this clause.'

Other words may have the same effect.

None of the current standard forms of contract in the building industry contains a *Scott v. Avery* clause but where one is included the parties have no right to litigate until arbitration has taken place. See also: *Arbitration; Stay of proceedings.*

**Seal**   Technically, a device affixed on wax or impressed on a wafer as a mark of authentication. Many building contracts are executed under seal in the form of deeds (q.v.), but today contracts under seal (called 'specialty contracts') differ little from ordinary or simple contracts made orally or in writing. Today it is not necessary to seal the document physically (*First National Securities Ltd v. Jones* (1975)) but specialty contracts differ from simple contracts in three respects:

— Under the Limitation Act 1980 the limitation period (q.v.) is 12 years as opposed to 6 years.

— Consideration (q.v.) is not necessary to support promises made under seal.

—In theory the parties cannot deny statements of fact contained in a deed, including its Recitals (q.v.). See also: *Attestation; Locus Sigilli.*

**Sealed offer**   In proceedings before the Lands Tribunal (q.v.) about compensation claims for compulsory purchase the acquiring authority may make an unconditional offer of compensation in a sealed envelope. If the sum eventually awarded is the same or less than the amount of the offer, then the claimant does not get his costs. It is the equivalent of a payment into court (q.v.). The existence of the sealed offer is not disclosed to the Lands Tribunal until it has given its decision. Sealed offers are sometimes used in arbitration (q.v.) and the practice was approved by Donaldson J. in *Tramountana Armadora SA v. Atlantic Shipping Co. SA* (1978). He said: 'A "sealed offer" is the arbitral equivalent of making a payment into court in settlement of the litigation or of particular causes of action in that litigation. Neither the fact, nor the amount, of such a payment into court can be revealed to the judge trying the case until he has given judgment on all matters other than costs. As it is customary for an award to deal at one and the same time both with the parties' claims and with the question of costs, the existence of a sealed offer has to be brought to the attention of the arbitrator before he has reached a decision. However, it should remain sealed at that stage and it would be wholly improper for the arbitrator to look at it before he has reached a final decision on the matters in dispute other than as to costs, or to revise that decision in the light of the terms of the sealed offer when he sees them.'

There are, in fact, substantial objections to the practice, which are usefully summarized in the Commercial Court Committee Report on Arbitration 1978 (Cmnd 7284), paras 62-5, the main objection being that 'the arbitrator, unlike a judge, will know that some offer of settlement has been made, although he will not know how much'.

An alternative course is to make an *open offer* on terms that its existence and contents must not be disclosed to the arbitrator until he has reached a final decision on liability when it will be drawn to his attention. It should offer to pay costs up to the time of its receipt and state whether or not it includes interest. The letter of offer should state that it is intended to have the effect of a payment into court. An example of such a letter is shown in Figure 32. At

**Figure 32**

Letter of offer: example

To – The other side                                      *Date*

Dear Sirs,

*Heading*

We hereby offer you the sum of £x in full and final settlement of all your claims in this matter, *(if appropriate* including the sum of £y in interest on the amount of your claim of £z, calculated at *state rate).*

This offer is intended to have the effect of payment into court pursuant to Order 22 of the Rules of the Supreme Court, and is made on terms that its existence and contents must not be disclosed to the arbitrator until he has determined all issues of liability and quantum herein.

If you do not accept it, we shall draw the arbitrator's attention to it as to costs after he has determined the issues between us.

In addition to the foregoing, we hereby offer to pay your costs (on a party and party basis *or* in the sum of £x) up to the date of receipt of this offer by you.

Yours faithfully,

the end of the hearing before the arbitrator he should be asked to make an interim award on liability and amount and, without the existence of the offer being disclosed, he should be asked to defer consideration of costs until he has made his interim award on the other issues. This procedure is commonly used and is suggested in Keating's *Building Contracts*, 4th edn., pp. 274-5.

An alternative procedure is to make a 'without prejudice' (q.v.) offer, backed up by a deposit of money in the joint names of the parties or their solicitors, and once again to ask the arbitrator to make an interim award on liability and amount. 'If the claimant in the end has achieved no more than he would have achieved by accepting the offer, the continuance of the arbitration after that date has been a waste of time and money. *Prima facie*, the claimant should recover his costs up to the date of the offer and should be ordered to pay the respondent's costs after that date': Donaldson J. in the *Tramountana* case.

| | |
|---|---|
| **Seizure and vesting** | See: *Vesting and seizure*. |
| **Serial contract** | If it is desired to carry out a number of contracts in succession, this type of contract may be employed. On the basis of the successful tender for the first contract, further contracts are negotiated. To operate properly, all the projects must be similar in construction and type so that negotiation for future contracts on the basis of the original contract is feasible. It is usual for the employer to make some sort of limited commitment to the successful tenderer for the whole series. However, it is not something which can be legally enforced since it is always subject to the successful outcome of negotiations. The advantage is that one set of tendering takes place and the contractor can use the experience gained on the first contract to improve efficiency thereafter. For maximum benefit for the employer, the basic terms for succeeding contracts in the series should be |

established when calling for the initial tender. An intended programme for all contracts in the series should be set down at the outset if the contractor is to be able to calculate the potential benefits to the full. The system should produce savings for both parties but it is often difficult to operate in practice.

**Service of notices, etc.**

All the standard forms of contract require the service of notices, certificates, etc., to follow certain procedures. In order to preserve the effect of such notices, employer, architect and contractor must carefully observe the procedure laid down. Although it may be considered doubtful whether a court would reject a notice served under JCT 80, clause 28.1.1 because a notice was served by hand for a receipt instead of by registered post or recorded delivery as prescribed, it is not worth taking the risk since courts can take a very literal view of the wording in the contract (see: *Removal of defective work*). JCT 80 deals with certificates (q.v.) in clause 5.8 and throughout the contract under the appropriate clauses. Notices are also dealt with under each clause as they arise. ACA 2 deals with notices in clause 23.1 and throughout the contract particularly as far as timing is concerned. GC/Works/1 deals with certificates under clause 42 and with notices throughout the contract. IFC 84 deals with certificates in clause 1.9 and, throughout the contract, notices are also dealt with as they arise.

**Set-off**

Most standard form building contracts contain a clause empowering the employer to set-off, by way of deduction from sums certified by the architect, certain specific and limited sums. The effect of such a clause depends entirely on its wording. For example, the JCT Standard Form of Nominated Sub-Contract (NSC/4), clause 23, is a comprehensive set-off clause. It contains the following provision:
'The rights of the parties to the sub-contract in respect of set-off are fully set out in the sub-contract NSC/4 and no other rights whatsoever shall be implied as

terms of the sub-contract relating to set-off.'
A right of set-off is implied by the general law, but it can be excluded by an appropriate contract term, and probably by necessary implication looking at the contract as a whole: *Gilbert-Ash (Northern) Ltd v. Modern Engineering (Bristol) Ltd* (1973); *Mottram Consultants Ltd v. Bernard Sunley & Sons Ltd* (1974). In the absence of the right being excluded, the employer is entitled to set-off against amounts certified by the architect. A set-off may also be pleaded as a defence under the Rules of the Supreme Court. See also: *Counterclaim*.

| | |
|---|---|
| **Setting out** | The procedure whereby the dimensions of a structure are transferred to the site by means of measuring tapes, theodolites, etc. The principal walls of a building, or the position of piles are indicated by pins, lines and profiles. The process calls for great accuracy and on large and complex works a specialized setting out engineer may carry out this part of the work. The architect is responsible for the accuracy of the drawings and for providing sufficient information to enable setting out to be completed ( JCT 80, clause 7). He is not responsible for the accuracy of the setting out itself. That is the contractor's responsibility. It is good practice for the architect to provide special drawings showing only the outline of the building on the site and such dimensions as are necessary for setting out. Unfortunately, it is common for drawings to be deficient in this respect necessitating the architect's visiting site and assisting the contractor to set out, if only by approving what has been done. The architect should avoid giving approval to the contractor's setting out by preparing properly dimensioned drawings, otherwise he runs the risk of accepting liability for any inaccuracies. |
| **Settlement** | 1. In construction terms, it is the movement of a building in response to alterations in the bearing capacity of the ground. |

2. In law, it is an arrangement of property in such a way as to create a trust. It is often done by will or by a deed.

3. An agreement, by parties in dispute, to compromise or otherwise put an end to their differences before any court or arbitration hearing takes place. It is always wise for litigants to settle if possible rather than run the risk and expense of court proceedings. It is also prudent to embody the terms of the settlement in contract form.

| | |
|---|---|
| **Shop drawings** | Short for 'workshop drawings'. Architect's and engineer's drawings are often not suitable for the manufacture of certain building components. Special drawings, termed 'shop drawings' must be produced to enable joinery, steelwork, sheet metalwork, etc., to be produced. These drawings are normally the responsibility of the manufacturer although he may, through the contractor, request the architect's approval to shop drawings before manufacture. The architect is under no obligation to give such approval – indeed it may be dangerous to do so – provided his own drawings contain all necessary information. It is usual, however, for the architect to examine any shop drawings sent to him and make any comments necessary while expressly reserving his approval. |
| **Shortage of labour and materials** | Grounds for extension of time under JCT 80, clause 25.4.10, provided that the shortage is for reasons beyond the control of the contractor which he could not reasonably have foreseen at the date of tender. IFC 84, clause 2.4.10 is an optional provision to the same effect. |
| **Shrinkages** | A term used in some of the standard forms of contract to indicate a type of defect which the contractor is liable to make good during the defects liability period (q.v.). The normal meaning of 'shrink' is to grow smaller in size. It is a characteristic of many materials used in building that they increase or decrease in size |

depending upon physical factors such as moisture or temperature, or chemical factors such as the reaction which takes place when mixing concrete or plaster. The contractor's liability for shrinkages is commonly misunderstood, not least by the contractor himself. He is liable to make good only if his workmanship or materials are not in accordance with the contract. For example: if the contract specifies the use of internal timber having a moisture content of 7%, and shrinkage of skirtings and architraves is found to have taken place at the end of the defects liability period, it may not be the contractor's liability. The excessive use of central heating may have reduced the moisture content of the timber, and hence the size, to 4%. It is a complicated point. It is easy to see that shrinkage has taken place but not easy to determine the cause. The architect will probably say that the timber brought onto site by the contractor was or was allowed to become of a greater moisture content than specified and that it was the drying out of the excess moisture which caused the shrinkage. The problem is not made easier by the fact that it is quite difficult to determine moisture content within 2 or 3% without removing a sample and testing under laboratory conditions. If a great deal of money is at stake, it may be worth the contractor's paying to have such a test carried out. If he proves to be correct and the architect had been withholding his certificate on account of the shrinkages, the contractor would have the basis of a sizeable claim at common law if he wished to press it.

Most contractors are extremely generous in making good shrinkages, probably because of the difficulty of proving the point and the retention money outstanding.

The contractor cannot refuse to make good a shrinkage on the ground that 'it is impossible to maintain a low moisture content in timber until the building is occupied'. It is in fact very difficult, but not impossible, and the contractor contracted to do it.

**Signature**

The name or mark of a person in his own writing, i.e., written by himself or by proxy (q.v.). The form is not prescribed and, therefore, it may be the full name, initials or any combination of the two. In some cases a signature may be valid if it is made by a mark properly witnessed, a rubber stamp or made by another with proper authority. The adding of a signature is taken as a sign of agreement. Many people, particularly those in public life, have an 'official' signature in an attempt to differentiate between an 'autograph' and their signatures on legal documents. Such attempts will only be effective, however, in so far as the parties likely to be affected are aware of the difference. For example, a bank may be informed that a particular form of signature must be the only form recognized for the drawing of cheques.

In Scotland the term 'signature' does not include marks, proxy or rubber stamp except in certain cases authorized by statute.

**Similar**

A word found in JCT 80, clause 13 and GC/Works/1, clause 9. For a discussion of its meaning see: *Fair valuation*.

**Simple contract**

A contract which is not under seal but made in writing and signed or made orally or by conduct. See also: *Contract*.

**Site**

Not always clearly defined in the contract, but a definition is given in clause 1(2) of GC/Works/1: '"the site" means the land or place which may be allotted or used for the purposes of carrying out the Contract'. A clear understanding of the extent of the site is important to the contractor in connection with possession (q.v.) and access (q.v.). Failure by the employer to give possession of 'the site' is a breach of contract. Adequate definition in the the contract documents (q.v.) is essential. See also: *Examination of site*.

**Site conditions**

In the absence of any specific guarantee or definite representations by the employer or his architect about site conditions, the nature of the ground, and related matters, the contractor is not entitled to abandon the contract or claim extra money on discovering the nature of the soil. Equally, under the general law, he has no claim for damages against the employer.

The position may be affected by the express terms (q.v.) of the contract. GC/Works/1, clause 2 reiterates the common law rule. It places on the contractor the risk that site and allied conditions may turn out more onerous than he expected.

In contrast, the optional clause 2.6 of ACA 2, gives the contractor a potential claim if he encounters 'adverse ground conditions or artificial obstructions at the Site' as work progresses. He must notify the architect immediately and the architect must issue an appropriate instruction. Compliance with this will rank for payment unless the ground conditions, etc., could have been reasonably foreseen by a skilled, experienced and qualified contractor at the date the contract was made.

Under JCT 80 and its derivatives the position is more complex, but where SMM 6 is used the contractor may well have a claim against the employer in respect of adverse ground conditions.

In *C. Bryant & Son Ltd v. Birmingham Hospital Saturday Fund* (1938), Bryant contracted to erect a convalescent home. The contract was in RIBA form with clauses equivalent to JCT 63 and JCT 80. The Bills formed part of the contract, clause 11 of which said 'the quality and quantity of the work ... shall be deemed to be that which is set out in the bills ... which ... shall be deemed to have been prepared' in accordance with the then current SMM.

This required that, where practicable, the nature of the soil should be described and that attention should be drawn to any trial holes, and that excavation in rock should be given separately. The bills referred the contractor to the drawings, a block plan and the site, to satisfy himself of the local conditions and the full nature and extent of the operations. The architect knew that there was rock on site, but it was not shown on the plans or referred to in the bills. They contained no separate item for excavation of rock.

The High Court held that Bryant was entitled to treat the excavation in rock as an extra and to be paid the extra cost of the excavation plus a fair profit. There is no material difference between the contract provisions in this case and those of JCT 80, clause 2.2.2.1 of which says that the Bills are to be prepared in accordance with SMM 6, unless otherwise stated. Various provisions in SMM 6, require the giving of information about ground conditions. For example, para. D3.2 states: 'If the above information is not available a description of the ground and strata which is assumed shall be stated.' In many cases a contractor working under JCT 80 will have a claim and may, under clause 2.2.2.2 treat corrections as a variation for 'any error in description or quantity'.

Other remedies may be available to the contractor, e.g., if there has been a misrepresentation (q.v.) about the ground conditions. For example, in *Morrison-Knudsen International v. Commonwealth of Australia* (1972), contractors were misled by site information provided by the employer. The employer may try to protect himself by a disclaimer of liability, but the case law establishes that this is not an easy thing to do and the courts seem prone to impose liability if it is possible to do so.

**Site manager**

A term used in ACA 2, clause 5.2, to describe the contractor's full-time representative on site in charge of the works. He must be appointed before work starts on site and the architect's consent to both his appointment and removal or replacement is necessary. Some of his duties are described in clause 5.3. He is to attend meetings convened by the architect in connection with the works, must keep complete and accurate records and make these available for inspection by the architect. Like all the contractor's employees under ACA 2 he must be properly skilled, qualified and experienced. His is a key appointment. See also: *Person-in-charge*.

**Sit-in**

An expression of industrial dispute in which people occupy some building or place (usually their place of work) until their demands are satisfied or they are forcibly evicted. It is trespass (q.v.). Although strike (q.v.) and lock-out (q.v.) are expressly stated in some contracts as grounds for extension of time, a 'sit-in' is not included.

| | |
|---|---|
| **Snagging list** | An expression commonly used on site for any list of defects. In an endeavour to be helpful, a clerk of works (q.v.) will often go beyond his duties and provide the contractor with a list of work requiring to be completed or rectified before, in the opinion of the clerk of works, the works will be ready for the architect to certify completion. The list is, of course, of no contractual significance and binds neither the architect nor the contractor. The contractor is under no obligation to take notice of the 'snagging list', only to fulfil his obligations under the contract. Nevertheless, contractors often welcome such a list and architects often encourage the clerk of works to prepare such a list before completion. There is a danger that the contractor will be persuaded to do more than is necessary and the architect should not become associated with such a list unless he wishes to be bound by it. The architect should never mention the clerk of works' snagging list in any correspondence. The 'contractor's list' and the 'architect's list' mentioned in ACA 2 (clause 12.1) are empowered by that contract. They are likely to be referred to indiscriminately on site as 'snagging lists'. The term is also commonly given to the 'schedule of defects' (q.v.) which the architect prepares at the end of the defects liability period (q.v.) under JCT 80. Although it is too much to expect that the expression will be obliterated from site conversation, the architect should be meticulous in using the correct terms to avoid confusion. |
| **Special case** | Prior to the Arbitration Act 1979 an arbitrator (q.v.) could state a special case on any point of law arising in the course of the reference. The award (q.v.) was given in the form of a special case. It is now replaced by a *limited* right of appeal See also: *Case stated; Point of law*. |

**Special damage(s)**     Damage of a kind which the law will not presume in the plaintiff's favour, but which must be specifically pleaded and proved at the trial or arbitration hearing, e.g., interest on money (q.v.) in some cases, loss of profit, medical expenses, etc. It is contrasted with *general damages* which are the damages the law presumes will have resulted from the defendant's act. See also: *Damages; Pleadings.*

**Specialist**     A person who concentrates on a particular facet of his trade or profession. Thus a lawyer may specialize in building contract law, an architect may specialize in the restoration of old buildings, etc. In the context of construction contracts, it refers to a person or firm who concentrates on a particular aspect of the construction process, e.g., lift installation, heating, lighting, etc.

**Specialty contract**     A contract under seal is so called. See: *Contract.*

**Specific performance**     Where damages (q.v.) would be inadequate compensation for breach of contract (q.v.) the contractor may be compelled to perform what he has agreed to do by a decree of specific performance. The court will not grant specific performance of an ordinary building contract which would, in effect, require supervision by the court (*Hepburn v. Leather* (1884); *Ryan v. Mutual Tontine Westminster Chambers Association* (1893)). However, if someone agrees to lease land and erect buildings on it, he may be granted a decree of specific performance provided:
— The building work is defined by the contract.
— The plaintiff has a substantial interest in the performance of the contract such that damages would be inadequate compensation for the defendant's failure to build.
— The defendant is in possession of the land.
Specific performance is a discretionary remedy (q.v.) and is commonly used to compel performance of contracts for the sale, purchase or lease of land. It will not be granted in the case of contracts of personal service.

| **Specification** | A document which, together with the drawings, describes in detail the whole of the workmanship and materials to be used in the construction of a building. In contracts which include bills of quantities (q.v.) as part of the contract documents (q.v.) the specification is not always a contract document but is merely to assist the contractor and amplify the drawings. Where no bills are included in the contract documents, such as JCT 80 Without Quantities Edition, the specification becomes a very important contract document. In this latter case, it will include preliminaries as for bills of quantities and preambles as part of the trade descriptions. |

The specification must describe:

— Quality of materials.
— Quality of workmanship.
— Assembly.
— Location.

The main body of the document is normally divided into trades or elements of construction in much the same sequence as they would be built. Where the specification is to be priced, every detail of the work must be described but not quantified.

The National Building Specification, published by NBS Services Ltd, provides a comprehensive range of standard clauses to simplify the production of both specifications and bills of quantities. See also: *Performance specification.*

| **Speed reply** | A system of answering letters particularly favoured by busy executives. In essence, the system works as follows. The answer to correspondence is typed or written on the bottom of the letter to which it refers. The letter is then photocopied and the copy sent to the correspondent. The original is sent to file. Advantages are, as the name suggests, speed, efficiency and saving on expense. Disadvantages are that it must be brief and may not be fully understood by the recipient. |

The system is said to have originated in South Africa.

**Stage payment**

A general term often used to indicate any payment made during the progress of the work. It is more accurately used for payments made at specific stages of work, e.g., DPC level, first floor level, eaves level, etc. This mode of payment is usually confined to relatively small lump sum contracts (q.v.) without quantities where a proportion of the total sum is agreed to be paid over in a number of stages. The proportions are fixed and do not depend upon any re-measurement of work.

The BPF System (q.v.) provides for stage payments of consultants (q.v.) in lump sums depending upon the stage reached in the design and development process. The BPF System also provides, in effect, for stage payments to contractors except that the contractor determines the stages and the amount payable in the Schedule of Activities (q.v.). See also: *Interim certificate; Interim payment.*

**Stamp duty**

Revenue which is raised by means of stamps fixed to conveyances, deeds, and so on. Stamp duty is normally paid by means of impressed stamps. Before the Finance Act 1985, a fixed stamp duty of 50p was payable in the case of a contract under seal. This was to be impressed by the Inland Revenue within 30 days of the execution of the contract. It is no longer normally necessary to stamp building contracts under seal unless they are complicated by other matters such as conveyances, in which case they must be stamped *ad valorem*. Formerly (until 1 August 1970) even contracts under hand required to be stamped, the duty in that case being 6d.

| **Standard forms of contract** | A printed form of contract containing standard conditions which are applicable (or can be made applicable by the use of alternatives) to a wide range of building projects. They are generally preferable to specially drafted contracts because they are intended to be comprehensive and avoid most of the pitfalls which surround contractual relations in the building industry. Examples of standard forms are:<br>— The JCT series of contracts (q.v.).<br>— The ACA contract (q.v.).<br>— GC/Works/1 and 2 (q.v.).<br>A comparison of some standard forms is shown in Table 25. |
|---|---|
| **Standard method of measurement (SMM)** | A document published by the Royal Institution of Chartered Surveyors and the Building Employers Confederation (formerly the National Federation of Building Trades Employers). Its purpose is to assist all connected with the construction industry by standardizing and rationalizing procedures for the preparation of bills of quantities (q.v.). It lays down rules governing the extent to which items should be separately identified or quantified in the Bills of Quantities or shall be deemed to be included, or separately referred to in the description of another item. The current edition is Number 6, but the document is revised at regular intervals to effect improvements and take account of developments in the industry. JCT 80 expressly states, at clause 2.2.2.1, that the contract bills (q.v.), unless otherwise specifically stated therein, are to have been prepared in accordance with the SMM. |
| **Standing offer** | Where tenders (q.v.) are invited for the carrying out of work or the supply or goods or services over a period of time at irregular intervals, the tenderer may make a standing offer. Whether or not he does so depends on the terms of his offer (q.v.) and the acceptance (q.v.).<br>If the tender is to the effect that the contractor will supply, e.g., 'bricks, if and when required between |

1 January and 31 December 1985' this is a standing offer. It is an offer to supply such quantities as may be required. A standing offer may be withdrawn at any time before it is accepted by placing a specific order. Once an order for a specified quantity is placed, the contractor must supply the goods ordered; the order is the acceptance: *Percival Ltd v. L.C.C. Asylums & Mental Deficiency Committee* (1918).

| **Standing orders** | Rules of procedure which apply in Parliament, local and public authority organizations, etc. Local authority standing orders may lay down rules which must be observed in the making of contracts, etc., e.g., as to when a performance bond (q.v.) is required or when a contract must be entered into under seal. They are internal procedures. For example, a local authority cannot rid itself of an onerous burden assumed under a contract by pleading that the contract is void because it was entered into contrary to standing orders. This situation must be distinguished from that where an authority has entered into a contract *ultra vires* (q.v.).
The Local Government Act 1972, s. 135, allows local authorities to contract in any way authorized by standing orders. Contractors dealing with local authorities are not affixed with notice of standing orders and so are protected if standing orders have not been complied with. The provision, however, does not validate an otherwise invalid contract, e.g., if in fact the local authority never consented to contract at all: *North West Leicestershire District Council v. East Midlands Housing Association Ltd* (1981). See also: *Local authority; Ultra vires*. |

| **Stare decisis** | Literally, to stand by things decided. It refers to the binding force of judicial precedent (q.v.) and is the basis of all legal argument and decision of the common law in England and other countries. In certain circumstances the judge is *bound* to stand by the decided cases, although the judges exercise considerable ingenuity in seeking to avoid the application of precedents which they dislike. |

| **Statement of claim;** **Points of claim** | The formal document in which the plaintiff in litigation or the claimant in arbitration set out all the facts which form the basis of the case, and a statement of the remedy required. This document is called a Statement of Claim in court proceedings and Points of Claim in arbitration. It needs to be drafted most carefully. See also: *Pleadings*. |
|---|---|
| **Statute** | An Act of Parliament (q.v.). |
| **Statute-barred** | Sometimes actions cannot be brought successfully because of lapse of time even though the cause of action may otherwise be sound. Such actions are said to be 'statute-barred' because of the time limits which are imposed by the Limitation Act 1980 in England and Wales and by the Prescription and Limitation (Scotland) Act 1973, as amended. See also: *Limitation of actions*. |
| **Statutory duty,** **breach of** | Many statutes impose duties on individuals to do something or not to do something and the statute itself may provide the only remedy (q.v.). In other cases, e.g., the Factories Act 1961 and related statutes, statute imposes general statutory duties in respect of classes of people, such as employees. Breach of statutory duty in this sense can give rise to a claim for damages in tort (q.v.) when – as a result of a breach of the statutory duty – a person is injured, e.g., *Quinn v. J. W. Green (Painters) Ltd* (1965). It is a question of interpretation whether the statute gives a special remedy or whether it co-exists with an existing common law remedy, e.g., an action for damages for negligence. In some cases the statutory duty is merely enforceable by sanctions of the criminal law. For example, the Health & Safety at Work, etc. Act 1974 imposes general duties on employers, employees, and others, but s. 47 of the Act makes it clear that such duties do not generally confer any right of civil action, i.e., if there is a breach of the Act's provisions, the injured person cannot bring a claim for damages for breach |

of the broken duty.

Statutory duties may be absolute (q.v.) but this is unusual. The position under the building regulations is not clear, but breach of a statutory duty imposed by these regulations is probably not an absolute offence. It has been held that breach of building bylaws does not give rise to liability in damages (*Perry v. Tendring District Council* (1985)).

Claims for damages for breach of stautory duty are very common and it is probable that the duty to comply with statutory requirements overrides even an express contractual obligation. See: *Street v. Sibbabridge Ltd* (1980).

| | |
|---|---|
| **Statutory instruments** | The most important class of subordinate or delegated legislation. For the most part they are regulations made by a Secretary of State, e.g., The Building Regulations 1985, for particular purposes. They have the force of law. |
| **Statutory rules and orders** | Regulations which were formerly made by the King in Council, Government departments and other authorities. In 1948 they were superseded by statutory instruments (q.v.). |
| **Statutory undertakers** | Organizations such as Water Authorities, Gas and Electricity Boards which are authorized by statute (q.v.) to construct and operate public utility undertakings. They derive their powers from statute, either directly or from previous authorities undertaking the function by virtue of statutory instruments (q.v.). Although their powers are extensive, they are not absolute, and constraints are placed upon the exercise of their powers. Failure to observe these constraints can lead to complaints being laid before the appropriate Minister or to an action for damages (q.v.) or an injunction being pursued in the courts.<br><br>Statutory undertakers may be involved in a building |

contract either in performance of their statutory obligations or as contractors or sub-contractors. When performing their statutory obligations they are not liable in contract (*Clegg Parkson & Co. v. Earby Gas Co.* (1896); *Willmore v. S. E. Electricity Board* (1957)), although they may be liable in tort (q.v.). Most standard building contracts draw a distinction between statutory undertakers performing their statutory duties as such and those cases where they are acting as contractors. JCT 80, clause 6.3 draws that distinction, which is also relevant in claims (q.v.) situations. In *Henry Boot Construction Ltd v. Central Lancashire New Town Development Corporation* (1980) the case was concerned with whether statutory undertakers were 'artists, tradesmen or others engaged by the Employer' for the purposes of clauses 23 (h) and 24 (1)(d) of JCT 1963, which are reformulated in JCT 80, clauses 25.4.8.1 and 26.2.4.1. The High Court held, on the facts, that the statutory undertakers there were within the phrase 'artists, tradesmen or others' because they were performing their work by virtue of a contract with the employer and not under statutory authority. The practical result was that, on the facts, the contractor was entitled to both an extension of time and to recover loss and/or expense (q.v.).

The judge said: 'If the employers contract with statutory undertakers, they can contract to provide for what is to happen if the undertakers are guilty of delay, just as they can so provide if they employ an artist or tradesman, and it is just that they should bear this risk, which they have had the opportunity of safeguarding themselves against. If, however, without having a contract, undertakers, using their statutory powers to fulfil their statutory obligations, came on the scene and hindered the works and caused delay, then the consequential loss would be one like *force majeure* which can be laid at the door' of neither party. It is, therefore, important to determine in which capacity the statutory undertakers are carrying out work. See also: *Boskalis Westminster Construction Ltd v.*

*Liverpool City Council* (1983), where it was held that a strike by workers employed by statutory undertakers engaged by the employer to execute work not forming part of the Works was not covered by JCT 63, clause 23(d) ( JCT 80, clause 25.4.4).

ACA 2 draws a similar distinction in clause 10, the result of which is the same as under JCT 80.

---

**Stay of proceedings**

The courts have very wide powers to put a stop, temporary or permanent, to proceedings brought before them, as part of their inherent jurisdiction. Specific powers are also conferred on them by statute (q.v.) in many cases.

So far as building contracts are concerned, the most important practical example is the general discretion conferred on the court under s. 4(1) of the Arbitration Act 1950 to stay proceedings brought in breach of a 'domestic arbitration agreement'.

Since the majority of standard form contracts contain an arbitration clause, this means in practice that if one party starts legal proceedings against the other e.g., for non-payment on a certificate, the defendant can apply to the court for the proceedings to be halted.

The rules governing this are complex, but the most important one is that the applicant must show a genuine wish to have the dispute resolved by arbitration. See also: *Arbitration*.

---

**Strict liability**

Liability irrespective of fault. It arises under the rule in *Rylands v. Fletcher* (1868). Negligence need not be proved where things likely to cause damage are kept on property. The rule is:

'A person who for his own purposes brings on to his land and collects and keeps there anything likely to do mischief if it escapes, must keep it at his peril and, if he does not do so, is *prima facie* answerable for all the damage which is the natural consequence of its escape.'

The following points should be noted:

— The rule only applies to a 'non-natural use of land',

e.g., blasting operations, demolition operations, water in a reservoir. It does not apply to things naturally on land or to the use of water, etc., for ordinary domestic purposes.
— There must be an *escape* from the land.
— Liability is strict but not absolute (q.v.) but it arises independently of either negligence (q.v.) or nuisance (q.v.).
— Various defences are available, e.g., Act of God (q.v.); that the damage was caused by the plaintiff's own act or default; that the escape was due to a third party, statutory authority, etc.

**Strike**

A simultaneous withdrawal of labour by the whole or a major part of an employer's workforce (employer used in the general sense). In many forms of building contract, it is a ground for extension of time, e.g., JCT 80, clause 25.4.4, IFC 84, clause 2.4.4, GC/Works/1, clause 28(2)(d), expressly stated. ACA 2 does not refer to strikes, but it is thought that an extension could be given under the head of *force majeure* (q.v.).

**Sub-contract**

A contract made between a main contractor and another contractor for part of the work which the main contractor has already contracted to carry out as part of his contract with the employer. Such other contractor is referred to as a sub-contractor. See also: *Assignment and sub-letting; Domestic sub-contractor; Named sub-contractor; Nominated sub-contractor.*

**Sub-contractor**

A person or firm to whom part of the main contract works are sub-let. See also: *Assignment and sub-letting.*

**Subject to contract**

In general, the use of the phrase 'subject to contract' indicates an intention not to be bound. There is no enforceable obligation until the contract (usually a formal document) is made. This is commonly the case in contracts for the sale of land.
However, where the parties are agreed on the terms of the contract and acceptance is made subject to the

execution of a formal document, it is a question of interpretation (q.v.) for the courts to decide whether or not there is a concluded contract: *Branca v. Cobarro* (1947). See also: *Acceptance; Conditional contract; Contract; Offer.*

| | |
|---|---|
| **Subpoena** | A writ issued by the High Court requiring the person to whom it is addressed to be present at a specified time and place and for a specified purpose, subject to a penalty (*subpoena*) should he fail to comply. A subpoena is normally used where a witness is not prepared to attend voluntarily. The writ takes two forms, *subpoena ad testificandum*, which is used for the purpose of compelling a witness to attend and give evidence, and *subpoena duces tecum*, when the witness is required to bring documents with him. In arbitration (q.v.) proceedings, application must be made to the High Court for a *subpoena*; the arbitrator (q.v.) himself has no power to compel the attendance of witnesses and the procedure is rarely used in arbitration. A witness summoned by subpoena who, without reasonable excuse, refuses to attend or refuses to answer questions is liable to be punished for contempt of court, provided that the writ has been properly served on him. |
| **Subrogation** | The substitution of one person or thing for another. Someone who discharges a liability on another's behalf is, in general terms, put in the place of that other person for the purpose of obtaining relief against any other person who is liable. The most important practical example arises in the field of insurance where an insurer who compensates a policy holder for loss is entitled to stand in the policy holder's shoes and recover from the person who caused the loss. |
| **Substantial completion** | In an ordinary lump sum contract (q.v.) provided the contractor has *substantially* performed his work, he will be entitled to recover the contract price, less a deduction in respect of defects: *Hoenig v. Isaacs* (1952). The nature of the defects must be taken into account |

414

as well as the proportion between the cost of rectifying them and the contract price: *Bolton v. Mahadeva* (1972). Substantial completion means complete in all major particulars and should be contrasted with 'practical completion' (q.v.).

The form of contract which comes nearest to requiring substantial completion is GC/Works/1, clause 28. The work is to be carried on and completed to the satisfaction of the SO. It is clear that the SO may accept a lesser state of completion than what is envisaged in the JCT forms. However, substantial completion implies that only very minor items will be outstanding. The SO's certificate marks the date at which:

— The contractor's liability for liquidated damages ends (clause 29(1)).

— The SO can require all copies of the specification, bills of quantities and drawings to be returned (clause 4(4)).

— The contractor's liability for frost damage ends (clause 32(2)).

— The contractor is entitled to receive the estimated final sum less one half of the retention (clause 41(1)).

— Reference to arbitration can be opened under clause 61(1).

— The maintenance period begins (Abstract of Particulars). See also: *Performance*.

| | |
|---|---|
| **Substantially** | To a considerable degree, not trivial. |
| **Substitute sub-contractors** | In the BPF variant of ACA 2, clause 9.6 makes provision for the situation where the contractor is unable, for any reason beyond his control, to enter into a sub-contract with a named sub-contractor (q.v.) or supplier. The contractor is given the duty to select another person to carry out the work or supply the materials which must be of equivalent standard and quality. The contractor is not entitled to any damage, loss and/or expense or any extension of time in complying with the provisions of this clause. |
| **Substituted contract** | A substituted contract arises where there is a novation (q.v.) and a new contract is substituted for the old. If the substituted contract incorporates or refers to the |

original one, the two will generally be read together (*A. Vigers Sons & Co. Ltd v. Swindell* (1939)), but the liabilities of the parties are always a question of interpretation.

## Suitability for purpose

Under s. 14 of the Sale of Goods Act 1979 there is an implied condition (q.v.) that goods are reasonably fit for the purpose required in circumstances where the buyer is relying on the seller's skill and judgment, as is normally the case. U ider the Unfair Contract Terms Act 1977 (q.v.) this – and other terms implied by the Act – can be excluded only to a limited extent. As regards building work generally, it is now settled law that, in the absence of some express term removing the liability, 'the builder will do his work in a good and workmanlike manner; that he will supply good and proper materials; and – at least where there is no architect – that (the completed structure) will be reasonably fit for the purpose required' – see, e.g., *Hancock v. B. W. Brazier (Anerley) Ltd* (1966). Where contractors and sub-contractors undertake to design (q.v.) the whole or part of a structure it is implied that they undertake to design a structure which is reasonably suitable for the purpose made known to them: *Independent Broadcasting Authority v. EMI Electronics Ltd & BICC Construction Ltd* (1980). 'In the absence of a clear contractual indication to the contrary' this obligation will be implied. It is to be equated with the statutory obligation of a seller of goods.

Many design and build contracts (q.v.) modify this liability, e.g., clause 2.5. of the JCT Form 'with contractor's design' cuts down the obligation severely and is, in effect, a plain exemption clause (q.v.). See also: *Supply of Goods and Services Act 1982.*

## Summary judgment

The plaintiff (q.v.) can issue a summons (q.v.) under Order 14 of the Rules of the Supreme Court, supported by an affidavit (q.v.) to obtain judgment summarily without going to trial. Provided that the Master (q.v.) is satisfied that the defendant has no defence which warrants a trial of the issue, the plaintiff will get judgment forthwith, together with his costs. The defendant can file an affidavit to resist the application, and must then attend a brief hearing before the Master to show that he has a triable defence. The Master has very wide powers and may give leave to defend. It is not his function, however, to try the dispute, but merely to decide whether the defence is other than frivolous.

It is a useful and, generally, quick way of obtaining judgment for the price of goods or services supplied. The usual defence is that the goods or services were defective.

| | |
|---|---|
| **Summons** | A formal document used in court procedure requiring a person, to attend court for a particular reason, e.g., to obtain directions, orders, etc. Actions in a County Court are commenced by summons. |
| **Superintending officer** | A term used in GC/Works/1 to indicate the person who will supervise the work, and there abbreviated to SO. He is very roughly in the same position as the architect under the JCT or ACA forms of contract. Clause 1(2) states that he will be designated in the Abstract of Particulars (q.v.) and indeed he may well be an architect or an engineer. His duties in relation to the contract are set out within the body of the contract. |
| **Supervising officer** | A term used in the JCT forms local authorities editions, ACA 2, and IFC 84. Its purpose is to enable an official in the local authority, who may not be an architect, to act in that capacity in relation to the contract. The title 'architect' is legally protected (see: *Architects Registration Council*) and the appropriate chief officer may be a chartered engineer or member of the Chartered Institute of Building. There is no equivalent provision in the Private editions of JCT 80. GC/Works/1 uses the term 'Superintending Officer' (q.v.). |

**Supervision of works**  Supervision implies constant inspection and direction. In building contracts, the duty lies principally with the contractor who will normally carry out this duty through his site agent, foreman, etc. It is not the responsibility of the architect under the terms of any of the standard forms, nor under the provisions of the RIBA Architect's Appointment (if used), which expressly states that if frequent or constant inspection is required, a clerk of works will be appointed. Note, however, that supervision is not one of the duties of the clerk of works. See also: *Inspector*.

**Supervisor**  A person who directs or oversees the works. Under the BPF System (q.v.) the supervisor is the firm or person responsible for monitoring that the works are built in accordance with the contract documents (q.v.). Under that system he may be an architect, engineer, building surveyor, clerk of works (q.v.), etc. The supervisor's main responsibility is to monitor the contractor's design, construction, commissioning and maintenance of the project, ensuring that the workmanship and materials are up to contract standard.

**Supplier**  A person or firm undertaking the supply of goods or materials to a contract. The supplier's contract is with the main contractor. See also: *Nominated supplier*.

**Supply of Goods and Services Act 1982**  Broadly speaking, this Act introduces statutory implied terms (q.v.) in contracts for the supply of goods and services which do not fall within the ambit of the Sale of Goods Act 1979. It applies, *inter alia*, to contracts for work and materials, hire, exchange or barter, as well as services. Contracts for the sale of goods and hire purchase are covered by other legislation.
Part I of the Act deals with the supply of goods, and its provisions affect building contracts, e.g., as regards materials supplied in the execution of the work.
Sections 1 to 5 cover 'transfer of goods' and extend to contracts for work and materials.

Hire of goods is covered by sections 6 to 10 and these provisions are important in the case of plant hired in by contractors.

Part II of the Act deals with the supply of services – which includes professional services. Where the supplier is acting in the course of business there is an implied term that he will carry out the service with reasonable care and skill – an obligation which is already implied at common law. Under s. 15, where no price is fixed for the service, there is an implied term that a reasonable charge will be paid (see: *Quantum meruit*).

Various exemption orders have been made excluding particular categories from the effect of Part II of the Act, e.g., arbitrators.

The Act seems unlikely to have any great impact in the field of building contracts and, to a large extent, it merely gives statutory effect to obligations that were already implied by the general law. See also: *Unfair Contract Terms Act 1977.*

---

**Support, right of**

An easement (q.v.) whereby the owner of one house has the right to have it supported by the adjoining house belonging to his neighbour (*Dalton v. Angus* (1881)). However, even where a right of support exists, the adjoining owner against whom the right is claimed ('the servient owner') is under no obligation to maintain his property in such a state of repair so that it gives support to the adjoining owner's property (*Bond v. Nottingham Corporation* (1940)). Where a right of support exists, the adjoining owner must provide equivalent support if the original support is removed. Without such a right or privilege there is no liability on an adjoining owner if he demolishes his property, although there might well be a claim in negligence (q.v.) if the demolition was undertaken in such a way that damage occurred to the neighbour's property. There is no natural right of support. The general rules may be affected and modified in the case of party walls (q.v.).

Even if there is a right of support, there is no right to

weatherproofing and the right to have one's house protected against the weather cannot exist as an easement (*Phipps v. Pears* (1964)). Some of the effects of this ruling are circumvented by sections 29, 29A, 29B and 29C of the Public Health Act 1961. Under those provisions a local authority may serve a notice on any person who has begun or who intends to begin a demolition, etc., requiring him (among other things) to:

— Shore up any building adjacent to the building to which the notice relates.

— Weatherproof any surfaces of an adjacent building which are exposed by the demolition.

— Repair and make good any damage to an adjacent building caused by the demolition or by the negligent act or omission of the person engaged in it.

The recipient of such a notice may appeal on the grounds that the adjoining owner ought to pay or contribute towards the expense of weatherproofing the exposed surfaces, and these provisions do not apply where the building to be demolished is less than 1,750 cubic feet.

| | |
|---|---|
| **Surety** | A person who agrees to be responsible to a third party for the debts or defaults of another. See also: *Bond; Guarantee and indemnity*. |
| **Survey** | The careful inspection and recording of something. Thus, a survey of land or buildings may involve taking and recording measurements and making notes about condition. In a wider sense, it will involve inspections and testing and the taking of samples and cores. Geotechnical surveys report on the ground conditions of a site by using boreholes and reference to geological maps. |
| **Suspension** | The employer has no power to direct suspension of the work under a building contract unless there is an express term in the contract empowering him to do so. Neither the JCT nor ACA standard forms confer an express power of suspension on the employer or |

the architect but, with the exception of JCT Minor Works 1980, all the JCT forms empower the architect to 'postpone the execution of any work to be executed under' the contract ( JCT 80, clause 23.2, IFC 84, clause 3.15) and the exercise of this power of postponement can amount in effect to suspension. GC/Works/1, clause 7 (1)(g) gives the Superintending Officer a general power to order 'the suspension of the execution of the works or any part thereof', while clause 23 confers power to order suspension of the work to avoid risk of damage from frost, inclement weather, or other like causes. ACA 2, clause 11.8, gives the architect power to 'postpone the dates shown on the Time Schedule for the taking-over of the works', etc. The contractor has no power to suspend execution of the work at common law and if he does so then this will amount to a breach of contract on his part: see *Canterbury Pipe Lines Ltd v. Christchurch Drainage Board* (1979). However, merely 'going-slow' will not amount to suspension amounting to a breach of contract under JCT terms: *J.M.Hill & Sons Ltd v. London Borough of Camden* (1980). None of the standard main contract forms commonly used gives the contractor a right to suspend work, although JCT 80, clause 34, ACA 2, clause 14, and GC/Works/1, clause 20(2) oblige him to take measures to preserve any objects of archaeological or related interest found during the construction operations and in the case of JCT 80 and GC/Works/1 an immediate obligation to cease work in the area of the find if this is necessary.

In contrast, the JCT related forms of sub-contract give the sub-contractor an express right to suspend work in the event of the main contractor failing to pay to the sub-contractor amounts properly due: DOM/1, clause 21.6; NSC/4, clause 21.8; NAM/SC, clause 19.6. Reference may be made to *Determination and Suspension of Construction Contracts* by V. Powell-Smith and J. Sims (Collins, 1985). See also: *Postponement.*

| **Taking-over** | See: *Practical completion*. |
|---|---|
| **Target cost** | In the BPF System (q.v.) this term is used to describe the amount which the client (q.v.) expects to pay for the design and construction of the completed building. The target cost includes all fees, costs of investigations and the forecast tender price (q.v.).<br><br>It is not a term of art nor does it appear in the BPF edition of the ACA Form of Building Agreement (q.v.). Target cost is also a term used to describe a contract in which the contractor is paid his prime cost (q.v.), but if this exceeds or falls short of an agreed target the difference is shared between contractor and the employer in pre-agreed proportions. |
| **Taxation of costs** | The process of going through and reducing as necessary the bill of costs of a solicitor. It has nothing to do with taxes imposed by the Inland Revenue. In the High Court the process is carried out by Taxing Masters in the Queen's Bench Division, while the Registrar performs that function in the County Court. In arbitration, the arbitrator has power to 'tax and settle' his own costs and also those of the reference (i.e., the costs of the parties) so as to avoid the need for taxation in the High Court: Arbitration Act 1950, s. 28(1). The usual practice is for the arbitrator to tax and settle the costs of the award (i.e., his own costs) and to leave taxation of the other costs to the High Court.<br><br>Taxation is not an automatic process. Either party may apply for taxation of costs, including the costs of the reference. |

| **Tender** | An offer (q.v.) by a contractor, usually in competition, which, if accepted by the employer, will form a binding contract. The architect usually invites a number of contractors to tender on a form specially provided for the purpose. The contractors have a stated time in which to prepare their tenders and a date and time by which these must be deposited with the architect. Tenders must be returned in unmarked envelopes. Sometimes a priced bill of quantities (q.v.) must also be provided in a separate envelope so that it can be returned unopened if the tender is unsuccessful. See also: *Code of procedure for single stage selective tendering 1977; Code of procedure for two stage selective tendering 1983; Invitation to tender.* |
|---|---|
| **Term contract** | Used when services may be required over a period of time at irregular intervals. The chief characteristics of term contracts are that the contractor: |

— Undertakes to carry out a particular category of work (e.g., plumbing, general repairs, etc.) within maximum and minimum individual job values.
— Undertakes to do the work for a particular time period.
— Undertakes to do the work within a particular geographical area.
— Undertakes to do the work at a particular rate.
The system finds its most useful application in maintenance work where the general scope of work and the area may be known but the precise jobs which have to be carried out are unknown until the need arises. The contractor agrees to a schedule of prices (q.v.) which are applicable for the duration of the contract. It requires a good deal of experience to decide upon the correct rate for each item of work because some items may be seldom required. The theory is that the contractor will even out his gains and losses over the contract period. Competitive tendering is used to select the successful contractor. Advantages are that contractors gain familiarity with the property, and lower costs can be achieved than by attempting to secure tenders for each job as it

arises.

Variations are the *Measured Term Contract* where the contractor has the opportunity of measuring the work before he tenders; the *Specialist Term Contract* where quotations, rather than a schedule of prices, are used for such things as lift maintenance, window cleaning, etc.; *Daywork Term Contracts* where the jobs are small and the pricing arrangements are somewhat more complex. See also: *National Schedule of Rates*.

**Term of the contract**　A provision or stipulation in a contract describing some aspect of the agreement. It may be express (written down), implied (included by the action of common law or statute) or incorporated (see: *Incorporation of documents*). Important terms are generally known as 'conditions' (q.v.), less important terms as 'warranties' (q.v.).

**Third party**　Any person who is not a party to a contract between two or more other parties. Contractual terms cannot bind third parties but third parties may be brought into a dispute by one of the parties who claims indemnity or joint liability. See also: *Privity of contract*

**Time at large**　Time is said to be 'at large' when there is no specific date for the completion of the contract. The contractor's duty is then to complete the works 'within a reasonable time' and, in the absence of an express term as to the date for completion (q.v.) the contractor's common law obligation is to complete 'within a reasonable time'. What is a reasonable time (q.v.) is a question of fact depending on all the terms of the contract and the surrounding circumstances. Time is not normally of the essence in building contracts (see: *Essence of the contract*): *Lucas v. Godwin* (1837). This is clearly the case where the contract itself provides – as do all the standard form contracts – for extension of time and liquidated damages for delay: *Lamprell v. Billericay Union* (1849). Under the normal standard form contracts, time may become at large because:

— The contractor has been delayed by the act or default of the employer or those for whom he is responsible in law and there is no contractual provision to cover the situation, e.g., a clause entitling the architect (on the employer's behalf) to grant an extension of time (q.v.).

— The architect fails properly to grant an extension of time under the contract.

Time will seldom become 'at large' under any of the standard form contracts in common use. If it does then, as indicated, the contractor's obligation is to complete within a 'reasonable time'. The employer forfeits any right to liquidated damages (q.v.) in these circumstances (*Wells v. Army & Navy Co-operative Society Ltd* (1902)).

The subject is extremely complex, especially where the architect awards extensions of time after completion of the works. It is a question of interpretation whether he is entitled to do so. Some contracts (e.g., JCT 80 and ACA 2) give him specific powers to do so. The general rule, however, is that any extensions of time (q.v.) must be awarded properly and in accordance with the express contract provisions; failure so to do will result in the completion date (q.v.) becoming 'at large' (see: *Fernbrook Trading Co. Ltd v. Taggart* (1979)).

| | |
|---|---|
| **Time schedule** | An appendix (q.v.) to the ACA 2 (and BPF variant) contract which sets out a number of matters which the parties are to insert. Among them are:<br>— Date for possession of the site.<br>— Date for Taking-Over of the works.<br>— Rate of liquidated damages.<br>— Maintenance period.<br>— Dates for issue of information.<br>There is an alternative where possession or completion in sections is desired. |
| **Title** | The right to ownership of property or the legal connection between a person and a right. The word is most commonly used in connection with land but |

applies to all kinds of property.

A title is said to be *original* where the person entitled does not derive his right from any predecessor, e.g., copyright. It is *derivative* where it is derived from someone else, e.g., by gift, purchase, inheritance or judgment of the court.

| | |
|---|---|
| **Tort** | A civil wrong other than a breach of contract or a breach of trust or other merely equitable obligation and which gives rise to an action for unliquidated damages at common law (Sir John Salmond).<br>Literally the word is French for 'wrong'. The essential point is that it is a breach of a civil duty imposed by the law generally.<br>The most important tort today is negligence (q.v.), but other torts include nuisance (q.v.), trespass (q.v.) and defamation (q.v.). |
| **Tortfeasor** | A person who commits a tort (q.v.). |
| **Trade custom/trade usage** | See: *Custom.* |
| **Trade discount** | A discount which is allowed by suppliers to members of the industry. Thus a building contractor will be able to purchase, say, timber at a price considerably below that at which it is available to members of the public. It is not the same as cash discount (q.v.). |
| **Treasure trove** | Gold or silver coin, plate, bullion or other valuable items hidden in a house or in the earth or other secret place, the true owner being unknown and undiscoverable. Treasure trove belongs to the Crown. If the property is merely lost or abandoned it is not treasure trove, and the finder acquires a possessory right to it. The finder of treasure trove must report the finding to the coroner for the area, and an inquest will be held to establish whether or not the objects found are treasure trove. If it is, the Crown awards its market value to the finder.<br>In building contracts, there is usually a specific clause |

426

dealing with objects found on site. JCT 80, clause 34 provides that as between the contractor and the employer 'all fossils, antiquities and other objects of interest or value' found on the site or during excavation are the property of the employer. GC/Works/1, clause 20(2) and ACA 2, clause 14 provide to much the same effect, but none of these clauses can affect the rights of third parties. See also: *Antiquities; Fossils.*

**Trespass**

A category of the law of tort (q.v.). There are several types of trespass, but trespass to land is of most concern to the construction industry. If a person enters upon, remains upon or allows anything to come into contact with the land of another, he is committing trespass. For there to be a cause of action, the person bringing the action must be in possession of the land. (Encroaching tree roots are not trespass but nuisance.) Trespass may take place under the land (e.g., foundations), on the surface of the land (e.g., fences and buildings generally) or in the air space for a reasonable height over the land (e.g., projecting cranes but not aircraft flying over). In order to sue for trespass, there is no necessity to prove damage. Remedies are to take action for damages (if any) and/or an injunction to prevent continuance. Another remedy which must be exercised with care is forcible eviction if the trespasser has refused to leave peacefully.

A builder is said to have a licence (q.v.) to be upon the site of the works. He may become a trespasser if he remains on the land or leaves materials there after his work is finished or after his employment has been determined. See also: *Occupiers' liability.*

**Trust**

The holding of property by one person for the benefit of another. The property is vested legally in one or more trustees who administer it on behalf of others. The law relating to trusts is set out in a number of Acts of Parliament. Trusts were the creation of equity (q.v.). See also: *Fiduciary.*

**Trustee in bankruptcy**

A person who takes charge of all the assets of a person who is declared bankrupt, and in whom the bankrupt's property vests. His duties are:

— To investigate the circumstances of the bankruptcy.

— To gather in all the bankrupt's discoverable assets.

— To investigate and decide the creditors' claims.

— To distribute the proceeds of the assets according to the statutory order of preference .

See also: *Bankruptcy; Insolvency.*

**Turnkey contract**

The term sometimes used to describe a contract where the contractor is responsible for both design and construction. Alternatively such contracts are called 'Package deal' contracts. They are sometimes encountered in the industrial field.

The term has no precise legal meaning (*Cable (1956) Ltd v. Hutcherson Brothers Pty. Ltd* (1969)) and its use is best avoided. The alleged advantages of such contracts are project cost, co-ordination and speed. Against this must be set the substantial disadvantage that the client is sometimes deprived of an impartial third-party check. 'Package deal' contracts are most suitable for specialist engineering fields where companies possessing highly developed expertise may offer such proposals as the only access to that expertise. See also: *Design and build contracts.*

| | |
|---|---|
| **Uberrimae fidei** | Of the utmost good faith. This expression is applied to a group of contracts where, contrary to the general rule, the party with knowledge of material facts must make full disclosure of those facts. Failure to do so makes the contract voidable (q.v.). Building contracts are not contracts *uberrimae fidei* nor are contracts for sale of goods. The requirement of utmost good faith applies to contracts of guarantee (q.v.), insurance (q.v.), partnership (q.v.) and certain others. If a contract is one of *uberrimae fidei* the party with special knowledge must disclose to the other every fact and circumstance which might influence him in deciding whether to enter into the contract or not. See also: *Good faith; Misrepresentation.* |
| **Ultra vires** | Beyond the powers. An act in excess of the authority conferred on a person or body whether by statute or otherwise. The doctrine is largely important in relation to the acts or contracts of local and other public authorities and companies. For example, local authorities may act *ultra vires* if they act in bad faith or exercise their powers for some unauthorized purpose. An architect will act *ultra vires* if he acts outside the terms of his appointment or in excess of the powers conferred upon him by the building contract. The employer is not liable to the contractor for acts of his architect which are not within the scope of the architect's authority, though the architect may be personally liable for breach of warranty of authority (q.v.) or otherwise. In *Stockport Metropolitan Borough* |

*Council v. O'Reilly* (1978) the position under JCT terms was aptly summarized:

'An architect's *ultra vires* acts do not saddle the employer with liability. The architect is not the employer's agent in that respect. He has no authority to vary the contract. Confronted with such acts, the parties may either acquiesce in which case the contract may be *pro tanto* varied and the acts cannot be complained of, or a party may protest and ignore them. But he cannot saddle the employer with responsibility for them.'

| | |
|---|---|
| **Uncertainty** | A court may find that a contract (q.v.) or deed is void because it is unclear about the intentions of the parties.<br>Certainty of terms is an essential requirement if there is to be a valid contract. See also: *Interpretation of contracts.* |
| **Unfair Contract Terms Act 1977** | This statute, which came into force on 1 February 1978, imposes limits on the extent to which 'civil liability for breach of contract, or for negligence or other breach of duty, can be avoided by means of contract terms and otherwise...' It deals with limitation of liability in contract and in tort. It does not outlaw 'unfair' contract terms as is often supposed. An important distinction is drawn between those who deal as 'consumers' i.e., private individuals, and those who are in business. The criteria for avoiding liability are more stringent for a businessman dealing with a consumer than a businessman dealing with another businessman.<br>The main provisions are:<br>— Liability for death or injury caused by negligence can never be excluded by any term in the contract or any notice (for example, displayed on a building site). 'Negligence' includes both the tort of negligence (q.v.) and situations in contract where one party has a duty to behave with reasonable care and skill:s.2(1). Thus, a notice displayed on a building site disclaiming responsibility for injury howsoever caused will be |

totally ineffective if the injury to a visitor is caused through the contractor's negligence.

— Any other loss or damage due to negligence can only be excluded if it satisfies the Act's requirement of *reasonableness* (see below): s.2(2). It should be noted that, as a result of the Occupiers' Liability Act 1984, the statutory duty of care owed by an occupier to visitors can be excluded altogether by means of an appropriately worded notice in the case of other entrants, e.g., trespassers.

— If one party deals as a consumer *or* not as a consumer but on the other party's *written standard terms of business*, the other party cannot:

1. exclude or restrict his liability in respect of any breach of contract, *or*

2. claim to be entitled to do something substantially different from that which he contracted to do or to do nothing at all, unless he satisfies the reasonableness test.

This is so no matter what terms he includes in the contract: s.3. This is an extremely important provision since it will affect any contract in the construction industry if one party can be said to be using his own written terms of business. The supply of goods is a common example where suppliers often have printed conditions. It is thought that the only main contract conditions to escape the provisions of the Act are the JCT and ICE forms, because they are negotiated between all sides of industry. Even these forms may fall under the Act if and in so far as they are amended by the employer to suit his special requirements. They would then become his written standard terms of business. For example, if an employer inserted a clause in JCT 80, clause 26, to the effect that he would not be liable for any claim for loss or expense above £10,000, it is unlikely that the court would support him if the contractor could prove that the employer had caused him £20,000 damage. Similarly, if a contractor attempted to show that a term in his standard terms of business allowed him to substitute an inferior material for what he had originally priced (say softwood in place of hardwood), he would be unsuccessful under this Act.

— Section 6 is also important in a construction context. No exemption clause can exclude liability in respect of claims brought under s.12 of the Sale of Goods Act 1979 (as to the title of the seller of the goods) and corresponding provisions in hire purchase contracts. Implied terms as regards description, sample or quality can only be excluded if *reasonable*. In consumer transactions the terms cannot be excluded at all. Section 7 is similar to section 6, but deals with transactions which do not fall under the Sale of Goods Act or hire purchase.

— Section 8 excludes all attempts to limit or avoid liability for misrepresentation (q.v.).

— Section 10 makes any term in a contract ineffective if it attempts to exclude liability on another contract. Although it is not thought that the point has been tested in the courts, it appears that GC/Works/1, clause 43, which attempts to give the authority (employer) power to deduct monies owing on the contract from any sums due on any other contract, may be such a term.

The test of 'reasonableness' is important. It has to be applied at the time the contract was made or, in the case of an excluding notice, when the liability arose. Section 11 and Schedule 2 of the Act deal with reasonableness. Schedule 2 lays down the guide-lines. The court is only required to have regard 'in particular' to them, they are not intended to be exhaustive. The burden of proof lies on the party who claims that a term is reasonable. The guide-lines are:

— The strength of the bargaining positions of the parties relative to each other, taking into account (among other things) alternative means by which the requirement could have been met.

— Whether the customer was induced to agree to the exemption clause or could have made a contract with someone else omitting the term in question.

— Whether the customer knew or ought reasonably

to have known of the term.

— Where the exemption clause only operates after non- compliance with a particular condition, whether at the time of the contract it was reasonable to expect that compliance would be practicable.

— Whether the goods were manufactured, processed or adapted to the special order of the customer. Section 11 (4) also provides added guide-lines in the case of a party seeking to limit his liability to a specified sum. Regard must be had to the resources he could expect to be available to him to meet the liability and the extent to which he could obtain insurance cover.

The Act does not apply to international transactions or to certain types of contract, e.g., insurance. It does contain provisions, in s. 13, to prevent people evading or contracting out of its requirements. For example, attempts to evade the Act by limiting remedies or restricting rules of evidence or procedure are specifically prevented. But agreements to submit disputes to arbitration (q.v.) are expressly excluded from this section.

The Act is of great importance to the construction industry, relying as it does upon a mass of contracts, sub-contracts and standard conditions. The Act attempts to make people shoulder and not evade their responsibilities unless it is reasonable to do so. There have been a number of reported cases on the Act (e.g., *Rees Hough Ltd v. Redland Reinforced Plastics Ltd* (1984)) which show that – so far as business transactions are concerned – it is difficult to satisfy the Act's requirement of reasonableness.

| **Unincorporated association** | A group of people not incorporated, under royal charter or statute, and which has no legal existence independent of the members of the association. Common examples are partnerships (q.v.) and some members' clubs. While partners may sue and be sued in the name of the firm, most other unincorporated associations cannot be so sued. Usually, the best procedure is by way of a 'representative action' when |

one (or more) of the individuals concerned is
authorized to appear on behalf of the group as a whole.
A judgment against representative defendants is
binding on them all.

| | |
|---|---|
| **Valuation** | The process by which the quantity surveyor arrives at the value (q.v.) of the work carried out by the contractor. It normally involves visiting site and checking that the work has been carried out by visual inspection and/or measurement (q.v.). |
| **Value** | The meaning of 'value' in the context of interim valuations is sometimes the subject of dispute. JCT 80, clause 30.2.1.1, for example, refers to the 'total value of work properly executed by the Contractor...' The contractor's view of the matter is that the value is to be found by reference to the bills of quantities (q.v.) and he is entitled to receive payment for what he has done at bill rates plus a proportion of the preliminaries. This appears entirely fair and reasonable and it is the system most commonly followed in practice. It has been argued, very convincingly, that this system does not represent the value of the work to the employer.<br><br>From the employer's viewpoint the value of the work done by the contractor is the value of the whole contract less the cost of completing the work with the aid of another contractor (which would include additional professional fees) if the first contractor went into liquidation immediately after the issue of the certificate. This could result in a minus figure in the early stages of a contract. Contractors argue that the retention fund is designed to take care of that sort of eventuality but the retention fund as provided in most modern contracts is quite insufficient to cover |

the additional cost involved in the finishing of a contract by another contractor.

Although there are difficulties in operating the latter system, not least the method of evaluating the cost of completion, it does have the merit of assuring the employer of adequate funds if the worst happened. However, in light of the decision of the Court of Appeal in *Townsend v. Stone Toms & Partners* (1985) it is suggested that the first view is the better one.

| | |
|---|---|
| **Value Added Tax (VAT)** | A tax on purchases, charged by the seller or purveyor and payable to HM Customs and Excise at the end of three-monthly periods in which the invoice was rendered. This last point is of crucial importance to businesses because it means that they have to pay the tax, often before they have collected it. To overcome this problem a firm will sometimes issue a statement showing the amount due, including VAT, with the words 'this is not an invoice' printed across. After payment, the receipted invoice is issued and the firm becomes liable for payment of the VAT at the end of that particular three-month period. A disadvantage is that the recipient of such a statement need not pay until he receives a proper invoice. |

VAT falls into three categories:

— Standard rated: 15% VAT is payable. In the case of buildings it means that the contractor charges the employer 15% of the cost of the building and the employer can claim the 15% from the Customs and Excise provided that he is VAT registered and his own VAT charges to others exceed the amount he is claiming. In effect, the amounts are set-off against one another.

— Zero rated: In the case of buildings it means that no VAT is charged by the contractor. He can claim any VAT payments he has made from Customs and Excise as above.

— Exempt: In the case of buildings it means that the contractor charges the employer 15% VAT but the employer cannot reclaim it.

The regulations governing VAT are constantly

revised. It is, therefore, important to check on the position before beginning any building work. Currently ( July 1984), the position is that all works of repair and alteration are standard rated. New building works are zero rated. Alterations become zero rated when only one façade of the original building is left standing.

Most standard form contracts provide for special VAT agreements to be signed between the parties. The contract sum (q.v.) is treated as being exclusive of VAT and the VAT transactions are dealt with separately from other contractual payments.

VAT can cause complications for contractors submitting estimates or quotations, as is shown by the decision of His Honour Judge Newey QC in *Franks & Collingwood v. Gates* (1985). There a contractor's quotation did not bear a VAT registration number and no mention was made as to whether the fixed and provisional sums set out in the quotation were inclusive or exclusive of VAT. The judge held that the contract was for sums which were inclusive of VAT saying: 'The quotation made no reference to VAT whatsoever. It was intended to be a competitive offer in respect of work to a single house ... It was perfectly proper for the plaintiffs to submit an inclusive offer, and in my view there is no reason why [the employer] should not regard it as such.'

| | |
|---|---|
| **Value cost contract** | In this type of contract, the contractor is paid only a fee which fluctuates depending upon the actual cost of work compared with a valuation made on the basis of an an agreed schedule of prices (q.v.). The fee is increased or reduced depending upon the contractor's success or failure in meeting the agreed valuation. The cost of the work is paid directly by the employer. A disadvantage is the complex accounting and measurement procedures required. The value cost contract is useful where a continuous programme of work is involved and time is at a premium. See also: *Cost Reimbursement contract; Management contract.* |
| **Variation of price** | See: *Fluctuations.* |

| **Variation order** | An outdated term still commonly used to describe an Architect's Instruction (q.v.) requiring additions, omissions or alterations in the works. |
|---|---|
| **Variations** | Alterations, additions or omissions in work, materials, working hours, work space, etc. See also: *Instructions; Variation order.* |
| **Vesting and seizure** | The majority of building contracts contain clauses dealing with the ownership of materials and/or plant (see: *Vesting clause*). Some contracts also contain an express provision dealing with seizure (sometimes 'vesting and seizure') of materials and plant, usually on determination of the contract or in the case of forfeiture (q.v.). |

For example, GC/Works/1, clause 3 – which is headed 'Vesting of Works, etc., in the Authority – Things not to be removed' is a vesting and seizure clause. Clause 3(1) transfers ownership of 'the Works and any things (whether or not for incorporation) brought on the site in connection with the contract and which are owned by the contractor or vest in him under any contract' though risk (q.v.) remains with the contractor.

The object of this provision (and similar clauses in other contracts) is to improve the employer's position in the event of failure by the contractor to complete the contract, especially where that failure is caused by the contractor's insolvency (q.v). It transfers the property in both plant and materials to the employer and is effective to defeat claims made by the contractor's trustee in bankruptcy (q.v.), liquidator (q.v.), etc., until the contract is completed.

However, although clause 3(1) provides that plant, etc. 'shall become the property of and vest in the employer', as regards things which will eventually be moved from site, the transfer is only temporary and so property will re-vest in the contractor on completion. Furthermore, in respect of plant, etc., owned by third parties, the clause cannot be effective against the third party owner, even if it is the intention

that it should be so.
Each such clause must be interpreted strictly and on its wording, against the background of the general law.

| | |
|---|---|
| **Vesting clause** | A clause in a contract which deals with the transfer of property in goods and materials (q.v.), e.g., JCT 80, clause 16. |

Such a clause can only be effective between the parties to the actual contract (see: *Privity of contract*) and cannot affect the rights of third parties, such as suppliers.

'Vesting clauses are inserted in contracts for the purpose of securing money advanced to the contractor or as security for the due performance of the contract': Emden's *Building Contracts & Practice*, 8th edn., vol. 1 p. 336. The effect of a vesting clause depends on its terms and also on the general law relating to the passing of property (q.v.). Even if the vesting clause is effective to transfer property in unfixed materials brought on site to the employer, this is qualified by the contractor's right to use the materials for the purpose of the works (*Bennett and White (Calgary) Ltd v. Municipal District of Sugar City No. 5* (1951)).

| | |
|---|---|
| **Vexatiously** | With an intention to annoy or embarrass. It is always wrong to take action vexatiously and, in litigation, may cause an action to be dismissed. JCT 80, clause 8.5, is one of many examples in the standard forms which contain an express prohibition on vexatious action (in that case, when the architect issues instructions to exclude a person from the works). |

| | |
|---|---|
| **Vicarious liability** | The liability of one person for the wrongs done by another. The liability generally arises in tort (q.v.). The most common examples are the liability of an employer for the actions of his employee and that of a principal for the acts of his agent. There will be no liability, however, if the employee is acting outside the course of his employment or if an agent is acting outside the scope of his authority. In general, the |

439

employer is not vicariously liable for the wrongful actions of an independent contractor engaged by him. An employer is, however, liable for the actions of an independent contractor if he is negligent in selecting him, where there is a breach of an absolute statutory duty, and in certain other limited cases, e.g., where the contractor's work involves operations on the highway (q.v.) and injury is caused. See also: *Agency; Master.*

| | |
|---|---|
| **Vicarious performance** | Performance of a contractual obligation by or through another person, e.g., performance of part of a contractual obligation by a sub-contractor (q.v.). English law draws a distinction between assigning duties (see: *Assignment*) and engaging someone else vicariously to perform them. Vicarious performance is generally permitted except when the nature of the contract calls for personal performance, which is not usually the case with building contracts, although it would be so in the case where the personality of the builder was important. |

Vicarious performance is only effective to discharge the contractor's duties if it is perfect. If the vicarious performance falls below the prescribed contractual standard, the original contractor is liable.

This concept is largely important in the context of sub-contracting and sub-letting. Most standard forms of contract deal with this matter expressly and, while such clauses prohibit vicarious performance of the *whole* contract, permit it in part with the written consent of the architect or the employer.

JCT 80, clause 19 is typical. Clause 19.1 deals with assignment (q.v.) of the contract, while clause 19.2 deals with the contractor's right of sub-letting. This right can be exercised only with the written consent of the architect.

| | |
|---|---|
| **Vis major** | Irresistible force whether of nature or act of man. It can be equated with *force majeure* (q.v.) and covers any overpowering force such as exceptional storms, earthquakes, riotous mobs, armed forces. It is an |

excuse for damage done or loss of property and is one of the excepted perils (q.v.) in certain insurance policies. See also: *Act of God*.

**Vitiate**

To make invalid. The word is used in JCT 80, clause 13.2, and in IFC 84, clause 3.6, to indicate that the variations stated will not invalidate the contract. MW 80 states the same thing in clause 3.6 and GC/Works/1 in clause 7(4), although the latter two contracts use the word invalidate instead of vitiate. Note that no action expressly allowed under the terms of a contract can invalidate that contract and the various standard forms appear simply to be stating the common law position. ACA 2 does not include a similar statement.

**Void; Voidable**

Void means of no legal effect, or a nullity. Thus, an illegal contract (q.v.) is void and cannot create any rights or obligations. A contract for an immoral purpose, e.g., to build a brothel, would be void at common law on grounds of public policy. In some cases the innocent party may be entitled to recover money paid or property transferred under a void contract, usually by way of *quantum meruit* (q.v.) see: *Craven-Ellis v. Canons Ltd* (1936).
Voidable, in contrast, means that the transaction is valid until one party exercises the right of rescission (q.v.), e.g., in the case of fraud (q.v.) or misrepresentation (q.v.). For example, a contract of partnership (q.v.) made by a minor (q.v.) is voidable at his option.

**Voucher**

A document which is evidence of something. Thus JCT 80, clause 13.5.4 requires vouchers specifying the time spent upon the works, workmen's names, etc., to be presented to the architect for verification. That type of voucher is commonly known as a 'daywork sheet'. ACA 2, clause 16.1 refers to the documents, vouchers and receipts necessary for computing the total amount due to the contractor.

| | |
|---|---|
| **Waiver** | The relinquishment of a right or remedy. It may be express, by a written statement (e.g., letter) to that effect, or implied, by inaction in enforcing a right. Care must be taken to avoid the latter situation which may easily arise on a building contract if the contractor commits a breach for which there is a clear remedy and the employer takes no advantage of the remedy. For example, if the contractor sub-lets part of the work without seeking the architect's consent in accordance with JCT 80, clause 19.2, the architect must immediately take action. If he does nothing, he may be said to have waived his right to object.
A waiver may be given by a planning authority in connection with satisfaction of the requirements of the building regulations (q.v.). Its effect is to remove the requirement to comply with the particular regulation to which it relates. The Secretary of State may also give a general waiver in certain circumstances. |
| **War** | Open, armed conflict between two or more nations or states, with the object of satisfying a claim. The outbreak of war makes all commerce between British subjects and alien enemies illegal. Any contract with an enemy alien is automatically dissolved by the outbreak of war and even in other cases war may well cause frustration (q.v.) of the contract.
JCT 80, clause 32 lays down the respective rights and duties of the parties to the contract in the event |

of 'an outbreak of hostilities', which covers the situation if war breaks out even if no formal declaration is made (clause 32.1). The criterion is to be general mobilization (q.v.) of the armed forces of the Crown.

Either party may give notice by registered post or recorded delivery to the other to determine the contractor's employment. Such notice may not be given:

— Less than 28 days after mobilization is ordered.

— After practical completion (q.v.) unless war damage (q.v.) has been sustained.

Clause 33 covers the situation if war damage is sustained.

ACA 2, clause 11.5, Alternative 2 makes war or hostilities (q.v.) a ground for extension of time. It is also a ground for termination of the contractor's employment under clause 21(c) if the contractor is prevented or delayed from executing the works for 90 consecutive days. A notice from one party to the other is all that is required.

GC/Works/1 makes no specific provision for war, but under clause 44 the Authority is given a discretionary power to determine the contract at any time, and that power might well be exercised if war broke out. In any event, as has been indicated, war may well result in frustration of the contract.

The JCT Agreement for Minor Works likewise has no specific provision. See also: *Force majeure; Frustration; Hostilities; War damage.*

---

**War damage**

Clause 33 of JCT 80 deals expressly with the situation if any part of the works 'or any unfixed materials or goods which are intended for, delivered to and placed on or adjacent to the Works' sustain war damage. The main provisions are:

— War damage must be disregarded in calculating monies payable to the contractor under the contract.

— The architect can issue instructions to the contractor to remove damaged work and debris and carry out protective work for which he will be paid.

— The contractor must make good the damage, for which he will be paid, and continue with the work.
— The architect will fix a later Completion Date.
— If a determination notice is served under clause 32, the provisions of that clause will take effect.
— The employer is entitled to any compensation provided by Parliament.
— War damage is defined by Section 2 of the War Damage Act 1943 in complicated terms and includes damage as a direct result of action taken by the enemy and damage occurring as a result of precautionary or other measures taken by proper authority. See also: *Frustration*.

**Warranty**

A subsidiary or minor term in a contract, breach of which entitles the other to damages (q.v.) but not to repudiate the contract. It should be contrasted with a condition (q.v.) which is a term going to the root of a contract. It is for the court to decide whether a contract term is a warranty or a condition. In *Thomas Feather & Co. (Bradford) Ltd v. Keighley Corporation* (1953), for example, a clause in a building contract forbidding sub-letting without the employer's consent was held to be a warranty as opposed to a condition. The court takes account of all the circumstances including the intentions of the parties.

**Warranty of authority, breach of**

Although the general rule of an agency (q.v.) is that the agent is not liable personally to the third party, this is subject to an important exception. If the agent exceeds his actual authority and the third party suffers damage as a result, the agent will be liable to the contractor for breach of warranty of authority (*Yonge v. Toynbee* (1910)). The architect's implied authority to bind his principal (the employer) is limited, but clearly if he exceeds his authority he is liable to the contractor in damages (*Randall v. Trimen* (1856)).

**Wayleave**

A right of way (q.v.) over, under or through land for such things as a pipeline, an electric transmission line, or for carrying goods across the land. The word is often used as a synonym for an ordinary right of way whether on foot, with vehicles or otherwise. Many statutory authorities (q.v.) such as Electricity Boards may apply to the appropriate Minister for a compulsory wayleave over land where the owner refuses his consent. A wayleave is a kind of easement (q.v.).

**Weather**

It can be a very important influence on the rate of progress of a job. Some contracts are more generous than others in giving the architect power to award extensions of time for delays caused by weather conditions. In the absence of such a provision, bad weather is at the contractor's risk unless it is of such magnitude as to amount to *force majeure* (q.v.). See also: *Adverse weather conditions*.

**Winding-up**

The process by which a limited liability company (q.v.) is brought to an end. The same term is used to describe the operation of putting an end to a partnership (q.v.).
Under the Companies Act 1985 there are several types of winding-up:
—Compulsory – by order of the court.
—Voluntary – either a *members'* or a *creditors'* winding-up. A voluntary winding-up may also be effected under the supervision of the court.
The winding-up of a limited company, except for the purposes of amalgamation or reorganization of the company's structure is a ground on which the contractor's employment may be determined under most standard forms of building contract, e.g., JCT 80, clause 27.2, ACA 2, clause 20.3, because of its connotations with insolvency (q.v.). The liquidator (q.v.) has the power of adopting or disclaiming any contract made by the company (Companies Act 1948, s. 323 (1)) but the wording of JCT 80, clause 27.2, effectively takes this option out of his hands by providing for automatic determination, although there is provision for re-instatement.

**Without prejudice**    A phrase used in correspondence or discussions seeking to negotiate a compromise and settle a dispute. Statements made 'without prejudice' for the purpose of settling a dispute cannot be given in evidence without the consent of both parties. The courts may imply consent if a party, wishing to rely upon the privilege (q.v.), seeks simultaneously to reveal part of the document which is to their advantage. The basis of the privilege is to be found in an implied agreement arrived at from marking the letter 'without prejudice' (*Rabin v. Mendoza & Co.* (1954)). It is important to note that 'without prejudice' statements and discussions will only be privileged if there is a dispute and an attempt to settle or compromise it. Architects and contractors alike must beware of heading letters 'without prejudice' indiscriminately, in the mistaken assumption that it gives them the opportunity to write whatever they wish with impunity. In arbitration proceedings a 'without prejudice' offer can never be referred to by either party at any stage of the proceedings, because it is in the public interest that there should be a procedure whereby the parties can discuss their differences freely and frankly and make offers of settlement without fear of being embarrassed by these exchanges if they do not lead to settlement: Donaldson J. in *Tramountana Armadora SA v. Atlantic Shipping Co. SA* (1978).

Letters written 'without prejudice' which do not result in agreement cannot, therefore, be looked at by the court even on the question of costs, unless both parties consent (*Computer Machinery Co. Ltd v. Drescher* (1983)). *Cutts v. Head* (1984) discussed the very limited exceptions to the general rule and held that an offer of settlement, made before trial, of an action contained in a 'without prejudice' letter which expressly reserved the right to bring the letter to the notice of the judge on the issue of costs after judgment is admissible without the consent of the parties, but only in cases where what is in issue is something more than a simple money claim in respect of which a payment into court

(q.v.) is appropriate.
The phrase 'without prejudice' is also used, in
JCT 80, clause 26.6 to mean that the foregoing
provisions are not to affect the contractor's common
law rights, which are preserved. See also: *Sealed offer.*

**Witness**

A person who has seen or who can give first-hand
evidence of an event or one who gives evidence (q.v.)
in arbitration or litigation of events or facts within
his own knowledge.
A person who attests to the genuineness of a signature,
etc., is also described as a witness. See: *Attestation;
Evidence; Expert witness.*

**Work and materials contract**

Building contracts are contracts for work and
materials, which means that they are not subject to
the provisions of the Sale of Goods Act 1979. The
distinction between contracts for the sale of goods
and those for work and materials was formerly more
important than it is today and there is a large volume
of case law on the topic, much of which is confusing.
See also: *Cost reimbursement contracts.*

**Working drawings**

The drawings which the contractor will use to
construct the works. They will be accurately
dimensioned and, together with the specification
(q.v.) or bills of quantities (q.v.), will contain all the
information the contractor requires. In practice,
schedules and tables may be included in the term.
The RIBA Plan of Work substitutes two stages, E:
Detail Design and F: Production Information, for
what used to be called the working drawing stage of
the architect's work. See also: *Drawings and details.*

**Workmanship**

Skill in carrying out a task. Building contracts
commonly use the word to differentiate between the
things – goods and materials – and the work done on
them to produce the finished building. Thus, JCT 80,
clause 2.1 refers to the quality of materials and the
standards of workmanship.
In the absence of an express term to the contrary, the

contractor is under an obligation at common law to carry out his work in a good and workmanlike manner. Express terms of the contract may sometimes impose a higher obligation, e.g., ACA 2, clause 1.2 and clause 5.4.

**Workpeople**

A term used in GC/Works/1, clause 11G(1)(a), and defined for the purpose of that clause only as: 'Workpeople means persons employed directly by the Contractor on the Site on manual labour, whether skilled or unskilled, and includes such persons chargeable to overheads, and "workperson" means one of such persons.'
Clause 11G is a limited provision for fluctuations in statutory tax and contributions.
The JCT contracts also use the term 'workpeople' for the purposes of the fluctuations clauses. JCT 80, clause 38.6.3, defines them as being 'persons whose rates of wages and other emoluments ... are governed by the rules or decisions ... of the National Joint Council for the Building Industry ...' or some other like body for associated trades. Labour-only sub-contractors are not workpeople for the purposes of this provision: *J. Murphy & Sons Ltd v. London Borough of Southwark* (1982).

**Works**

The operation on site required to produce a building or structure. Works includes, not only the building itself at various stages of construction but also, all ancillary works necessary such as scaffolding, site huts, temporary roads, etc., even though they may not form part of the finished structure.
Most building contracts draw a distinction between 'the Works' and 'work'. Thus, under JCT 80, 'the Works' means either the work contracted for (Article 1) or the site, as in clause 8.5. In contrast, 'work' means 'work carried out under the contract' as in clause 13.1.1.1.

**Writ**

An order issued in the name of the Queen requiring the performance of an act. In most cases, actions in the High Court are commenced by a *writ of summons*, and this is generally referred to merely as 'a writ'. This is a royal command to the person named (called 'the defendant' (q.v.)) to enter an appearance to the action instituted by the plaintiff (q.v.). The writ must be issued using the prescribed form which is completed in duplicate and taken to the Central Office of the High Court or to one of the several district registries throughout the country. A fee is payable on issue and one copy is sealed and returned to the plaintiff. The action has now been commenced for the purposes of the Limitation Act 1980. A writ is valid for 12 months beginning from the date of issue and must generally be served during that period.

**Writing**

Many building contracts require certificates, notices, instructions, etc., to be given in writing, e.g., ACA 2, clause 23.1. This requirement is satisfied by any process which represents the words in visible form and includes handwriting, typewriting, printing, etc., although a particular contract may distinguish writing from printing. As a noun, 'writing' means a document produced in permanent form as contrasted with oral communication. Certain contracts are required to be in writing, e.g., assignments of copyright (q.v.) or to be evidenced in writing, e.g., contracts for the sale of land. See also: *Notices*.

**Year** A period of 12 calendar months or 365 consecutive days in ordinary years or 366 days in leap years. From 1 January 1753 in England the year has commenced on 1 January. The regnal year commences on the accession of the Sovereign. The income tax year runs from 6 April to 5 April and the Government financial year runs from 1 April to 31 March. The accounting year of limited companies (q.v.) runs from any date convenient to the company.

451

**Bramall & Ogden Ltd v Sheffield City Council** (1985), 1 Con LR 30
45, 48, 129, 280

**Branca v Cobaro**, [1947] 2 All E.R. 101     414

**British Russian Gazette & Trade Outlook Ltd v Associated Newspapers Ltd**,
[1933] All E.R. Rep 320     23

**British Steel Corporation v Cleveland Bridge & Engineering Co Ltd** (1981),
24 BLR 94; *BCCB* 3     269, 271, 362

**Brodie v Cardiff Corporation**, [1919] A.C. 337     254

**Brunswick Construction Ltd v Nowlan** (1974), 21 BLR 27; *BCCB* 56
162

**Bryant (C) & Son Ltd v Birmingham Hospital Saturday Fund**, [1938] 1 All
E.R. 503     188, 401

**Burden (RB) Ltd v Swansea Corporation**, [1957] 3 All E.R. 243; *BCCB* 186,
289     60, 317

**Butler Machine Tool Co Ltd v Ex-Cell-O Corporation (England) Ltd**, [1979] 1
All E.R. 965     144

**Bywaters v Curnick** (1906), HBC, 4th edn., vol. 2, p. 393     79


**Cable (1956) Ltd v Hutcherson Brothers Pty Ltd** (1969), 43 ALJR 321;
*BCCB* 50     428

**Candler v Crane, Christmas & Co**, [1951] 1 All E.R. 426     177

**Canterbury Pipelines Ltd v Christchurch Drainage Board** (1979), 16 BLR
76     421

**Carlill v Carbolic Smoke Ball Co**, [1893] 1 QB 256     319

**Catalina v Norma** (1938), 82 SJ 698

**Cawley & Co Ltd, *In re*** (1889), 42 Ch D. 207  .  183

**Chandris v Isbrandtsen-Moller Co Inc**, [1950] 2 All E.R. 613     180

**City of Manchester v Fram Gerrard Ltd** (1974), 6 BLR 70     155

**Clegg Parkinson & Co v Earby Gas Co**, [1896] 1 QB 56     411

**Clough Mill Ltd v Martin**, [1984] 3 All E.R. 982     379

**Collingwood v Home & Colonial Stores Ltd**, [1936] 3 All E.R. 200     234

**Colls v Home & Colonial Stores**, [1904] A.C. 185     382

**Computer Machinery Co Ltd v Drescher**, [1983] 3 All E.R. 153     446

**County & District Properties Ltd v C Jenner & Son Ltd** (1976), 3 BLR 41
233

**Wraight Ltd v PH & T (Holdings) Ltd** (1968), 13 BLR 26; *BCCB* 214     167, 288

**Yonge v Toynbee**, [1910] 1 KB 215     444

**Young & Marten Ltd v McManus Childs Ltd** (1969), 9 BLR 77; *BCCB* 62 205, 229

The following abbreviations of Reports are used:

| | |
|---|---|
| **A.C.** | Law Reports, Appeal Cases |
| **App.Cas.** | |
| **All. E.R.** | All England Law Reports |
| **All E.R. Rep.** | All England Law Reports Reprint |
| **ALJR** | Australian Law Journal Reports |
| **B & S** | Best and Smith's Reports |
| **Beav.** | Beavan's Reports |
| **BLR** | Building Law Reports |
| **C & P** | Carrington & Payne's Reports |
| **Ch** | Law Reports, Chancery Cases/Division |
| **Ch D.** | |
| **Co. Rep.** | Coke's Reports |
| **Com. Cas.** | Commercial Cases |
| **Con LR** | Construction Law Reports |
| **D.L.R.** | Dominion Law Reports (Canada) |
| **Ex.** | Law Reports, Exchequer Cases/Division |
| **Ex. D.** | |
| **E.R.** | English Reports |
| **HBC** | Hudson's Building Contracts, *4th edn.* |
| **I.C.R.** | Industrial Cases Reports |
| **Ir. Jur.** | Irish Jurist |

| | |
|---|---|
| **JP** | Justice of the Peace & Local Government Review |
| **KB** | Law Reports, King's Bench |
| **LGR** | Local Government Reports |
| **LJ Ex.** | Law Journal Reports, Exchequer |
| **LJ Ch** | Law Journal Reports, Chancery |
| **Lloyds' Rep.** | Lloyds' Law Reports |
| **LR HL** | Law Reports, House of Lords |
| **LR CP** | Common Pleas |
| **LR Exch** | Exchequer |
| **LT** | Law Times Reports |
| **NZLR** | New Zealand Law Reports |
| **Ph** | Phillips' Reports |
| **QB** | Law Reports, Queen's Bench |
| **SC (HL)** | Session Cases (House of Lords) |
| **SJ** | Solicitor's Journal |
| **TLR** | Times Law Reports |
| **TR** | Term Reports |
| **WLR** | Weekly Law Reports |
| **WR** | Weekly Reporter |

Many of these series of Reports will be found only in the specialist law libraries. Where a case is reported in *Building Law Reports* or *Construction Law Reports* those are the references given in preference to any other.

The major cases affecting building contracts are collected in *A Building Contract Casebook* by V. Powell-Smith and M. Furmston (Granada Publishing, 1984) and the reference to that book is the abbreviation **BCCB**.

**S.Bickford-Smith and E. Freeth (eds)**, *Emden's Building Contracts and Practice*, 8th edn, 3 vols, with supplement, Butterworth, 1980.

**D.M. Chappell**, *Contractor's Claims: an architect's guide*, Architectural Press, 1984.

**D.M. Chappell**, *Contractual Correspondence for Architects*, Architectural Press, 1984.

**D.M. Chappell and V. Powell-Smith**, *JCT Intermediate Form of Contract*, Architectural Press, 1985.

**D.M. Chappell and V. Powell-Smith**, *JCT Minor Works Form of Contract*, Architectural Press, 1986.

**D.L. Cornes**, *Design Liability in the Construction Industry*, 2nd edn, Collins, 1985.

**M.P. Furmston**, *Cheshire & Fifoot's Law of Contract*, 10th edn, Butterworth, 1981.

**M.P. Furmston and V. Powell-Smith**, *Construction Law Reports*, 5 vols and continuing, Architectural Press, 1985ff.

**A.G. Guest et al**, *Chitty on Contracts*, 25th edn, 2 vols, Sweet & Maxwell, 1983.

**D. Keating,** *Building Contracts*, 4th edn, with supplement, Sweet & Maxwell, 1978.

**H. Lloyd and C. Reese**, *Building Law Reports*, 32 vols and continuing, George Godwin/Longmans, 1976ff.

**M.J. Mustill and S. Boyd**, *The Law and Practice of Commercial Arbitration in England*, Butterworth, 1982.

**J. Parris**, *The Standard Form of Building Contract: JCT 80*, 2nd edn, Collins, 1985.

**J. Parris**, *Retention of Title on the the Sale of Goods*, Granada, 1982.

**J. Parris**, *Arbitration: Principles and Practice*, Granada, 1983.

**V. Powell-Smith**, *The Standard Form of Building Contract 1980* edn, IPC Business Press, 1983.

**V. Powell-Smith**, *The Model Conditions for the Hiring of Plant*, IPC Business Press, 1981.

**V. Powell-Smith**, *The General Conditions of Government Contracts for Building and Civil Engineering Works (GC/Works/1)*, IPC Business Press, 1984.

**V. Powell-Smith**, *The Intermediate Form of Building Contract*, IPC Business Press, 1984.

**V. Powell-Smith**, *The Standard Form of Nominated Sub-Contract*, IPC Business Press, 1985.

**V. Powell-Smith**, *Guide to the Second Edition 1984 ACA Form of Building Agreement 1982*, Architectural Press, 1985.

**V. Powell-Smith and M. Billington**, *The Building Regulations Explained and Illustrated*, 7th edn, Collins, 1981.

**V. Powell-Smith and D.M. Chappell**, *Building Contracts Tabulated and Compared*, Architectural Press, 1986.

**V. Powell-Smith and M.P. Furmston**, *A Building Contract Casebook*, Collins, 1984.

**V. Powell-Smith and J. Sims**, *Building Contract Claims*, Collins, 1983.

**V. Powell-Smith and J. Sims**, *Contract Documentation for Contractors*, Collins, 1985.

**V. Powell-Smith and J. Sims**, *Determination and Suspension of Construction Contracts*, Collins, 1985.

**G. Trickey**, *The Presentation and Settlement of Contractors' Claims*, Spon, 1983.

**D.M. Walker**, *The Oxford Companion to Law*, Clarendon Press, 1980.

**I.N.D. Wallace**, *Hudson's Building and Engineering Contracts*, 10th edn, with supplement, Sweet & Maxwell, 1970.

# Construction Law Reports

**Edited by Michael Furmston and Vincent Powell-Smith**

Case law relating to the construction industry is continually developing, as new cases are tried or go to appeal, or previously unexamined problems receive judicial consideration. Many of these cases come before the Official Referees' court, which has come to specialise in this area. This series will report Official Referees' decisions and appeal cases arising from them, and will be of vital concern to those involved in construction law. The aim will be to publish three volumes per year.

*234 × 148 mm*      *160 pp*      *ISBN (for volume 1) 0–85139–780–8*      *cloth*
*(for volume 2) 0–85139–781–6*

# AJ Legal Handbook
# Fourth edition

**Edited by Anthony Speaight and Gregory Stone**

Law affects the practice of architecture in more and more ways, and to an increasing degree. This book has become a standard text for students and an essential office reference for architects and related professionals in the building industry.

The contents of the fourth edition reflect the various new developments in case law, particularly land law, the law of negligence and the law of limitations. Forms of contract such as the JCT form have been amended, and professional codes of practice have been revised.

## Contents

Introduction to English law
Introduction to Scots law
English land law
Scottish land Law
Building contracts
Building contracts in Scotland
The liability of architects
Arbitration
Statutory authorities in England and Wales
Statutory authorities in Scotland

Planning law
English construction regulations
Construction regulations in Scotland
Copyright
Architects and the law of employment
Legal organisation of architects' offices
Architect's appointment
Professional conduct in England
Professional conduct in Scotland

'This is undoubtedly a comprehensive and authoritative guide to those areas of law of particular concern to architects and other professions involved in the building industry.'

*Local Government Chronicle*

*297 × 210 mm*      *254 pp*      *ISBN 0–85139–751–4*      *paper*

# Professional Liability

**Ray Cecil**

Architects are now more than ever vulnerable to legal actions, which may occur long after a building has been completed, and due to inflation may involve far larger sums than the cost of the original building. The law here is complex; how to practise safely while still providing a professional service has become a major concern of the whole profession.

Ray Cecil is an architect writing for architects, to 'advise, guide and horribly warn' them. The reader is taken through various situations and is shown what the law seemed to be, and what actually happened. The author deals in depth with the problems of suitable and adequate insurance. He offers a combination of experienced professional advice and real-life example, with practical checklists of what to do to avoid or minimise trouble.

Lastly, Ray Cecil provides a vigorous discussion of the injustices of the present system and describes the changes the future should bring.

**Contents**
An outline of the law
The main areas of risk
Minimising the impact
Something has to change

'What the practitioner has been waiting for: a book written by an experienced practising architect and one who, by his own account, has been through the fire. It is well researched, and written in a highly readable style . . . I have no hesitation in saying that every practising architect should have a copy of this book.'

*The Architects' Journal*

*234 × 148 mm*     *172 pp*     *ISBN 0–85139–956–8*     *cloth*

# Contractor's Claims

**David Chappell**

No two contractor's claims ever seem to be quite the same; they are a
potential source of embarrassment to the architect and need to be
understood if they are to be dealt with speedily, accurately and fairly.
This book gives practical guidance on ways to assess and determine a
claim, and on what action to take once the decision is reached. Simple
flow charts guide the reader through all the principal procedures.
Model letters are provided, supporting chapters discuss related issues.
Here is a desk-top companion for working architects; and indeed for
contractors too, since it indicates how claims may be most effectively
presented. It also points up areas of risk, and outlines the good
management measures necessary to minimise the need for claims to
arise at all.

**Contents**
What is a claim?
Roles
Contractor's duties
Evidence
Techniques for dealing with extensions of time
Techniques for dealing with loss and/or expense
Claims from sub-contractors
Liquidated damages, penalties and bonus clauses
Architect's certificates
Employer's decisions

'In a claims-conscious age this is an invaluable book for both the
inexperienced and the experienced reader. It is a guide . . . which deals
with the subject matter in clear and concise terms.'

*The Architects' Journal*

*210 × 148 mm*     *136 pp*     *ISBN 0–85139–778–6*     *cloth*

# JCT Intermediate Form of Contract: An Architect's Guide

**David Chappell and Vincent Powell-Smith**

The IFC was welcomed by those who found the longer JCT80 unwieldy for use on contracts larger than those covered by the Minor Works form. Certainly, every architect who has not already done so will need to become familiar with it. Clearly written by two experienced authors, this guide is primarily aimed at the architect: it follows the contract through every stage, using a wealth of explanatory material such as sample letters, action flow charts and comparative tables.

## Contents

*234 × 148 mm*      *208 pp*      *ISBN 0–85139–885–5*      *cloth*

# Professional Indemnity Claims

**N. P. G. Thomas**

More and more claims are being made against architects. This book is written for the architect who is concerned both to understand the ramifications of these claims and how best to avoid their arising in the first place.

The steps in resolving a claim, either by litigation or by arbitration, are described by following a hypothetical case, and simple language is employed to explain the terms used. The author goes on to point out how professional liabilities may arise; he discusses whether they can be avoided, and explains the working of the professional indemnity insurance industry.

He also draws on his experience of claims and provides a checklist of what to avoid and where to take special precautions. This book offers valuable reading for any architect, whether student or long qualified.

**Contents**

Litigation in the high court
The alternatives to litigation in the high court
The architect as plaintiff
Professional indemnity insurance
The concept of liability
Common causes of liability and their avoidance

'This is a book to be read by all architects. It avoids legal jargon and tedious description . . . Architects, having read this book, should then keep it as quick reference whenever storm clouds appear on the horizon. It might just help avoid getting very wet.'

*Building Design*

*210 × 148 mm      99 pp      ISBN 0–85139–748–4      cloth*